MW00911859

Genealogical record of Nathaniel Babcock, Simeon Main, Issac Miner, Ezekiel Main,

Cyrus Henry Brown

BIBLIOLIFE

Genealogical Record

OF

NATHANIEL BABCOCK
SIMEON MAIN   ISAAC MINER
EZEKIEL MAIN

COMPILED BY

CYRUS H. BROWN

WESTERLY, R. I.

BOSTON
THE EVERETT PRESS
1909

To

My Cousins

JOHN RUSSELL BABCOCK

AND HIS SISTER

SUSAN H. BABCOCK

This Record Is

Gratefully Dedicated

By the Author

PREFACE.

AFTER publishing the Brown Genealogy, in 1907, the author of this genealogy took up first the records of his great-great-grandfather Nathaniel Babcock, Sr., in lineal descent from James Babcock, who settled in Portsmouth, R. I., in 1642, but removed to Westerly, R. I., in 1662, where his second son, John, who married Mary Lawton, had settled; thus through regular lines of descent, and giving more *particular* records than were given when that part of the Babcock Genealogy was published, in 1903, bringing the records down to 1910. Stephen Babcock, of Yonkers, N. Y., has granted me permission to use as much of the early history of the Babcock Family as may be of interest to the descendants of Nathaniel Babcock, Sr. This Babcock record is also supplemented by the descendants of Simeon Main and Martha York, carrying the records on from the last given in the Brown Genealogy; also by the descendants of Isaac Miner and Katurah Brown.

The Ezekiel Main Family has received by far the most extended research. Ezekiel Main removed to Stonington, Conn., about 1670. The records begin on page 49. My plan of research has been to search town records, to visit burying-grounds, to send hundreds of personal letters with blanks to be filled out, and to make personal visits. This all means labor and expense, which the author has personally assumed, soliciting no subscriptions except from John D. Babcock's family (51), page 26. To this family belongs the credit of financial support in commencing this work; but it has been extended far beyond my expectations. Much of the matter has been submitted to the persons interested for their approval and correction, thus making the genealogy as reliable as possible, but taking much added time to complete the book.

The compiler believes he has succeeded in collecting a vast amount of material that has never before been printed; also in establishing several lines of descent connecting with the progenitor, Ezekiel Main.

In the preparation of this work the compiler of this volume has been assisted by many families who are deeply interested in knowing this work is being done. Therefore he desires to make further acknowledgment of valuable assistance rendered by:

Stephen Main Family, Westerly, R. I.
Mrs. Lydia E. Harris, Eagleville, Conn.

PREFACE

Robert Palmer Main's descendants, Wisconsin.
Lewis Avery Main, Cedar Rapids, Ia.
Mrs. Lillian M. Porter, Brockton, Mass.
Dr. Frank D. Maine, Springfield, Mass.
Dr. C. Wesley Hale, Springfield, Mass.
Hubert P. Main, Newark, N. J.
Eli Gilbert Main, Waterbury, Conn.
Alonzo Main, Old Mystic, Conn.
Mrs. Nathan T. Main, Laurel Glen, Conn.

The writing of this genealogy has been a labor of *love;* and, like most genealogical works, an expensive gratification, which I do not regret. If the living families mentioned in this volume but appreciate my untiring labors in placing in a tangible form the records of the fathers, mothers, sons, and daughters I shall feel my labors have not been in vain.

CYRUS HENRY BROWN,

March, 1910.   Westerly, R. I.

INTRODUCTION.

" People will not look forward to posterity who never look backward to their ancestry."
— EDMUND BURKE.

When we were young we were looking toward the future; in middle life we are too busy to give any attention but to the present; but as years progress we begin to look backward to our ancestors.

More than twoscore years have passed since the Civil War, yet that terrible struggle abides in the memory of many now living; but more than three times as many years have passed since the movement began which resulted in American Independence. As we look back still farther to the landing of the Pilgrim fathers we catch but glimpses of our ancestry in all these decades which have passed in the Colonial and Revolutionary periods. So the distance widens that separates us from our ancestors. Yet we can better understand our own times if in youthful days we came in personal contact with those who, in those stirring events, were shaping our history and marching towards civilization in social, political, and religious liberty.

The people of the West whose family history was left behind them in old New England need to be reminded of the priceless heritage of their fathers and mothers, and restore the same to their descendants, so that the West may be indissolubly connected with the development of the East.

The study of genealogy would convince most of us that our ancestors were every-day sort of people, who were more familiar with blacksmithing, hewing timber, constructing houses and barns, and who knew more about raising cattle than buying and selling stocks. Their farms and stone walls are monuments still standing, reminding us of the strong hands and brawny arms that built them; their long hours of toil are a legacy left to their children and children's children. Some who read these pages will remember in the early part of the nineteenth century the home-spun articles made in our New England homes. The scene is realistic: it is a winter evening; in the fireplace is built the huge fire; the family has gathered in semicircle and, by the light of it, the knitting goes on, while at the back of the circle, the buzz of the spinning-wheel is heard; the ponderous loom is there ready to weave the cloth for every-day garments or for the wedding attire.

Lest these primeval days be forgotten by the children and the grandchildren, this genealogy is written, that the deeds of the fathers and mothers may be kept sacredly in remembrance.

Before laying down my pen, I want to extend sincere and hearty thanks to all who have contributed in furnishing data for this book. Many will find under their own names my appreciation of their contributions.

C. H. B.

Westerly, R. I., January, 1909.

ABBREVIATIONS.

b., born.
bapt., baptized.
Bapt., Baptist.
B. G., Brown Genealogy.
Cong., Congregational.
d., died.
dau., daughter.
m., married; m.(1), married first; m. (2), married second.
p., page.
res., resides, or residence.
unm., unmarried.
Other abbreviations in common use need no further explanation.

EXPLANATIONS.

After the name of a parent will follow their original number in parentheses; by turning backward, his or her number will be found with their parents.

The children of parents who have numbers in parentheses at the right of their names can be found by corresponding numbers carried forward.

After the name of the parents of the head of a family there will follow in brackets the names of the ancestors in genealogical order.

The larger part of these records was obtained by correspondence, but town records, family Bibles, and tombstones have contributed much to these data.

Nathaniel Babcock Genealogy.

James[1] Babcock (1), b. 1612, probably in Essex Co., England; d. June 12, 1679; m. (1) Sarah, who d. 1665 or later; m. (2), 1669 (?), Elizabeth; she m. (2), Sept. 22, 1679, Wm. Johnson, and settled in Stonington, Conn. His residence for the first twenty years was in Portsmouth, R. I. James Babcock moved to Westerly, R. I., in March, 1662. June 29, 1660, a tract of land, estimated to be twenty miles by ten miles, known as Misquamicut, afterwards Westerly, was purchased from the Indian Chief Sosoa by a company headed by William Vaughn. The company, numbering sixty or more, was organized at Newport, R. I. The following March, 1661–62, the company made their first permanent settlement at Misquamicut (Westerly). The records of Westerly show that James Babcock was a man of sterling integrity and of strong convictions. He was respected by his neighbors, honored and trusted as a citizen, and ready to serve the community in whatever capacity he was appointed.

Children by first m.:

  2. James[2], b. 1641; m. Jane Brown (7–7e).
  3. John, b. 1644; m. Mary Lawton (8–15).
  4. Job, b. 1646; m. Jane Crandall.
  5. Mary, b. 1648; m. William Champlin.

Children by second m.:

  6. Joseph, b. 1670; m. (1) Dorothy Key; m. (2) Mrs. Hannah Coats.

  Nathaniel, date of birth unknown.

  Elizabeth, date of birth unknown.

James[2] Babcock, Jr. (2), son of James and Sarah Babcock, b., Portsmouth, R. I., 1641; d., Westerly, now Woodville, R. I., 1698; m. Jane, dau. of Nicholas Brown. She d. 1719. James was a blacksmith and a farmer in that part of Westerly which is now Woodville, Hopkinton, R. I., where he manufactured iron from bog ore and from black sand found on the seashore.

Children:

  7. James[3], m.——.
  7a. Sarah, m. James Lewis, son of John Lewis. They settled in Exeter, R. I. She d. 1740.

7b. Jane, m., Richmond, R. I., 1696, Israel Lewis.

7c. Mary, m. George Brown.

7d. Hannah, m. Roger Larkin.

7e. Elizabeth, m. Daniel Lewis, brother of James. She d. 1716.

John² Babcock (3), second son of James, Sr., and Sarah Babcock, b., Portsmouth, R. I., 1644; d., Westerly, R. I., 1685; m. Mary Lawton, dau. of George and Elizabeth (Hazzard) Lawton, of Portsmouth. Mary m. (2), Apr. 21, 1698, Erasmus Babbitt; d., Westerly, Nov. 8, 1711.

Tradition says that John and Mary eloped from Newport, R. I., in a boat, and married themselves, calling on the moon and stars to witness the solemn vow. They settled on the east bank of the Pawcatuck River, on Massatuxet Cove, two and one half miles from Westerly, on the Watch Hill road, with no neighbors but the friendly Indians, and were not found till several months after, when the parents made inquiry of the Indians, who helped to locate them at Massatuxet Cove. The Indians told them they had a "papoose."

This elopement story is classed by some as fiction. If any wish to study these early records they can do so by examining the full and exhaustive reports found in the Babcock Genealogy by Stephen Babcock, New York City, who says: "The town records of Westerly show that in 1669 John Babcock was given the twenty-seventh lot. It is certain he settled in Westerly, on the banks of the Pawcatuck River, near what is now Avondale, R. I., and that his oldest son, James, inherited and occupied the homestead. Some of the homestead land has never passed from the ownership of the descendants of John, as the widow of Ezra Babcock, son of Daniel and Nancy (Babcock) Babcock, owns and occupies the house at Avondale, which it is claimed stands upon the same lot on which John and Mary (Lawton) Babcock built their first house. In the burying-ground on the east side of the road, about half way up the hill from the brook (Massatuxet), are buried many of these early settlers, where the stones and tablets that mark their last resting-place are in a good and legible state of preservation."

As John and Mary (Lawton) Babcock are our direct progenitors, this ancient burying-ground is of peculiar interest. John Babcock d. probably in May or June, 1685. The inventory of his personal property is dated June 4, 1685, and the property amounted to £790, 3s., and was the largest recorded in the town of Westerly for many years.

The children of John² Babcock (3) and Mary (Lawton) Babcock are mentioned in a will in the order given.

"John and Mary"

By Calvin Thurbur, Westerly, R. I.

Reproduction from a water-color sketch of a painting made for George H. Babcock, of Plainfield, N. J.

Tradition — which is often as authentic as the official record, and always more interesting — says that John Babcock, a young man working for Lawton, of Newport, R. I., fell in love with his employer's daughter Mary, — a condition of affairs not pleasing to the father, who forbade all thought of his daughter becoming the wife of a poor laborer.

But "Love laughs at locks and bars." The young people cleared away, taking a boat, early one summer morning, sailed along the coast past Point Judith until they rounded Watch Hill and came to what we now know as the mouth of the Pawcatuck River; up this till they reached Massatuksett Cove, where they landed, made friends with the Indians, and made their permanent home — the first of the Babcocks coming to Westerly, R. I.

Children, all b. in Westerly:

8. James³, b. 1663; m. (1) Elizabeth ——— (16–22); m. (2) Content Maxson (24–27).

    Ann, b. 1665 (?).

    Mary, b. 1667 (?).

9. John, b. 1669 (?); m. Mary Champlin.

10. Job, b. 1671 (?); m. Deborah ———.

11. George, b. 1673; m. Elizabeth Hall.

12. Elihu, b. Dec. 19, 1675; unm. Tradition says the "day of the Great Swamp Fight."

13. Robert, b. 1678 (?); m. Lydia Crandall.

14. Joseph, b. 1681 (?); m. Rebecca Stanton.

15. Oliver, b. 1683 (?); m. (1) Susanna Clark; m. (2) Deborah Knowles.

James³ Babcock (8), better known as Captain James, eldest child of John and Mary (Lawton) Babcock, b., Westerly, R. I., 1663; d. there Jan. 17, 1736-37. He was buried in the Babcock burying-ground at Massatuxet, as described under John Babcock (3) His grave is covered by a horizontal tablet, six feet long and four feet wide. The inscription upon the tablet is as follows: "In memory of Capt. James Babcock, who died Jan. ye 17th 1736, in ye — year of his age. Having been in his life of extensive charity and beneficence and not wholly silent at his death." The year of his death has been completely obliterated.

Tradition says that James was the first white male child born in Misquamicut (Westerly). He m. (1), 1687, tradition says, Elizabeth Saunders, dau. of Tobias Saunders. Another tradition says her name was Elizabeth Babbit. Upon her tombstone, which is near her husband's grave, is inscribed the following: "Here lieth intered ye body of Elizabeth, ye wife of Capt. James Babcock, died March ye 3rd 1730-1 in the 69th year of her age."

James m. (2), in Westerly, by Theodoty Rhodes, Justice, July 7, 1731, Content, eldest child of Jonathan and Content (Rogers) Maxson, b., Westerly, Jan. 28, 1708-09. She was in the twenty-third year of her age. Captain James's last will, written Jan. 9, 1736-37, provides that his infant son James should receive a collegiate education.

The family burying-ground is reserved from this farm, "for a buryingplace of my relations and as many others as they shall see cause to accept of." No doubt his parents and grandparents were buried upon the same grounds. It has been said of Captain James Babcock that he was as good as he was rich, a true philanthropist, who lived for God and his fellow men.

Children by first m.:

16. James⁴, b., Westerly, Dec. 23, 1688; m. Sarah Vose (28–35).
17. Elizabeth, b. Feb. 8, 1691; m. Elder Thomas Clark.
18. Samuel, b. Feb. 15, 1697; m. Ann Pendleton.
19. Daniel, b. Apr. 23, 1699; m. Abigail Thompson.
20. Anna, b. Nov. 29, 1701; m. Elder Joseph Clark.
21. Sarah, b. Dec. 13, 1704; d. Nov. 13, 1705.
22. Joshua, b. May 17, 1707; m. (1) Hannah Stanton (35a–35i); m. (2) Ann Maxson.

Children by second m., all b. Westerly:

24. Ann, b. Mar. 23, 1732; m. Simon Rhodes.
25. Colonel James, b. Nov. 1, 1734; m. (1) Sarah Stanton; m. (2) Joanna McDowell.
27. Jonathan, b. Oct. 11, 1736; m. Esther Hazard.

James⁴ Babcock, Jr. (16), son of Captain James³ (8) and Elizabeth Babcock, b., Westerly, R. I., Dec. 23, 1688; d., Stonington, now No. Stonington, Conn., Apr. 9, 1731; m., Milton, Mass., June 12, 1706, by Peter Thatcher, pastor, Sarah Vose, dau. of Edward and Abigail Vose; b., Milton, Aug. 30, 1684; d., Stonington, Dec. 25, 1758. Her father, Edward Vose, was b. in England in 1636; d., Milton, Jan. 29, 1716. Abigail, the mother of Sarah Vose, d., Milton, May 18, 1712, aged sixty-five years. Her grandfather, Robert Vose, b. in Lancaster, England, about 1599, came to America with his three sons, Edward, Thomas, and Henry, and bought land in Milton July 13, 1654.

James⁴ Babcock, Jr., and his wife Sarah (Vose) Babcock settled upon a farm in that part of Stonington which is now Pendleton Hill, No. Stonington. It was owned by his father, Capt. James Babcock, and was found afterwards to lie partly in Stonington and partly in Voluntown. Much of the land was retained in the family for more than a hundred and fifty years. James and wife Sarah joined Stonington Church (Congregational), Rev. James Noyes, pastor, Aug. 8, 1708, and left with others to form the No. Stonington Church 1727. Records of births, deaths, and baptisms found on town and church records.

James, Jr., d. in the forty-third year of his age, and was buried on the farm upon which he lived; later his widow, children, and grandchildren were buried near him. The burying-ground having been overgrown with bushes and briars, and being in a desolate, neglected spot remote from the highway, Col. Andrew J. Babcock, of Springfield, Ill., and Stephen Babcock, of New York City, the comprehensive compiler of the Babcock

Genealogy, in the autumn of 1900, caused the remains of James and his wife, their sons Oliver and Timothy and their wives, to be removed to a well-kept cemetery adjacent to the Pendleton Hill Meeting-house, which was about a mile from the original burying-ground. All of these bodies were found in a measure preserved, although one of them had lain in the ground one hundred and seventy years. Ten years previous to this removal the remains of Capt. Oliver Babcock, grandson of James and Sarah (Vose) Babcock, and that of Oliver's brother Joshua and wife had been removed to the same cemetery at Pendleton Hill.

Children:

28. James⁵, b. May 29, 1708; m. Phebe Swan (35j–350).
· 29. Nathaniel, b. Mar. 6, 1709–10; m. Sarah Billings (36–41).
30. Elias, b. Feb. 20, 1711–12; m. Anna Plumb.
   Sarah, birth not recorded on Stonington records; bapt., Jan. 11, 1714, recorded on Stonington church records.
31. Elizabeth, b. Aug. 25, 1715; m. John Davidson.
   Martha, b. March, 1717; d. Apr. 18, 1717.
32. Isaiah, b. Jan. 29, 1719; m. Elizabeth Plumb. The records of the descendants of Isaiah appear in the records compiled by Stephen Babcock, carefully prepared by Mr. A. Emerson Babcock, of Brighton, N. Y.
33. Oliver, b. July 27, 1720; m. Anna Avory.
34. Grace, b. Dec. 31, 1722; m. Samuel Plumb.
35. Timothy, b. Oct. 12, 1724; m. (1) Lois Billings; m. (2) Thankful Read.

The above-mentioned children were all doubtless born in what is called now, in 1908, and has been for more than one hundred years, "The Capt. Nathan Pendleton House." This is the same house where James, Jr., and Sarah (Vose) Babcock lived. The store was burnt in 1866, and was not attached to the house as now.

Dr. Joshua⁴ Babcock (22), son of Captain James and Elizabeth Babcock [John, James], b., Westerly, R. I., May 17, 1707; d., Westerly, Apr. 1, 1783; m. (1), Aug. 11, 1735, Hannah, dau. of Joseph Stanton (granddau. of Thomas Stanton, Sr., who was an Indian interpreter); b., Stonington, Conn., 1714; d. Sept. 19, 1778; m. (2), May 28, 1780, Ann, dau. of Elder John and Tacy (Rogers) Maxson, of Newport, R. I. (She was a great-granddau. of Elder John Maxson, b. 1638–39, who was the first white child born on the island of Rhode Island, and who was the first pastor of the Seventh Day Baptist Church of Westerly.) Ann Babcock d. Aug. 25,

1812, aged seventy-one years. She was buried in what is now the First Hopkinton Cemetery. Her grave is a few rods northwest of the "Ministers' Monument" (see Brown Genealogy, p. 95).

Joshua Babcock graduated at Yale College in the class of 1724, and was the first graduate of this college from Rhode Island. Soon after his graduation he began the study of medicine and surgery in Boston, and about 1730 went to London to attend the hospitals there. On his return he settled in Westerly (being admitted a freeman of the colony Apr. 30, 1734), and for nearly twenty-five years practised his profession extensively. He also opened a retail country store, which it is said did as much business as any like establishment between Boston and New York, and thus increased his already large estate. He represented his town in the Colonial Legislature in the years 1740, 1747, 1749, 1752, 1758, 1759, 1773, 1776, and 1778, serving repeatedly as Speaker. He was Chief Justice of the Supreme Court of the colony from May, 1747, to May, 1749, and from May, 1750, to May, 1764. In this capacity he pronounced the sentence of death upon Thomas Carter for the murder of Jackson. He was one of the original corporators of Brown University, in 1764, and continued on the Board of Fellows until his death. He is recorded in the History of the University as a Seventh Day Baptist. He was connected with that church early in life, but later became a Unitarian in his religious belief.

The large colonial mansion which he owned is still standing (1908) upon Quarry Hill, in Westerly, and has just the same appearance it had when the writer saw it in 1851, with the two rows of box each side of the front walk. Benjamin Franklin, when on his official tours through the country as Postmaster-General, frequently made Dr. Babcock's house his resting-place. Tradition says that the favorite sport of the two men was catching blackfish from the ocean, at a place then called Noyes Rocks, now known as Weekapaug. The place is still a favorite fishing-ground.

Dr. Franklin established the first post-office in the town in 1776, and appointed Dr. Babcock postmaster. The receipts of the office for this year were £1, 3s, 8d. Prior to the Revolution the nearest post-office was New London, Conn., twenty miles distant.

It is said that George Washington, when passing between New York and Boston, stopped more than once at the home of Dr. Babcock.

Dr. Babcock was one of the signers of the Declaration of Independence passed by the Legislature of Rhode Island more than two months prior to July 4, 1776 (Arnold's History of Rhode Island).

In May, 1775, Joshua Babcock was appointed to carry proceedings of the Rhode Island Assembly to Connecticut. In November, 1775, by Act of the General Assembly of Rhode Island, he was appointed Major-General of the colony's forces. This position he held until December, 1776, when he was appointed as a member of the Council of War. He was reappointed to the latter position in the years 1778 and 1779.

The Rhode Island records of Revolutionary times show that no man was more active in the service of his country, or held more responsible positions, than did Dr. Joshua Babcock. A history of his remarkable career and merits would fill an interesting volume.

His remains were buried near the graves of his parents in the ancient Babcock burial-ground of Westerly. A large and finely sculptured tablet covers his grave. The inscription in part is as follows:

THIS STONE COVERS THE MORTAL

PART OF

THE HON. JOSHUA BABCOCK,

OF WESTERLY,

WHO DIED APRIL 1, 1783, AGED 75 YEARS.

Children, recorded in Westerly:

35a. Colonel Henry[5], b. May 25, 1736; m. Mary Stanton.

35b. Luke, b. July 6, 1738; m. Grace Isaacs.

35c. Adam, b. Sept. 27, 1740; m. (1) Abigail Smith; m. (2) Martha Hubbard.

35d. Hannah, b. Jan. 22, 1742–43; m. John Bours.

35e. Frances Nancy, b. May 11, 1745; m. Commodore Dudley Saltonstall.

35f. Paul, b. Dec. 5, 1748.

35g. Amelia, b. Apr. 19, 1751.

35h. Sarah (or Sally), b. Oct. 18, 1753.

35i. Harriet, b. May 18, 1756.

James[4] Babcock (28), son of James, Jr., and Sarah (Vose) Babcock, b., No. Stonington, Conn., May 29, 1708; bapt., Stonington, Conn., Aug. 1, 1708; m., Stonington, by Justice Palmer S. Clark, May 7, 1730, Phebe Swan; May 13, 1733, he joined the No. Stonington Church at Milltown.

By will of his grandfather, Capt. James Babcock, of Westerly, R. I., dated Jan. 9, 1736, he received two certain tracts of land in Westerly, each containing one hundred acres. This land he sold, Oct. 15, 1741, to Stephen Babcock, of Westerly. In the deed he, James, is mentioned as residing in Stonington. He built a house on this land in 1740, as an inscription, on a board three feet long, over the door in the inside, reads: "THIS HOUSE WAS BUILT BY JAMES BABCOCK, 1740."

This land is located half way between Stonington and Westerly, on what is now known as "The Daniel Brown Farm." The house stands about one hundred rods east of the road.

Children (Wheeler):

    ·   35j. Phebe[6], b. May 2, 1731; m. Rufus Palmer.

    35k. Sarah, b. Feb. 12, 1733.

    35l. James, b. Feb. 22, 1735; m., July 21, 1757, Lucretia[5] Babcock, dau. of Elder Stephen and Anna (Thompson) Babcock, of Westerly, b. Nov. 2, 1734.

    35m. Elias, b. Dec. 16, 1736; m. Ann Plumb, b. Nov. 10, 1737.

    35n. Abel, b. Apr. 28, 1739; m. (1) Hannah Lewis; m. (2) Elizabeth Williams.

    35o. Martha, b. Feb. 22, 1741.

Captain Nathaniel[5] (29), son of James, Jr., and Sarah (Vose) Babcock, b., No. Stonington, Conn., Mar. 6, 1709–10; bapt., Stonington, Conn., Mar. 6, 1710; joined No. Stonington Congregational Church 1738; d. before Oct., 1772; m., Nov. 20, 1733, Sarah Billings, of Preston, Conn.; b. 1715; d., Petersburg, N. Y., Feb. 25, 1794.

March 13, 1735-36, he bought for £300, of John Gallup and John Dixon, the west half of the farm previously deeded to him by his grandfather, a survey having shown that part of the farm lay in Voluntown, Conn., hence Captain James had no good title to it.

February 25, 1760, Nathaniel Babcock conveyed to his son Nathaniel, Jr., "the east part of the land the grantor now lives on, in Voluntown, bounded on the south by Stonington land."

The second Thursday of Oct., 1772, the General Assembly of Connecticut authorized Nathaniel Babcock and Sarah Babcock, joint administrators of the estate of the late Nathaniel Babcock, to sell forty and one-half acres of land. March 25, 1773, the land was sold to Elias Babcock (30). The following day Elias Babcock sold the same land to Nathaniel Babcock, Jr.

Nathaniel was commissioned Ensign in Connecticut Militia in 1740; Captain, 1750, by the General Assembly of Connecticut (Book 1735-43, p. 291, C. R. of Connecticut).

Records gathered from town records and No. Stonington (Congregational) Church.

Children:

    36. Nathaniel[6], Jr., b. Jan. 24, 1735; m. Mary Larrison (42–44).

    36a. Jonas, b. Feb. 21, 1737; d. Oct. 15, 1755.

The following was copied from a journal left by Nathaniel Babcock, Sr.:

"June, the 9th day, 1755, my well-beloved son Jonas Babcock left home, and June 11, he set out for Norwich (Ct.) and Crown Point, and Sept. 5 he arrived at Lake George, and the 8th of the month they had a battle with the French and Indians; 24th of Sept. he was taken sick. The 4th of Oct. he left Lake George and came to Albany. He died Oct. 15, about 2 o'clock at night, being in the 19th year of his age. Oct. 18, 1755, I got to Albany in four days to see my son's grave and fetch his clothes, which almost broke my heart. I was gone eight days and half from home."

37. Sarah, b. Apr. 18, 1739; d., Petersburg, Aug. 27, 1792; m. Joseph Hewitt. They had a son Joseph and a dau. Polly.
38. Lucy, b. Feb. 12, 1742; m. Benjamin Randall.
39. Comfort, b. July 3, 1746.
40. Amy, b. Apr. 14, 1749; d., Genesee Co., N. Y., Jan. 18, 1826.
41. Reuben, b. Mar. 2, 1758; m. Hannah Hendricks.

For complete and exhaustive records of James[4] Babcock, Jr., and Sarah Vose's children see Stephen Babcock Genealogy, pp. 52–59 of that book. Records also supplied by Col. Andrew J. Babcock, great-grandson of Timothy and Thankful (Read) Babcock. Page 58 of Stephen Babcock's Genealogy says, "Timothy was a farmer and a merchant, having a country store adjoining his house." This original store was sufficiently far removed from the house that when it was destroyed by fire, in 1866, the house was not burnt, but is the same house that is probably more than two hundred years old. It stands partly in No. Stonington and partly in Voluntown.

The writer of these records (C. H. B.) with his father visited the store burnt in 1866, which was kept by the sons of Capt. Nathan Pendleton in about 1838. The writer's mother, Elizabeth Stewart Babcock, as late as 1886, owned by inheritance a farm one mile west of this famous house now known as "The Capt. Nathan Pendleton House."

Here on these farms lived and died, and were buried, east of the road, in the Babcock burying-ground, our great-great-grandfather, James[5], Nathaniel, Elias, Isaiah, Oliver, and Timothy. As many as could be identified have been removed to a better kept cemetery, adjacent to the Pendleton Hill Meeting-house.

Nathaniel[6], Jr. (36), son of Nathaniel and Sarah (Billings) Babcock, b., No. Stonington, Conn., Jan. 24, 1735; bapt. Sept. 14, 1735; d., No. Stonington, Apr. 19, 1813; buried on the Larrison Farm, just three miles from Westerly, R. I. Disinterred by Cyrus W. Brown and his grandson John D. Babcock, and buried in the Union Cemetery near the Miner Meeting-house, No. Stonington. He m., Dec. 1, 1756, Mary, dau. of Thomas and Mary (Landphear) Larrison, b., No. Stonington, 1741; d. Oct. 15,

1801. They lived for a time at Canterbury, Conn. They settled on the Larrison Farm, No. Stonington, where he and his wife d. The house stood half a mile east of the first burying-ground, mentioned above.

"Feb. 25, 1760, Nathaniel Babcock, Sr., conveyed to his son Nathaniel land where the grantor now lives in Voluntown, bounded on the south by Stonington land."

"June 14, 1772, Nathaniel Babcock, of No. Stonington, conveyed to Amos Babcock, of Voluntown, land bounded west upon land which belonged to Capt. Nathaniel, deceased."— *From Voluntown Records.*

May, 1778, Nathaniel Babcock Jr., of Canterbury, Windham Co., administrator of the estate of Nathaniel Babcock Sr., deceased, was given permission to sell Land in Voluntown belonging to the estate.— *From Records of Connecticut by Hoadley.*

Nathaniel was living in Canterbury as late at 1798. For his Revolutionary War record, see Brown Genealogy, p. 28.

Children:

> 42. Jonas', b. 1757; d. in army at Valley Forge, in the Revolutionary War.
>
> 43. Mary, b. 1759; m., Stonington, Conn., Sept. 8, 1776, Nathaniel Hinckley, son of Samuel and Mary (Wyatt) Hinckley.
>
> 44. Stephen', b., Stonington, June 13, 1765, who became insane in the latter part of his life (45-53).

Lucy⁶ (38), dau. of Nathaniel and Sarah (Billings) Babcock [James, James, John, James¹], b., Stonington, Conn., Feb. 12, 1742; d., Berlin, N. Y., Mar. 9, 1824; m. Benjamin Randall, d. June 17, 1816.

Children, order of births not known:

> Ichabod, b.——
>
> Nathaniel, b.——
>
> Benjamin, Jr., b.——; d. June 23, 1847; m. Sarah ——. She d. Dec. 30, 1817. (He was a soldier in the Revolutionary War.)
>
> Stephen, b ——
>
> Eunice, b.——; d. Sept. 27, 1829; m. Sanford Hewitt.
>
> Sally, b.——; d. Dec. 20, 1829; m. Luke Hull.
>
> Lucy, b.—— 1861 Archibald Thomas
>
> Eleanor, b.——
>
> Lois, b. —— Abel Thomas
>
> Betsey, b. ——
>
> Abigail, b. ——

Reuben[6] (41), son of Nathaniel and Sarah (Billings) Babcock [James, James, John, James[1]], b., Stonington, Conn., Mar. 2, 1758; d., E. Poestenkill, N. Y., Feb. 24, 1849; m., Mar. 6, 1788, Hannah, dau. of Moses or Reuben Hendricks; b., Petersburg, N. Y., Apr. 4, 1763; d., E. Poestenkill, Mar. 7, 1849.

Children:

    (1) Reuben[7], Jr., b. Oct. 24, 1789; m. Susanna Gould.

    (2) Nathaniel, b. Apr. 15, 1791; m. Polly Blivin.

    (3) Sarah, b. June 23, 1794; m. Ophir Gould.

    (4) Jonas, b., Petersburg, Apr. 7, 1796; d., Hartland, N. Y., Oct. 31, 1835. Children: Polly, Rachel, Emily, Alfred, and Leroy, who lived in Kendall, N. Y.

    (5) Polly, b. Dec. 25, 1797; m. James Murray.

    (6) Rufus, b. Aug. 23, 1800; m. Elma E. Walker.

    (7) Infant dau., b. Apr. 22, 1806; d. same day. (Continued Babcock Genealogy, p. 180.)

Reuben Babcock (41) served in the Revolutionary War as a private and sergeant in the Continental Army. The Troy *Budget* of Sept., 1900, had an account of old records in the courthouse, dated 1840, including a list of pensioned Revolutionary soldiers then (1840) living in the County of Rensselaer, N. Y. Among them were the names Reuben Babcock, Sandlake (that part now called E. Poestenkill), and Moses Kendricks, Berlin, same county.

After the Revolution Reuben returned to Stonington or Voluntown, for the following record is found:

"Reuben Babcock, of Voluntown, conveyed to Anna Langworthy, of Stonington, for twenty-five pounds, land lying partly in Voluntown and partly in Stonington."

Sept. 20, 1783, he conveyed to Anna Langworthy for £30 his whole right, title, and interest in his part, as he said, "of my honored mother's thirds in the real estate of my honored father, Capt. Nathaniel Babcock, as set off by the probate court of Plainfield, Ct." In the same sale he conveyed the whole of the share of his thirds "which I bought of Mr. Stephen Hull Jr., and Comfort Hull, his wife, being one fifth part of said thirds of the real estate of my said father lying in three lots containing by estimation 25 acres."

Reuben Babcock left Stonington Oct. 16, 1786, and came to New York State. After marriage he bought a farm near Petersburg, and, Nov., 1796, purchased another in that part of Sandlake now called E. Poestenkill, where he lived the rest of his life.

Stephen[3] Babcock (44), son of Nathaniel, Jr., and Mary (Larrison) Babcock [Nathaniel, James, James, John, James[1]], b., Stonington, Conn., June 13, 1765; d., No. Stonington, Conn., Aug. 30, 1845; m. (1) 1790 (?) Mercy Hinckley, b. 1771; d. Oct. 22, 1802; m. (2) Elizabeth Stewart, of Voluntown, Conn., dau. of William and Elizabeth (Fish) Stewart, of Voluntown; d. Jan. 19, 1807, aged twenty-nine years; m. (3) Mercy Davis, dau. of Bill Davis, of Preston, Conn.; d. Sept. 26, 1854. He was a farmer; lived in No. Stonington, three miles north of Westerly, R. I. Interments, Union Cemetery.

Children by first m., all b. No. Stonington:
45. Eunice[6], b. 1791; m. Ethan Crandall (54-56).
46. Stephen, Jr., b. 1793; m. Emma Bentley (57-60).
47. Samuel H., b. 1798; m. Caroline Stanton (61-61c).
48. Henry, b. Jan. 19, 1800; m. Mary C. Ross.

Dau. by second m.:
49. Elizabeth Stewart, b. Dec. 28, 1806 (62-71). See Brown Genealogy, pp. 27, 28 (259-268).

Children by third m.:
49a. Nathaniel S., b. Mar. 7, 1813; d. Feb. 27, 1894; unm.
Charles, m. Betsey Richmond. No issue.
50. Mercy Ann, b. Dec. 8, 1815; d. Sept. 20, 1845; m. Thomas M. Brown. Had four sons (72-75). See Brown Genealogy, p. 51 (427-430).
51. John Davis, b. Feb. 5, 1818 (76-81).
52. Jonas Larrison, b. Mar. 1, 1820; m. Abby C. Stanton.
53. William Stuart, b. Mar. 20, 1822 (82-87).

Eunice[6] Babcock (45), dau. of Stephen and Mercy (Hinckley) Babcock [Nathaniel, Nathaniel, James, James, John, James], b. 1791; d. Aug., 1877; m. Ethan Crandall, of Potter Hill, R. I.
Children:
54. Wealthy M.[9], b. Sept. 23, 1820; d. June 7, 1878.
55. Nancy M., b.——; m. William D. Brown (B. G. 714, p. 95).
56. Caroline P., b. 1825; d. Oct. 28, 1852, aged twenty-seven years; unm.

Wealthy M. Crandall (54), m., June 21, 1855, John P. Babcock. She was his second wife. John P. Babcock was son of Jesse and Sally (Sheffield) Babcock, b., New Shoreham, R. I., Aug. 17, 1811; d., Mystic, Conn., Jan. 20, 1868; m. (1), No. Kingston, R. I., Sept. 3, 1838, Lydia Case Wightman, b., No. Kingston, Apr. 4, 1812; d., Wickford, R. I., Aug. 29, 1850; dau. of Benj. and Patience (Allen) Wightman.

Children by first m., b. No. Kingston:

  56a. Melissa Jane, b. Aug. 27, 1839; unm. Res., 1908, Wickford.

  Jesse, b. July 10, 1843; d., Wickford, May 28, 1846.

Dau. by second m.:

  56b. Carrie P., b. Aug. 11, 1856; m., Mystic, Apr. 3, 1878, Charles
  B. Gallup. Children: (1) Benj.[1] Gallup, b. Sept. 4, 1881; m.,
  Dec. 7, 1901, Florence L. Lewis. Dau.: Susan Carrie, b. May
  1, 1903. (2) John B. Gallup, b. May 16, 1889; d. Oct. 20,
  1890.

Stephen Babcock, Jr. (46), son of Stephen (44) and Mercy (Hinckley)
Babcock [Nathaniel, Nathaniel, James, James, John, James], b., Stonington, Conn., 1793; d. Nov. 10, 1870, aged seventy-seven years; m., Dec. 23,
1819, Emma Bentley, d. Jan. 14, 1876, aged eighty years. He owned a fine
farm two miles north of Westerly, R. I., now owned by Chas. F. Champlin,
where they lived the most of their days and their children were born. The
burial-place is on the homestead. He was in the War of 1812, and responded
to the call for the defence of Stonington, Aug. 9, 10, 1814, in the Third
Company,— Jesse Breed, Captain; Wm. Frink, Lieutenant; Dudley Brown
(205), Ensign.

  Children, b. Stonington:

    57. Mary Ann[9], b. June 15, 1821 (88-91).
        Stephen L., b. 1822; d. Jan. 28, 1824.
        Lucy G., b. Mar. 9, 1825; d. Aug. 30, 1827.
    58. Frank W., b. Nov. 5, 1827 (91a).
    59. Ira Bentley, b. July 24, 1830 (92-93a).
    60. Lucy A., b. July 28, 1834; d. Nov. 13, 1900; m., Feb. 26, 1862,
        Obed P. Miner. No issue.

Samuel Hinckley[8] Babcock (47), son of Stephen (44) and Mercy (Hinckley) Babcock, b., No. Stonington, Conn., 1798; d. Apr. 3, 1877; m., Feb. 28,
1832, Caroline S., dau. of Amos and Amelia (Babcock) Stanton, of No.
Stonington; b. Oct. 19, 1808; d. Jan. 11, 1867. He lived all his days in the
immediate vicinity where he was born, and for several years on the Amos
Stanton farm. Afterwards owned the Larrison farm and bought the place
owned by Nathan Thompson, adjacent to his father's homestead, where
he was born. He rebuilt the Thompson house, improving all the outbuild-
ings, making a comfortable home, which afterwards was owned by his son
Samuel Avery, and now (1908) is occupied by his widow and children.
He was a man of very quiet nature, unassuming, that loved his home and
family; much esteemed and highly respected.

Children, b. No. Stonington:

    61. Samuel Avery[8], b. Dec. 29, 1832 (94–96).

    61a. Daniel Hix, b. July 2, 1834; d. Nov. 28, 1857; unm.

    61b. Horace S., b. June, 1837; unm. Res., 1908, No. Stonington, on the Stanton farm, where he was born.

    61c. Albert Clinton, b. Dec. 12, 1840. He responded to the call of the Civil War, enlisting in the 21st Regiment, Conn. Volunteers; d., New Haven Hospital, Jan. 31, 1863.

        These four sons, cousins of the compiler, attended the district school together until 1845. They were much esteemed and greatly beloved.

Henry Babcock[8] (48), son of Stephen and Mercy (Hinckley) Babcock, b. Jan. 19, 1800; d., No. Stonington, Conn., Sept. 16, 1875; m., Feb. 4, 1839, Mary Ross, of Westerly, R. I. He had a broken hip and was lame all his life. He learned the boot and shoe making business, and had a shop near his father's house, which was afterwards moved to Westerly and located where the Peleg Barber Hose Co. Building now stands. Afterwards he opened a boot and shoe store on the west end of Pawcatuck Bridge, and successfully carried on that store for many years.

Dau.:

    Mary Esther, b.——; m. Edwin Goss. Res., New York City. Dau.:

        Virginia P. Goss, b.——; m. — Dugliss. Res.,Westerly, R. I.

Elizabeth Stewart Babcock[8] (49), dau. of Stephen and Elizabeth (Stewart) Babcock, of Voluntown, Conn. [Nathaniel, Nathaniel, James, James, John, James], b., No. Stonington, Conn., Dec. 28, 1806; d., No. Stonington, Sept. 22, 1886; m., No. Stonington, Dec. 21, 1826, Cyrus Williams Brown, Jr., b. Mar. 11, 1806; d., No. Stonington, Nov. 27, 1875. (B. G. 253, pp. 27, 28.) Mrs. Brown was a woman of great strength of character, generous and lovable in all her relations. She was a loyal and earnest Christian, a member of the Second Baptist Church, of which her husband was a deacon. At the time of her death she was reading the Bible through in regular course for the thirteenth time. On my visits to her she would hand me her Bible to read and pray with her. Her hospitality was unbounded, her heart and home always open to friend and stranger. Her nature was one of rare unselfishness and sympathy, by which she greatly endeared herself to all with whom she came in contact. She gave herself in unstinted measure to her large family. Her children and grandchildren helped to make her home a home of loveliness and unbounded joy, when the old homestead would resound with songs from the Gospel Hymns. "Her children rise up to call her blessed."

"A solemn proverb haunts my mind,
     With meaning deep and vast:
     The mill will never grind again
         With waters that are past.

" Leave no tender word unsaid;
     Love, love while life shall last.
     The mill will never grind again
         With waters that are past."

For particular records and history, see Brown Genealogy, pp. 57–62.

Children, b. No. Stonington (continued, Appendix I.):

62. Emily Elizabeth[9], b. Jan. 16, 1828; m. Thomas W. Wheeler.

63. Cyrus Henry, b. Nov. 24, 1829; m. Sarah C. Maxson.

64. Louisa A., b. Mar. 21, 1832; m. Dr. Edwin R. Lewis.

65. Gideon Perry, b. Aug. 3, 1834; m. (1) Mary Lewella Hollis; m. (2) her sister, Martha Corrina Hollis.

66. Benadam Williams, b. Apr. 4, 1836; m. Almira McGlaflin; she d., Prairie City, Ia., July 27, 1907.

67. Thomas Shailer, b. June 28, 1838; m. Mary A. Colby.

68. John Babcock, b. Feb. 3, 1841; m. Lovinia Richardson.

69. Sarah Ellen, b. May 23, 1843; m. Allen Barber.

70. Wm. Stewart, b. July 11, 1845; m. Carrie L. P. Colby.

71. James Stone, b. Mar. 2, 1848; m. Mary E. Brayton.

Additional records of this family (see B. G. 480, p. 91; also Appendix I.):

Wilfred M. Brown (480), son of Cyrus H. and Sarah C. (Maxson) Brown, b. Apr. 4, 1870; m. Annie Cutler Bradley. Dau: Lois Bradley, b., Roxbury, Mass., Feb. 20, 1908.

Horace Clifford Brown (481), brother of the preceding, b., Boston, Mass., June 22, 1873; m. Aldeane Kilmer. Children: (1) Horace Clifford, Jr., b., Melrose, Mass., Jan. 8, 1906; (2) Lois Theda, b., Newburyport, Mass., Sept. 9, 1907.

Mercy Ann Babcock[8] (50), dau. of Stephen and Mercy (Davis) Babcock [Nathaniel, Nathaniel, James, James, John, James], b., No. Stonington, Conn., Dec. 8, 1815; d. Sept. 20, 1845; m. Thomas M. Brown. Mrs. Brown was a very beautiful woman, the idol of the family. Her early death was a shock to family and friends, she dying of quick consumption. (See records B. G. 420, pp. 51–54.)

Children, b. No. Stonington (continued, Appendix I.):

72. Thomas Harrison, b. Oct. 16, 1839.

73. William Ellsworth, b. July 13, 1841.

74. Hermon Clinton, b. Jan. 22, 1843.

75. Stephen Edwin, b. May 27, 1845.

Additional records of this family (see B. G. 431, p. 52; also Appendix I.):

Carrie E. Brown (431), dau. of Thomas H. and Amanda A. (Wilbur) Brown, b. Jan. 22, 1873; m., Oct. 19, 1900, Frank I. Dawley. Son: Irwin Frank, b. Apr. 1, 1907.

Bessie Mae Brown (437), sister of the preceding, b. Apr. 13, 1882; m., Westerly, R. I., Oct. 24, 1907, Herbert Pomeroy Clark, son of George F. and Mary Olive (Spicer) Clark. He is a member of the Seventh Day Baptist Church, and a compositor on the Westerly *Daily Sun.*

John Davis Babcock (51), son of Stephen and Mercy (Davis) Babcock [Nathaniel, Nathaniel, James, James, John, James], b., No. Stonington, Conn., Feb. 5, 1818; d. Jan. 11, 1887; m. (1), No. Stonington, Jan. 5, 1843, Harriet D. Bentley, b. Jan. 1, 1824; d. Jan. 31, 1889; dau. of Russel and Susan (Stanton) Bentley; m. (2), No. Stonington, Jan. 24, 1854, Eunice A. Maine, b., No. Stonington, Aug. 20, 1829; d. Apr. 30, 1876; dau. of Prentice and Anna (Miner) Main (B. G. 1151, p. 161); dau. of Isaac and Katurah (382b) (Brown) Miner [Deacon Zebulon (74), James (38), Eleazer (11), Thomas]. Mr. Babcock was chosen to represent his native town in the State Legislature, 1864. He was an energetic business man and farmer in Stonington, Conn., and No. Stonington.

Children by first m., b. Stonington:

76. Susan[9] H., b. Oct. 21, 1845; unm. Miss Babcock is a very industrious woman, of a retiring disposition, and withal a woman adorned with all the Christian graces; benevolent, seeking the comfort and happiness of others, with a kind, gentle spirit. She is deeply interested in all the things pertaining to the kingdom of God, and is a valuable member of the First Baptist Church, Groton, Conn. (Old Mystic). Res., 1908, Old Mystic, Conn.

77. John Russell, b. June 17, 1848; m., Old Mystic, Mar. 19, 1896, Martha Eliza Chipman, b. Mar. 11, 1875; dau. of Collins Chipman, b., Mystic, Aug. 22, 1833, d. May 8, 1906, and Jane E. Chapman, b., Ledyard, Conn., Mar. 20, 1834. Mr. Babcock is a well-known and highly respected man of Mystic and adjoining towns. He is known for his honesty, integrity, and industry; he combines farming with other industries, notably a grain and feed store. He is one of the energetic, persevering kind, having success in view in all he does. Dau.: Emily Chipman, b., Old Mystic, Nov. 2, 1899.

Children by second m., b. No. Stonington:

78. William Prentice[9], b. July 14, 1855 (97–102).

79. Wealthy E., b. Feb. 24, 1858; d. Oct. 5, 1880.
80. Betsey Anna, b. Feb. 24, 1861; d. Aug. 26, 1863.
81. Abby Lathrop, b. Mar. 26, 1865; m., Old Mystic, May 22, 1890, Wallace A. Phillips, b., E. Lyme, Conn., Apr. 13, 1858; son of Chester and Ellen (Haynes) Phillips, of E. Lyme. Mr. Phillips is a Republican in politics. He is a carriage-maker and both he and his wife are members of the Second Baptist Church. Mrs. Phillips is beneficent and very active in church work in its various branches. She is a member of the D. A. R. She is especially interested in genealogy, and her records should have followed her grandmother Anna Miner (B. G. 1151, p. 161). No issue. Res., Bridgeport, Conn.

Jonas Larrison[8] Babcock (52), son of Stephen (44) and Mercy (Davis) Babcock, b. Mar. 1, 1820; d. Apr. 21, 1855; m. Abby C. Stanton, of Stonington, Conn.; b. Mar. 1, 1822; d. Nov. 12, 1853. Mr. Babcock was very gentlemanly, agreeable to everybody, and a favorite in the family. For a number of years he was engaged in carrying cheese to Providence, R. I., by his own team, making regular trips during the summer and late into the autumn. He built the house where he lived and died, opposite the West Broad St. schoolhouse in Westerly (Pawcatuck), R. I. He was a member of the Congregational Church near his home, where the funeral services were held. In his will he remembered this church.

Son:

Edwin Lewis, b. Sept. 5, 1843; d. Apr. 8, 1849.

Wm. Stuart[8] Babcock (53), son of Stephen and Mercy (Davis) Babcock [Nathaniel, Nathaniel, James, James, John, James], b. Mar. 20, 1822; d. May 8, 1899; m., Oct. 4, 1859, Frances E. Maine, b. June 15, 1840. Mr. Babcock was captain of a militia company in 1845, and was a farmer in Stonington and Plainfield, Conn., where he died.

Children, b. Plainfield, Conn.:

82. William Payson[9], b. Feb. 5, 1862 (114-116).
83. Frances Nella, b. July 28, 1865 (117-119).
84. Anna E., b. Jan. 16, 1867 (120-123).
85. Stephen R., b. Feb. 6, 1870 (124-126).
86. Callia Maine, b. Nov. 16, 1871 (127-130).
87. Telley Eugene, b. Oct. 22, 1876 (131).

Mary Ann[9] Babcock (57), b. June 15, 1821; d. Mar. 24, 1892; m., June 20, 1844, Edwin P. Berry, d. Feb. 4, 1874.

Children, b. Stonington, Conn.:

    88. Emma A.[10], b. June 10, 1845 (103-108).

    89. Sarah G., b. Aug. 16, 1846; d. Nov. 17, 1881.

    89a. Charles W., b. ———; d. young.

    90. Lucy Marion, b. Feb. 22, 1849 (109-113).

    91. Edwin P., b. Oct. 10, 1850; d. Apr. 23, 1873.

Frank W.[9] Babcock (58), son of Stephen, Jr., and Emma (Bentley) Babcock [Stephen, Nathaniel, Nathaniel, James, James, John, James], b. Nov. 5, 1827; d. May 31, 1893; m., Feb. 28, 1877, Mrs. Sarah Thompson, née Wilbur. He was a farmer in Stonington, Conn.

    Dau.:

    91a. Christine Evalena[10], b. Nov. 21, 1878; m., Apr. 17, 1897, Henry J. Spencer. Children: (1) Edith Louise, b., Westerly, R. I., Jan. 4, 1898; (2) William Clifford, b., Chester, Mass., June 11, 1901. Res., Mystic, Conn.

Ira Bentley[9] Babcock (59), brother of the preceding, b. July 24, 1830; m., W. Torrington, Conn., Feb. 22, 1857, Maria C. Green, b., Canaan, Conn., Oct. 22, 1835; dau. of Samuel Green, b., Ancram, N. Y., Apr. 16, 1812, d. Aug. 11, 1873, and Sally A. Packard, b., Hartford, Conn., Feb. 23, 1814; m. Nov. 24, 1834; d. Oct. 4, 1864.

    Children, b. Goshen, Conn.:

    92. Edwin Stephen[10] Babcock, b. Mar. 15, 1859; m., Naugatuck, Conn., Dec. 20, 1885, Laura Candee, b. Dec. 20, 1865; dau. of Henry and Sarah (Scoville) Candee. Bookkeeper and manager for the N. E. Engineering Co. of Waterbury, Conn., for eight years. No issue. Occupation, Automobiles. Res., 1908, Brooklyn, N. Y.

    93. Ida Maria[10] Babcock, b. Sept. 14, 1864; m., Torrington, May 8, 1888, George Luman Harrison, b., Cornwall, Conn., Dec. 3, 1859; son of Heman Harrison, b., Cornwall, Feb. 12, 1812, and Mary E. Judd, b., Canaan, Conn., Dec. 1, 1825. He is a farmer. Children: (1) Lee H., b. June 3, 1891; (2) Ramond F., b. Aug. 27, 1893. Res., 1908, Torrington, Conn.

    93a. Roena Babcock, b. Feb., 1867; d. Nov. 18, 1869.

Samuel Avery Babcock[9] (61), son of Samuel H. and Caroline (Stanton) Babcock [Stephen, Nathaniel, Nathaniel, James, James, John, James], b., No. Stonington, Conn., Dec. 29, 1832; d. Mar. 10, 1892; m., So. Kingston, R. I., Dec. 14, 1863, Mary J. Barber, b. Nov. 27, 1842. He was a successful teacher in the public schools in Rhode Island and Connecticut for twenty-

Jonas L. Babcock (52) and wife, Abby C. Stanton

Page 27

Mrs. Lydia E. Harris

(377)

Eagleville, Conn.

Page 67

five years, and afterwards a farmer in his native town. Res., No. Stonington, Conn.

Children:

94. Emma E.[10], b. Feb. 3, 1869.

95. Edwin A., b. Sept. 5, 1872.

96. Frank H., b. Nov. 4, 1878.

William Prentice[9] Babcock (78), son of John D. and Eunice A. (Maine) Babcock [Stephen, Nathaniel, Nathaniel, James, James, John, James], b. July 14, 1855; m., No. Stonington, Conn., Sept. 24, 1882, Mary E. Burdick, b. May 30, 1863; dau. of Horace F. Burdick, a soldier in the Civil War. Mr. Burdick, son of Jonathan and Ann (Coon) Burdick, b. Nov. 2, 1840; m. Mary Frances Sherley, b., No. Stonington, Mar. 1, 1844; d. Mar. 20, 1904; dau. of Geo. W. and Nancy A. (Peckham) Sherley. Mr. Babcock is a farmer, and has always lived in his native town. He is devoted to his family and derives his greatest happiness in his home, surrounded by his family. He easily recalls names and events, and is interested in genealogical data. His wife is a member of the Baptist Church.

Children, b. No. Stonington:

97. Allis M.[10], b. Oct. 16, 1883.

98. Ida B., b. Jan. 21, 1885.

99. Anna L., b. Aug. 20, 1886.

100. Betsey F., b. July 9, 1889.

101. Susan V., b. Dec. 29, 1890.

102. Frances A., b. Sept. 6, 1892.

Emma A. Berry[10] (88), dau. of Edwin P. and Mary Ann (Babcock) Berry, b., Stonington, Conn., June 10, 1845; m., Apr. 6, 1866, Edward Taylor Pitcher, son of Joel and Pauline (Peckham) Pitcher, of No. Stonington. He was a private in the Civil War, Co. G., 21st Conn. Regiment Vol. Infantry (see Ezekiel Main record, 541).

Children, b. No. Stonington, Conn.:

103. Lucy Marion Pitcher,[11] b. Feb. 4, 1868; d. June 3, 1898; m., Aug. 26, 1894, Thomas Lewis Peabody, son of Newland and Sarah (Lewis) Peabody. Children: Benjamin Lewis[12], b. Aug. 25, 1895; Frank Carroll, b. June 2, 1898.

104. Nellie M. Pitcher, b. May 23, 1871; m., No. Stonington, Feb. 9, 1890, Thomas Edwin Brown (B. G. 450, p. 53). Dau.: Marion Louise, b. July 8, 1893; d. Sept. 10, 1893.

105. Grace Louise Pitcher, b. Mar. 18, 1873; m., No. Stonington, May 25, 1892, George A. Thompson (B. G. 4498, p. 522).

Children: (1) Sarah Palmer, b. July 11, 1899; (2) Ruth Gladys, b. July 30, 1903. Res., 1908, No. Stonington, Conn.

106. Sarah Evelyn Pauline Pitcher, b. May 28, 1880; m., No. Stonington, Oct. 25, 1900, Fred K. Schwenk. Dau.: Marion Kienzel, b. Oct. 13, 1901. Res., 1908, Westerly, R. I.

107. Edward Waldo, b. Feb. 21, 1884.

108. Henry Earl, b. Aug. 16, 1887.

Lucy Marion Berry[10] (90), dau. of Edwin P. and Mary Ann (Babcock) Berry, b., Stonington, Conn., Feb. 22, 1849; m., Dec., 1868, William A. Potter, b. Mar. 29, 1842, son of Alfred Warren and Deborah (Chase) Potter. Res., Waterbury, Conn.

Children, first four b. Meriden, Conn.:

109. Willie[11], b. Oct. 23, 1869; d. Jan. 1, 1871.

110. Emma May, b. Sept. 23, 1872; m., June 23, 1898, Albert Horton Miller, b. Feb. 23, 1872.

111. Clara Louise, b. Dec. 27, 1875.

112. Lillian Berry, b. Mar. 31, 1887.

113. Ruth Marion, b., Waterbury, Conn., Jan. 7, 1890.

William Payson[9] Babcock (82), son of William Stuart and Frances E. (Maine) Babcock [Stephen, Nathaniel, Nathaniel, James, James, John, James], b. Feb. 5, 1862; m., May 11, 1892, Gracie A. Green. Mr. Babcock is a mechanic and repairs all kinds of machines; wood-worker and metals. Res., 1908, Plainfield, Conn.

Children, b. Plainfield:

114. Frances E.[10], b. June 26, 1894.

115. Lillian C., b. Aug. 3, 1898.

116. William E., b. Nov. 3, 1901.

Frances Nella Babcock (83), sister of the preceding, b., Plainfield, Conn., July 28, 1865; m., Plainfield, Jan. 1, 1890, George Lester Bradford, b., Canterbury, Conn., Aug. 5, 1865; d., Plainfield, Apr. 5, 1906; son of John and Jane C. (Congdon) Bradford, of Canterbury. He was a Republican and combined blacksmithing with farming. His wife completed her education at the Plainfield Academy, and taught school until her marriage. Mr. Bradford was a direct descendant in the eighth generation of George Bradford, who came over in the *Mayflower*. He was also a cousin of the gifted Burleigh family of Plainfield. He served in many offices of his town, and was chosen to represent it in the State Legislature in 1895.

Children, b. Plainfield:

117. Alice Nella[10], b. Oct. 3, 1891.

118. John William, b. Aug. 16, 1895.
119. Cecil Babcock, b. July 19, 1897.

Anna Evenor Babcock (84), dau. of Wm. S. and Frances E. (Maine) Babcock, sister of the preceding, b., Plainfield, Conn., Jan. 16, 1867; m., Plainfield, Apr. 25, 1889, Nathan Exley, Jr., b., Westerly, R. I., Jan. 5, 1866; son of Nathan and Janett (Riddell) Exley, of Canterbury, Conn. He is a farmer and a Republican. His wife was educated in the public schools and at the Plainfield Academy, teaching before marriage in Canterbury, Plainfield, and W. Greenwich, R. I. Res., 1908, Plainfield, Conn.

Children, b. Canterbury:
  120. William Stuart, b. Jan. 14, 1891.
  121. Edith Maine, b. Sept. 18, 1893.
  122. Florence Riddell, b. Sept. 27, 1896.
  123. Lucius Morgan, b. Sept. 1, 1901.

Stephen Richard Babcock (85), son of William S. and Frances E. (Maine) Babcock [Stephen, Nathaniel, Nathaniel, James, James, John, James], b., Plainfield, Conn., Feb. 6, 1870; m., Canterbury, Conn., Apr. 6, 1898, Birdie May Kenyon, b., No. Stonington, Conn., Dec. 29, 1879; dau. of Henry B. and Harriet Ada (Park) Kenyon, of Canterbury. He is a farmer and Republican. They attend the Canterbury Congregational Church, and his wife is a member. He was educated in the public schools and at the Plainfield Academy. They reside with his mother on the homestead of his father, in Plainfield.

Children, b. Plainfield:
  124. Ella May, b. Jan. 25, 1899.
  125. Ruby Ada, b. July 22, 1903.
  126. Richard Stuart, b. Oct. 31, 1906.

Callia Maine Babcock (86), dau. of William S. and Frances E. (Maine) Babcock, sister of the preceding, b., Plainfield, Conn., Nov. 16, 1871; m., Plainfield, Oct. 6, 1897, Albert Exley, brother of the husband of her sister, b., Westerly, R. I., May 30, 1867; son of Nathan and Janet (Riddell) Exley, who were b. in England. Mr. Exley is a locomotive engineer, and a Republican. They attend the Baptist Church, Poquonoc Bridge, Conn. Res., 1908, Groton, Conn.

Children:
  127. Bertha E., b., Norwich, Conn., Nov. 10, 1898.
  128. Clarice C., b., Norwich, Nov. 20, 1900.
  129. Martha M., b., New London, Conn., Oct. 15, 1903.
  130. Maybell E., b., Poquonoc Bridge, May 20, 1907.

Telley Eugene Babcock (87), son of William Stuart and Frances E. (Maine) Babcock, brother of the preceding b., Plainfield, Conn., Oct. 22, 1876; m., Boston, Mass., Aug. 15, 1906, M. Elizabeth Geeson, b., Nottingham, England, Feb. 29, 1876; dau. of John and Mary J. (Harrison) Geeson, of Tewksbury, Mass. Mr. Babcock is an attorney at law in Plainfield and Norwich, Conn. He secured his early education in the public schools of his native town, and later attended the Norwich Business College. He taught school for a time at Westminster, and in 1897 he entered the Norwich Free Academy, but on account of illness was absent one school year. Nevertheless, he graduated in June, 1901, receiving honorable mention for his work in science. In October of the same year he entered the Boston University Law School, graduating in 1904 with the degree of LL.B. The same year he passed the Connecticut State Bar Examinations. Mr. Babcock was chosen to represent his town in the State Legislature for the term of 1907-08; served on the Committee of Cities and Boroughs, and as clerk of that committee; and clerk of the County Representatives of his county. He is modest and gentlemanly, and has before him a bright future.

Dau.:

    131. Anita Marion, b., Plainfield, July 11, 1907.

Telley Eugene Babcock

(87)

Residence of Susan H. Babcock, 1902 1910

(76)

Old Mystic, Conn.

Page 96

The Simeon Main Family.[*]

See p. 51. (2. 72 - 3. 192).

These records that now follow belong in the Brown Genealogy, but they were not traced until that book was published. Several of these married into the Babcock family.

Martha, or Patty, York (B. G. 1299, p. 171), dau. of Bell York (B. G. 1254), b., Stonington, Conn., Dec. 16, 1780; d. Feb. 15, 1878; m. (1), by Elder Simeon Brown, Stonington, June 23, 1794, Simeon Main, b., Stonington, Sept. 16, 1772; d., No. Stonington, May 1, 1821; m. (2) Dea. John Stanton.

The No. Stonington Town Records say: "Simeon Main, b. Nov. 27, 1768; m. Martha York, b. Dec. 16, 1777."

Children, b. No. Stonington:

132. Prentice, b. Feb. 22, 1797; m. Anna Miner (B. G. 1151), (141, 142).

133. Prudence, b. —; d. July 8, 1806, aged seven years.

134. Joanna, b. Dec. 29, 1801; m. De Wooley. They went West in early life and he became an eminent lawyer.

135. Phœbe, b. July 27, 1803; m. Dudley Mitchell (143, 144).

136. Hulda, b. Oct. 11, 1806; m. Zebulon B. Miner (187–191).

137. Richard Holmes, b. Feb. 27, 1809; m. Mrs. Abby (Stanton) Hewitt, née Crandall (145–148).

138. Adam, b. Oct. 29, 1811; m. Lucy M. Main (149–152).

139. Daniel, b. June 21, 1814; d.——, aged two years.

140. Christopher G., b. 1819; d. Sept. 7, 1861; m. Lydia E. Miner (179), dau. of Isaac and Katurah (Brown) Miner, b. Aug., 1815; d. June 14, 1884. Son: Miner Main, b. Sept. 2, 1840; unm. Res., No. Stonington, Conn.

Prentice Main (132), son of Simeon Main and Martha York (B. G. 1299, p. 171) [Katurah Brown (B. G. 382b, p. 161), Dea. Zebulon (74), James (38), Eleazer (11), Thomas], b., Stonington, Conn., Feb. 22, 1798; d., No. Stonington, Conn., Feb. 4, 1890; m., No. Stonington, 1825, Anna Miner (B. G. 1151), b., Stonington, Dec. 11, 1803; d., No. Stonington, May 25, 1888; dau. of Isaac Miner, b., Stonington, Mar. 2, 1773, and Ka-

[*]This family originally spelled their names Main, but *some* of the later generations have added *e*, Maine. The compiler has as nearly as possible conformed to their wishes.

33

turah Brown (B. G. 382b). Mr. Main spent his whole life in his native town, was a farmer, and both he and his wife were members of the Second Baptist Church. By strict economy and prudent forethought he accumulated a large property from small beginnings. He loaned his money to Dudley R. Wheeler, and after the savings banks in Westerly were inaugurated he placed with his family in the Westerly banks all the law would allow, and then in the Norwich banks.

Children, b. No. Stonington.

    141. Eunice Ann Maine, b. Aug. 20, 1829; m John D. Babcock (78–81).

    142. Isaac Maine, b. July 8, 1833 (163–171).

Phœbe Main (135), sister of the preceding, b , No Stonington, Conn., July 27, 1803; d , Old Mystic, Conn., Oct. 6, 1890; m. Dudley Mitchell
    Children, b Old Mystic:

    143. Amos Mitchell.

    144. Wm. Henry Mitchell. Children and grandchildren res. at Old Mystic, Conn. Did not answer queries.

Richard Holmes Main (137), son of Simeon and Martha, or Patty, York Main, b., No. Stonington, Conn., Feb. 27, 1809; d., No. Stonington, Sept. 24, 1901, aged ninety-three years; m Mrs. Abby Stanton Hewitt, née Crandall, b. Nov. 24, 1805; d. Sept. 9, 1851. Mr. Main was a farmer in his native town, on Winnechuck Hill, a member of the Second Baptist Church, and devout in his Christian duties, He was named for Richard Holmes, b. 1774, d. Apr. 6, 1851, who was a prominent man and lived where Adam Main spent his days, and on the same farm is the Holmes burying-ground of about sixty graves. The schoolhouse, at the south, was always known as "The Holmes Schoolhouse."

Children, b. No. Stonington:

    144a. George Washington, b. Dec. 28, 1833 (241–243).

    145. Charles Henry, b. Jan. 3, 1837 (158–162)

    146. Frances E., b June 15, 1840; m. Wm. S. Babcock (82–87).

    147. Mary Abbie, b. July 26, 1844; m. Geo. A. Avery (record follows 162).

    148 John D., b. Aug. 14, 1846; d. Sept. 1, 1851.

Adam Main (138), son of Simeon and Martha, or Patty, (York) Main (B. G. 1299, p. 171), b. Oct. 29, 1811; d., No Stonington, Conn., Mar. 31, 1893; m., Apr. 6, 1843, Lucy M. Main, b. 1821; d. Jan 19, 1890, dau of Jesse Main, who lived near Dea. Allen Wheeler. Mr. Main was a farmer and passed his whole life in his native town, a quiet, unassuming, and respected citizen. The children that follow spell their names Maine

Children, b. No. Stonington:

149. Lucy A. Maine, b. June 14, 1845 (153-157.)

150. Park Benjamin Maine, b. Sept. 8, 1847; m. (1), No. Stonington, June 30, 1872, Emma L. Woodmansee; after her death he m. (2), Aug. 1, 1882, Lillie A. Main, b. July 20, 1861; dau. of Amasa and Lucy (Frink) Main. No issue by either m. Res., No. Stonington, Conn.

151. Herman Maine, b. Mar. 8, 1850; m., No. Stonington, 1881, Sarah E. Campbell, b., Stonington, June 9, 1850; dau. of John and Margaret (Cornell) Campbell, of Stonington. She is a member of the Methodist Church. No issue. Res., Old Mystic, Conn.

152. Nellie A. Maine, b. Jan. 8, 1864; m., No. Stonington, June 29, 1886, George C. Brown, b. July 30, 1864 (B. G., p. 153); son of Clark L. and Sabrina (Maine) Brown. He is a farmer and a Democrat; attends the Third Baptist Church, No. Stonington. Res. on the homestead of his father-in-law, Adam Main.

Lucy A. Maine (149), dau. of Adam (138) and Lucy M. (Main) Main [Martha York (B. G. 1299), Katurah Brown (B. G. 382b), Dea. Zebulon (74), James (38), Eleazer (11), Thomas], b. June 14, 1845; m. (1), No. Stonington, Conn., Sept. 25, 1861, William E. Coon, b. Oct. 1, 1841; d. No. Stonington; son of William E. and Phœbe (Frink) Coon. He was a farmer, and they attended the Second Baptist Church, No. Stonington. She m. (2) Amos C. Burdick, d., No. Stonington, May 8, 1895; son of Amos and Wealtha (Allen) Burdick. Res., 1908, No. Stonington, Conn.

Children by first m., b. No. Stonington:

153. Chauncey E. Coon, b. Apr. 28, 1863; m. Julia Kelly. Children: (1) Nellie, deceased; (2) Willie E.; (3) John T.; (4) Katie; (5) Mary D.; (6) Jesse W.; (7) Annie M.; (8) Frank; (9) Julia A.; (10) Fanny.

154. Frank Eugene Coon, b. Feb. 9, 1867; m., Old Mystic, Conn., July 3, 1895, Melissa Green, b., Perryville, R. I., Apr. 2, 1876; dau. of Albert C. and Agnese M. (Burdick) Green, of Green Hill, R. I. Mr. Coon received a public-school education, and was in company with A. D. Miner in the grocery business for four years; Selectman in No. Stonington in 1894; in Stonington, Conn., in 1901; Assessor in Stonington two years. In 1908 employed in Campbell's mill in Westerly, R.I. Children, b. Stonington: (1) Marion Reba, b. June 5, 1899;

(2) Raymond, b. Dec. 3, 1901; (3) Anis Louise, b. Oct. 19, 1904; (4) Alice Della, b. Nov. 22, 1906; (5) Carroll Evans, b. Mar. 13, 1908.

155. Jessie A. Coon, b. June 12, 1869; d. Dec. 10, 1897; m. Robert C. Miller. Children: (1) Willie Woodward; (2) Ethel Campbell.

156. Delia A. Coon, b. Mar. 16, 1871; d., Norwich, Conn., May 29, 1894; m. Edward J. Duro. Children: (1) Archibald E., b. Sept. 4, 1886, a machinist in Norwich; (2) Amy D., b.—, d. Apr. 12, 1893, aged three years; (3) Lucy Dorothy, b. July 31, 1892, a student at Wheeler High School, No. Stonington, 1908.

Dau. by second m.:

157. Alida M. Burdick, b. Aug. 25, 1883; graduated from Pawcatuck High School, Westerly, R. I. She is now [1908] bookkeeper and cashier in Westerly.

Charles Henry Main (145), son of Richard H. and Mrs. Abby S. Hewitt, née Crandall, Main, b., No. Stonington, Conn., Jan. 3, 1837; m. (1), 1860, Louisa Miner, b. Apr. 17, 1844; d. Sept. 12, 1875; m. (2), Mar. 30, 1877, Lovisa Miner, twin sister of first wife, and dau. of Palmer N. and Martha P. (York) Miner (B. G., p. 161). Mr. Main owns large and productive farms on Winnechuck Hill, including the farm that was his father's. Children by first m., b. No. Stonington:

158. Mary Alice, b. Aug. 16, 1861; m., Mar. 6, 1883, Dea. Thomas W. Avery. Children: Albert T., b. Jan. 25, 1899; John D., b. Dec. 29, 1895. Two children d. in infancy.

159. Abby Crandall, b. Dec. 16, 1865; m., No. Stonington, Sept. 25, 1894, Rev. John G. Stanton, b., Mystic, Conn., July 7, 1867; son of Amos G. and Betsey (Williams) Stanton. Mr. Stanton spent two years at the Mystic Valley Institute, and taught school at Preston, Groton, and Montville, Conn., taking private instruction; and finally entered Newton Baptist Theological Institute, graduating with the class of 1894. He settled for seven years over the Baptist church at No. Oxford, Mass.; two years at Woodville, Mass. He is now [1908] pastor at Plainfield (Moosup), Conn., in his sixth year. He has been on the School Board of Plainfield for three years. Mrs. Stanton received instruction in her native town and the M. V. Institute, and took a partial course at the New Britain Normal School. She taught school in No. Stoning-

ton two years, and for five years was a successful grammar-school teacher at Mystic. Children: (1) Gladys E., b., No. Oxford, June 25, 1895; (2) Paul M., b., No. Oxford, June 12, 1898, d. in infancy; (3) Ruth M., b , Woodville, Nov. 11, 1901; (4) Donald H., b., Moosup, May 12, 1906.

160. Martha Lovisa, b. Dec. 19, 1867; m., No. Stonington, Sept. 25, 1894, Frank R. Green, b., Seekonk, Mass., June 9, 1867; son of Edwin H. and Mary A. (Briggs) Green, of Coventry, R. I. Mr. Green is superintendent of cloth finishing, and both he and his wife are members of the Congregational church. Children: (1) Lila Beatrice, b., River Point, R. I., Jan. 31, 1897; (2) Florence Inez, b., Shelton, Conn., Sept. 21, 1899, d. Apr. 23, 1904; (3) Edwin Maine, b., Saylesville, Apr. 4, 1901; (4) Charles Elton, b., Saylesville, July 18, 1904. Res., Saylesville, R. I.

161. Charles E., b. Dec. 16, 1870; unm. Res., Providence, R. I.

162. Nancy E., b. Oct. 10, 1872; d. Sept. 28, 1875.

Mary Abbie Maine (147), dau. of Richard H. and Mrs. Abby S. Hewitt, née Crandall, b., No. Stonington, Conn., July 26, 1844; m., No. Stonington, Mar. 24, 1869, George Albert Avery, b., Groton, Conn., Mar. 4, 1840; d., No. Stonington, Mar. 14, 1893; son of Albert L. and Joanna B. (Wheeler) Avery. Mr. Avery was a farmer, a deacon of the Congregational church at No. Stonington, and was a soldier in the Civil War in Co. A, 25th Regiment of Connecticut Vol. No issue. Her res., Plainfield, Conn.

Isaac Maine (142), son of Prentice and Anna (Miner) Main, b., No. Stonington, Conn., July 8, 1833; m., No. Stonington, July 31, 1877, Betsey Ann Maine, b., Ledyard, Conn., Apr. 11, 1858; dau. of Amasa and Lucy (Frink) Maine. He is a Democrat and farmer, and all his life has lived on the farm that was his father's. He is a member of the Second Baptist Church.

Children, b. No. Stonington:

163. Isaac, Jr., b. July 6, 1878.

164. Lucy M., b. Oct. 18, 1879; d. Aug. 22, 1883.

165. Amasa M., b. Apr. 13, 1882.

166. James W., b. June 19, 1883; d. in infancy.

167. Arthur P., b. June 11, 1885; d. in infancy.

168. Truman Parks, b. July 30, 1888. He attended the Wheeler High School, and graduated from the New London Business College; is a bookkeeper in New London, Conn.

169. Jennie Lind, b. Apr. 19, 1891.

170. Adlia E., b. Aug. 18, 1892; d. Nov. 23, 1893.

171. Daisy G., b. Oct. 8, 1894; d. in infancy.

Isaac Maine, Jr. (163), son of Isaac and Betsey Ann (Maine) Maine, b., No. Stonington, Conn., July 6, 1878; m., No. Stonington, Nov. 14. 1902, Nellie J. Chapman, dau. of Truman and Sophia (Maine) Chapman. Res., No. Stonington, Conn.

Children:

(1) Dorothy Evelyn, b. Oct. 1, 1903.

(2) Dorris Irene, b. Feb. 24, 1905.

(3) Violette Marie, b. Aug. 16, 1907.

Amasa M. Maine (165), brother of the preceding, b. Apr. 13, 1882; m. Nettie B. Benjamin.

Children:

(1) Nettie Bell.

(2) Jennie Emeline, d. young.

The Isaac Miner Family.

The Stonington Town Records give over four hundred by the name of Miner. (See Brown Genealogy, pp 161–163.) Wheeler says, "The surname of Miner originated in England during the reign of King Edward the Third, whose reign continued from 1327 to 1377. When preparing for war with France he took progress through Somersett, and came to Mendippe Hill, where lived a man by the name of Bullman, whose extraordinary and successful efforts to aid the king in the munitions of war, with one hundred powerful men volunteers in the service, so pleased the king that he granted him a coat-of-arms, with the name of Henry Miner thereon, in recognition of his loyalty and patriotic devotion to him and his cause." From his grandson Thomas, b. Apr. 23, 1608, m. Grace Palmer, dau. of Walter Palmer, descended General and President Ulysses S. Grant. (See note, Brown Genealogy, p. 11.)

Katurah Brown (B. G. 382b), dau. of Dea. Zebulon (74) and Anne (Main, 808) Brown [James (38), Eleazer (11), Thomas], b 1775, d. Apr. 10, 1854, aged seventy-nine years; m., Stonington, Conn., Mar. 3, 1795, Isaac Miner (B. G. 1139), b. Mar. 2, 1773; d. Dec. 31, 1836; son of Christopher and Mary (Randall) Miner [Data taken from tombstones in an old burying-ground located west of the road that leads from the turnpike to Angwilla, near the farm of the late Deacon Ezra Miner. The farm is now [1908] owned by Hermon C. Brown (429).]

Children, b. Stonington:

172. Katurah, b. Sept. 28, 1797; d. Apr. 23, 1878, aged eighty years; m. Jesse Chapman. No issue. She was his third wife. Interment, Union Cemetery.

173. Isaac Williams, b. Feb. 11, 1799; m. Eliza Green (180–186).

174. Zebulon Brown, b. Jan. 13, 1801, m. Hulda Main, 136 (187–191).

175. Anna, b. Dec. 11, 1803, m Prentice Main (141, 142).

176. Palmer Niles, b. July 29, 1805; m. Martha P. York (192–202).

177. Denison W., b. Dec. 13, 1809; m. Clarissa M Park (203–207).

178. Mary E., b ——, d. Sept 6, 1852; m. Luke Chesborough. Children: (1) Luke Palmer, b. 1836; (2) Mary Matilda, (3) Martha Esther All d., of typhoid fever, in 1864.

179. Lydia E., b. Aug., 1815; m Christopher Main. (See 140.)

39

THE ISAAC MINER FAMILY

Isaac Williams Miner (173), son of Isaac and Katurah (Brown, 382b. B. G., p. 161) Miner, b., Stonington, Conn., Feb. 11, 1799; d. Feb. 14, 1888; m., Mar. 29, 1829, Eliza Green, b. Nov. 3, 1805; d. Sept. 26, 1870. Interment, Elm Grove, Mystic, Conn.

Children:
180. Calvin G., b.——; d. Montrose, Pa.
181. Hiram, b.——; d. Binghamton, N. Y.
182. Jane, b.——; d. New London, Conn.
183. Ellen, b.——; d. Binghamton.
184. Harriet Newel, b. Nov. 28, 1837; d. Mystic, Conn.
185. Emma, b.——; m. Jesse Y. Hull. Res., 1908, Tuckahoe, N. J.
186. Arthur, b.——; still living.

Harriet Newel Miner (184), b., Stonington, Conn., Nov. 28, 1837; d., Mystic, Conn., Nov. 26, 1893; m., Aug. 2, 1864, Dr. Alfred W. Coates, of Mystic. She was his third wife.

Dau.:
Annie Eliza, b., Mystic, July 31, 1867; m. William Dudley Breaker. Children, b. Brooklyn, N. Y.: (1) Helen, b. Mar. 6, 1897; (2) William Dudley, Jr., b. Mar. 15, 1894; (3) Lewis Coates, b. Jan. 27, 1906. Res., Brooklyn, N. Y.

Zebulon Brown Miner (174), son of Isaac Miner and Katurah Brown (B. G., p. 161), b., Stonington, Conn., Jan. 13, 1801; m. Hulda Main (136), b., No. Stonington, Conn., Oct. 11, 1806; dau. of Simeon and Martha (York) Main (B. G. 1299, p. 171). He was a farmer, and spent his whole life in No. Stonington. He was a member of the Second Baptist Church. Interments, Union Cemetery.

Children, b. No. Stonington:
187. Phebe Ann, b. ——; d. ——, aged nineteen years.
188. Amos Prentice, b. Nov. 20, 1838; m. Susan E. Wilkinson (210–216).
189. Frances E., b. Apr. 5, 1840; m. Nathan Benjamin (217–223).
190. Isaac Dwight, b. Aug. 8, 1842; m. Susan K. Main (224, 225).
191. Etna, b. ——; d. young.

Palmer Niles Miner (176), son of Isaac and Katurah (Brown) Miner, brother of the preceding, b. July 29, 1805; d. June 2, 1883; m., No. Stonington, Conn., 1830 Martha Pauline York (B. G. 4340, p. 501), b., No. Stonington, June 7, 1814; d. Dec. 27, 1894; dau. of Nathan and Martha, or Patty, (Breed) York. Mr. Miner owned the farm where Irving W. Miner now lives, which he sold to his brother Denison, and removed to the

40

farm where his son George W. now [1908] lives. On this farm he spent his last days. Both he and his wife were members of the Second Baptist Church. Interment, Union Cemetery.

Children, b. No. Stonington:

192. Marita, b. May 14, 1831; m. Orrin B. Allen (232a–232d).

193. Mary Ann, b. Nov. 1, 1833 (233, 234).

194. Courtland Palmer, b. Feb. 20, 1836; m. Lucy U. Slocum (235–240).

195. Lucy Brown, b. Oct. 26, 1838; m. George W. Main (241–243).

196. George Wilson, b. Apr. 25, 1841; m. Mary A. Chapman (244–247).

197. Louisa, twin, b. Apr. 17, 1844; m. Charles H. Main (158–162).

198. Lovisa, twin, b. Apr. 17, 1844; m. Charles H. Main, husband of her twin sister. No issue.

199. Martha Altana, b. July 12, 1847; m. Harva C. Burdick; d. ninety days after her marriage. His res., Ashaway, R. I.

200. Emeline, b. July 28, 1850; d. Dec. 20, 1874; m. James A. Pendleton.

201. Thomas P., b. Dec. 6, 1852; d. Mar. 5, 1860.

202. Nellie Wheeler, b. June 28, 1856. Her record follows (247).

Denison W. Miner (177), son of Isaac and Katurah (Brown) Miner, brother of the preceding, b. Dec. 13, 1809; d. May 27, 1886; m., No. Stonington, Conn., May 20, 1832, Clarissa M. Park, b., No. Stonington, Dec. 13, 1814; d. Dec. 29, 1897; dau. of Israel Park. Mr. Miner was a farmer, and a member of the Second Baptist Church. His farm was located a short distance east of the Miner Church. He was a most excellent neighbor and friend. Interment, Union Cemetery.

Children, b. No. Stonington:

203. Orrin Eugene, b. Sept. 29, 1834 (208, 209).

204. Clarissa, b. July 26, 1836; m. Elias Miner (B. G., p. 162).

205. Elmina, b. Dec. 13, 1838; d. Oct. 25, 1839.

206. Fanny, b. May 30, 1844; d. Jan. 25, 1861. She was a member of the Second Baptist Church.

207. Irving Wilson, b. July 19, 1857; m., Brooklyn, N. Y., Sept. 23, 1884, M. Annette Stillman, b. May 11, 1859; dau. of John C. and Emeline (Lewis) Stillman, and granddau. of Beriah Lewis, of No. Stonington. No issue. Mr. Miner is a farmer on the homestead of his father. The house is pleasantly located overlooking a valley to where Mrs. Miner's grandfather spent his days, now owned by Horace G. Lewis.

THE ISAAC MINER FAMILY

Dr. Orrin E. Miner (203), son of Denison W. and Clarissa M. (Park) Miner, b. Sept. 29, 1834; m., May 19, 1859, Abby J. Latham, dau. of James and Abby (Palmer) Latham. Dr. Miner was a practising physician at Noank, Conn.

Children, b. Noank:

>208. Orrin Eugene, Jr., b. Nov. 28, 1860. He is in the employ of the U. S. R. R. Postal Service, and has held that position for twenty years. He is married and they have no issue. Res., New London, Conn.

>209. Fanny M., b. Jan. 10, 1870; unm. Res., Noank, Conn.

Amos Prentice Miner (188), son of Zebulon B. Miner (B. G., p. 161) and Hulda Main (136), dau. of Simeon and Martha (York) Main (B. G. 1299, p. 171), b., No. Stonington, Conn., Nov. 20, 1838; m., Westerly, R. I., Dec. 27, 1869, Susan E. Wilkinson, b., Ledyard, Conn., Nov. 2, 1850; dau. of George F. and Sarah I. (Fish) Wilkinson. Mr. Miner is a grocer and farmer, a Republican, and formerly a member of the Second Baptist Church. He received a common-school education, and held the offices of Assessor, Board of Relief, Registrar of Voters, and Trustee of School. Res., No. Stonington, Conn.

Children, b. No. Stonington:

>209a. Susan Alida, b. Nov. 11, 1871; d. Oct. 1, 1896. She was educated at E. Greenwich, R. I., and the Wheeler High School. She was a school-teacher, and a member of the Second Baptist Church. She was a young lady highly esteemed, and of much promise.

>210. Amos Prentice, Jr., b. July 10, 1873; m. Jennie M. M. Deane.

>211. Chester, b. May 12, 1875; m. Fannie Fenner.

>212. Willie, b. Jan. 10, 1879; m. Jennie A. Wilkinson.

>213. Belle, b. June 28, 1880. She is a cashier and bookkeeper, Westerly, R. I.

>214. Parker, b. Jan. 21, 1882; d. Apr. 5, 1883.

>215. Helen Hulda, b. Aug. 20, 1886; m. Birdsey G. Palmer.

>216. Roscoe Revere, b. July 18, 1893.

Amos Prentice Miner, Jr. (210), son of Amos P. and Susan E. (Wilkinson) Miner, b. July 10, 1873; m., No. Stonington, Conn., Dec. 16, 1897, Jennie M. M. Deane, b., No. Stonington, May 26, 1881; dau. of Randolph and Carrie (Green) Deane. Both received common-school education. Mr. Miner took a course at the Wheeler High School. They attend the Second Baptist Church.

Children, b. No. Stonington:

(1) Alvin Prentice, b. Mar. 3, 1899.

(2) Elsie Merial, b. Nov. 9, 1900.

Chester Miner (211), brother of the preceding, b. May 12, 1875; m., Westerly, R. I., Apr. 5, 1897, Fannie Fenner, b., Stonington (Pawcatuck), Conn., Aug. 21, 1876; dau. of Joseph and Mary (Lawler) Fenner. Mr. Miner is a Republican, educated in the common schools and at the Wheeler High School. His wife was educated in the schools of E. Providence and Westerly, R. I. Res., No. Stonington, Conn.

Children, b. No. Stonington:

(1) Olive May, b. June 25, 1901.

(2) Raymond Chester, b. May 11, 1904.

Willie Miner (212), brother of the preceding, b., No. Stonington, Conn., Jan. 10, 1879; m., Voluntown, Conn., Oct. 19, 1897, Jennie A. Wilkinson, b., No. Stonington, Nov. 4, 1882; dau. of Walter A. and Annie (Rathbone) Wilkinson, of No. Stonington. Mr. Miner is a farmer, a Republican, and they both attend the Second Baptist Church. Res., No. Stonington, Conn.

Son:

William Harold, b. Oct. 6, 1898.

Helen Hulda Miner (215), sister of the preceding, b., No. Stonington, Conn., Aug. 20, 1886; m., Pendleton Hill, Conn., June 26, 1907, Birdsey G. Palmer, b., Voluntown, Conn., Aug. 8, 1873, son of Edgar and Harriet (Wheeler) Palmer, of Voluntown. Mr. Palmer had a common-school education, is a Democrat, a Constable, is on the School Board, and Trustee. He is a farmer, combining with it the grocery business. His wife was a student of the Wheeler High School, and a graduate of the Home Correspondence School of Massachusetts. They attend the First Baptist Church. Res., Pendleton Hill, Conn.

Child:

Amelia Miner Palmer, b. Oct. 8, 1908.

Frances E. Miner (189), dau. of Zebulon B. and Hulda (Main 136) Miner, b., No. Stonington, Conn., Apr. 5, 1840; d., Preston, Conn., Nov. 7, 1903; m., No. Stonington, Aug. 27, 1862, Nathan Benjamin, b., Preston, Jan. 19, 1834; son of Nathan H. and Hannah (Cook) Benjamin, of Preston. Mr. Benjamin is a farmer, a Democrat, and his wife is a member of the Baptist Church. Res., Norwich, Conn.

Children, b. Preston:

217. Nellie F. Benjamin, b. June 25, 1863; d., Preston, Feb. 10,

1887; m., Preston, Sept., 1881, Frank D. Turner, of No. Stonington.

218. Henry B. Benjamin, b. July 26, 1866. He is a farmer in Preston.

219. Nathan W. Benjamin, b. Oct. 11, 1868; m., E. Greenwich, R. I., Nov., 1893, Mary A. Shaw, of E. Greenwich. He is in the grocery business in Providence, R. I. Son: Arthur D., b. Feb., 1895.

220. Mary A. Benjamin, b. Sept. 1, 1870; m., E. Greenwich, Mar. 4, 1895, Arthur W. Savage, of Rockland, Me. Both are book-keepers for W. L. Main, Mystic, Conn. Dau.: Marguerite May, b., Preston, Dec. 2, 1898; d. Feb. 10, 1899.

221. Sarah A. Benjamin, b. July 4, 1872; d., Preston, Nov. 20, 1900.

221a. Elizabeth A. Benjamin, b. Feb. 5, 1877; m., Mystic, Aug. 27, 1901, William L. Main, of Ledyard, Conn.; son of Leeds Main, whose father was Wm. Leeds Main, who lived west of Lantern Hill, Conn. He conducts a large grocery business in Mystic.

222. Frank A. Benjamin, b. Dec. 28, 1880. He is a farmer. Res., Preston, Conn.

223. Albert D. Benjamin, b. July 8, 1886. He is a grocer in Stonington, Conn.

Isaac Dwight Miner (190), son of Zebulon B. and Hulda (Main 136), Miner, b., No. Stonington, Conn., Aug. 8, 1842; m., No. Stonington, Sept. 7, 1864, Susan K. Main, b., Staten Island, N. Y., June 14, 1846; dau. of Stephen and Lydia (York) Main. Lydia York (B. G. 1326, p. 172), dau. of Jeremiah and Thankful (Thurston) York, b. Nov. 24, 1812; d. Aug. 8, 1846; she was the second wife of Stephen Main, son of Rufus and Sabra (Wells) Main. Susan K. Main, when two months old, after the death of her mother, lived with her grandparents until her marriage. Mr. Miner has been a successful business man; he owned at one time the Nathaniel M. Crary farm in No. Stonington, where he started a store, but removed to the village later. Afterwards he owned and operated stores in different localities, the last at E. Greenwich, R. I., which he sold to his son. He conducted his business with marked success, and now [1908] has retired from active service. Res., Norwood, R. I.

Children, b. No. Stonington:

224. Albert D., b. June 23, 1867 (226–230).

225. John Durward, b. Dec. 10, 1869 (231,232).

Albert D. Miner (224), son of the preceding, m., Scituate, R. I., Feb. 12, 1887, Mary E. Arnold, b., Scituate, Aug. 7, 1867; dau. of Simeon C. and Alzada (Tourtellot) Arnold, of Scituate. Both he and his wife are members of the Baptist Church. They completed their education at the E. Greenwich Academy, R. I. Mr. Miner bought out the grocery store at E. Greenwich conducted by his father in 1890, and has since operated it with good success, also two stores of like character in Westerly, R. I. Res., E. Greenwich, R. I.

Children, b. E. Greenwich:

226. Florence May, b. Jan. 27, 1889.
227. Isaac Dwight, b. May 24, 1890.
228. Harold Cranston, b. Sept. 8, 1893.
229. Ralph W., b. May 9, 1897.
230. Wilfred A., b. Aug. 16, 1903.

John Durward Miner (225), son of Isaac D. and Susan K. (Main) Miner, b., No. Stonington, Conn., Dec. 20, 1869; m., E. Greenwich, R. I., Oct. 30, 1902, Bertha Alice Owen, b., E. Greenwich, July 1, 1877; dau. of William Aldrich and Mary (Morris) Owen, of E. Greenwich. Mr. Miner resided in his native town the first fourteen years of his life, afterwards in E. Greenwich. He is a graduate of Brown University, class of 1891; his wife is a graduate of the State Normal School of Providence, class of 1896. Mr. Miner has a department store, and both are members of the Baptist Church. Res., E. Greenwich, R. I.

Children, b. E. Greenwich:

231. John Durward, Jr., b. Oct. 3, 1903.
232. Irving Owens, b. June 12, 1905.

Marita Miner (192), dau. of Palmer N. and Martha P. (York) Miner, b., No. Stonington, Conn., May 14, 1831; m., No. Stonington, Orrin B. Allen, d. Oct. 5, 1881, aged fifty-five years.

Children, b. No. Stonington:

232a. Eva A., b. ——; d. Nov. 9, 1878, aged twenty-four years.
232b. Ida E., b. ——; d. Apr. 13, 1882, aged sixteen years and nine months.
232c. Jennie L., b. ——; d. May 4, 1883, aged fourteen years and ten months.
232d. Emma G., b.——; d. Jan. 29, 1884, aged twenty-four years and eleven months. [Data taken from Union Cemetery. Mrs. Allen's res., 1908, No. Stonington, Conn.]

THE ISAAC MINER FAMILY

Mary Ann Miner (193), dau. of Palmer N. and Martha P. (York) Miner,
b., No. Stonington, Conn., Nov. 1, 1833; d., Lebanon, Conn., Aug. 3, 1875;
m., No. Stonington, Nov. 11, 1854, Horace Wells, of Ashaway, R. I., b.
Feb. 12, 1833. Mary A. Miner and her sister Marita were schoolmates of
the compiler.

Children, b. Ashaway:

    233. Clara Pauline Wells, b. Nov. 6, 1859; d. Nov. 11, 1885.

    234. Maryette Wells, b. July 27, 1864; m., No. Stonington. Sept. 1,
           1886, James Winslow Maine, b., No. Stonington, Sept. 26,
           1863; son of Orrin T. and Mary (Johnson) Maine. Mr. and
           Mrs. Maine are members of the Baptist Church; in politics he
           is a Republican. Mr. Maine was clerk in a store at Hope
           Valley and Arctic, R. I.; manager of a store at Fiskville, and
           has been in the employ of B. B. & R. Knight & Co. at Natick,
           R. I., for twenty years, and manager of one of their stores for
           fifteen years. Children, b. Natick, except the first: (1) Clar-
           ence Elsworth, b., Arctic, June 11, 1888; (2) Arline, b. Oct.
           22, 1894, d. Nov. 24, 1894; (3) Mildred, b. Oct. 12, 1895;
           (4) Dorothy, b. Oct. 8, 1896; (5) Chester Brackett, b. Aug.
           25, 1899; (6) Ruth Marion, b. Sept. 13, 1902; (7) Norman
           York, b. Sept. 24, 1907. Res., Natick, R. I.

Courtland Palmer Miner (194), son of Palmer N. and Martha P. (York)
Miner, b., No. Stonington, Conn., Feb. 20, 1836; m., No. Stonington, May
20, 1866, Lucy U. Slocum, b., No. Stonington, May 1, 1846; dau. of Jesse
B. and Lucy Caroline (Park) Slocum, dau. of Israel Park. Mr. Miner is a
farmer and has resided in No. Stonington all his life.

Children, b. No. Stonington:

    235. George Palmer, b. Feb. 20, 1867; unm. He is an alderman in
           Preston, Conn.

    236. Charles Elbert, b. Aug. 31, 1868; m. Maria Gore (248–250).

    237. William Jesse, b. Aug. 4, 1872; m. Addie R. Pierce (251–253).

    238. Nellie May, b. May 16, 1875; m. S. Curtis Eggleston (254, 255).

    239. Anna Grace, b. Jan. 3, 1880; m. Charles H. C. Miner (256).

    240. Arthur Courtland, b. Oct. 26, 1885; m. Anna M. Chapman (257).

Lucy Brown Miner (195), dau. of Palmer N. and Martha P. (York)
Miner, b., No. Stonington, Conn., Oct. 26, 1838; m. George W. Main
(144a), b., No. Stonington, Dec. 28, 1833; d., Hop River, Conn., Apr. 26,
1904; son of Richard H. Main and Mrs. Abby (Stanton) Hewitt, née Cran-

dall. Mr. Main was a farmer, a Democrat, and attended the Congregational Church. Her res., 1908, Hop River, Conn.

Children:

241. George Henry Main, b., Stonington, Conn., Nov. 12, 1857; d., Hop River, Nov. 3, 1901.

242. Mary Jane Main, b., Hop River, Aug. 15, 1863; m., So. Coventry, Conn., Frank Collins.

243. Susan Pearl Main, b., Hop River, July 25, 1882; m., Willimantic, Conn., May 1, 1907, Claud Griggs. Res., Hop River, Conn.

George Wilson Miner (196), brother of the preceding, and son of Palmer N. and Martha P. (York) Miner, b., No. Stonington, Conn., Apr. 25, 1841. m., No. Stonington, Feb. 27, 1887, Mary A. Chapman, b. June 10, 1859; dau. of Wm. D. and Lois A. (Chapman) Chapman, and granddau. of Jesse Chapman, who m. Katurah Brown (172) for his third wife. Mr. Miner lives on the homestead that was his father's. The house is well preserved, and on one of the chambers and bedroom the wall-paper has been on one hundred years and is in a good state of preservation. They are members of the Second Baptist Church.

Children, b. No. Stonington:

244. George Franklin, b. Sept. 5, 1889.

245. Maurice Chapman, b. Feb. 28, 1891.

246. Palmer William, b. Feb. 1, 1894.

247. Herbert Allen, b. Aug. 20, 1898.

Nellie Wheeler Miner (202), youngest dau. of Palmer N. and Martha P. (York) Miner, b. June 28, 1856; m. Thomas Franklin Richardson, b. Feb. 23, 1852; son of Benadam and Sarah (Burdick) Richardson. No issue. Mr. Richardson is a farmer, and owns the farm one mile north of Westerly in Stonington, Conn., known as "The Thomas Hinckley Farm." He is a prudent, industrious man and a model farmer.

Charles Elbert Miner (236), son of Courtland P. and Lucy U. (Slocum) Miner, b., No. Stonington, Conn., Aug. 31, 1868; m., Preston, Conn., Apr. 1, 1893, Abby Maria Gore, b., Preston, July 19, 1864; dau. of Joseph Albert and Elizabeth (Fitch) Gore, of Preston. Res., Norwich, Conn.

Children;

248. Lillian Maria, b., No. Stonington, Feb. 3, 1894.

249. Charles Amos, b., Preston, Sept. 17, 1898.

250. Grace Edna, b., Preston, Jan. 3, 1904.

William Jesse Miner (237), brother of the preceding, b., No. Stonington,

Conn., Aug. 4, 1872; m., Preston, Conn., July 19, 1893, Addie R. Pierce, b., Griswold, Conn., Mar. 4, 1871; dau. of William and Sarah (Penry) Pierce, of Griswold. Mr. Miner is a mechanic in the blacksmithing business. Res., Griswold, Conn.

Children:

251. Minnie, b., No. Stonington, July 8, 1894.

252. Dora, b., Griswold, Aug. 25, 1899.

253. Lucy, b., Griswold, June 21, 1905.

Nellie May Miner (238), sister of the preceding, b., No. Stonington, Conn., May 16, 1875; m., No. Stonington, July 16, 1893, S. Curtis Eggleston, b., No. Stonington, Oct. 22, 1865; son of Silas P. and Louisa A. (Maine) Eggleston, of No. Stonington. Mr. Eggleston is a graduate of the Mystic Valley Institute, class of 1886. He taught school, and represented his native town in the State Legislature in 1892 and 1893. He has held other positions of trust and honor at Canonchet, Rockville, and Woodville, R. I., until he removed to So. Lyme, Conn., where he now resides. Mrs. Eggleston taught school several terms in No. Stonington. They attend the So. Lyme church.

Children:

254. Gladys May, b., Rockville, Sept. 10, 1897.

255. Ethel Curtina, b., So. Lyme, Aug. 17, 1903.

Anna Grace Miner (239), sister of the preceding, b., No. Stonington, Conn., Jan. 3, 1880; m., No. Stonington, Apr. 27, 1898, Charles H. C. Miner, b., No. Stonington, May 21, 1873; son of James H. and Mary A. (Owen) Miner, of No. Stonington. Mr. Miner is a Democrat and a farmer. Res., No. Stonington, Conn.

Dau.:

256. Bernice Charline, b. Jan. 15, 1905.

Arthur Courtland Miner (240), brother of the preceding, and son of Courtland P. and Lucy U. (Slocum) Miner, b., No. Stonington, Conn., Oct. 26, 1885; m., Westerly, R. I., June 25, 1905, Anna M. Chapman, b., So. Lyme, Conn., May 4, 1888; dau. of Frederick and Marie Louise (Griswold) Chapman, of So. Lyme. Mr. Miner took a three years' course at the Wheeler High School, and Mrs. Miner took a course at the Morgan High School at Clinton, Conn., and is a graduate of the New London Business College; she is also a member of the Episcopal Church. Mr. Miner is Superintendent of the Oil Department of the Niantic Menhaden and Guano Co. Res., So. Lyme, Conn.

Son:

257. George Arthur, b. Jan. 9, 1907.

The Ezekiel Main Family

The first record of the Main family is John Maine (Mayn, Mayne, Main), b., York, England, 1614. He came to America with the early settlers, in 1629, and settled at York, Me., on the site of the present city of York. His son Ezekiel, born in 1641, is next heard from in this country as living at Scituate, Mass.; in 1669 he removed to Stonington, Conn , and received in 1670 and in 1672 land grants from the town. He subsequently purchased other land, and in 1680 received another town grant of land, all of which extended from the old goldsmith-shop of David Main nearly to the residence of Nathaniel M. Crary, which is now No. Stonington, Conn.; bounded all the way by Shunoc River on the south and on the north in part by lands of Joshua Holmes.

Children:

258. Ezekiel, b.——
259. Mary, b.——; bapt. July 1, 1677; d. young. *no had family*
260. Jeremiah, b. 1678
261. Thomas, b.——; bapt. Sept. 22, 1679; d. young.
262. Phebe, b ——; bapt Aug. 7, 1681, m. Kingsbury.
263. Hannah, b.——

Jeremiah Main (260), son of Ezekiel and Mary Main, m. Mrs. Ruth Brown It is not certainly known whose daughter she was; but she, with her daughter Ruth, were admitted to the first church of Stonington, Conn , and baptized July 16, 1699. Mr. Jeremiah Main was admitted May 18, 1712; d. Nov. 11, 1727; m. Oct. 11, 1699. On Feb 22, 1727, a church was formed in what is now No. Stonington, Conn., and, among others, Mr. Jeremiah Main and wife Ruth were dismissed by request, in order to be embodied in church estate in No. Stonington, in which society they were residing — *Wheeler.*

Children (from B G., p. 113):

264. Thomas, b. July 19, 1700, m. Annah Brown (B. G 40) (275–283).
265. Hannah, bapt. May 17, 1702.
266. Elizabeth, b. Feb. 22, 1702–3; m Ebenezer Brown (B. G. 41) (284)

49

267. Lydia, b. Apr. 19, 1705.
268. Sarah, b. May 19, 1706.
269. Jeremiah, b. Apr. 10, 1708; m. (1) Abigail Worden; m. (2) Thankful Brown (B. G. 71) (284a-291).
270. Hepzibah, b. Mar. 24, 1710.
271. Nathaniel, b. Aug. 4, 1714.
272. Anna, b. Aug. 21, 1715.
273. John, b. May 20, 1716; m. Sarah Morgan (1151-1155).
274. Peter, b. Aug. 5, 1718; m. Mary Egglestone (1156-1166).

Dea. Thomas Main (264), son of Jeremiah and Mrs. Ruth (Brown) Main, b. July 19, 1700; m., Stonington, Conn., Apr. 20, 1720, Annah Brown (B. G. 40, p. 113), b. Feb. 1, 1700; dau. of Eleazer Brown and Ann Pendleton. Eleazer Brown was the son of Thomas Brown and Mary Newhall, of Lynn, Mass. (B. G., pp. 9, 12).
    Children, b. Stonington (B. G., p. 113).
        275. Thomas, b. Feb. 12, 1721; m. Mary Pendleton (312a-312g).
        276. Andrew, b. Aug. 5, 1723; m., Jan. 5, 1743, Fear Holmes.
        277. Timothy, b. Apr. 8, 1727; m. Elizabeth Brown (292-300).
        278. Joshua Main, b. Apr. 5, 1729; m. (1) Rachel Peckham, Nov. 2, 1752, and removed to Patterson, Putnam Co., N. Y.; m. (2) Elizabeth Hovey (1988-1991).
        279. Anne, b. July 31, 1731; m. Dea. Zebulon Brown (301-312).
        280. Jonas, b. Feb. 7, 1735; m. (1) Patience Peckham; m. (2) Content Bromley (475-485).
        281. Elizabeth, b. ——; d. young.
        282. Ezekiel, b. July 8, 1742; m., Nov. 25, 1761, Deborah Meacham. Son: Ezekiel, b. Aug. 17, 1762.
        283. Phebe, b. Nov. 16, 1747; m. Samuel Meacham, Mar. 31, 1763.

Elizabeth Main (266), dau. of Jeremiah and Mrs. Ruth (Brown) Main, b. Feb. 22, 1702; m., Stonington, Conn., Apr. 5, 1723, Ebenezer Brown, b., Stonington, June 28, 1702; d. Mar. 4, 1725; son of Eleazer and Ann (Pendleton) Brown (B. G. 41, p. 13).
    Son:
        284. David Brown, b. Feb. 23, 1724.

Jeremiah Main (269), son of Jeremiah (260) and Mrs. Ruth (Brown) Main, b., Stonington, Conn., Apr. 10, 1708; m. (1), Stonington, Jan. 4, 1727, Abigail Worden, dau. of Thomas and Sarah (Butler) Worden. She

d. Nov. 13, 1741. He m. (2), Apr. 26, 1742, Thankful Brown, b. Oct. 22,
1720; dau. of James Brown and Elizabeth Randall (B. G., p. 114).

Children by first m.:

284a. Thankful, b. Sept. 14, 1727.

284b. Ruth, b. Dec. 12, 1729; m. Bell York. They had thirteen
children (B. G., p. 168).

284c. Jeremiah, b. Apr. 13, 1732.

284d. Amos, b. Sept. 2, 1735; m. Abigail Brown (486-494).

284e. Abigail, b. Sept. 21, 1740.

Children by second m.:

285. James, b. Jan. 27, 1743 (495-498).

286. Lydia, b. Apr. 11, 1745.

287. Thankful, b. Jan. 14, 1748; m. Edward Thurston.

288. Bridget, b. June 14, 1749.

289. David, b. Aug. 26, 1752 (499-507).

290. Nathaniel, b. July 12, 1754; m. Abigail Thurston (870-879).

291. Daniel, b. Jan. 26, 1761; m.,July 21, 1797, Grace Main (297);
dau. of Timothy (277) and Elizabeth (Brown) Main.

Timothy Main (277), son of Dea. Thomas (264) and Annah (Brown)
Main, b., Stonington, Conn., Apr. 8, 1727; m., Stonington, Jan. 27, 1750,
Elizabeth Brown, b., Stonington, July 31, 1732; dau. of James and Elizabeth
(Randall) Brown (B. G. 75, p. 114).

Children, b. Stonington:

292. Elizabeth, b. Nov. 2, 1750.

293. Timothy, b. Apr. 7, 1752.

294. Nathaniel, b. July 12, 1754.

295. Lydia, b. Aug. 31, 1756.

296. Rufus, b. Nov. 15, 1758; m. Sarah York (313-317).

297. Grace, b. Apr. 22, 1761; m., July 21, 1779, Daniel Main, 291.

298. Laban, b. Jan. 27, 1764 (318-322).

299. Luther, b. Apr. 18, 1766.

300. Lucy, b. Dec. 9, 1768.

Anne Main (279), dau. of Dea. Thomas (264) and Annah (Brown)
Main, b., Stonington, Conn., July 31, 1731; d. Dec. 14, 1822, aged ninety-
one years; m., Stonington, Dec. 20, 1749, Dea. Zebulon Brown, b., Stonington, Nov. 20, 1730; d. July 14, 1814, aged eighty-four years; son of James
and Elizabeth (Randall) Brown, son of Eleazer, son of Thomas and Mary
Newhall, of Lynn, Mass. (B. G., p. 43). Deacon Brown was the first deacon

of the Second Baptist Church, No. Stonington, Conn., when his brother, Elder Simeon, was pastor of the same church. (See Appendix IX., B. G., p. 554.) Interments in Brown Cemetery, No. Stonington.

Children, b. Stonington:

    301. Anne, b. May 3, 1751.
    302. Elizabeth, b. Sept. 15, 1752.
    303. Marvin, b. July 4, 1754.
    304. Zebulon, b. May 20, 1756; m. Theda York (1675, 1676).
    305. James, b. Mar. 19, 1758.
    306. Oliver, b. Feb. 9, 1760.
    307. Hannah, b. June 15, 1761.
    308. Nabbe, b. Dec. 11, 1762.
    309. Thomas, b. Nov. 26, 1764.
    310. Mathew, b. 1766 (B. G., p. 44) (1910–1912).
    311. Phebe, b. 1770; m. Elias Miner (B. G., p. 161) (1913–1918).
    312. Katurah, b. 1775; m. Isaac Miner (Family, p. 39).

Thomas Main (275), son of Dea. Thomas (264) and Annah (Brown) Main, dau. of Eleazer and Ann (Pendleton) Brown (B. G., pp. 12, 13); b. Feb. 12, 1721; m., Stonington, Conn., Feb. 3, 1742, Mary Pendleton.

Children: ✱

    312a. Mary, b. Apr. 19, 1743.
    312b. Sarah Foster, b. Aug. 19, 1745. *married name.*
    312c. Thomas, b. Aug. 8, 1747; m., Griswold, Conn., Lucy Tyler.
    312d. Benajah, b. Sept. 5, 1749; m. Dolly Woodward (2134–2141).
    312e. Prudence Benjamin, b.——
    312f. Abigail Ecclestone, b.—— } *married names.*
    312g. Lucy, b.——; and probably others.
    312h. William. (named in will)

Andrew Main (276), brother of the preceding, b. Aug. 5, 1723; m., Jan. 5, 1744, Fear Holmes, b. July 8, 1722; dau. of Joshua and Mary (Richardson) Holmes.

Children:

    312h. Bethiah, b. Apr. 6, 1745.
    312i. Fear, b. Aug. 13, 1747.
    312j. Anne, b. Nov. 18, 1748.
    312k. Andrew, b. July 6, 1749.
    312l. Ruth, b. Sept. 23, 1750.
    312m. Rachel, b. Jan. 8, 1753.
    312n. Molly, b. Aug. 6, 1755.

✱ See Pendleton Geneal. p. 120.

Matilda (Brown) Miner
(1911)
From a daguerreotype taken in 1852
Pages 52 and 224

This house, in North Stonington, Conn., was built by Dea. Zebulon Brown, who married Anne Main (279), and here their children were born. It was occupied by their son Mathew (310), and after him by his son Mathew (1912); then by his daughter Lucy E. Brown (1963), who married Dea. Reuben W. York, whose children were born here. The farm is now owned by Richard B. Wheeler. The buildings are in better condition in 1910 than they were seventy-five years ago.

3120. Joshua, b. Oct. 3, 1757.

312p. Elias, b. Oct. 6, 1760.

312q. Reuben, b. Jan. 22, 1762.

312r. Eunice, b. Mar. 17, 1764.

Rufus Main (296), son of Timothy (277) and Elizabeth (Brown) Main, b., Stonington, Conn., Nov. 15, 1758; m. Sarah York, b. Jan. 22, 1761; dau. of Bell York and Ruth Main, dau. of Jeremiah Main and Abigail Worden. Jeremiah Main was son of Jeremiah Main and Mrs. Ruth Brown; son of Ezekiel Main, the first mentioned in this historical record of the Main family.

Children:

313. Rufus, b.——; m. Sabra Wells (323–334).

314. Stephen, b., Stonington, Jan. 27, 1781; m. Lucinda Ray (335–337).

315. Lewis, b., Preston, Conn., 1783; m. Hannah Ray (364–371).

316. Sanford, b.——; m. Rebecca Billings (1543–1548).

317. Ruth, b.——; m. Joseph Chapman.

Also three other children, Edith, Prudence, and Polly, d. young.

Laban Main (298), son of Timothy (277) and Elizabeth (Brown) Main, b., Stonington, Conn., Jan. 27, 1764; d. 1842; m. Mary, or Polly Brown, b., Stonington, Feb. 28, 1771; d. 1855; dau. of Elder Eleazer Brown and Ann Green (B. G., p. 19).

Children, b. Stonington:

318. Mary, or Polly, b. Jan. 12, 1795; m. John Partelo (1602–1606).

319. Harry, b. 1797; unm.

320. Maranda, b. 1799; unm.

321. Alfred, b. Apr. 26, 1804; m. Samantha Stillman (1607–1611).

322. Erastus, b. 1806; m. Dorcus Perry. Children: Lucien, b. about 1837; Edward and Edgar (twins), b. about 1839; Alice, b. 1842; John, b. 1845. Not further mentioned.

The grandchildren of Laban Main (298) are carried forward to (1602–1611). The family tree, with its branches, is there extended to the present time.

Rufus Main (313), son of Rufus (296) and Sarah (York) Main, b. about 1780; m. Sabra Wells.

Children, b. No. Stonington, Conn.:

323. Rufus Wells, b. 1803; m. Mary A. Miner (372–376).

324. Stephen, b. June 8, 1805 (377-385).
325. Thomas J., b. Mar. 14, 1806; m. (1) Abigail Barton; m. (2) Henrietta Williams (386-389).
326. Edith, b. Dec., 1808; m. Rowland Kenyon (399).
327. William, b.——; m. Elizabeth Williamson.
328. Timothy, b.——; unm.
329. Nancy, b.——; m. Porteous Park (405-408).
330. Phebe, b. Nov. 15, 1814; m. James E. Wilson (409, 410).
331. Sarah, b. July, 1816; m. Abel Palmer (411-413).
332. Mary, b.——; m. Charles Coats.
333. Reuben Palmer, b. Sept. 29, 1824; m. Mattie E. Neal (420-427).
334. Abby E., b. May 24, 1836; m. James E. Rider (432-439).

Stephen Main (314), son of Rufus and Sarah (York) Main, b., Stonington, Conn., Jan. 27, 1781; d. Dec. 19, 1863; m., Jan. 10, 1810, Lucinda Ray.
Children, b. No. Stonington, Conn.:

335. Stephen Nelson Main, b. June 5, 1815; m. Cornelia A. Pratt (338-342).
336. Erastus F. Main, b. May 28, 1818 (343, 344).
337. Lucy Wheeler Main, b. May 11, 1823; m. Asa Randall Main (345-349).

Stephen Nelson Main (335), son of Stephen (314) and Lucinda (Ray) Main, b., No. Stonington, Conn., June 5, 1815; m., Ontario, N. Y., Sept., 1842, Cornelia A. Pratt, b., New York, 1824; d., Ontario, 1878; dau. of Alva and Ann (Peck) Pratt, of Ontario.

Mr. Main moved to Ontario in 1836, and taught district schools winters for twenty-five years. He was superintendent of schools for six years and supervisor of town. Now [in 1908] lives with his daughter on the homestead which he purchased in 1837. He was one of the pioneers of Ontario, and prominent in the affairs of the town. He is a member of the Baptist Church.
Children, b. Ontario:

338. Palmer Nelson, b. 1845; d., Ontario, 1849.
339. Alva Pratt, b. Sept. 21, 1846 (350).
340. Jennie A., b. June 9, 1848 (351, 352).
341. Erastus A., b. 1856; d., Ontario, 1857.
342. Frank N., b. 1860; d., Webster, N. Y., 1881.

Erastus F. Main (336), son of Stephen (314) and Lucinda (Ray) Main, b. May 28, 1818; d., Ontario Center, N. Y., June 18, 1905; m. (1), West Walworth, N. Y., Apr. 2, 1845, Mary Ann Palmer, of West Walworth, b. Aug. 19, 1824; d., Three Mile Bay, N. Y., Jan. 8, 1883; dau. of Nathan and Dolly (Lamb) Palmer, of West Walworth. He m. (2), Sandy Creek, N. Y., Jan. 30, 1884, Addie Hannah Carlisle, b. July 17, 1834; she is living in 1908. Mr. Main was a Baptist minister, having pastorates at West Walworth, Webster, Adams Center, Three Mile Bay, Mexico, and Sandy Creek, N. Y. He was an active, intelligent man, and proclaimed the gospel for fifty-five years. It is difficult to realize the sum-total of the good which sprang from all those years of tireless service for the Master. It is only when all secrets shall be disclosed that he will receive his full reward, "a crown of glory that fadeth not away." After a life of great usefulness and abundant labors, he rested from his toils in a good old age.

Children, by first m., b. West Walworth:

    343. Delia, b.—— 1847–8; d. in infancy.

    344. Franklin Erastus, b. Nov. 4, 1856; m. (1) Mary E. Hoag; m.
        (2) Cora I. Thayer (353, 354).

Lucy Wheeler Main (337), sister of the preceding, b., No. Stonington, Conn., May 11, 1823; d., Perryville, N. Y., Feb. 21, 1873; m., Jan. 13, 1845, Asa Randall Maine.

Children, b. Perryville:

    345. Marion Augustine Maine, b. Oct. 28, 1845; m. Horatio K.
        Vedder (355–357).

    346. Paul S. Maine, b. Dec. 13, 1847; m. Florence A. Keeler (358).

    347. Frank L. Maine, b. Feb. 20, 1853; m. Sarah E. King (359–361).

    348. Nellie Maine, b. Nov. 29, 1854; d. Perryville, Aug. 31, 1865.

    349. Ida Philura Maine, b. Nov. 29, 1861; m. Charles H. Dick (362,
        363).

Alva Pratt Maine (339), son of Stephen Nelson (335) and Cornelia A. (Pratt) Main, b., Ontario, N. Y., Sept. 21, 1846; m. (1), Palmyra, N. Y., Mar. 22, 1871, Maria M. Smith, b., Farmington, N. Y., July, 1843; d., Webster, N. Y., Apr. 28, 1903; dau. of Alanson and Harriet (White) Sheffield, of Farmington. Mr. Maine m. (2), Rochester, N. Y., June 10, 1904, Clara D. Vanderwrof, b., Penfield, N. Y., May 17, 1864.

Mr. Maine was educated at Macedone Academy, and graduated from the Medical Department of the University of Pennsylvania in 1870. He practised medicine at Vernon Center, N. Y., until 1878. He is health officer of Webster, where he is physician and surgeon, in 1908. He is a Republican, and both he and his wife are members of the Presbyterian Church.

THE EZEKIEL MAIN FAMILY

Adopted son:

> 350. Alva F. Maine, b., New York City, Nov. 2, 1878. He is a physician and surgeon. Res., 1908, San Francisco, Cal.

Jennie A. Maine (340), dau. of Stephen Nelson (335) and Cornelia A. (Pratt) Maine, b., Ontario, N. Y., June 9, 1848; m., Ontario, Dec. 25, 1868, Benjamin H. Hoag, b. in 1849. Mr. Hoag is a farmer and a Republican. They attend the Baptist Church, and his wife is a member. Res., 1908, Ontario Center, N. Y.

Children:

> 351. Cora B., b., Walworth, N. Y., 1871.
> 352. Grace E., b., Ontario, 1876.

Franklin Erastus Maine (344), son of Erastus F. (336) and Mary Ann (Palmer) Main, b., West Walworth, N. Y., Nov. 4, 1856; m. (1), West Walworth, July 17, 1878, Mary Ella Hoag, b., West Walworth, July 17, 1856; d., Auburn, N. Y., Jan. 26, 1896; dau. of Hiram C. and Sally Ann (Wyman) Hoag. Mr. Maine m. (2), Newport, Ky., June 23, 1897, Cora I. Thayer, b., Richmondville, N. Y., Jan. 10, 1864; dau. of George and Rosanna (Boyle) Thayer, of Auburn. Dr. Maine is a physician, and a consulting specialist in abdominal and pelvic disorders. He is an author of several papers on medicine; a graduate of the University of Pennsylvania in 1878. In politics he is a Republican, and both he and his wife are members of the Presbyterian Church.

Children, by first m.:

> 353. Anna Beth Maine, b. Apr. 28, 1882; m., Auburn, Oct. 9, 1901, Joseph Huckney Colclough, b., England, Jan. 10, 1873; son of Joseph Colclough, of Pennsylvania. Mr. Colclough is a Presbyterian clergyman. Son: Franklin Simister, b.——. Res., 1908, Deposit, N. Y.
> 354. Frank Elfleda Maine, b. Aug. 21, 1888.

Marion Augustine Maine (345), dau. of Asa Randall and Lucy Wheeler (Main) Maine, b., Perryville, N. Y., Oct. 28, 1845; d., Ingham's Mills, N. Y., May 6, 1872; m., Perryville, Mar. 20, 1867, Horatio K. Vedder, b., Ingham's Mills.

Children, b. Ingham's Mills:

> 355. Florence L., b. June 13, 1868.
> 356. Frank A., b. Jan. 14, 1870.
> 357. Marion A., b. May 1, 1872.

56

Paul S. Maine (346), son of Asa Randall and Lucy Wheeler (Main) Maine, b., Perryville, N. Y., Dec. 13, 1847; m., Perryville, July 2, 1872, Florence A. Keeler, b., Fenner, N. Y., Jan. 12, 1850; dau. of Harvey L. and Lauraette (Allen) Keeler, of Fenner. He was educated in district schools and at Cazenovia Seminary, and began teaching when seventeen years of age, and continued until 1872. He was appointed school commissioner to fill vacancy, and later elected for full term. In 1876 he entered mercantile business, which he conducted until July 1, 1902. He was postmaster of Perryville from 1876 to 1903, except during part of President Cleveland's two administrations. He served the town twelve years as supervisor, resigning Jan. 1, 1898, to take the office of county clerk of Madison County. He owns and manages the farm that was his father's, where his brother and sisters were born. He is a Past Master in Masonry and Past Grand in Odd Fellowship. He is a Republican, and both he and his wife attend the Methodist Church. Res., Perryville, N. Y.

Dau.:
358. L. Ethelyn, b., Perryville, June 30, 1874; m., June 26, 1901, Frank G. Armstrong. Son: J. Paul, b. Sept. 20, 1902.

Frank L. Maine (347), brother of the preceding, b., Perryville, N. Y., Feb. 20, 1853; d., Manlius, N. Y., Jan. 5, 1906; m., West Walworth, N. Y., Feb. 2, 1881, Sarah E. King, dau. of Henry King and Ruth E. White, of West Walworth. Mr. Maine studied law and graduated from the Law College at Ann Arbor, Mich. He was in law practice at Fayetteville, N. Y., for a few years. He assumed the management of, and edited, *The Fayetteville Recorder* for a few years. At the solicitation of the business men of Manlius, he removed to that place and started *The Manlius Eagle*, being editor and proprietor. He held the office of Justice of the Peace for several terms. He was prominent in Masonry and Odd Fellowship, and was Past Master and Past Grand Master.

Children, b. Fayetteville:
359. Eloise Grace, b. Sept. 17, 1883.
360. Paul Henry, b. July 4, 1885.
361. Murray Asa, b. Oct. 3, 1887.

Ida Philura Maine (349), sister of the preceding, b., Perryville, N. Y., Nov. 29, 1861; m., Sept. 9, 1880, Charles H. Dick, b. Three Mile Bay, N. Y. His occupation was blacksmithing, but, being unable to work at his trade, on account of ill-health, he removed from Three Mile Bay to Watertown, N. Y. Mrs. Dick holds the appointment of matron in the County Orphan

Asylum of that city. Mr. Dick is a Republican, and both are members of the Baptist Church. Res., 1908, Watertown, N. Y.

Children, b. Three Mile Bay:

362. Lucy Maine, b. Aug. 21, 1881; m., Aug. 2, 1905, Warden Clinton Hayes. He is a dentist at Watertown.

363. Homer Eugene, b. Mar. 22, 1884. He is a lawyer at Rochester, N. Y.

Lewis Main (315), son of Rufus (296) and Sarah (York) Main, b., Preston, Conn., May 17, 1783; d., Voluntown, Conn. (near the No. Stonington line), Nov. 20, 1870; m., Oct. 17, 1803, Hannah Ray, b. Jan. 29, 1784; dau. of Gersham Ray.

Children, b. Voluntown:

364. Lewis, Jr., b. June 9, 1804; m. Cyntha Stewart (1410–1415).

365. Avery, b. Aug. 29, 1806; m. Laura A. Baldwin (1429–1436).

366. Edgar Ray, b. Sept. 24, 1808; accidentally killed, Dec. 13, 1826.

367. Charles Henry, b. Feb. 4, 1811; m. Elmira B. Eccleston (1467–1472).

368. Jesse Palmer, b. Feb. 13, 1813; m. Abby Benjamin (1489-1493).

369. Gersham Albert, b. Dec. 23, 1815; m. Susan A. Billings (1494–1496).

369a. Hannah Marilla, b. Feb. 28, 1819; unm.

370. Esther Stafford, b. June 14, 1821; m. William Chapman (1501–1504).

371. Mary Ann, b. June 27, 1825; m. (1) Stanton Main (860–862).

Rufus Wells Main (323), son of Rufus and Sabra (Wells) Main, b., No. Stonington, Conn., about 1803; d. Rochester, N. Y.; m., Pendleton Hill, Conn., by her father, Apr. 22, 1827, Mary Ann Miner, b., Mystic, Conn.; d. Rochester; dau. of Rev. Jonathan and Eunice (Park) Miner. Rev. Mr. Miner was the fourth pastor of the First No. Stonington Baptist Church from 1814 to 1834. His labors were followed by very powerful revivals. He was a man of strong native talents, fervent piety, and was a superior preacher. He died in New York in 1844. (See B. G., p. 552.) Mr. Main was the owner of the Frankford Flour-mills, Rochester.

Children:

372. Eliza Ann, b., Pendleton Hill, May 27, 1830.

373. Harriet Louise, b., Pendleton Hill, Jan. 27, 1833; d. Dec. 6, 1896.

Stephen Main
(324)
North Stonington, Conn.
Page 59

Elizabeth Stewart, wife of Stephen Main
(321)
Page 59

374. Charles George, b. Mar. 10, 1835; d. July 10, 1853.
375. Maria Antoinette, b. May 11, 1839; d. Aug. 29, 1890.
376. Sarah Frances, b. Oct. 6, 1846.

Stephen Main (324), son of Rufus and Sabra (Wells) Main, b., No. Stonington, Conn., June 8, 1805; d., No. Stonington, July 22, 1886; m. (1), No. Stonington, Apr. 21, 1833, Susan K. Chapman, b., Griswold, Conn., Sept. 10, 1815; d. Sept. 5, 1841, aged twenty-six years; dau. of Andrew and Wealth Chapman. Mr. Main m. (2), No. Stonington, Mar. 6, 1842, Lydia York, b., No. Stonington, Mar. 24, 1812; d., No. Stonington, Aug. 8, 1846; dau. of Jeremiah and Thankful (Thurston) York (B. G., p. 172). Mr. Main m. (3), No. Stonington, June 8, 1847, Elizabeth Stewart, b., No. Stonington, Apr. 25, 1831; dau. of George P. Stewart, b. Apr. 6, 1786, d. May 1, 1851, and Polly, or Mary, Hewitt, b. July 26, 1790; d. Mar. 15, 1870. Mr. George P. Stewart and wife settled in New York State in early life; but wolves and fevers and ague were such disastrous neighbors they returned to Connecticut and spent the remainder of their days at No. Stonington, on Stewart Hill.

At the age of seventeen Mr. Main went to New York City to work for his uncle, teaching school evenings. Later he became proprietor of a butter-stall in Washington Market, remaining there twenty-three years, and he was very successful in business. He removed from there to Port Richmond, Staten Island, N. Y., and while there held several offices of trust. He was also an extensive dealer in real estate, owning and renting at one time ten houses in New York City. In 1856 he sold his residence at Port Richmond, and removed with his family to the town of his nativity, where he built and conducted a grist and shingle mill. He assisted with his brothers, and had the supervision in building a commodious house for his father and mother, about 1844, on the site of the old homestead, half a mile south of Pendleton Hill Meeting-house. He was a highly respected citizen, friend, and neighbor, and a valuable member of the Third Baptist Church, leaving the precious legacy of Christian manhood to his sons and daughters and grandchildren, worthy of emulation.

Mrs. Main is a woman of unusual strength of character, and has a warm heart, ever manifesting true motherly affection and self-sacrificing interest for the welfare of her children and grandchildren. The same hands that cared for the first-born are rendering loving service to the third generation. She is much pleased that these family records are to have a place in history for future generations.

Son by first m.:

Stephen, b.——; d. aged three years.

Children by second m.:

377. Lydia E., b., New York City, Jan. 14, 1843 (444–446).

378. Achsah M., b., Staten Island, July 12, 1844; m. Amos P. Chapman (447–449).

379. Susan K., b., Staten Island, June 14, 1846; m. Isaac D. Miner (224, 225).

Children by third m.:

380. Theodore S., b., Staten Island, Apr. 15, 1849 (450–452).

381. George Irving, b., Staten Island, Mar. 30, 1852; d. Feb. 28, 1860.

382. Hattie Isadore, b., No. Stonington, May 22, 1857 (453).

383. William Dean, b., No. Stonington, May 21, 1860 (454–456).

384. Jennie Eveline, b., No. Stonington, July 16, 1863.

385. Anna Belle, b., No. Stonington, July 12, 1867.

Thomas J. Main (325), son of Rufus and Sabra (Wells) Main, b., Stonington, Conn., Mar. 14, 1806; d., Grand Round Valley, Ore., Apr. 25, 1862; m. (1) Albany, N. Y., Abigail Burton, b. Albany. He m. (2), Feb. 13, 1837, Henrietta Williams, b. New London, Conn.; d., Stonington, Ill., Sept. 24, 1854.

Mr. Main was a Whig in politics, a Baptist, and his wife was a Methodist. He was in the produce business in New York and Philadelphia until 1848. He removed to Cincinnati, and later to Pittsburg, Ill. In 1851 he went to California across the plains; from there to Oregon, where he died.

Son by first m.:

386. Joseph D. Main, b., Albany, June 3, 1835; m., Greenville, Floyd Co., Ind., Mar. 6, 1859, Margaret A. Green, b., Greenville, Feb. 2, 1838; d., New Albany, Ind., Feb. 3, 1908; dau. of William and Sophia (Ford) Green. Dau.: Lulu Abigail Main, b., New Albany, Dec. 13, 1859. Res., 1730 E. Oak St., New Albany, Ind.

Children by second m.:

387. Susan Amelia Main, b., New York City, Feb. 13, 1838 (389a–389k).

388. Stephen Palmer Main, b., New York City, Nov. 20, 1839 (390–398).

389. Elizabeth Main, b., Stonington, Ill., Aug. 25, 1850 (713–717).

Susan Amelia Main (387), dau. of Thomas J. (325) and Henrietta (Williams) Main, b. Feb. 13, 1838; d., Petersburg, Mich., June 7, 1892; m., Bridgeport, Nevada Co., Cal., Oct. 13, 1857, Benjamin Franklin Rose, b., So. Kingstown, R. I., May 7, 1831; d., Petersburg, Mar. 20, 1891; son of Oliver Tenant and Eliza A. (Mumford) Rose, of So. Kingstown. He was a farmer and a Republican, and both he and his wife were members of the Methodist Church.

Children, the last nine b. Petersburg:

389a. Mary Elizabeth, b., Eureka, Cal., Aug. 6, 1858; d. Aug. 22, 1858.

389b. Tirzah Amelia, b., Greenville, Cal., Oct. 28, 1859; d., Peacedale, R. I., July 5, 1878.

389c. Frances Olive, b. June 7, 1862; d., Petersburg, Dec. 23, 1879.

389d. Minnie Adelaide, b. Jan. 31, 1864; m. John W. Gramkie (720, 721).

389e. Harriet Elizabeth, b. Oct. 14, 1865; d., Petersburg, Feb. 8, 1870.

389f. Sylvia Jennie, b. Oct. 31, 1867; d., Petersburg, Feb. 17, 1870.

389g. Franklin Main, b. Feb. 15, 1869; d., Petersburg, Feb. 23, 1870.

389h. Oliver Tenant, b. Oct. 5, 1871; m. Ada C. McLachlin (722–724).

389i. Laura Julia, b. Aug. 13, 1874; received high-school education; unm.

389j. Elizabeth Main, b. July 22, 1877 (725–730).

389k. Jennie Eliza, b. Apr. 21, 1880; d., Toledo, O., Jan. 27, 1905.

Stephen Palmer Main (388), son of Thomas J. (325) and Henrietta (Williams) Main, b., New York City, Nov. 20, 1839; m., Washington Co., Ind., June 2, 1867, Amanda J. Davis, b., Harrison Co., Ind., Dec. 14, 1848; dau. of Robert and Jane (Pennington) Davis. Mr. Main is a plow-manufacturer, a Republican, and both he and his wife are members of the Methodist Church. Res., 919 11th St., New Albany, Ind.

Children, b. New Albany, except the last two:

390. Henrietta J., b. Feb. 17, 1869.

391. Anna Gertrude, b. Apr. 12, 1870; m. Franklin Rogers. No. issue.

392. Clara May, b. June 29, 1871; d. Feb. 24, 1872.

393. Susan A., b. Mar. 29, 1873; d. Mar. 10, 1874.

394. Harry Davis, b. Dec. 9, 1874; d. July 21, 1876.

395. Rilda May, b. May 25, 1878; d.——

396. Joseph Raymond, b. Nov. 12, 1880; m. Nov. 11, 1907.
397. Carl Stephen, b., Greenville, Ind., May 24, 1884.
398. Mary Irene, b., Greenville, June 17, 1887.

Ede Main (326), dau. of Rufus and Sabra (Wells) Main, b., No. Stonington, Conn., Dec., 1808; d. (Pendleton Hill), No. Stonington, July 25, 1890; m., No. Stonington, Rowland Kenyon, b. Charlestown, R. I. Mr. Kenyon was a farmer, and both he and his wife were members of the First Baptist Church, Pendleton Hill.

Dau.:

399. Mary Ann Kenyon, b., Pendleton Hill, Sept. 25, 1830; d., Pendleton Hill, Aug. 17, 1868; m., Voluntown, Conn., Dec. 8, 1860, James Monroe Cook, b., Preston, Conn., June 24, 1840; d., Voluntown, Oct. 25, 1907; son of Albert and Susan (Perégo) Cook. No. issue. James M. Cook m. (2), Hopkinton, R. I., Feb. 22, 1881, Mary Annie Rider (441), b., Pendleton Hill, Aug. 26, 1864; dau. of Abby E. Main (334) and James E. Rider.

Miss Rider was educated in the public schools of Jersey City, N. J., and No. Stonington, Conn. Mr. Cook had lived in Voluntown (Pendleton Hill) since he was nineteen years old, and he and his wife were prominent members of the Baptist Church, Pendleton Hill. Mr. Cook was well acquainted with public matters, and represented Voluntown for three years in the State Legislature and one term in the Senate. For thirty years he was first selectman. Mr. Cook possessed a kind and whole-souled disposition, and every person who called at his home, either friend or stranger, found a warm welcome. He was a farmer, and a Republican.

Children, by second m., b. Voluntown (Pendleton Hill):

400. Reuben D. Cook, b. Sept. 21, 1881; m., Hopkinton, May 10, 1903, Edna V. Maine, b., Waltham, Mower Co., Minn., Sept. 13, 1876; dau. of James M. and Sarah (Smith) Maine, of No. Stonington. Mr. Cook is a farmer, and a Republican. His wife is a member of the Baptist Church. No issue. Res., 1908, Westerly, R. I.

401. Mary Edith Cook, b. Mar. 26, 1883. She was educated in the public schools and at the Wheeler High School, and has taught school eight years in Voluntown.

402. Charles A. Russell Cook, b. June 2, 1885.

403. James Morton Cook, b. Mar. 19, 1891.

404. Susan A. Cook, b. May 18, 1897.

Nancy Main (329), dau. of Rufus and Sabra (Wells) Main, b. No. Stonington, Conn.; d. Jersey City, N. J., m. Porteous Park, b.——; d.——, Jersey City. Mr. Park was a merchant.

Children:

405. Frank, b.——; d. young.

406. George, b.——

407. Theodore, b.——; m. Miss Palmer, and has one daughter.

408. Porteous, b.——; d. young.

Phebe Main (330), sister of the preceding, b., No. Stonington, Conn., Nov. 15, 1814; d., No. Stonington, June 28, 1875; m., New York, James E. Wilson, who d. in California. Mr. Wilson was a carpenter.

Children, b. No. Stonington:

409. James Wilson, b. Apr. 22, 1850.

410. Hattie Wilson, b.——; d. in childhood.

Sarah Main (331), dau. of Rufus and Sabra (Wells) Main, b., No. Stonington, Conn., July, 1816; d., Pendleton Hill, Conn., Aug. 10, 1866; m., Pendleton Hill, Abel Palmer, b., Pendleton Hill, Feb., 1801; d., Pendleton Hill, Feb. 17, 1872; son of Gersham and Zeruiah (Palmer) Palmer, of Pendleton Hill; son of Dr. Joseph Palmer, who m. Zipporah Billings July 10, 1737; son of George and Hannah (Palmer) Palmer; m., Mar. 24, 1711, son of Dea. Gersham Palmer, who was twice married. Soon after his last m. he fixed his permanent abode on the eastern slope of Taugwonk in Stonington, now known as Angwilla, locating his house on the present site of the residence of Elias H. Miner. In Mr. Palmer's house were frequently held the Stonington town meetings. A stone marked "G. P." was preserved by Mr. Miner, which is set in the underpinning of the present house. The lineage of the Palmer family of Stonington is of peculiar interest, as they were of sterling worth who placed their good names among the best citizens of Stonington.

Children, b. Stonington (Pendleton Hill):

411. Alonzo A. Palmer, b. Sept., 1836; d., Pendleton Hill, Dec. 13, 1866. He graduated from the Connecticut Literary Institution at Suffield and from medical college at Ann Arbor, Mich., and later from the University of New York. He practised medicine in Ohio and Rhode Island. Unm.

412. George C. Palmer, b. Dec., 1837 (414, 415).
413. Caius C. Palmer, b. Jan. 3, 1846; m. Mary P. Billings (416-419).

George C. Palmer (412), b. Dec., 1837; d., Flint, Mich., Aug. 17, 1894; m., Detroit, Mich., Mary S. Macarty, who was living in 1908. Mr. Palmer was a graduate of the Connecticut Literary Institution at Suffield, and from the Ann Arbor Medical College of Michigan, and from there he went to the Michigan Insane Asylum at Kalamazoo, Mich., where he remained for twenty-five years, first as physician, then as superintendent. From Kalamazoo he went to Flint, where he founded a private asylum, where he died. Both he and his wife were members of the Episcopal Church. Res., 665 Woodward Ave., Detroit, Mich.
Children:
414. Mary, b., Kalamazoo, Aug. 23, 1889.
415. George Culver, b., Flint, Oct. 18, 1892.

Caius C. Palmer (413), son of Abel and Sarah (Main) Palmer, b., Pendleton Hill, Conn., Jan. 3, 1846; d., Pendleton Hill, Dec. 14, 1885; m., Stonington, Conn., Feb. 25, 1867, Mary P. Billings, b., Griswold, Conn., July 23, 1845; dau. of Hon. Benjamin F. and Ann P. (Palmer) Billings. He was a merchant and farmer; in politics he was a Democrat. They attended the first Baptist Church, No. Stonington, Conn., and his wife is a member. Mr. Palmer was educated at the Connecticut Literary Institution, where he prepared to enter Yale College, but on account of illness was obliged to give up professional life.
Children:
416. Winifred I. Palmer, b., Pendleton Hill, Aug. 23, 1869. She was educated at the Westerly High School, and has been a teacher in the public schools of Connecticut and Rhode Island for nineteen years; unm. Res., Pendleton Hill, Conn.
417. Mary C. Palmer, b., Westerly, R. I., July 23, 1875. She was educated at the Attleboro, Mass., High School, and has been engaged in teaching in public and private schools the past ten years. Res., Pendleton Hill.
418. Annie M. Palmer, b., Stonington, Sept. 11, 1877; d. Apr. 26, 1881.
419. Cecile C. Palmer, b., Pendleton Hill, Feb. 28, 1886. She graduated from the Wheeler High School in 1903; now (1908) is a student of the Rhode Island Normal School.

THE EZEKIEL MAIN FAMILY

Mary Main (332), dau. of Rufus and Sabra (Wells) Main, b. No Stonington; d. No. Stonington; m. Charles Coats. There were two children, Charles and Hattie; both d. young.

Reuben Palmer Main (333), son of Rufus and Sabra (Wells) Main, b., No. Stonington, Conn , Sept 29, 1824; m. (1), New Albany, Ind., Sept 2, 1860, Mattie E. Neal, b., Salem, Ind., Jan. 6, 1841; d , New Albany, 1871; dau. of Charles and Maria Neal, of Louisville, Ky. Mr. Main m. (2), New Albany, Feb. 1, 1872, Hattie J. Knepfly, b., New Albany, June 4, 1849; dau. of John and Magdaline (Snyder) Knepfly. Mr. Main has been an active business man, conducting a wholesale grocery business, and had other outside extensive business enterprises which he conducted successfully. He owned and operated the Phenix Flouring-Mill of New Albany. He has now retired to his farm, twelve miles from New Albany, where he looks backward to a successful business life In politics he is an independent Republican His first wife was a member of the Episcopal Church. His second wife is a member of the Baptist Church. Res., Greenville, Ind

Children by first m., b. New Albany:
  420. Pauline, b. Aug. 2, 1861; d. Mar. 10, 1863.
  421. Raymond Palmer, b. Feb 16, 1863; d., Corydon, Ind , Apr. 4, 1902; m., Greenville, Emma Shappenfield, b. Greenville He was a farmer, and both he and his wife members of the Christian Church. No issue Her res , Corydon, Ind.
  422. Reuben Franklin, b Oct. 4, 1865; m. Hope Brown (428-430).
  423. Erminnie Victoria, b. Oct. 14, 1867; m. Jesse N Morris (431).
  424. Charles Augustus, b. Feb. 18, 1869, d. July 18, 1870
Children by second m., b. New Albany.
  425. Hattie Leona, b. May 24, 1873; d. July 2, 1876.
  426. John Knepfly, b. Apr. 18, 1875.
  427. William Lawrence, b. May 6, 1877; m., Greenville, Oct 12, 1903, Lois Coffman, of Greenville. Mr. Main is a dentist, and both he and his wife are members of the Methodist Church. Res., Greenville, Ind.

Reuben Franklin Main (422), son of Reuben P. (333) and Mattie E (Neal) Main, b., New Albany, Ind., Oct 4, 1865; m., Greenville, Ind., Feb. 20, 1890, Hope Brown, dau. of John N. and Mary A. (Hayburn) Brown. Mr. Main is a farmer, and both he and his wife are members of the Methodist Church. Res., Greenville, Ind.

65

Children:

428. Ruby Pearl, b. June 15, 1891.
429. Palmer William, b. June 10, 1893.
430. Hattie Vera, b. Mar. 4, 1895.

Erminnie Victoria Main (423), sister of the preceding, b., New Albany, Ind., Oct. 14, 1867; m. Jesse N. Morris, son of George and Sarah (Woods) Morris. Mr. Morris is route agent for Adams Express Company for Michigan, Ohio, and Indiana. Res., 1908, Fort Wayne, Ind.
Son:

431. Reuben Main Morris, b. Feb. 10, 1891. He is a student at Ohio Northern University.

Abby E. Main (334), dau. of Rufus and Sabra (Wells) Main, b., No. Stonington, Conn., May 24, 1836; d., No. Stonington, Apr. 30, 1875; m., Jersey City, N. J., James E. Rider, b., Jersey City, Nov. 28, 1830; d., Jersey City, Aug. 10, 1883; son of Bargill W. and Hannah (Warren) Rider. Mr. Rider was a provision merchant in Jersey City, and both he and his wife were Baptists, his wife a member of the church.
Children, b. No. Stonington:

432. Emily A., b. June 2, 1854; d., No. Stonington, Aug. 2, 1856.
433. Sabra E., b. July 6, 1860; m. John C. Thompson (440–443).
434. Phebe G., b. Sept. 1, 1862; d., Jersey City, Aug. 15, 1863.
435. Mary Annie, b. Aug. 26, 1864; m. James M. Cook (413–417).
436. Carrie A., b. Sept. 6, 1867. She was educated at the East Greenwich Academy, R. I., and has been a teacher over twenty years in the schools of No. Stonington.
437. Weston B., b. Oct. 31, 1869. He is a farmer.
438. Sarah, b. Nov. 23, 1872; m., Voluntown, Conn., June 30, 1907, Harlan P. Brown, b., Danielson, Conn., Oct. 27, 1840; son of Jeremiah and Phebe (Brightman) Brown, of Danielson. Mr. Brown is a provision dealer at Niantic, R. I.
439. James Edward, b. Apr. 22, 1875; m., at Lincoln Park, Conn., Sept. 18, 1906, Mabel Jenkins, b. Nov. 24, 1872; dau. of Charles and Helen (Whipple) Jenkins, of Apponaug, R. I. Mr. Rider was educated at the Wheeler High School, and is a merchant, and both he and his wife are members of the Episcopal Church. Res., Apponaug, R. I.

Sabra Elizabeth Rider (433), dau. of James E. and Abby E. (Main) Rider, b., No. Stonington, Conn., July 6, 1860; m., Hopkinton, R. I., May

5, 1877, John C. Thompson, b., No. Stonington, Apr. 23, 1859; adopted son of Benjamin and Frances (Hillard) Thompson. Mr. Thompson was educated at Ashaway High School, R. I. He was superintendent of the Sunday school at Pendleton Hill, Conn. Mrs. Thompson was educated at Jersey City, N. J., and No. Stonington. Mr. Thompson is a farmer, and a Republican. He and his wife are members of the Baptist Church.

Children, b. No. Stonington:

440. Elmina B., b. June 25, 1878. She was educated at the Wheeler High School and at the State Normal School at Willimantic Conn. Now [1908] a teacher in the grammar schools at Wellesley, Mass.

441. Bertha G., b. Apr. 23, 1880; m., June 29, 1904, James Brooks. She was educated at the Wheeler High School, and was a teacher up to the time of her marriage. Mr. Brooks was a division superintendent in the Saylesville, R. I., bleacheries. Now [1908] at Jewett City, Conn.

442. Malcom E., b. Feb., 1882. He was educated at the Wheeler High School, and is a farmer and contractor.

443. Maud O., b. Sept. 23, 1886. She was educated at the Wheeler High School and is a teacher.

Lydia E. Main (377), dau. of Stephen (324) and Lydia York Main, b., New York City, Jan. 14, 1843; m. (1), No. Stonington, Conn., Nov. 28, 1861, Francis J. Bentley, b. Hartford, Conn.; d., Willington, Conn., Apr. 4, 1882; son of Daniel Bentley, of Goshen, Conn., and Julia Marble, sister to Emily Marble, who m. John Richardson, whose dau. Lovinia m. John B. Brown (B. G., p. 60). Another sister also, Laura Marble, m. Mr. McGlaflin, of Hartford, whose dau. Almira M. m. B. W. Brown (B. G., p. 60). Mr. Bentley received special education at Bakerville, Conn. He was a farmer and a Republican, and both he and his wife were members of the Baptist Church. Mr. Bentley responded to the call for volunteers in the Civil War and enlisted in the 4th regiment of Connecticut Volunteers, and was discharged Dec. 6, 1861.

Mrs. Lydia E. Bentley, née Main (377), m. (2), Mansfield, Conn., July 10, 1887, George H. Harris, b., No. Windham, Conn., Sept. 23, 1828; d., Eagleville, Conn., Nov. 16, 1897; son of Parker Harris, of Mansfield, and Annie Bettis. Her father, D. M. C. Bettis, was celebrated for his herds of Alderney cows and Marino sheep. He was the propagator of the Early Rose potato, which became so famous throughout the country, being the best variety up to that time. He was fond of flowers, and when unable, on account of age and ill-health, to be out-of-doors he had choice flowers planted in front of his bay window, where he could look out and see their flowering beauty. He was an upright, honest man and an obliging neighbor, passing away at the ripe age of eight-four years. Mr. Harris was a farmer. He served in the Civil War in the 21st Connecticut regiment until it was discharged. No issue by last marriage. Her res., 1908, Eagleville, Conn.

Children, by first m., b. No. Stonington:

    444. Charles F., b. May 23, 1865; m. Clara E. Arnold (457, 458).

    445. William T., b. Dec. 8, 1866; m. Christiana Bogue (459–466).

    446. Herbert G., b. Aug. 17, 1868; m. Lillie Heck (467–472).

Achsah Maria Main (378), dau. of Stephen and Lydia (York) Main, b., Staten Island, N. Y., July 12, 1844; d., Westerly, R. I., Nov. 15, 1876; m., Westerly, Jan. 1, 1864, Amos Palmer Chapman, b., Westerly, July 20, 1840; son of Sumner and Sarah (Brightman) Chapman, of Westerly. In early years he was a farmer. In politics he was a Republican. He was a member of the Episcopal Church and his wife was a member of the Baptist Church.

Mrs. Chapman's childhood was spent in New York City, but she came to No. Stonington, Conn., and lived until her marriage; then lived in Westerly until her death. Mr. Chapman enlisted in the Civil War Sept. 21, 1861, and was honorably discharged July 27, 1862. He m. (2), Jan. 18, 1876, Mrs. Sarah S. Brewster, née Johnson.

Children, by first m., b. Westerly:

    447. Fred S., b. Dec. 25, 1867; m. Emma C. Schrader (473, 474).

    448. Theodore Stephen, b. Mar. 18, 1874; m. Therese M. Gundersen.

    449. Achsah M., b. Mar. 10, 1876; unm.

Theodore S. Main (380), son of Stephen and Elizabeth (Stewart) Main, b., Staten Island, N. Y., Apr. 15, 1849; d., Westerly, R. I., Feb. 28, 1905; m. (1), Voluntown, Conn., Aug. 11, 1867, Mary E. Main, dau. of Charles H. and Almira (Eggleston) Main; d. Oct. 19, 1873. Mr. Main m. (2), New Albany, Ind., Sept. 18, 1877, Elizabeth Young, b., New Albany, July 1, 1857; dau. of Jacob and Katharine (Dice) Young, of New Albany. Mr. Main was educated in the public and private schools of New York and No. Stonington, Conn., also at the Suffield, Conn., Literary Institution. He spent considerable time in Texas as civil engineer. In 1865 he was with Reuben P. Main, and manager of his flour-mill; later was partner with his cousin Palmer Parks in the coal business in New Albany. In 1888 he was employed by the Singer Sewing-Machine Company in the Paterson, N. J., office; later in the Hartford, Conn., office, where his health broke down. He spent the remainder of his days in No. Stonington and Westerly, R. I. Interment, River Bend, Westerly.

Mrs. Main was a student of the German Lutheran School at New Albany, also of the business college. Res., No. Stonington; address, Preston, Conn.

Children, by second m.:

450. Anna Kate Main, b., No. Stonington, July 21, 1878; m., No. Stonington, June 12, 1900, Irving C. Eccleston, b., No. Stonington, Jan. 1, 1878; son of H. Clinton and Louisa B. (Bailey) Eccleston, of No. Stonington. Mr. Eccleston is a farmer, a Democrat, and a Methodist. He is a graduate of the Wheeler High School, class of 1898, and has been selectman of his native town. Mrs. Eccleston is a graduate of the Wheeler School, and before her marriage taught in the schools of Westerly and other towns with marked ability and success. Res., No. Stonington, Conn.; address, Preston, Conn.

451. Iona Main, b. Feb. 15, 1880; d. June 3, 1881.

452. Jennie Cleveland Main, b., New Albany, Ind., Oct. 14, 1887. She is a graduate of the Wheeler High School and of the Westerly High School; also of the Bryant and Stratton's Business College, Providence, R. I. She taught school in Westerly, Richmond, and Hopkinton, R. I. She is now [1908] stenographer in the office of the Waterhouse Worsted Company, Providence.

Harriet Isadora Main (382), dau. of Stephen and Elizabeth Stewart Main, b., No. Stonington, Conn., May 22, 1857; m., No. Stonington, Sept. 1, 1875, Henry Chesebrough Greene, b., Voluntown, Conn., May 5, 1853; son of Charles B. and Ruth Mary (Palmer) Greene. Mr. Greene was educated in the schools of No. Stonington; was clerk in Westerly, R. I., for three years; was proprietor of a store in No. Stonington and held the offices of town clerk and treasurer in 1881; and afterwards was connected with a store for three years at Millville, Mass. Selling his interest, he returned to Westerly, conducting the same business until 1888. Since that time he has been manager and salesman for a Providence, R. I., wholesale grocery house.

Mrs. Greene was educated in public and private schools of No. Stonington; studied art in Providence, and practised since 1887. Both Mr. and

Mrs. Greene are members of the First Baptist Church, Westerly. Res., Westerly, R. I.

Son:

453. Fred Stewart, b., No. Stonington, June 23, 1876. He is an artist, and has a studio at Westerly.

William Dean Main (383), brother of the preceding, b., No. Stonington, Conn., May 21, 1860; m., at Mystic, Conn., June 15, 1881, Almira Perron, dau. of Frank and Helen (Wilbur) Perron. Mr. Main attended the schools at No. Stonington and the East Greenwich Academy, R. I. He was clerk in the Boston Store, Westerly, R. I., until 1888, when he entered the employ of the Singer Sewing-Machine Company as assistant manager; in 1890 became manager of the Westerly office, and in 1908 retains that position. He is a Republican, and he and his wife are members of the Baptist Church.

Children:

454. Wilbur Stewart, b., Mystic, Feb. 19, 1883.
455. Priscilla Green, b., Westerly (Pawcatuck), Apr. 27, 1900.
456. Grace Marguerite, b., Westerly (Pawcatuck), Mar. 7, 1902.

Jennie Evelyn Main (384), sister of the preceding, b., No. Stonington, Conn., July 16, 1863; m., No. Stonington, Sept. 12, 1900, John William Beaton, b. Prince Edward Island; son of Venus Beaton, of Providence, R. I., and Frances Kaye. Mr. Beaton is a clerk in Westerly, R. I. Mrs. Beaton was educated in the public schools and at the Rhode Island State Normal School. For many years she was a teacher in the public schools of Rhode Island and Connecticut. She joined the Third Baptist Church at No. Stonington at the age of nine years, where her membership is still retained. No issue. Res., Westerly, R. I.

Anna Belle Main (385), dau. of Stephen and Elizabeth (Stewart) Main, b., No. Stonington, Conn., July 12, 1867; m., No. Stonington, June 12, 1900, Chester Grant Savage, b., Rockland, Me., June 25, 1869; son of Asbury C. and Abbie L. (Crane) Savage, of Rockland. Mr. Savage attended the schools of his native city, and was a student at Kimball Academy, Me., and Dartmouth College. He is a graduate of the Newton Theological Institution, class of 1893. Ordained to the Baptist ministry at Meriden, N. H., June, 1893, with pastorate at No. Stonington. He studied medicine at Baltimore University and graduated in April, 1898. Dr. Savage is a practising physician at Westerly, R. I. Both he and his wife are members of the Baptist Church. No issue.

Charles Frank Bentley (444), son of Francis J. and Lydia E. (Main) Bentley, b., No. Stonington, Conn., May 23, 1865; m., No. Scituate, R. I., Feb. 15, 1892, Clara E. Arnold, b. No. Scituate; dau. of Simeon and Alzada Tourtellot Arnold, of No. Scituate. Mr. Bentley is a farmer, a Republican, and both he and his wife are members of the Baptist Church. Res., East Greenwich, R. I.

Children, b. East Greenwich:

    457. Laurence A., b. Oct. 20, 1894; d. Apr. 12, 1895.

    458. Alice May, b. June 16, 1897.

William T. Bentley (445), brother of the preceding, b., No. Stonington, Conn., Dec. 8, 1866; m., Mansfield, Conn., Oct. 25, 1890, Christina Bogue, b., Groton, Conn., Apr. 26, 1872; dau. of Holan and Elizabeth (Allen) Bogue, of Groton. He is a farmer, and a Republican. They have lived at Mystic, Eagleville, and Tolland, Conn. Res., West Wellington, Conn.

Children, first three b. Mystic; next four at Eagleville:

    459. Harold F., b. Aug. 31, 1891; d. July 9, 1903.

    460. Frederick York, b. Oct. 29, 1893.

    461. Cora Harris, b. Feb. 28, 1895.

    462. William Lloyd, b. Feb. 23, 1899.

    463. Grace Viola, b. Apr. 30, 1901.

    464. Ruth May, b. May 26, 1902.

    465. Elsie W., b. Feb. 22, 1905.

    466. Lydia, b., Tolland, June 5, 1908.

Herbert G. Bentley (446), brother of the preceding, b., No. Stonington, Conn., Aug. 17, 1868; m., Jersey City, N. J., July 14, 1890, Lillie Heck, b., Jersey City, Jan. 17, 1869; dau. of John and Agnes (Horr) Heck, of New York. Mr. Bentley is a farmer; in politics he is a Republican. Res., Eagleville, Conn.

Children:

    467. Florence Agnes, b., Mystic, Conn., Sept. 19, 1891.

    468. Mabel Viola, b., Mystic, June 8, 1893.

    469. Mildred May, b., Willington, Conn., July 29, 1895.

    470. Alace Lillian, b., Willington, Oct. 29, 1896.

    471. Esther Marguerite, b., East Greenwich, R. I., Jan. 17, 1898.

    472. Gertrude M., b., Eagleville, Dec. 8, 1904.

Fred S. Chapman (447), son of Amos P. and Achsah M. (Main) Chapman, b., Westerly, R. I., Dec. 25, 1867; m., Clay Center, Kan., May 1,

1892, Emma C. Schrader, b., Ackley, Ia., Nov. 10, 1872. Mr. Chapman is a stereotyper, a Republican, and both he and his wife are members of the Episcopal Church.

Mrs. Chapman, when six years old, moved with her parents to Clay Center, and attended the public schools, and graduated from the grammar schools when sixteen years old. Res., 35 Willard Ave., Woodhaven, N. Y.
Children:

    473. Kenneth S., b., New York City, June 22, 1894.
    474. Elmer, b., Queens Co., N. Y., Dec. 8, 1898.

Theodore Stephen Chapman (448), brother of the preceding, b., Westerly, R. I., Mar. 18, 1874; m., White Plains, N. Y., Sept. 1, 1904, Therese Magrethe Gundersen, b., Christiana, Norway; dau. of Arne and Amabe Gundersen, of Christiana. Mr. Chapman's early life was spent in Westerly; since 1899 in New York City and Brooklyn. He is an engineer, a Republican, and both he and his wife are members of the Episcopal Church. No issue. Res., Brooklyn Manor, Woodhaven, N. Y.

Jonas Main (280), son of Dea. Thomas Main (264) and Annah Brown, dau. of Eleazer Brown and Ann Pendleton. Eleazer Brown, son of Thomas Brown and Mary Newhall, of Lynn, Mass. (B. G., pp. 9–12.)

Jonas Main, b., Stonington, Conn., Feb. 7, 1735–6; d., Stonington, Jan. 24, 1804; m. (1), Westerly, R. I., June 3, 1756, Patience Peckham, b. Feb. 13, 1732; d. July 23, 1758 (Bibles say 1757); m. (2), Apr. 14, 1760, Content Bromley, dau. of William and Elizabeth (Dewey) Bromley; d. Aug., 1825, aged eighty-nine years. She is believed to have passed her last days and died at the home of her son Jabish (483).

Elizabeth Dewey was dau. of Israel, 2d; son of Israel and Abigail (Drake) Dewey. Israel Dewey 1st, a son of Thomas Dewey, the settler, of Windsor, Conn., the first of the name in the New World, and from whom descends Admiral George Dewey. Abigail Drake was a dau. of Sergeant Job Drake, who m. Mary Wolcott, dau. of Henry Wolcott, of Windsor, ancestor of the Connecticut Wolcotts.

REVOLUTIONARY RECORD.

Jonas Main (280) was of Capt. Hungerford's Company, Col. Samuel McClellan's Regiment; was appointed Ensign Nov. 5, 1780; and received his discharge Jan. 3, 1781. The regiment was ordered on a tour of duty at New London and Groton, Conn. (See Adjutant-General's Records of Connecticut's War of the Revolution, p. 579.)

This will qualify the descendants of Jonas Main to become Sons and Daughters of the American Revolution.

NOTE.— The descendants of Jonas Main (280) spelled the name "Maine," adding final "e."

Children by first m., b. Stonington, Conn.:

    475. Sibius, b. Mar. 23, 1757; d. young. (This name is spelled in various ways.)

Children by second m.:

    476. Content, b. Feb. 7, 1761; d. June 2, 1825; m. Hakes.

    477. Reuben Peckham, b. Jan. 5, 1763; m. Sally Burdick (508–516).

    478. Patience, b. Mar. 7, 1765; m. Thomas Hazard Peckham (533–542).

    479. Lyman, b. Mar. 14, 1767; m. Fanny Burdick (543).

    480. Dewey, b. Sept. 14, 1770; m. Lucinda Colgrove (544–553).

    481. Jonas M., b. Mar. 15, 1772.

    482. Thomas, b.——; m. Hannah Chapman, b. Nov. 28, 1776 (553a–553i).

    483. Jabish Breed, b. July 4, 1774; m. Freelove Edwards (554–566).

    484. Nancy, b.——; m. John Gray (567–570).

    485. Paul B., b. Apr. 1, 1782; m. Lydia Miner (570a–570g).

The names of Thomas (482), Nancy (484), and Paul (485) do not appear in the old Jonas Main Bible.

Amos Main (284d), son of Jeremiah (269) and Abigail (Worden) Main, b. Sept. 2, 1735; m., May 19, 1756, Abigail Brown. He was in the Revolutionary War.

Children:

    486. Naboe, b. Aug. 8, 1757.

    487. Esther, b. July 1, 1759.

    488. Keturah, b. Jan. 23, 1762.

    489. Thankful, b. Aug. 12, 1764.

    490. Tryphenia, b. May 8, 1767.

    491. Anne, b. Aug. 11, 1769.

    492. Desire, b. Mar. 31, 1772; m. Gilbert Sisson.

    493. Betsey, b. May 3, 1777.

    494. Amos C., b. July 3, 1779 (1095–1101).

James Main (285), b. Jan. 27, 1743; son of Jeremiah (269) and Thankful (Brown) Main, dau. of James Brown and Elizabeth Randall; m., Stonington, Conn., Mar. 4, 1763, Hannah Wallace.

Children:

495. Hannah, b. Dec. 12, 1763.

496. James, b. Apr. 3, 1766.

497. Gilbert, b. Jan. 10, 1768.

498. Lucinda, b. July 28, 1770.

David Main (289), brother of the preceding, and son of Jeremiah (269) and Thankful (Brown) Main, b. Aug. 26, 1752; d. Dec. 27, 1843; m. (1), Apr. 26, 1773, Hannah Worden; d. Nov. 27, 1779. Mr. Main m. (2), Apr. 29, 1780, Judeth Palmer; d. Nov. 16, 1783. He m. (3), Jan. 8, 1787, Mrs. Esther Palmer, widow of Dr. Asher Palmer; dau. of Rev. Seth Dean; d. Feb. 24, 1824, aged sixty-eight years. He m. (4), Feb. 7, 1825, Philena Sawyer; d. Apr. 8, 1845, aged seventy-two years.

Children by first m., b. Stonington, Conn., in the north part:

499. Hannah, b. Jan. 27, 1774; d. Aug. 8, 1776.

499a. Thankful, b. Apr. 9, 1775; d. Jan. 12, 1777.

500. Patty, b. Feb. 10, 1778.

Children by second m.:

501. David, Jr., b. July 26, 1781; d., New Orleans, La., Sept. 20, 1810.

502. Robert, b. Jan. 19, 1783; d. Aug. 30, 1810.

Children by third m., b. Stonington:

502a. Ira, b.——; d. Sept. 12, 1789.

503. Rial, b. May 27, 1788; m. Eunice Palmer (731–738).

504. Chandler, b. Jan. 29, 1790; m. Nancy Brown (B. G., p. 32) (832, 833).

505. Fenner, b. Oct. 29, 1791; m. Lucrecia Main (835–844).

506. Rhoda, b. May 16, 1794; m. Joseph Holmes (852–856).

507. Saxton, b. Aug. 27, 1796; m. Sophronia Stanton (857–859).

Records corrected by David Main's Bible, bought in 1796.

Reuben Peckham Maine (477), son of Jonas (280) and Content (Bromley), b., Stonington, Conn., Jan. 5, 1763; d., Adams, N. Y., at the home of his son Perez, June 2, 1842; m., in 1785, Sally Burdick, b. Sept. 7, 1763; dau. of John and Elizabeth (Babcock) Burdick; d., Guilderland, N. Y., Jan. 28, 1837. (Perez Maine's Bible says she died in her seventy-second year.) Mr. Maine was a farmer in Guilderland.

Children:

508. Perez, b. Jan. 29, 1786; m. Sally Burdick (same name as his mother) (517–522).

509. Jonas, b. Apr. 1, 1788; m. Lydia Porter (523–525).

510. John Burdick, b. July 15, 1790; d., Guilderland, 1873; m. and
lived at Guilderland, where were born children: John, James
R., and Sally.

511. Fanny, b. Jan. 3, 1792; d., Ellisburg, N. Y., Mar. 22, 1856; m.
James Thayer, of Ellisburg. Children (all of whom are deceased): Joseph, Lewis, Mariette, Lucy, Royal C., Frank,
and Francis.

512. Lewis, b. Apr. 3, 1795; d., Richfield, N. Y., Nov. 3, 1840; m.
Mrs. Moore. Children: Stephen and Charles.

513. Asher H., b. Sept. 29, 1798; d., Guilderland, Oct. 4, 1842; m.
and had five children.

514. Sophia, b. Nov. 8, 1799; d., Petersburg, N. Y., Oct. 30, 1834;
m. Seth Worthington, of Petersburg. Children: Aaron,
John M., Thomas, Maryline J., Harvey R., and David
Mortimer.

515. Franklin Brown, b. Apr. 5, 1802; m. Zeruiah Maine (526–
532).

516. Adam W., b. Sept. 12, 1804; d., Torrington, Conn., Oct. 13,
1882; m. (1) Jerusha C. Fielding; m. (2) Harriet N. Ingraham.
Children, by second m. only: Edwin, Frank, Harriet, and
Jennie.

NOTE.— The old Bible of Perez Maine, which is replete with family records and in
good state of preservation, is now in the hands of Dr. C. Wesley Hale (1067), of
Springfield, Mass.

Perez Maine (508), son of Reuben P. (477) and Sally (Burdick) Maine,
b., Stonington, Conn., Jan. 29, 1786; d., Adams, N. Y., Sept. 8, 1877; m.
Sally Burdick, b. Jan. 5, 1786; d. Dec. 5, 1841.

Children:

517. Betsy Babcock, b. Apr. 22, 1807; d. Mar. 5, 1882.
518. Hiram Ledyard, b. Nov. 28, 1809; d. 1856.
519. Celia Meria, b. June 14, 1812; d. 1835.
520. Harriet Melissa, b. Jan. 5, 1816; d. 1845.
521. Hannah Burdick, b. Oct. 5, 1819; d. aged eighty-two years.
522. Ira Kilbourn Burdick, b. Nov. 12, 1822; d. 1859.

Jonas Maine (509), brother of the preceding, b. Apr. 1, 1788; d., Henderson, N. Y., Aug. 27, 1823; m. Lydia Porter.

Children:

523. Frances, b. March 4, 1812; d., Nunda, N. Y., Apr. 10, 1891; m.
Rev. Joseph F. Aspinwall and had family.

75

524. Amanda, d., Porter, Rock Co., Wis., Apr. 23, 1853, in the thirty-fifth year of her age; unm.
525. Mortimer P., d., St. Paul's, Ia., in 1856, in the thirty-seventh year of his age; m. Sarah Drummond and had family.

Franklin Brown Maine (515), brother of the preceding, b., Plainfield, N. Y., Apr. 5, 1802; d., Bolton, Conn., Aug. 1, 1882; m., No. Stonington, Conn., May 23, 1824, Zeruiah Maine (557), dau. of Jabish (483) and Freelove (Edwards) Maine; b., No. Stonington, Dec. 20, 1801; d., Bolton, July 1, 1872. She possessed a remarkable memory of dates and events, was of strong religious convictions, and conscientious to the extreme. Mr. Maine was a blacksmith and wagon-maker by trade, was keen of wit and interesting in conversation. They passed their last years in Bolton, and are buried there, in the Quarryville Cemetery.
Children:
526. Reuben Selim, d. in infancy.
527. Frank Carolus, d. in infancy.
528. Sarah Marcia, b., Coventry, Conn., 1826; d. 1842; bur. Bolton Hill Cemetery.
529. Ralph Brown, b., So. Bolton, 1833; d. 1838; bur. Bolton Hill Cemetery.
530. Jerusha Sophia, b., Andover, Conn., July 15, 1836; m. Charles W. Richardson (532a–532e).
531. Frank Duane, b., No. Coventry, Conn., Nov. 19, 1839; m. Eliza B. Julian.
532. Isabel Imilda, b., No. Coventry, Conn., Oct. 18, 1842; m. (1), Bolton, May 20, 1867, John Lane, of Rockville, Conn., d. June 3, 1868, aged forty-five years; m. (2), Springfield, Mass., Oct. 16, 1878, Herman Henry Poskey, b. Cincinnati, O., May 30, 1852. Res., 1909, Worcester, Mass.

Jerusha Sophia Maine (530), b., Andover, Conn., July 15, 1836; m., Deerfield, Mass., Oct. 12, 1861, Charles Wesley Richardson, of Conway, Mass., b. Oct. 12, 1833; d., Conway, June 26, 1882. He was a veteran of the Civil War, enlisting in 1st Bat. Conn. Vol. Light Artillery in 1861; discharged in 1865. Mrs. Richardson res., 1909, in Springfield, Mass.
Children, last four born Conway:
532a. Charles Fernando, b., Bolton, Conn., May 22, 1862; m. Mrs. Emma O'Connor. Res., 1909, New Britain, Conn.
532b. Isabel Augusta, b. Mar. 8, 1869. Res., 1909, Springfield, Mass.

Dr. Frank D. Maine
(531)
Springfield, Mass.
Page 77

The Deacon's Chair

This chair was used by Deacon Thomas Main (261), page 50, in the
old Meeting-House (Raccoon Box). See Appendix V. It is now
owned by Dr. C. Wesley Hale (1067)

532c. Frank Gilbert, b. Apr. 12, 1871; m. ——. Children: Leroy Wesley and Gilbert Thomas.

532d. Kathaline Maria, b. Mar. 5, 1873; d. aged nineteen months.

532e. Eunice Waite, b. Apr. 21, 1876; m. John Douglas. Res., 1909, Greenfield, Mass.

Dr. Frank Duane Maine (531), brother of the preceding, b., No. Coventry, Conn., Nov. 19, 1839; m., Rockville, Conn., May 20, 1862. Eliza B. Julian, dau. of John and Julia (Bramwell) Julian, d., Windsor Locks, Conn., Oct. 13, 1890, aged fifty-one years. Buried Rockville. No issue.

Dr. Maine graduated from the New York Medical College in 1872, and practised successfully for twenty years at Windsor Locks, since which time he has devoted himself to travel and literary pursuits. He has written at some length descriptive of his travels; also upon lines of religio-historic and scientific research. He served in the Civil War, being a member of Co. D., 14th Regt. Conn. Vol. Infantry; was disabled at Antietam, and later discharged. Res., 1909, Springfield, Mass.

Here end the family records of Reuben Peckham Maine (477).

Patience Maine (478), dau. of Jonas (280) and Content (Bromley), b. Mar. 7, 1765; d., No. Stonington, Conn., May 20, 1863, being over ninety-eight years of age; m., Stonington, May 15, 1784, Thomas Hazard Peckham, b. July, 1766; d. Sept. 22, 1822, both of Stonington, Corn. Mrs. Peckham is remembered in 1909, by a few of the older people in No. Stonington, as "Granny" Peckham; the last years of her life she lived with her daughter Nancy (Peckham) Wheeler and her grandsons John Owen and Thomas W. Wheeler. Here in this quiet, pleasant home she was lovingly cared for, and in her old age she passed much of her time knitting. The compiler remembers, in August, 1858, placing in her arms his oldest daughter, who is now the wife of Ex-Governor George H. Utter, of Westerly, R. I. He remembers also how she laughed, and how delighted she was to have a baby in her arms; she was then ninety-three years old. She passed away as a candle burns down to the socket, flickers, and goes out.

Thomas H. Peckham had brothers: Benjamin, b., So. Kingstown, R. I., 1755; d., Groton, Conn., now Ledyard, Apr. 5, 1833; m., Feb. 19, 1778, by Simeon Brown, Elder, (2) Lucy, b. 1759, dau. of Capt. Nathan Wilcox and wife Tabitha Prosser. They had fifteen children. Isaac Peckham, b. 1773; d., Ledyard, Jan. 31, 1843; m. Mary ——, b. 1773; d. Apr. 15, 1849. They had a dau. Fanny, who m. Dea. Thomas Prosser; a dau. who m. Taft and went to Vermont. Thomas H. Peckham had a sister Mary, b. 1756; m. Hillard ——. She makes an affidavit Dec. 30, 1836.

Children, b. in what is now (since 1807) No. Stonington:

533. Thomas Hazard Peckham, Jr., b. Aug. 24, 1785; m. Sophia Stanton (603-611).
534. William, b. Oct. 10, 1787; m. Cynthia Lewis (617).
535. Patty or Martha, b. June 2, 1789; m. Benjamin Peabody (618-624).
536. Hannah, b. May 10, 1791; m. Augustus L. Babcock.
537. Nancy, b. July 31, 1793; m. Jesse Wheeler (625-628).
538. Fanny, b. Nov. 12, 1795; d. a young lady.
539. Esther, b. Aug. 15, 1799; m. George W. Little.
540. Philura, b. July 5, 1801; m. Jedediah Wheeler Randall (645-653).
541. Pauline, b. July 20, 1803; m. Joel Pitcher (654-660).
542. Stephen Van R., b. Apr. 30, 1805; m. Mary Ann Hill (661-665).

Lyman Maine (479), son of Jonas (280) and Content (Bromley), b. Mar. 14, 1767; m., Dec. 14, 1789, Fanny Burdick.
Son:

543. Isaac, b. Oct. 17, 1793.

Dewey Maine (480), brother of the preceding, b. Sept. 14, 1770; d. Jan. 31, 1847; m., Aug. 18, 1793, Lucinda Colgrove.
Children:

544. Lucinda, b. Dec. 22, 1795.
545. Sheffield, b. Mar. 22, 1798.
546. Susan, b. Feb. 17, 1800.
547. Milton, b. Mar. 4, 1802.
548. Sebius, b.——
549. Prentice, b.——
550. Silas, b.——
551. Nancy, b.——
552. Julia, b.——
553. Levantia, b.——

John[1] Peckham, b.——; d. 1681; lived at Newport, R. I.; m. (1) Mary Clark, b. 1607; d. 1645; he m. (2) Elinor ——
John[2] Peckham, b., Newport, R. I., 1645; d. 1712; m. (1) Elizabeth ——; m. (2) Sarah ——. Their first child b. 1668.

Jabish Breed Maine (483) and wife, Freelove (Edwards)

North Stonington, Conn.

Picture taken about 1850

Page 79

Collins (555)
Cynthia Louesa (558)
Christopher Ira (561)

Freelove (556)
Jonas Chapman (559)
Sebeus Colver (562)
Diantha Harriet (566)

Zeruiah (557)
Clarinda Wells (560)
Sidney Orrison (565)

Timothy³ Peckham, b. June 19, 1673; m. (1) Dinah ——; m. (2) Rachel ——; m. (3) Content Drake, a widow.

Reuben⁴ Peckham, b. 1709; m., Dec. 16, 1730, Patience Hathaway.

(1) Rachel⁵ Peckham, b. Sept. 5, 1731; m., Nov. 2, 1752, Joshua Main (278), son of Dea. Thomas Main (264). He removed to Patterson, Putnam Co., N. Y. (1988–1991).

(2) Patience⁵ Peckham, b. Feb. 13, 1732; d. July 23, 1758; m. (1), June 3, 1756, Jonas Main, and had one child, Sabius, b. Mar. 23, 1757. Jonas Main (280) m. (2) Content, dau. of William Bromley, and had ten children.

(3) Timothy⁵ Peckham, b. Nov. 6, 1734; d. Apr. 5, 1822; m., Sept. 19, 1754, Mary, dau. of Benjamin and Johanna (Sprague) Barber, of Westerly, R. I. They had thirteen children.

Thomas Maine (482), brother of the preceding, b.——; m. Hannah Chapman, b. Nov. 28, 1776, dau. of Joseph and Prudence (Lewis) Chapman.

Children (order of birth not ascertained):

553a. Thomas.
553b. Aaron.
553c. Fleet.
553d. Joseph.
553e. Polly.
553f. Hannah.
553g. Content.
553h. Nancy.
553i. Sophia.

NOTE.— The town of Stonington was divided in 1807, the north part being called North Stonington. It then had 2,700 inhabitants; now [1909] it has 1,200.

Jabish Breed Maine (483) (this name has been spelled also Jabez), son of Jonas (280) and Content (Bromley), b., No. Stonington, Conn., July 4, 1774; d., No. Stonington, Oct. 30, 1856; m., No. Stonington, Mar. 15, 1795, Freelove Edwards, b., No. Stonington, Sept. 6, 1776; d., No. Stonington, Apr. 10, 1856. Interments in the family cemetery, a few rods south of the homestead, where are buried also Hiram and Fanny, the two children who died young, and Diantha the youngest child.

Mr. Maine's farm, situated about two miles south of Pendleton Hill, was not large, as he devoted much of his time to his trade as a stone and plaster mason. He helped build the old Stonington lighthouse, and there are yet many specimens of his skill which testify that he was "a workman that needeth not to be ashamed." He and his two oldest sons were in the War of 1812, and participated in the defense of Stonington.

Freelove Edwards was the daughter of Christopher and Amy (Hall) Edwards, who lived near Billings Pond. He was son of Thomas and Jerusha (Brown) Edwards, a dau. of Capt. Thomas Brown. Amy Hall was dau. of Thomas and Hannah (Fellows) Hall, the latter a dau. of Dea. Ephraim Fellows, of Rhode Island. Mrs. Maine was rarely endowed with superior natural literary ability, which was evidenced in her children and grandchildren. She was noted for the composition of poetry on striking events. "Aunt Freelove," as she was commonly called, was also well known for her skill in the care of the sick and injured, using chiefly medicaments of her own preparation.

The Maine homestead, which had become old and neglected, has been purchased and put in excellent condition by a great-grandson, Dr. C. Wesley Hale (1067), of Springfield, Mass., who uses it as a summer residence. The family Bible, which was also the Bible of Mrs. Maine's mother, Amy (Hall) Edwards, and printed in Edinburgh in 1749, is in the hands of Dr. Hale, who has rendered valuable service in collecting these family records.

The following poem was prepared by Dr. Frank D. Maine, and read by him upon the occasion of the reopening of the Jabish Maine homestead, in No. Stonington, Conn., in October, 1908. On this occasion there were present *grandchildren* of Jabish and (Freelove) Maine, *great-grandchildren*, *great-great-grandchildren*, and one *great-great-great-grandchild*. There were four generations in one line.

HALLOWED REMINISCENCES OF DEAREST KITH AND KIN.

By Frank D. Maine, M.D., Springfield, Mass.

A reminiscence of the past, of pleasure and of pain,
Is to us mortals quite as real as sunshine and the rain;
It is the warp and woof of life, donned by us every day;
The very act or thought expressed; yea, every word we say.

Let us, in reminiscent mood, revert to scenes of yore:
To the aged sire, his consort, who many children bore;
And to the mansion where they lived, and where their race was run;
Made hallowed by their presence here, in old North Stonington.

Who were this aged man and wife, I greeted when a boy,
And such a two-weeks visit made, of unalloyèd joy?
Within these very portals here I find myself again,
With memories of grandparents, Jabish and Freelove Maine.

This Jabish Breed, on July fourth, in seventeen seventy-four,
First saw the light and two years lived, plus eighty years and more:

THE EZEKIEL MAIN FAMILY

In eighteen hundred fifty-six, that year, he passed away,
Amid the autumn's falling leaf, October, thirtieth day.

Freelove in seventeen seventy-six, September sixth, was born;
A blushing maiden at eighteen, on March fifteenth, at morn,
Was married, seventeen ninety-five, and was a handsome bride;
In eighteen hundred fifty-six, on April tenth, she died.

Grandfather he was broad and stout, six feet in height and more,
While "granny" was a slight *petite*, with pluck and nerve galore,
Jabish was slow, conservative, mild-mannered, and sincere,
But Freelove was a "four-in-hand," and was at times severe.

Her life, though ever strenuous, yet was she just and true;
Within the home and for her friends did all that could she do;
With roots and "yarbs" she ministered, assuaged their griefs and pain —
A good Samaritan, indeed, this Freelove Edwards Maine.

Disparity as aforesaid, of size and weight and vim,
We rarely note in mating choice, in her, in it, or him;
But when we do, as in these two, you oftentimes will find
A progeny of good physique and of judicial mind.

Now Jabish, junior, was the *first*, born seventeen ninety-six,
April twentieth was the day, and never was betwixt
The right and wrong of anything — from guile was ever free;
On April eighth he breathed his last, in eighteen forty-three.

Collins, he was the *second* born, in seventeen ninety-seven;
The month December, sixteenth day, so is the record given;
Was able and of sterling worth, sanguine, alert, alive;
He died the sixteenth day of June, in eighteen seventy-five.

Freelove, the *third*, on tenth of June, in eighteen hundred born;
The only maiden of the girls, and only one forlorn;
However, she was good as gold, as all who knew her say;
In eighteen hundred seventy died, eleventh day of May.

To bless this union, Zeruiah, the *fourth* to see the sun,
December twentieth was born, in eighteen hundred one;
She was the fairest of the girls, as was well understood;
Religious, pensive, always sad, superlatively good.
Her memory was very great, excelled by only few; —
On July first she passed away, in eighteen seventy-two.

Cynthia's advent, the *fifth*, occurred in eighteen hundred four;
The month was June, the twenty-third, as has been told before;
As wife and mother none excelled; years since her work was done; —
June sixth she yielded up the ghost, in eighteen ninety-one.

Jonas Chapman, March the seventh, in eighteen hundred six,
Midway between the first and last, do we his advent fix;
Though was the *sixth* in date of birth, he was the first in wit;
As doctor, lawyer, poet, too, was never a misfit.
Quite late in life at Colchester he lived, and passed away
In eighteen hundred seventy-seven, July, seventeenth the day;
For years he was an invalid, had heart-disease and gout; —
And died, as oft expressed the wish, "as goes the candle out."

81

THE EZEKIEL MAIN FAMILY

Clarinda Wells, March thirtieth, born eighteen hundred eight;
Unlike the rest, when was full-grown, in breadth, in flesh, and weight;
And none so sanguine of the girls, so full of hope and cheer; —
A benediction to her friends, throughout the livelong year.
With hallowed memories of her life, the *seventh* in point of birth; —
June tenth, in eighteen eighty-eight, she bade farewell to earth.

Christopher Ira, November fifth, in eighteen hundred ten,
The *eighth*, was born into the world, and of distinguished men
He well compared in mental strength, — of constitution strong;
Both brain and brawn which he possessed to him of right belonged.
He loved and practised medicine, in which his race was run; —
Fifteenth November passed away, in eighteen eighty-one.

In the year eighteen hundred twelve, June, twenty-second day,
Sebeus Colver *ninth* in line was born, the records say;
A lawyer and distinguished judge, his parents' joy and pride; —
In eighteen hundred eighty-seven, twenty-fifth November, died.

The *tenth* was Hiram Leonard born, eighteen fourteen the year;
'T was on September twenty-sixth he did at first appear;
Three years ten months, of record clear, he lived, and passed away
In eighteen eighteen, month July, and twenty-seventh the day.

Fanny Mary, *eleventh*, was born, eighteen seventeen, 't is said;
When only nineteen days had passed was this sweet angel dead;
February twenty-third were both the month and day
When first this seraph saw the light; March thirteenth passed away.

In eighteen eighteen, May the sixth, the next and *twelfth* in line,
Was Sidney Orrison, the wit, and all was superfine
Of whatsoever was produced, of poetry or prose;
Besides, taught school successfully, as everybody knows.
August it was, the twentieth, in eighteen ninety-four,
When he was summoned straightway hence — as we say, "gone before."

Diantha Harriet, the last, though not the least to be;
The *thirteenth*, born on June the eighth, in eighteen twenty-three.
She was in truth superior to many of her kind,
And withal was she well possessed of an enlightened mind;
As teacher of the village school, in mem'ry will survive; —
She died in July, on the fifth, in eighteen sixty-five.

Except the infants that died young, and Jabish, eldest son,
I knew these uncles and these aunts; yes, knew them every one;
Their faces, forms, and habits, too, I personally knew,
And their idiosyncrasies — so consequently drew
Just inferences of them all, and much could truly say
Of mental and of moral worth, as shown from day to day.
They wrestled with the world, the flesh, and with Satanic strength;
Just as all other mortals do — but overcame at length.

In many ways they differed much, but of a truth can tell
They had in common this one trait, — all told a story well;
The reason why lies in the fact, good memories they had
Of what they saw and heard and read, of either good or bad.

82

Irony, sarcasm, to this add, and repartee besides,
Together with shrewd tactfulness, which with the race abides,
Than the major part of mortals can show by taking pains,
And in this summary you have the facts about the Maines.

And why not, since the following reveals in full the cause?
Ezekiel Maine of Stonington did help to make the laws.
From Thomas Dewey, pioneer, did Jabish Maine descend,
And from Henry Wolcott the first, both good and able men.

From Major Brian Pendleton, and Captain James his son,
For whose heroic services were all their laurels won;
There's kinship in Eleazer Brown, it is of record clear;
Grit, wit, and grace from all this stock doth in the Maines appear.

Then Edwards is another name, Freelove the maiden bore,
From Thomas, first, or settler came, who lived in days of yore;
The blood of *all* these ancestors coursed freely through the veins
Of these thirteen sons and daughters, which every gift explains.

But time and space forbid detail, in reminiscent speech,
Of Jabish B. and Freelove Maine, their children, all or each;
Grandparents, will we simply say, before I close these lines,
Lie buried but a stone's throw hence, beneath the lovely pines.

Not only did *they* live, grow old, and from earth pass away —
Their domicile of early years was subject to decay;
What great dilapidation marked this frame of long ago,
As witnessed by the lookers-on, in passing to and fro!

And as *they* have the Jordan crossed, now dressed in living green,
So resurrected is the house as visibly is seen;
It stands complete upon the site it occupied before,
And near it is the same old well as in the days of yore.

To whom are we indebted most, these pleasures to afford,
For what is witnessed here and now, the former home restored?
Viewed whether in the aggregate, or surveyed in detail?
To the great-grandson, be it said, Doctor Charles Wesley Hale!

Let us who are of kith and kin of those who now are dead
Their good deeds ever imitate, and speak the truths they said;
By dint of effort higher climb than possibly they could,
And so be recognized by all as strong and kind and good!

The children that follow lived near the father of the compiler of these records, and attended the same district school, the "Ash House."

Children, b. No. Stonington:

554. Jabish (or Jabez), b. Apr. 20, 1796; m. Lydia Edwards (965-973).

555. Collins, b. Dec. 16, 1797; m. Susan Peabody (1017-1030).

556. Freelove P., b. June 10, 1800; d., Bolton, Conn., May 11, 1870; unm. Buried Quarryville Cemetery. Was school-teacher and nurse by occupation.

557. Zeruiah, b. Dec. 20, 1801; m. Franklin Brown Maine (526–532).

558. Cynthia Louesa, b. June 23, 1804; m. Alfred Turner (1031–1038).

559. Jonas Chapman, b. Mar. 7, 1806; m. (1) Melinda Turner; m. (2) Mrs. Julia Wells (1039, 1040).

560. Clarinda Wells, b. Mar. 30, 1808; m. (1) Elias Sprague; m. (2) Capt. William Hunt (1041–1047).

561. Christopher Ira, b. Nov. 5, 1810; m. Electa Randall (1070–1075).

562. Sebeus Colver, b. June 22, 1812; m. Julia Octavia Stevens (1076, 1077).

563. Hiram Leonard, b. Sept. 26, 1814; d. July 27, 1818 (tombstone says July 21).

564. Fanny Mary, b. Feb. 23, 1817; d. Mar. 13, 1817.

565. Sidney Orrison, b. May 6, 1818; m. Eliza Lucinda Wentworth (1078–1082).

566. Diantha Harriet, b. June 8, 1823; d., Voluntown, Conn., July 5, 1865; m., Mar. 12, 1865, Joseph T. Rood. She possessed superior natural gifts, and was for several years before her marriage a successful school-teacher. No issue.

Nancy Maine (484), dau. of Jonas (280) and Content (Bromley), b.——; d. May 1, 1804; m., Nov. 2, 1794, John Gray, b., Stonington, Conn.; d., No. Stonington, Conn., Sept. 12, 1858, aged eighty-three years. Interment, Peabody Cemetery.

Children, b. Stonington, north part:

567. John Gray, b.——; m. Lucy Main and went West.

568. Lyman M. Gray, b.——; m. Eunice P. Leray (591–596).

569. Nancy Gray, b.——; m. William Whipple. Children: (1) Sarah, (2) Erastus, (3) Annie. Sarah m. William Grant. Erastus m. Louisa Gould. Children: Annie, Nancy, Charles, and Phebe Whipple.

570. Lucy Gray, b.——; m. Daniel Thompson.

Paul B. Maine (485), son of Jonas (280) and Content (Bromley), b. Apr. 1, 1782; d. Dec. 19, 1867; m. Lydia Miner. Lived in Madison and Chenango Counties, N. Y.

Children (order uncertain):

570a. Eliza.

570b. Clara.

570c. Mary.

570d. Grace.

570e. Julia.

570f. William.

570g. Henry.

After the death of Nancy (Maine) Gray (484), John Gray m. (2) Lucy York, b. Jan. 29, 1782; d. Mar. 1, 1869; dau. of James and Lucy (Palmer) York.

Children, b. No. Stonington, Conn.:

571. Dr. Alvah Gray, b. Mar. 12, 1805; m. Wheeler.

572. Melissa P., b. Sept. 17, 1806; m. Asher M. Ray (579-582).

573. William W., b. Dec. 20, 1809; m., went to Ohio, had three children, and d. there.

574. Van Renesselaer, b. Jan. 5, 1812; m., late in life, Charlotte Hunter. Mr. Gray was a school-teacher of ability, and very successful. His beautiful handwriting is seen in many family Bibles, written with a quill pen in No. Stonington. He was a teacher of the compiler. No issue. Interment, Peabody Cemetery.

575. Jirah Ishman, b. Sept. 6, 1814; m. Nancy Palmer. They had six children.

576. Daniel Packer, b. June 18, 1817; m. and had several children; lived and d. in New York.

577. Mary W., b. July 13, 1820; m. Charles W. Rouse. They had one child.

578. La Fayette, b. Oct. 14, 1824; m. Martha York Palmer (583-586).

Melissa P. Gray (572), sister of the preceding, b. Sept. 17, 1806; m. Asher M. Ray.

Children:

579. Rev. Charles Walker Ray. He was a Baptist minister at No. Stonington, Conn., for a number of years. He was a composer of music, and a fine singer. Res., Pennsylvania.

580. Rev. La Fayette Ray. He was a minister in Norwich, N. Y.

581. George W. Ray. He was a lawyer and member of Congress, Norwich, N. Y.

582. Walace Ray. He was an undertaker; lived in Hamilton, N. Y.

La Fayette Gray (578), b. Oct. 14, 1824; d. June, 1871; m. Martha York Palmer, b. Feb. 22, 1822; d. Oct. 22, 1905.

Children, b. No. Stonington, Conn.:

> 583. George Fayette, b. June 29, 1850; d. Jan., 1871; m. Sarah Newton. They had one child who d. young.
>
> 584. Murray, b. Apr. 22, 1852; m., Ashaway, R. I., Nov., 1877, Margaret Matilda Hoxie, b., Westerly, R. I., Aug. 21, 1859. Children: (1) Iona Grace, b. Oct. 10, 1879; m. Lyman Hall. Children: John Murry, b. Mar. 6, 1907; Helen Eca, b. June 17, 1908; d. Nov. 4, 1908. (2) Howard Victor, b. Dec. 6, 1881; unm. Mr. Gray is in the employ of the New York, New Haven, and Hartford Railroad. Res., Westerly, R. I.
>
> 585. Earnest Eugene, b. Mar. 2, 1854; d. Nov. 12, 1905: unm.
>
> 586. Charles Cressingham, b. May 22, 1859: m., Feb. 22, 1883, Emma Rebecca Chapman, b., New London, Conn., June 22, 1861; dau. of Rev. Daniel F. Chapman and Rebecca Getchell. Mr. Gray is a farmer and member of the Second Baptist Church, No. Stonington, and was superintendent of the Sunday school. He is a man of ability and credit to the community.

Children:

> 587. Cressingham Lafayette, b. May 22, 1884.
>
> 588. Lyle Chapman, b. Aug. 2, 1886.
>
> 589. Leslie Jennings, b. Mar. 23, 1895; d. Mar. 6, 1908. He was a student at the Wheeler High School, and was a youth of rare abilities, and much beloved.
>
> 590. Charley Earnest, b. Dec.26, 1898.

Lyman M. Gray (568), son of John Gray and Nancy Main (484), b. Stonington, Conn.; m., No. Stonington, Conn., Jan. 8, 1821, Eunice P. Leray.

Children, b. No. Stonington:

> 591. Eunice Ann, b. Oct. 7, 1822 (597-600).
>
> 592. Nathan S., b. Dec. 2, 1825.
>
> 593. Thomas Wattles, b. Nov. 11, 1829; d. young.
>
> 594. William C., b. Dec. 19, 1832; m. Sarah Jane Richardson (601).
>
> 594a. Thomas Hull, b. Mar. 21, 1839. Always lived in No. Stonington. He was in the Civil War for three years, in Co. G, 21st Reg. Conn. Vol.; honorably discharged at the close of the war: unm. Res., No. Stonington, Conn.

595. Abby M., b. June 20, 1842; d. 1865; unm.

596. Latham H., b. Oct. 3, 1845; m., July 25, 1871, Lois P. Hood. No issue.

Eunice Ann Gray (591), dau. of Lyman M. (568) and Eunice P. (Leray) Gray, b. Oct. 7, 1822; d. Mar. 17, 1895; m. (1) Gilbert Sisson, b. 1800; d. July 26, 1876, aged seventy-five years, and ten months; m. (2) Augustus Terwilliger.

Children, by first m.:

597. Dudley W., b. Apr. 2, 1847; d. Apr. 14, 1906; m. Mary Jane Dinsmore. Son: Elmer G.

598. Jennie Lind, b. Mar. 27, 1851 (602).

599. Oliver Avory, b. Sept. 26, 1855; d. Sept. 12, 1880; unm.

600. Mary Elizabeth, b. Jan. 5, 1858; d. Apr. 11, 1882; unm.

William C. Gray (594), son of Lyman (568) and Eunice P. (Leray) Gray, b., No. Stonington, Conn., Dec. 19, 1832; d., No. Stonington, 1904-5; m., No. Stonington, Sarah Jane Richardson, dau. of Benadam Richardson.

Son:

601. W. Henry Gray, b. Sept. 16, 1862; m., Mystic, Conn., December, 1892, M. Sada Barnes, b. 1868, dau. of Amos T. and Mary (Browning) Barnes. Dr. Gray is a physician in Mystic; a graduate of Columbia Medical College, New York, 1889. Children: A. Louise, b. Oct. 26, 1893; Marion and Mildred (twins), b. June 16, 1897.

Jennie Lind Sisson (598), sister of the preceding, b., No. Stonington, Conn., Mar. 27, 1851; m., Hartford, Conn., Jan. 14, 1873, Frank Webb Ripley, b., Windham, Conn., Sept. 7, 184; 8d., New Haven, Conn., Mar. 27, 1873. Mr. Ripley was a bookkeeper at Norwich, Conn. He enlisted Jan. 19, 1865, as a private in the Civil War. Mrs. Ripley m. (2), Nov. 25, 1882, Charles B. Caswell, b., No. Stonington, Apr. 28, 1849. He is a carpenter and painter. Res., No. Stonington, Conn.

Son:

602. Clifford W., b. Oct. 20, 1890. He was two years at Wheeler High School; graduated from Westerly Business College, December, 1907.

Thomas Hazard Peckham, Jr. (533), son of Thomas H. and Patience Main (478) Peckham; b. Aug. 24, 1785; d. May 4, 1867, aged eighty-one years; m. Sophia Stanton, b. 1793; d. Mar. 27, 1860. Mr. Peckham lived in

No. Stonington, Conn., northwest corner, until 1837, when he removed to Norwich, Conn., where he d.

Children, b. No. Stonington:

    603. Emily Ann, b. May 30, 1814; m. Ebenezer W. Woodworth (612-615).

    604. Isaac Miner, b. Apr. 19, 1815; d., Norwich, Mar. 18, 1876; unm.

    605. Harriet De Coursey, b. Nov. 25, 1818; d. Jan. 25, 1844; unm.

    606. William, b. Jan. 19, 1821; d., Norwich, Dec. 3, 1869; m. Fanny Woodworth. Children: Helen Malvina, b.——; d. Nov. 13, 1862, aged twelve years and ten months; son, b.——; d. young.

    607. Enoch Stanton, b. Feb. 8, 1823; d. May 31, 1874; unm.

    608. Albertus, b. Nov. 11, 1825; m. Nancy G. Dolbeare (616).

    609. Stephen Hazard, b. Nov. 4, 1827; d. Jan. 25, 1867; unm.

    610. Nancy Wheeler, b. Aug. 19, 1831; d. Apr. 15, 1835.

    611. Nancy H., b. Oct. 25, 1836; d. Aug. 3, 1839.

Emily Ann Peckham (603), sister of the preceding, b. May 30, 1814; d., Norwich, Conn., Sept. 11, 1875; m. Ebenezer Williams Woodworth, of Montville, Conn., b. Oct. 17, 1815; d., Norwich, Feb. 24, 1889. Mr. Woodworth was a contractor on stone work, and both spent their married life in Norwich.

Dau.:

    612. Harriet Peckham Woodworth, b., Norwich, Oct. 16, 1846; m. Martin Frances Bent, b., Wareham, Mass., Mar. 17, 1835; son of Isaac Bent, b., Wareham, Aug. 4, 1799, and Sophia Bartlet, b., Plymouth, Mass., Mar. 3, 1809. Res., W. Thames St., Norwich, Conn.

Children, b. Norwich:

    613. Helen Sophia Bent, b. Sept. 9, 1867; d. Jan. 1, 1873.

    614. Francis Peckham Bent, b. Mar. 13, 1872.

    615. William Woodworth Bent, b. Apr. 17, 1883. Graduated from Yale Law School, and is lawyer at Bridgeport, Conn.; unm.

Francis Peckham Bent (614), brother of the preceding, m., Brooklyn, N. Y., Dec. 10, 1902, Gertrude May Fowler. Mr. Bent is a dealer in real estate, stocks, and bonds. He is an alderman in 1908, from the 61st district of Brooklyn.

Dau.:

Gertrude Knight, b. Oct. 8, 1903.

Albertus Peckham (608), son of Thomas Hazard (533) and Sophia (Stanton) Peckham, Jr., b., No. Stonington, Conn., Dec. 11, 1825; d., Norwich, Conn., Apr. 7, 1901; m., Norwich, Nov. 7, 1859, by Elder Charles Weaver, Nancy Gleason Dolbeare, b. Jan. 15, 1836; dau. of William and Nancy (Raymond) Dolbeare. Mr. Peckham removed with his parents, when he was twelve years old, from No. Stonington to Norwich, where he resided the remainder of his life. He attended school at the northwest corner of No. Stonington. His teacher was Hibbard M. Brown (B. G. 4139). In politics he was a Democrat. He was a farmer and a contractor in stone masonry.

Dau.:
616. Annie Sophia, b., Norwich, July 12, 1862. She was educated in the schools of Norwich; unm.

William Peckham (534), son of Thomas H. and Patience (Main 478) Peckham, b. Oct. 10, 1787; d. June 10, 1820; m. Cynthia Lewis, b. Oct. 21, 1790; d. Apr. 8, 1844; dau. of Ichabod and Cynthia (Bailey) Lewis.

Son:
617. William L. Peckham, b. May 15, 1819; m., May 20, 1839, Lucy Ann Dickinson, b. Nov. 17, 1816; d. Nov. 19, 1893. No issue. Res., Waterford, Conn. Mr. Peckham, in 1873, published a book, entitled "The Evangelist; or, Life and Labors of Rev. Jabez S. Swan," which had a wide circulation in the churches of Connecticut, Rhode Island, and Madison County, New York. Mr. Peckham recalls with much pleasure the benefit his book has done in awakening a deeper spiritual interest in the churches where Elder Swan's influence was and still is felt.

Patty, or Martha, Peckham (535), dau. of Thomas H. and Patience (Main 478) Peckham, b., Stonington, Conn., June 2, 1789; d. May 13, 1848; m., No. Stonington, Conn., Mar. 5, 1812, Benjamin Peabody, b. Apr. 29, 1772; son of Thomas and Ruth (Babcock) Peabody. She was his second wife. (Mayflower Records, Appendix II.)

Children, b. No. Stonington:
618. Thomas H., b. Mar. 10, 1813; d. in young manhood; unm.
619. Francis S., b. Apr. 29, 1815 (666-668).
620. Martha E., b. Apr. 24, 1819; m. John I. Miner. (See Appendix II.)
621. Mary, b. May 2, 1822; m. Cyrus W. Crary (G. B., p. 469).
622. Fanny A., b. June 29, 1825; m. Russell Welles.

623. Nancy, b. Sept. 5, 1828; m. (1)—— Cook; m. (2) Ralph Partelo.
624. James Alden, b. May 30, 1831; m. Augusta Josephine Crumb
(675–683).

Nancy Peckham (537), dau. of Thomas H. and Patience (Main) Peckham, b., Stonington, Conn., July 31, 1793; d., No. Stonington, Conn., Mar.
9, 1885; m., May 30, 1811, Jesse Wheeler, b., Stonington, May 28, 1786;
d. Jan. 16, 1852; son of Lester and Eunice (Bailey) Wheeler, dau. of David
Bailey and Eunice Brown.

Mr. Wheeler was a blacksmith in No. Stonington, and after his death
the business was conducted successfully by his sons John O. and Thomas
W., until their death. Mrs. Wheeler lived and died in the pleasant village
of her native town, endeared to all who came under the charm of her sweet
nature; and here in her home, with her two sons and wife of Thomas W.,
she lovingly cared for her aged mother for many years, who died aged
ninety-eight years and two months. It was their will that the last survivor
should give the property to the Baptist Church. It was so given. (B. G.,
p. 561).

Children, b. No. Stonington:

625. Stephen Hazard, b. Mar. 6, 1812; m. Harriet N. Williams
(629–631).
626. Elisha Packer, b. Dec. 15, 1815; m. Emeline E. Clark (632–
634).
627. John Owen, b. June 5, 1818; d. July 30, 1900; unm.
628. Thomas William, b. Oct. 20, 1822; m. Emily Elizabeth Brown
(635).

Stephen Hazard Wheeler (625), son of Jesse and Nancy (Peckham) (537)
Wheeler, b. Mar. 6, 1812; d., Old Mystic, Conn., Mar. 5, 1886; m. Harriet
Newell Williams. Mr. Wheeler was a blacksmith at Old Mystic, following
the line of his father in No. Stonington, Conn.

Children:

629. Thomas Eldredge, b. Feb. 1, 1834; m. Mary Briggs (636).
630. Harriet Newell, b. June 20, 1839; m. Edwin W. French.
631. Julia Hickox, b. Jan. 25, 1846; m. Albert Taylor Chapman
(640, 641).

Elisha Packer Wheeler (626), son of Jesse and Nancy (Peckham) Wheeler
b., No. Stonington, Conn., Dec. 15, 1815; d., Carolina, R. I., Aug. 1, 1857;
m., Richmond, R. I., June 7, 1838, Emeline E. Clark, b. Richmond; d.,

Patience Maine (478), wife of Thomas Hazard Peckham
Stonington, Conn.
Page 77

Nancy Peckham (537), wife of Jesse Wheeler
North Stonington, Conn.
Page 90

Hope Valley, R. I., Apr. 8, 1886; dau. of Peter and Mary (Clark) Clark. Mr. Wheeler was a blacksmith, and both he and his wife were Baptists.

Children, b. Richmond:

632. Van Rensselaer, b. Aug. 9, 1842; m. Sarah Hannah Starr (642).

Edgar ⎱ twins, b. June 15, 1844; d. in infancy.
Ellen ⎰

633. Edward Lillibridge, b. Apr. 18, 1848; d., Hopkinton, R. I., Nov. 20, 1865.

634. Joseph Green, b. Aug. 6, 1850; m. Mary Hopkins. No issue.

Thomas William Wheeler (628), son of Jesse and Nancy (Peckham) Wheeler, b. Oct. 20, 1822; d. Oct. 12, 1900; m., Nov. 7, 1844, Emily Elizabeth Brown, b. Jan. 16, 1828; d. Jan. 29, 1905; dau. of Cyrus W. and Elizabeth S. (Babcock) Brown.

Dau.:

635. Nancy Mary, b., No. Stonington, Conn., Sept. 2, 1847; d. Jan. 5, 1902; m., Dec. 3, 1878, William Horace Hillard, b. Aug. 8, 1826; d. Mar. 19, 1908 (B. G., pp. 57–8). Interments in River Bend, Westerly, R. I.

Thomas Eldredge Wheeler (629), son of Stephen H. (625) and Harriet N. (Williams) Wheeler, b. Feb. 1, 1834; d. Nov. 1, 1864; m., Voluntown, Conn., Oct. 19, 1857, Mary W. Briggs.

Son:

636. Thomas Everett Wheeler, b., Old Mystic, Conn., Jan. 16, 1862; m., Utica, Ill., May 15, 1884, Alace Dunan, b., Peru, Ill., May, 1864; dau. of Hayes and Fanny (Hutchins) Dunan, of Peru. Mr. Wheeler is a druggist. Res., Utica, Ill.

Children, b. Utica:

637. Besse Briggs Wheeler, b. July 3, 1885; m., Utica, May 15, 1906, John Franklin Huffstodt, b., Princeton, Ill., Oct. 10, 1876. Son: Robert Wheeler, b. Srurea, Ill., Apr. 1, 1907.

638. Ray Dunan, b. Dec. 5, 1889.

639. Ethel Gallup, b. Nov. 15, 1892.

Harriet Newell Wheeler (630), dau. of Stephen H. (625) and Harriet (Williams) Wheeler, b., Mystic, Conn., June 20, 1839; d., Mystic, May 8, 1906; m., Mystic, Apr. 5, 1859, Edwin W. French, b., Glastonbury, Conn , Mar. 11, 1837. Mr. French was in the Civil War and served from private to captain in the Connecticut Cavalry. He is insurance agent, Republican, and a Unitarian. Res., Old Mystic, Conn.

Julia Hickox Wheeler (631), dau. of Stephen H. (625) and Harriet N. (Williams) Wheeler, b., Old Mystic, Conn., Jan. 25, 1846; d., Old Mystic, Jan. 5, 1896; m., Old Mystic, June 10, 1868, Albert Taylor Chapman, b., No. Stonington, Conn., July 21, 1839. Dr. Chapman graduated, in 1864, from the College of Physicians and Surgeons in New York City, and since has practised at Old Mystic. He became blind in 1885. Res., Old Mystic, Conn.

Children, b. Old Mystic:

640. Gertrude Wheeler, b. Sept. 17, 1869.
641. Julia Maud Chapman, b. July 10, 1879; m., Old Mystic, Jan. 20, 1903, William D. Harris, of New London, Conn.

Van Rensselaer Wheeler (632), son of Elisha P. (626) and Emeline E. (Clark) Wheeler, b., Richmond, R. I., Aug. 9, 1842; m., Mystic, Conn., Sept. 8, 1860, Sarah Hannah Starr, b. Yonkers, N. Y.; d., Providence, R. I., Jan. 14, 1897; dau. of Vine A. and H. Sally (Sullivan) Starr. Mr. Wheeler is an insurance agent; in politics, a Democrat. He and his wife are members of the Methodist Episcopal Church. Before his marriage he lived at Carolina, R. I.; afterwards at Baltic, Mystic, and New London, Conn. He was in the carriage business at New London eighteen years and was steward and trustee in the Methodist Church; is now a member of the Executive Committee of the Willimantic, Conn., Camp Meeting Association. Res., Providence, R. I.

Son:

642. Edward Mallory Wheeler, b., Mystic, Dec. 2, 1869; m., June 11, 1895, Harriet Beldin Goodrich, b., East Hartford, Conn., Mar. 25, 1871.

Children:

643. Edward Van R., b. June 12, 1896.
644. Dorothy Goodrich, b. June 9, 1899.

Philura Peckham (540), dau. of Thomas H. and Patience (Main 478) Peckham, b. July 5, 1801; m., Stonington, Conn., Oct. 27, 1822, Jedediah Wheeler Randall, b., Stonington, Feb. 21, 1802; son of Hon. William and Eunice (Wheeler) Randall.

Children, the first five b. in Stonington:

645. John Dean, b. Aug. 9, 1823; m. Mary Louisa Barnes (694–696).
646. James Wolf, b. Nov. 25, 1825; m. Nancy A. McLaughlin (697–701).
647. Mary Alace, b. June 26, 1828; m. Peleg S. Winslow (702–704).

648. Dudley, b. Feb. 17, 1832; m. Ellen Chamberlain (705-709).

649. Roswell, b. May 31, 1835; d., Sugar Grove, Ill., Mar. 7, 1844.

650. Russell William, b. New Berlin, N. Y., June 21, 1837 (710-712).

651. Cyrus Wheeler, b. New Berlin, June 21, 1838; d., Andersonville, Ga., Oct. 12, 1864.

652. Jerome Anderson, b. New Berlin, Sept. 25, 1840; d., Aurora, Ill., Feb. 15, 1861.

653. Harriet A., b., Sugar Grove, Jan. 8, 1846; d. Apr. 14, 1847.

Pauline Peckham (541), dau. of Thomas H. and Patience (Main) Peckham, b. July 20, 1803; m. Joel Pitcher, of No. Stonington, Conn.

Children, b. No. Stonington:

654. Lucy E., b. Oct. 16, 1826; m. Fred Maynard. They had one dau., Martha.

655. Joel W., b. Nov. 14, 1828; unm. He was in the Civil War.

656. Harriet N., b. May 16, 1830; m. James Buddington. They had one dau.

657. Ann E., b. Dec. 16, 1834; unm.

658. Emily W., b. Dec. 17, 1837.

659. Henry Harrison, b. Mar. 12, 1840; unm.

660. Edward Taylor, b. Nov. 3, 1843; m., Apr. 6, 1866, Emma A. Berry (103-108). (See Babcock Record, p. 29.)

Stephen Van R. Peckham (542), son of Thomas H. and Patience (Main) Peckham, b. Apr. 30, 1805; d., Moosup, Conn., Sept. 6, 1884; m., Packerville, Conn., 1836, Mary Ann Hill, b. Stonington, Conn., d., Moosup, 1872; dau. of John and Rebecca (Davis) Hill, of Groton, Conn. Mr. Peckham enlisted, in 1863, in the Civil War as a musician in the 21st Conn. Regt. He was a machinist and a Baptist.

Children, b. Packerville, except the last one. None were married:

661. Stephen H., b. May 3, 1837; d., Center Village, Conn., Aug. 27, 1906.

662. Mary E., b. Apr. 8, 1839; d., Jewett City, Conn., June 21, 1858.

663. Fannie E., b. Jan. 6, 1842. Res., 51 Atlantic Ave., Providence, R. I.

664. John O., b. Apr. 16, 1844; d., Washington, D. C., 1863.

665. Charles B., b., Jewett City, Mar. 17, 1851; d., Moosup, May 30, 1867.

Francis Starr Peabody (619), son of Benjamin and Martha (535) (Peckham) Peabody, b. Apr. 29, 1815; d., No. Stonington, Conn., Oct. 1, 1900;

m., Preston, Conn., by Rev. N. E. Shailer, Oct. 9, 1836, Martha Almira Phillips, dau. of Bradford Phillips, of No. Stonington. Mr. Peabody devoted the most of his life to school-teaching, and was at that time one of the most successful teachers that No. Stonington ever sent out. He taught private schools to qualify young men and ladies for teaching. He made himself a real force in the education of the young during his many years of teaching. He passed the last ten or more years of his life in Westerly, R. I., with his son Thomas H. Peabody; but he died at the homestead in No. Stonington, where he was born.

Children, b. No. Stonington:

666. Francis Newland, b. Sept. 6, 1837; m. Sarah E. Lewis (669-672).

667. Thomas Hazard, b. Sept. 23, 1839; m. Lucy Ella Briggs.

668. Sarah Ellen, b. Sept. 30, 1843; d. Oct. 2, 1865; unm.

Francis Newland Peabody (666), b. Sept. 6, 1837; d., No. Stonington, Conn., Jan. 18, 1907; m., No. Stonington, Nov. 11, 1860, Sarah E. Lewis, b. about 1842; d. about 1904; dau. of Thomas W. and Almira (Slocum) Lewis, sister of Simeon Slocum, of No. Stonington.

Children, b. No. Stonington:

669. Sarah Ellen Peabody, b.——; m. Henry W. Lanphear (673, 674).

670. Frank S. Peabody, b.——; m.

671. Thomas Lewis Peabody, b.——; m., No. Stonington, Aug. 26, 1894, Lucy Marion Pitcher, b. Feb. 4, 1868; d. June 3, 1898; dau. of Edward T. and Emma A. (Berry) Pitcher. Children: Benj. Lewis, b. Aug. 25, 1895; Frank Carroll, b. June 2, 1898. Res., No. Stonington, Conn. (See Babcock Record, p. 29.)

672. Howard W. Peabody, b.——; unm.

Sarah Ellen Peabody (669), sister of the preceding and dau. of Francis N. and Sarah E. (Lewis) Peabody, b., No. Stonington, Conn., 1866; d., Westerly, R. I., Dec. 25, 1890; m., Westerly, Sept. 20, 1887, Henry Warren Lanphear, b., Shannock, R. I., 1859; son of William Earl and Caroline Patience (Green) Lanphear. Both were members of the Baptist Church.

Children, b. Westerly:

673. Elma Almira, b. June 28, 1889.

674. Nellie Caroline, b. Nov. 12, 1890.

Thomas Hazard Peabody (667), son of Francis Starr and Martha Almira (Phillips) Peabody, b., No. Stonington, Conn., Sept. 23, 1839; m., Voluntown, Conn., Sept. 8, 1874, Lucy Ellen Briggs, b., Scituate, R. I., Oct. 2, 1850; dau. of Ira G. and Lydia (Andrews) Briggs. Mr. Peabody in early life was a school-teacher; later he took up the study and profession of the law. In politics he is an Independent. Both he and his wife are members of the Baptist Church. He has retired from active duties. No issue. Res., Westerly, R. I.

James Alden Peabody (624), son of Benjamin and Martha (535) Peckham Peabody, b., No. Stonington, Conn., May 30, 1831; d., Stonington (Pawcatuck), Conn., Apr. 28, 1908; m., Stonington, Conn., Nov. 10, 1856, Augusta Josephine Crumb, b., Westerly, Apr. 7, 1841; dau. of Arnold and Lucinda (Lamphere) Crumb. Mr. Peabody attended school in the Rufus Williams district, No. Stonington, with the compiler of these records for three winters, 1845–1848. Later he went to the Connecticut Plainfield Academy; there he became acquainted with Stephen H. Crary (B. G., p. 473), with whom he engaged in gold-mining in California in 1852. He told of his perils gold-hunting and with the Indians. Soon after returning to the States he was route mail agent from Westerly, R. I., to Voluntown, Conn. He was in the Civil War, Co. G, 8th Regt. Conn. Vols. The remaining part of his life he spent with the Adams Express Company, as their trusted agent, until his death.
Children, b. Stonington (Pawcatuck):
- 675. Charles Alden, b. May 24, 1857 (684, 685).
- 676. Benjamin Arnold, b. Aug. 20, 1860 (686–688).
- 677. John Edward, b. Nov. 11, 1863; unm.
- 678. Frances Stillman Tinker Augusta Josephine, b. May 6, 1866 (689, 690).
- 679. Carrie Louella Eva Louise, b. June 15, 1868; m. Edward Johnson (690a–690d).
- 680. George Bird, b. Nov. 29, 1870 (691, 692).
- 681. Martha Eudora Noyes, b.——; m. William Rowe (692a–692c).
- 682. Charlotte Le Valley, b. May 25, 1879; m. Lewis Stanton (693).
- 683. Irene Bailey, b.——; unm.

Charles Alden Peabody (675), son of James Alden (624) and Augusta J. (Crumb) Peabody, b., Westerly, R. I., May 24, 1857; d., Bridgeport, Conn., Dec. 10, 1892; m., Mystic, Conn., Jan. 26, 1882, Annie Barns, b., Mystic, June 18, 1856; dau. of Nathan W. and Harriet M. (Way) Barns. Mr. Peabody, after leaving the high school at Westerly, entered the Adams Express office with his father as clerk at Westerly; later he held positions

for the Adams Express Company at Providence and Newport, R. I.   The
last agency was at Bridgeport, where he died, highly esteemed and honored
by the company and his many friends. Res., 189 Harriet St., Bridgeport,
Conn.

Children:

 684. Arthur Alden, b., Mystic, Mar. 12, 1883; d., Bridgeport, Apr.
   9, 1901.

 685. Ethel, b., Bridgeport, Aug. 23, 1885.

Benjamin Arnold Peabody (676), brother of the preceding, b. Aug. 20,
1860; m., Narragansett Pier, R. I., Nov. 8, 1886, Elizabeth Caswell, b.,
Peacedale, R. I., Aug. 19, 1865; dau. of James D. and Annie (Davidson)
Caswell. Mr. Peabody for a number of years has been his father's assistant
at the Adams Express office; and after his death was promoted to the agency
of the Westerly office.

Children:

 686. Mary Stanton Peabody, b., Narrangasett Pier, Feb. 9, 1888;
   m., Westerly, R. I., Feb. 19, 1908, Arthur Robert Irvine.

 687. Benjamin Arnold Peabody, Jr., b., Westerly, May 14, 1889.

 688. Annie Davidson Peabody, b., Westerly, Feb. 10, 1898.

Frances Stillman Tinker Augusta Josephine Peabody (678), sister of the
preceding, b., Stonington (Pawcatuck) Conn., May 6, 1866; m., Stonington,
Conn., Dec. 19, 1888, James Archbald Reaves, b., Pittston, Penn., Oct. 11,
1857; son of P. A. A. and Mary (Love) Reaves, of Pittston. Mr. Reaves is a
druggist at 572 Westminster St., Providence, R. I. They attend the Baptist
Church. Mrs. Reaves is a member.

Children, b. Providence:

 689. Dorothy Mae, b. Nov. 27, 1890.

 690. Margaret Love, b. May 25, 1899.

Carrie Luella Eva Louisa Peabody (679), dau. of James Alden and
Augusta J. (Crumb) Peabody, b., Stonington (Pawcatuck), Conn., June 15,
1868; m., Stonington, Nov. 25, 1897, Edward Johnson, b. Norwich, Conn.,
Sept. 19, 1869; son of Samuel and Emily (Crandall) Johnson, of Norwich.
Mr. Johnson is an Independent in politics. He is superintendent of Yale
Dining-Club and a member of the Governor's Foot Guards. His wife is a
member of the Baptist Church. Res., New Haven, Conn.

Children, the last three b. in New Haven:

 690a. Walter Peabody, b., Washington, D. C., Sept. 3, 1898.

690b. Harriet Augusta, b. Aug. 15, 1900.
690c. Emily Louisa, b. Dec. 9, 1903.
690d. Christine, b. Nov. 13, 1905.

George Bird Peabody (680), brother of the preceding, b., Stonington (Paw-catuck), Conn., Nov. 29, 1870; d., Attleboro, Mass., Jan. 3, 1905; m.,Wor-cester, Mass., June 5, 1900, Grace Ella Jerome, b., Worcester, Aug. 17, 1873; dau. of Edward and Helena Gertrude (Elliot) Jerome. Mr. Pea-body was agent for the Adams Express Company at Attleboro. In politics he was a Republican. Both he and his wife were church-members. Mrs. Peabody's ancestry is traced to John Elliot, the apostle to the Indians. Res., 22 Lagrange St., Worcester, Mass.

Children:

691. Gertrude Augusta, b., Providence, R. I., Oct. 31, 1901.
692. Priscilla Alden, b., Attleboro, Jan. 19, 1904.

Martha Eudora Noyes Peabody (681), sister of the preceding, m. William Rowe. He is a memorial architect.

Children, b. Mount Vernon, N. Y.:

692a. Muriel Eudora, b. May 22, 1904.
692b. Lora, b. Aug. 2, 1906.
692c. Gladys, b. Nov. 4, 1908.

Charlotte Le Valley Peabody (682), sister of the preceding, b., Stonington (Pawcatuck), Conn., May 25, 1879; m., Stonington, Conn., Oct. 7, 1905, Lewis Stanton, b., Westerly, Jan. 5, 1880; son of Courtland G. and Mary E. (Lewis) Stanton. Mr. Stanton is teller in the Westerly branch of the In-dustrial Trust Company of Providence, R. I. Res., Westerly, R. I.

Dau.:

693. Mary Augusta, b. June 4, 1908.

John Dean Randall (645), son of Jedediah W. and Philura (540) (Peck-ham) Randall, b., Stonington, Conn., Aug. 9, 1823; m., Geneva, Ill., Apr. 24, 1851, Mary Louisa Barnes, b., Alexandria, N. Y., Nov. 2, 1829.

Children:

694. Frank John, b., De Kalb, Ill., Mar. 6, 1852.
695. Martha Maria, b., De Kalb, Dec. 24, 1854.
696. S. Wallace, b., Aurora, Ill., Nov. 1, 1861.

James Wolf Randall (646), brother of the preceding, b., Stonington, Conn., Nov. 25, 1825; d., Batavia, Ill., Apr. 2, 1875; m., Dover, Ill., Apr. 18, 1850, Nancy A. Laughlin, b., Washington, Penn., May 25, 1831.

Children:

    697. Sarah Frances, b., Burean, Ill., Mar. 20, 1851.

    698. Charles Dudley, b., Aurora, Ill., Apr. 12, 1853.

    699. Jay Cook, b., Batavia, Ill., May 7, 1863.

    700. Jennie, b., Batavia, Dec. 24, 1866; d. in infancy.

    701. Park Benjamin, b., Aurora, May 29, 1874.

Mary Alace Randall (647), sister of the preceding, b., Stonington, Conn., June 26, 1828; m., Sugar Grove, Ill., May 6, 1847, Peleg S. Winslow, b. Mar. 3, 1823.

Children, b. Big Rock, Ill.:

    702. Mary Isabella, b. Oct. 28, 1849; d. Mar. 30, 1850.

    703. Frank L., b. Aug. 16, 1851.

    704. Mary Belle, b. Nov. 25, 1853.

Dudley Randall (648), brother of the preceding, b., Stonington, Conn., Feb. 17, 1832; m., Emporia, Kan., July 2, 1860, Ellen Chamberlain, b., McHenry, Ill., Jan. 4, 1842.

Children, the last three b. in Aurora, Ill.:

    705. Marna A., b., Janesville, Wis., May 7, 1861.

    706. Elmer Albert, b., Janesville, Apr. 16, 1863.

    707. Lena Mabel, b. Aug. 1, 1866.

    708. Etta Eva, b. Apr. 15, 1869; d. May 24, 1871.

    709. Alace Eva, b. Jan. 15, 1873.

Russell William Randall (650), brother of the preceding, b., New Berlin, N. Y., June 21, 1837; m., Americus, Kan., Feb. 14, 1861, S. Miller, b., Lawrence, Pa., Jan. 9, 1841.

Children:

    710. Emma, b., Janesville, Wis., Aug. 1, 1863.

    711. Anna, b., Americus, May 28, 1866.

    712. Mary Alace, b., Americus, July 29, 1870.

Elizabeth Main (389), dau. of Thomas J. (325) and Henrietta (Williams) Main, b., Stonington, Ill., Aug. 25, 1850; m., Dundee, Mich., July 12, 1868, Horace J. Breningstall, b., Dundee, July 18, 1843; son of Horace J. Breningstall. Elizabeth Main received a common-school education having a meager chance to attend school "in those days when schools were few and far between." She resided for a time in Burke Co., Cal., with her father. After her marriage she resided at Laporte, Ind., and Bay City, Mich.; since 1875, at Petersburg, Mich. Mr. Breningstall, at the age of seventeen, June 20,

1861, enlisted in Co. A., 4th Regt. Mich. Vol. Infantry, serving four years in the Civil War. He participated in fifty-one engagements, serving in the 2d Brigade, 1st Division, 5th Army Corps, Army of the Potomac. He was postmaster for four years under President Harrison; Commissioner of Highways; now [1909] serving the sixteenth year as Justice of the Peace and Notary Public for his town. Res., Petersburg, Mich.

Children, b. Petersburg:

    713. Reuben Grant, b. Mar. 31, 1869 (718, 719).

    714. Susan Amelia, b. Nov. 18, 1873; d. July 21, 1907.

    715. Adalaid, b. Mar. 14, 1880.

    716. Lucy May, b. May 31, 1887.

    717. Gertrude Main, b. Dec. 11, 1890.

Reuben Grant Breningstall (713), son of Horace J. and Elizabeth (Main) Breningstall, b. Mar. 31, 1869; m., Detroit, Mich., Nov. 22, 1894, Bertha Idella McDowell, b. Detroit; dau. of Joseph McDowell, of Detroit. Mr. Breningstall is a druggist, and both he and his wife are members of the Presbyterian Church. He received his early education in the public schools of his native town. At the age of fourteen he began the drug business. He passed the examination of the Michigan Board of Pharmacy in 1888. He served two years in the Michigan National Guard as Brigade Hospital Steward. He joined the Masonic order, and is a thirty-second degree Mason and a member of the Mystic Shrine. He engaged in the drug business for himself in 1898, and has enjoyed success in business and home life. He enjoys outdoor sports.

Children, b. Detroit, Mich.:

    718. Joseph Horace, b. Aug. 29, 1895.

    719. Ideria Loucele, b. Aug. 30, 1904.

Minnie Adelaide Rose (389d), dau. of Benjamin F. and Susan Amelia (Main 387) Rose, b., Petersburg, Mich., Jan. 31, 1864; d. Aug. 12, 1896; m., Petersburg, Dec. 3, 1884, John W. Gramkie. He is a farmer. His wife was a member of the Methodist Episcopal Church. She was educated in the high school of Petersburg, where she always lived.

Children, b. Petersburg:

    720. Grace Rose Gramkie, b. May 27, 1889.

    721. Hermon Gramkie, b. May 14, 1892; d. July 29, 1893.

Oliver Tenant Rose (389h), brother of the preceding, b., Petersburg. Mich., Oct. 5, 1871; m., Petersburg, Oct. 4, 1893, Ada C. McLachlin, b. Petersburg; dau. of H. C. and Hattie A. McLachlin, of Petersburg.

Mr. Rose is a banker, a stalwart Republican, and both he and his wife are members of the Methodist Episcopal Church. They were educated in the high school. Mr. Rose completed his education in the Normal Department of the N. I. N. S. and B. I. at Valparaiso, Ind. Mrs. Rose finished her musical education at the State Normal College at Ypsilanti, Mich. After marriage they lived at Owosso, Mich., where Mr. Rose was cashier and chief clerk in the local office of the Michigan Central R. R. Co. Since Nov. 1, 1897, he has been in the banking business, and is one third owner, and cashier of the Exchange Bank, Petersburg. He has held all positions on the School Board, and is serving the third term as president in 1909.
Children:

      722. Dean McLachlin, b., Owosso, Dec. 9, 1894; d. Jan. 12, 1896.

      723. Laura Blanche, b., Petersburg, May 31, 1902.

      724. Henry C., b., Petersburg, Feb. 22, 1906.

Elizabeth Main Rose (389j), sister of the preceding, b., Petersburg, Mich., July 22, 1877; m., Petersburg, Jan. 1, 1896, Charles D. Fillmore. Both were educated in the high school, finishing their education at Adrian, Mich. Mr. Fillmore took the course at Brown's Business College; and Mrs. Fillmore, by private instruction in music. He is a farmer, a Prohibitionist, and both he and his wife are members of the Methodist Episcopal Church.
Children, b. Petersburg:

      725. Millard, b. July 16, 1897.

      726. Frank, b. Apr. 2, 1899.

      727. Dale, b. Oct. 4, 1901.

      728. Jennie, b. Sept. 20, 1903.

      729. Frances, b. Jan. 2, 1907.

      730. John, b. Apr. 19, 1908.

Rial Main (503), son of David (289) and Mrs. Esther Palmer, née Dean, b., Stonington, Conn., May 27, 1788; d., Madison, Wis., Mar. 4, 1861; m., No. Stonington, Conn., Eunice Palmer, b. July 4, 1791; d., Madison, Nov. 19, 1852. Mr. Main resided in his native town over sixty years, and was a man of more than ordinary abilities. His education was limited to what the district schools could furnish in those days. He taught school a number of terms in the winter season. He led the singing in the old Miner Church, Second Baptist, in the early forties. He was a man of positive ideas, with strong native talents. He, with his wife and two daughters, and his wife's sister, Lydia Palmer, removed in 1851 to Wisconsin, where his sons had located before him. He built a house at Madison, where he lived with his family, his wife passing away the next year. He taught school in his adopted State several terms. At the time when Mr. Main and his sons went West the tide of emigration was strong and the song was:

> "Away to Wisconsin a journey to go,
> To double my fortune, as other folks do."

Refrain by the older people:

> "Oh, stay on your farm and suffer no loss:
> For the stone that keeps rolling will gather no moss."

Nevertheless they went; for No. Stonington, with 2,700 people, was being crowded, and some of the more courageous pushed out in the first half of the nineteenth century.

Children, b. No. Stonington:

731. David Chester, b. Nov. 8, 1810 (739-743).
732. Eunice Ann, b. June 11, 1813. Her records follow 743.
733. Robert Palmer, b. May 13, 1816 (744-751).
734. William H., b. Dec. 23, 1818. His records follow 751.
735. Edwin C., b. July 26, 1821 (752-755).
736. Elias P., b. Oct. 16, 1823; d. May 15, 1826.
737. Fanny E., b. Jan. 13, 1827; d. Oct. 15, 1828.
738. Mary Louisa, b. Dec. 20, 1833; d. Aug. 9, 1871. She went with her parents to Oregon, Wis., in 1851, to the home of her brother Robert. She lived with her sister Mrs. Atwell and lovingly cared for her until her death; then she performed the same kind offices for her aunt Lydia Palmer, her mother's sister. It was her lot to serve others with Christian fortitude and good cheer, during her short life; unm.

David Chester Main (731), son of Rial (503) and Eunice (Palmer) Main, b., No. Stonington, Conn., Nov. 8, 1810; d., Morristown, Tenn., Nov. 12, 1852; m., Barborville, Ky., 1839, Eliza Messer, b., Kentucky, 1824; d., Tennessee, Aug. 11, 1851. He taught school in Rhode Island and New Jersey, and soon after went with his brother Robert on an adventure, in 1832 or 1833, to Virginia, visiting Washington, D. C., repairing clocks and selling nutmegs to pay expenses, and both taught school in their journeyings, going as far south as Tennessee. Both had suits of clothes made by Andrew Johnson, who afterwards became President of the United States. Mr. Main married and made his permanent home in Tennessee, while his brother Robert continued his travels to Wisconsin.

Children, b. Morristown:

739. Mary Elizabeth, b. 1841; m. C. B. Havely (760-766).

740. Louisa Jane, b. Mar. 15, 1843; d., Jefferson City, Tenn., May, 1877.

741. Martha Ann, b. 1845; d. Dec. 11, 1898.

742. William Henry, b. Aug. 11, 1847; d., Jefferson City, 1872; m., Jefferson City, 1870, Margaret McDaniel. Mr. Main was a merchant and a member of the church. Res., Jefferson City, Tenn.

743. Susan Campbell, b. Apr., 1849; d., White Pine, Tenn., Mar., 1877.

Eunice Ann Main (732), dau. of Rial (503) and Eunice (Palmer) Main, b., No. Stonington, Conn., June 11, 1813; d., Madison, Wis., 1889; m., Madison, about 1852, Benjamin Arthur Atwell, b., Annapolis, Md., 1814; d., Hutchings, Tex., 1891. Mr. Atwell was a merchant in Texas, and in politics he was a Republican. Both he and his wife were members of the Baptist Church. This was his second marriage. By his first marriage he had two sons, Benjamin D. and William Arthur Atwell. Both were officers in the Civil War, and both graduates of the State University of Wisconsin. Res. of Benj. D. Atwell, 1909, Hutchings, Tex. Wm. A. Atwell is American Consul at Ghent, Belgium. No issue by second m.

Robert Palmer Main (733), brother of the preceding, b., No. Stonington, Conn., May 13, 1816; d., Oregon, Wis., Apr. 24. 1882; m., Oakland, Clinton Co., O., Sept. 30, 1838, Cordelia A. Desdemona Dakin, b., Oakland, May 11, 1813; d., Oregon, July 4, 1902; dau. of Preserved and Elizabeth (Prosser) Dakin, of Oakland. Both were Baptists; but as there was no Baptist Church they attended the Presbyterian. Mrs. Main was reared a Quaker, but they were liberal in their views, and later in life joined the Methodist Church, and Mr. Main was superintendent of the Sunday school at the time of his death. He was a Republican and an active Abolitionist. He was a member of the State Legislature in 1857. He was a master Mason and a member of the local order. He was a prominent campaign speaker, Justice of the Peace for many years; was known as Esq. Main. He was strictly temperate in all his habits, and an ardent worker along these lines. He had traveled extensively in nearly all the States and in Canada. His home was a model Christian home, and in every relation of life he proved himself one of God's own gentlemen. His widow placed a memorial window in the Methodist Episcopal Church: "Add to knowledge, temperance and industry."

Robert Palmer Main

(733)

Page 102

He blazed the trees and opened the way whereby *all* his father's family took up the trail and made their homes in Wisconsin.

Mrs. Harriet E. (Maine) Glass, Mrs. Frances F. (Faulkes) Oleson
(746)   (786)

Page 106

Children, the last four b. in Oregon:

744. Mary Frances, b., Oakland, July 27, 1839. Miss Maine has furnished complete records of her grandparent's family, and was helpful in many details from which extracts were made of interest to all the Maine kinship. She has been successfully engaged in school-teaching for thirty-eight years, in Wisconsin, Iowa, and So. Dakota; unm.

745. Louisa Adelaide, b., Oakland, Mar. 15, 1841; m. Lloyd S. Kniffen (777–785).

746. Harriet Elizabeth, b., Oakland, Jan. 30, 1843; m. Charles H. Faulkes (786).

747. Martha Emily, b., Danville, Ill., Oct. 3, 1845; m. George Smith (790–796).

748. Edwin Dakin, b. Nov. 6, 1847; m. Juliett Chapin (797–801).

749. Anna Maria, b. Sept. 23, 1849; m. Edgar W. Comstock (802–806).

750. Alice Cordelia, b. Dec. 27, 1851; m. Francis M. Ames (807–812).

751. Robert Walter, b. Sept. 17, 1854; m. Susan Morrison.

William H. Main (734), son of Rial (503) and Eunice (Palmer) Maine, b., No. Stonington, Conn., Dec. 23, 1818; d., Baraboo, Wis., Oct. 10, 1898; m., Baraboo, about 1884, Mrs. Hattie Barker, née Converse, b. in Massachusetts. Mr. Main was a school-teacher in No. Stonington and the State of Michigan. The compiler remembers him as his teacher in the early forties. He removed to Wisconsin about 1860, and resided at Madison for a number of years. He had a poetical turn of mind, and was the author of considerable poetry. He lived with his sister Mrs. Atwell about fourteen years. After his marriage he settled on a farm, where he lived the remainder of his life. He was a stalwart Republican, and both he and his wife were members of the Methodist Church. Res., Baraboo, Wis.

Edwin C. Main (735), brother of the preceding, b., No. Stonington, Conn., July 26, 1821; d., Portage, Wis., July 27, 1883; m., No. Stonington, June 13, 1852, Ellen Wheeler, b., No. Stonington, Apr. 13, 1833; d., Portage, Oct. 16, 1901; dau. of Dea. Allen and Jemima A. (Wheeler) Wheeler, of No. Stonington. Mr. Main in his younger days was a school-teacher. He taught the same school in Exeter, R. I., as the compiler of these records, previous to 1848. He studied medicine and removed to Wisconsin, where he practised until his death. He was a Republican, and both he and his wife were members of the Baptist Church.

Children, the last three b. in Portage:

752. Lilla F. Maine, b., Madison, Wis., June 14, 1854; unm. Res., La Crosse, Wis.

753. Clinton DeWitt Maine, b. Dec. 11, 1857; m. Emma R. Potter (756-759).

754. Thurlow W. Maine, b. Apr. 14, 1860; d., Portage, Oct. 4, 1883.

755. Jessie L. Maine, b. ——; d. No. Stonington.

Clinton De Witt Maine (753), son of the preceding, b., Portage, Wis., Dec. 11, 1857; m., Sparta, Wis., Oct. 29, 1881, Emma R. Potter, b., Johnstown, N. Y., Aug. 16, 1856; dau. of George and Jane (Montoney) Potter, of Sparta. Dr. Maine is a magnetic physician, and a stalwart Republican. He and his wife are members of the Baptist Church. Res., La Crosse, Wis.

Children, the last three b. in Portage:

756. George Edwin, b., Sparta, Nov. 24, 1882; m., Seattle, Wash., Dec. 15, 1907, Margaret Wilson, dau. of Mr. and Mrs. John D. Wilson, of La Crosse.

757. Frank Thurlow, b. Sept. 20, 1887.

758. Spurgeon De Witt, b. Mar. 29, 1892.

759. Malcom Potter, b. May 29, 1895.

Mary Elizabeth Main (739), dau. of David Chester (731) and Eliza (Messer) Main, b., Morristown, Tenn., 1841; m., Morristown, Nov. 8, 1866, Charles Benton Havely, b., Lee Co., Va., Nov. 10, 1840; son of C. H. Havely and Elizabeth Ely, of Lee Co., Va. Mr. Havely is a farmer, and in politics he is a Democrat. Both he and his wife are members of the Baptist Church. Mr. Havely was in the Civil War, enlisting in the Confederate Army, at Tazewell, Tenn., early in 1862, and was in seventeen battles; among them the siege of Knoxville, Bean Station, and Rogersville, Tenn.; also Wathwale, Sailor's Creek, and Drury's Bluff, Va., where he was taken prisoner in 1864 and sent to Point Lookout, Md., and from there to Elmira, N. Y., where he remained in prison until the close of the war. Res., Morristown. Tenn.

Children, b. Morristown:

760. Maggie Elizabeth, b. Sept. 5, 1867; m. W. H. B. Graves (767-772).

761. James Chester, b. May 5, 1869; m. Sara I. Austin (773-776).

762. Lura Josephine, b. Sept. 30, 1870; unm.

763. Charles Sidney, b. Dec. 31, 1871; m., Russellville, Tenn., June

8, 1905, Lucy Lee, of Russellville. Son: Paul, b. June 20, 1907. Mr. Havely is a bookkeeper. His wife is a member of the Baptist Church. Res., Morristown, Tenn.

764. Jerome Felix, b. Aug. 23, 1874; unm.

765. Isham Harris, b. Jan. 24, 1877; m., Morristown, May 28, 1904, Bessie Sullenbarger, of Morristown. Mr. Havely is a hardware clerk. Both he and his wife are members of the Baptist Church. Res., Morristown, Tenn.

766. Anna Belle, b. Dec. 27, 1878; d. June 29, 1880.

Maggie Elizabeth Havely (760), dau. of Charles B. and Mary Elizabeth (Main) Havely, b., Morristown, Tenn., Sept 5, 1867; m., Morristown, Sept. 17, 1891, W. H. B. Graves, b., Rogersville, Tenn., 1850; son of Rev. William Graves. Mr. Graves is a farmer; in politics, a Democrat. Both he and his wife are members of the Methodist Church. Res., Morristown, Tenn.

Children, b. Morristown:

767. Thomas Jason, b. Nov. 20, 1892.

768. Benton Havely, b. Apr. 14, 1894.

769. Mary Orena, b. Mar. 27, 1895.

770. William Carroll, b. Aug. 5, 1897.

771. Henry Bascom, b. Dec. 12, 1898.

772. Pauline, b. Sept. 28, 1900.

James Chester Havely (761), brother of the preceding, b., Morristown, Tenn., May 5, 1869; m., Morristown, May 7, 1897, Sara Isabelle Austin, b., Morristown, 1866; dau. of William and Jane (McBride) Austin, of Grainger Co., Tenn. Mr. Havely is a public road contractor. Both he and his wife are members of the Methodist Church. Res., New Market, Tenn.

Children, b. Morristown

773. Frank S., b. July 10, 1899.

774. William Benton, b. Feb. 6, 1902.

775. Earl, b. Mar. 16, 1904.

776. Alice Josephine, b. Nov. 28, 1906.

Louisa Adelaide Main (745), dau. of Robert Palmer (733) and Cordelia A. Desdemona (Dakin) Main, b., Oakland, Clinton Co., O., Mar. 15, 1841; d., Lime Springs, Ia., May 16, 1895; m., Rutland, Wis., Mar. 3, 1864, Lloyd S. Kniffen, b., Ohio, Mar. 15, 1841; son of James Plat and Esther (Bowker) Kniffen, of Rutland. Mrs. Kniffen was educated in common and select schools, and was a teacher. Mr. Kniffen was educated in public schools and at the Albion Academy. He is a farmer, a Republican, and both he and his wife are members of the Methodist Church. Res., Cresco, Ia. Children, the first six b. in Rutland:

 777. Mary Belinda, b. Apr. 22, 1865; m. Fred Hill (818–821).
 778. Hattie C., b. Oct. 16, 1866; m. Charles Dykeman. No issue.
 779. Archie Platt, b. Aug. 22, 1870; unm.
 780. Jessie Esther, b. Sept. 4, 1872; m. Charles Dykeman (822–827).
 781. Frank Main, b. Jan. 22, 1875; m. Edith D. Tibbals (828–831).
 782. Fred Dakin, b. Mar. 25, 1878; unm.
 783. Iva, b., Darien, Wis., Dec. 24, 1881; d. Mar. 3, 1887.
 784. Louisa Melinda, b., Darien, Aug. 4, 1883. Record follows 831.
 785. Roy Stanley, b., Darien, Nov. 4, 1886; unm. He is employed
   by the Great Northern R. R. Co. Res., Skykomish, Wash.

Harriet Elizabeth Maine (746), sister of the preceding, b., Oakland, O., Jan. 30, 1843; m. (1), Madison, Wis., Jan. 1, 1873, Charles H. Faulkes, b., Buffalo, N. Y., Feb. 28, 1844; deceased; son of John and Nancy (Ford) Faulkes, of Cornwall, England. Mrs. Faulkes was a teacher, and a member of the Congregational Church. Both were educated in common schools and the University of Wisconsin. Mrs. Faulkes m. (2), Harvard, McHenry Co., Ill., June 15, 1904, Elias Glass, b., Rome, N. Y., Mar. 10, 1821; d., Harvard, Mar. 21, 1908; son of Alexander and Lucinda (Hawley) Glass. Both were members of the Baptist Church. Mr. Glass removed to Illinois in 1843; bought government land which he owned at the time of his death. Her res., 1909, Colville, Wash.

Dau., by first m.:

 786. Frances Felicia Faulkes, b., Oregon, Wis., Jan. 2, 1876; m.,
   Riceville, Ia., Nov. 8, 1899, John Oleson, b., Christiana,
   Norway, Oct. 16, 1865; son of Eric and Carol (Jensen) Oleson, of Christiana. Mr. Oleson is a Republican. He is a tele-
   grapher, and has been in the employ of the C. M. and St. Paul
   R.R. since 1883. Both are members of the Congregational
   Church. Miss Faulkes was educated in the high school and
   the State Normal School at Cedar Falls, Ia.; she afterwards
   taught in So. Dakota and Iowa for four years. Res., Hern-
   don, Ia.

Children, b. Le Roy, Minn.:

 787. Charles Main, b. Sept. 27, 1900.
 788. Carl Valiant, b. Oct. 18, 1901.
 789. James Rush, b. July 25, 1903.

Martha Emily Main (747), dau. of Robert Palmer (733) and Cordelia A. Desdemona (Dakin) Main, b., Danville, Ill., Oct. 5, 1844; d., Vernon, Wis., Feb. 3, 1885; m., Oregon, Wis., Oct. 28, 1869, George Smith, b., Easingwold, Yorkshire, England; son of Martin and Mary A. (Dunford) Smith, of Easingwold. Mr. Smith in politics is a Democrat, attending the English Lutheran Church. After marriage they lived in Philadelphia, Penn., for three years, where he was private for Allen Pinkerton and superintendent of his police force in Philadelphia and New York City and official superintendent of Pinkerton's Detective Agency. Thereafter, making farming his business, he went up to Wisconsin and later to Chester, Ia., where he now resides.

Children:

790. Mary Emily, b., Philadelphia, Nov. 10, 1870; unm.

791. Grace Darling, b., Oregon, Jan. 11, 1873; d., Chester, Oct. 11, 1896.

792. Frances Cordelia, b., Blanchardville, Wis., Jan. 8, 1875; m. John A. Johnson (813–815).

793. Gertrude, b., Blanchardville, Oct. 6, 1876; d., Chester, Dec. 7, 1897.

794. Alice, b., Spencer, Ia., Nov. 18, 1878; m. Charles Shrode (816, 817).

795. Walter Clark, b., Verona, Wis., Jan. 23, 1883; unm.

796. Dale Stanley, b., Verona, Jan. 20, 1885.

Edwin Dakin Main (748), brother of the preceding, b., Oregon, Wis., Nov. 6, 1847; m., Madison, Wis., Nov. 26, 1872, Juliet Chapin, b. June 2, 1853. Mr. Main had the advantages of the common schools and the high school of Oregon, and has been president of the Board of Education and the County Board, and has held several offices of trust. Mrs. Main was educated in the common schools and the Evansville Seminary. Mr. Main is a real-estate broker, a Republican, and both he and his wife attend the Presbyterian Church. Res., Oregon, Wis.

Children, the last four b. in Fitchburg, Wis.:

797. Celia H. Main, b., Oregon, Sept. 15, 1875. She is a graduate of the Oregon High School, Beloit Business College, and the Capital City Commercial College of Madison. She is a stenographer at Madison.

798. Florence E. Main, b. Nov. 23, 1880; d., San Antonio, Tex., July 18, 1908. She graduated from the high school, attended the Northwestern University School of Oratory of Evanston, Ill., and the College of Madison. She was a teacher for sev-

eral years, teaching in part elocution for some time. In the midst of her usefulness she was suddenly called to lay down her earthly duties.

799. Idell May Main, b. Nov. 11, 1885. She is a graduate of Oregon High School and the University of Wisconsin, taking a three years' course in music, in connection with other duties, and is now a teacher of music.

800. Stanley D. Main, b. Jan. 4, 1890. He is in the high school, class of 1910.

801. Lillian H. Main, b. June 19, 1892. She is in the high school, class of 1911.

Ann Maria Main (749), dau. of Robert P. (733) and Cordelia A. D. (Dakin) Main, b., Oregon, Wis., Sept. 23, 1848; m., Oregon, Dec. 23, 1867, Edgar W. Comstock, b., Oregon, Aug. 9, 1846; son of William Comstock, b., Rhode Island, 1808, and Fanny Chapin, b., Otsego Co., N. Y., 1810; m., Otsego, 1837. E. W. Comstock and wife were educated in public and private schools of Oregon. After marriage they lived for three years at the homestead. In 1870 they moved to Sioux Rapids, Ia., remaining four years; then returned to his father's farm at Oregon. He owned a farm at Paoli, Wis., twenty years, where he lived; then bought the lumber business at Oregon, which he conducted successfully with his three sons. He has now retired from active business, and has travelled, with his wife and daughter Lenora, west, and east as far as Connecticut. Mrs. Comstock when living at Paoli held the prominent offices of the W. C. T. U. and is a prominent worker in the Methodist Episcopal Church. Res., Oregon, Wis.

Children:

802. William Robert, b., Oregon, Nov. 2, 1871; m., Oct. 18, 1893, Jessie Wineland, of Paoli, Dane Co., Wis. He is in the lumber business. Son: Merl Ivan, b., Oregon, May 26, 1895. Res., Marmarth, N. D.

803. Jay Main, b., Sioux Rapids, Mar. 31, 1873; m. (1), Lodi, Wis., Sept. 6, 1900, Marie Slater. Children, b. Church's Ferry, N. D.: (1) Cedric Charles, b. Dec. 27, 1902, d., Chicago, Ill., Nov. 23, 1905; (2) Gertrude Rosemary, b. Sept. 29, 1904. He m. (2), Marmarth, May 10, 1908, Gertrude Ellsworth, of Minneapolis, Minn.

804. Ethel Violet, b., Oregon, Dec. 31, 1875; m., Oregon, Sept. 6,

The home of Francis Marion Ames and Alice Cordelia Main (750), his wife.
Rutland, Wis.

House built in 1892 on the site of old homestead purchased in 1844

Page 109

Family group of Francis Marion and Alice Cordelia (Main) Ames

(730)

Picture taken at their home, Brooklyn, Wis., where all the children were born

1899, Roy C. Richards. She is a graduate of Oregon High School. Children, b. Oregon: (1) Curtis Ward, b. Nov. 6, 1901, (2) Mernon Cumstock, b. Dec. 3, 1904; (3) Dowell Spencer, b. Mar. 20, 1907.

805. Frank Chapin, b. Paoli, Jan. 28, 1879; m., Oregon, Sept. 24, 1902, OrRell Morrison. Children: (1) Mervilla May, b. Dec. 19, 1903; (2) Lamoine Attolee, b. Oct. 18, 1905, d. May 12, 1906; (3) Reginald Morris, b. Feb 2, 1909

806. Lenora Emogene, b., Paoli, July 3, 1882. She graduated from the Oregon High School and is a milliner; unm.

Alice Cordelia Main (750), dau. of Robert Palmer (733) and Cordelia A. Desdemona (Dakin) Main, b., Oregon, Wis., Dec. 27, 1851; m., Oregon, Aug 15, 1876, Francis Marion Ames, b., Oregon, Mar. 23, 1847, son of John Norton and Mary A. (Ball) Ames, of Oregon. Mr. Ames attended common and select schools and the University of Wisconsin. He taught school for five years after his marriage, then he purchased two hundred and fifty acres of land, adding later two hundred and fifty acres more. Both Mr. and Mrs. Ames are members of the Methodist Church and are Prohibitionists. Mrs. Ames is a member of the W. C. T. U. and the Woman's Suffrage Society. She was educated in common, select, and high schools, teaching for five years. Mr. Ames was nominated for Congress on the Prohibition ticket in 1888. He served as chairman of township and school boards several years, has been secretary of Farmers' Mutual Benefit and Trading Company for years. He travelled extensively through the Western and Southern States and Canada. His father, John N. Ames, and grandfather, David Ames, were both born at Steuben, N. Y. David Ames was a soldier in the War of 1812, and his father, Nathaniel Ames, son of David, Sr., was born in Killingly, Conn., Apr. 25, 1761, and at the age of six years moved to No. Stonington, Conn., to live with his grandfather, Cornelius Waldo. Nathaniel Ames enlisted in the War of the Revolution in 1778, and served one month as guard at Stonington and Groton, Conn. He assisted in building Ft. Griswold at Groton Bank. He witnessed the execution of Major Andre. He located later at Steuben, and spent his later days at Oregon, where he located in 1845. He died at the age of one hundred and two years After leaving the army he became a Methodist minister. He is buried in the Oregon cemetery. Thus this whole line of the Ames family are sons and daughters of the American Revolution. Francis M. Ames and family reside on the farm at Rutland, Wis., where their children were all born.

Children

807 Frances Marion Ames, b. May 8, 1877, unm She was educated in the Brooklyn schools and the Evansville Seminary,
and graduated from Commercial College, Madison, Wis
Employed as bookkeeper by Baker Manufacturing Co,
Evansville, Wis

808. John Quincy Ames, b. Oct. 4, 1878, m, Madison, June 28,
1907, Edna Lora Graves, dau of H. E and Arvilla S (——)
Graves, of Madison Mr Ames is a graduate of Yale College, and has travelled round the world. He is now general
secretary of the Y M. C A at New Haven, Conn, and is a
member of the Methodist Church. Res, Campbell Ave,
West Haven, Conn.

809. Hallie Alice Ames, b. July 13, 1880, m, Mar 29, 1907, Owen
Lincoln Jones, b, Union, Wis, Apr 1, 1881; son of David
and Mary (Allen) Jones, of Evansville Mr Jones is a mercantile clerk, in politics is a Democrat, attends the Methodist Episcopal Church with his wife, who is a member She
was educated at Evansville Seminary and the business college
of Madison She was a teacher and cashier of bank. Dau.,
——, b. and d. Oct. 23, 1908. Res., Evansville, Wis

810. Fanny Tressa Ames, b. Oct. 4, 1882; m, Brooklyn, Wis,
June 26, 1906, Robert Lothrop Templeton, of Chicago, Ill.;
son of John and Mary (Lothrop) Templeton, of Chicago
He is a salesman for Marshall Field, in politics is a Democrat
Both he and his wife are members of the Methodist Episcopal
Church Mrs. Templeton is a graduate of Evansville Seminary and the State Normal School, Whitewater, Wis She
was a teacher, and is a member of the W. C T U Res,
1548 Fulton St, Chicago, Ill.

811 Paul Main Ames (twin), b Apr. 15, 1888. He is a graduate of
Evansville High School and a member of the Methodist Epis-
copal Church. Sales manager of the Baker Manufacturing
Co, at Evansville.

812 Sadie Minnie Ames (twin), b Apr 15, 1888
These twins were named for the twin cities of St Paul and
Minneapolis, Minn She is a graduate of Evansville High
School and a member of the Methodist Episcopal Church.
A student at the Kindergarten College of Chicago.

810a Robert Parke Ames, b Aug 28, 1884. m, Union, Wis, Oct
16, 1907, Burnice Franklyn, b, Union, Jan 23, 1885, dau
of Arthur and Mary (Wall) Franklyn, of Union. Mr Ames
was educated at Evansville Seminary and Madison Busi-

THE EZEKIEL MAIN FAMILY

Robert Walter Main (751), son of Robert Palmer (733) and Cordelia A. Desdemona (Dakin) Main, b., Oregon, Wis., Sept. 17, 1854; m., Aug. 12, 1890, Susan Morrison. They had two children that died in infancy at Columbia Falls, Mont. Mr. Main has large stores at Columbia Falls and Whitefish, Mont.

Frances Cordelia Smith (792), dau. of George and Martha Emily (Main 747) Smith, b., Blanchardville, Wis., Jan. 8, 1875; m., Chester, Ia., Mar. 12,1901, John A. Johnson, b., Stoughton, Wis., Dec. 4, 1874; son of Charles A. and Isabella (Greig) Johnson, of Harmony, Minn. He graduated from the business college at Decorah, Ia., in 1897. In politics he is a Republican, and he and his wife attend the Presbyterian Church. Mrs. Johnson was educated in the public schools of Iowa; also the high school at Decorah. For eight years previous to her marriage she taught school in Iowa, Wisconsin, and Minnesota. They are settled on a farm at Chester, Ia.

Children, b. Chester:
    813. Lucile Isabella, b. Feb. 25, 1903.
    814. Clarice Norine, b. Apr. 12, 1905.
    815. Mabel Frances, b. July 9, 1907.

Alace Smith (794), sister of the preceding, b., Spencer, Ia., Nov. 18, 1878; m., Riceville, Ia., Mar. 18, 1903, Charles Shrode, b., Riceville, Oct. 17, 1877; son of Conrad and Barbara (Workman) Shrode, of Riceville. Mr. Shrode is a farmer; in politics he is a Republican. Miss Smith lived with her parents in different towns,— Spencer, Chester, and Riceville, Ia.; and for three years in Verona, Wis. She attended the Markato State Normal School of Minnesota, and taught school for three years in Iowa and Minnesota.

Children, b. Riceville:
    816. Dorothy Maria, b. May 5, 1904.
    817. Ethel Pauline, b. Dec. 5, 1907.

Mary Belinda Kniffen (777), dau. of Lloyd S. and Louisa Adelaide (Main 745) Kniffen, b., Rutland, Wis., Apr. 22, 1865; m., Darien, Wis., June 17, 1885, Fred Hill, b., Waterloo, Wis., July 18, 1844; son of Bradford and Catherine (Cummings) Hill, of Waterloo. Bradford Hill b., New Haven, Vt., July 8, 1805; m., Covington, Genesee Co., N. Y., Aug. 22, 1833, Catherine Cummings. He d. in Lime Springs, Ia., Aug. 31, 1885. Reuben Hill, father of Bradford, b., Woodbury, Conn., Sept. 3, 1766; m., New Haven, Vt., Oct., 1794, Jane Bradley, b., Salisbury, Conn., Aug. 15, 1774; dau. of Miles and Jane Bradley. Belias Hill, father of Reuben, was called

Captain of Artificers and planned and laid out the works at West Point on the Hudson, N. Y.

Mr. Fred Hill is a Republican, a farmer, and in the milling business, but is now retired on account of ill-health. Both he and his wife affiliate with the Presbyterian Church. Mrs. Hill was educated in the public and high schools of Oregon, Wis.; Mr. Hill, at Waterloo and State University of Wisconsin, and he served in the 40th Regt. Wis. Vol. in the Civil War. Res., Lime Springs, Ia.

Children, b. Lime Springs:

  818. Henry Kniffen, b. June 10, 1886.

  819. Gertrude Eloise, b. Sept. 14, 1887.

  820. Helen Winifred, b. Nov. 4, 1893.

  821. Marion Cecile, b. May 1, 1905.

Hattie C. Kniffen (778), dau. of Lloyd S. and Louisa A. (Main 745) Kniffen, b., Rutland, Wis., Oct. 16, 1866; d., Fairfield, Rock Co., Wis., Sept. 10, 1890; m., Darien, Wis., Mar. 7, 1889, Charles Dykeman, b., Fairfield, May 6, 1867; son of John and Anna (Byers) Dykeman, of Fairfield. Mrs. Dykeman was educated at the Oregon High School and taught four years in Rock Co., until her health failed. Mr. Dykeman after the death of his wife m. (2), Crescoe, Ia., Sept. 19, 1891, Jessie Esther Kniffen (780), sister of first wife, b. Sept. 4, 1872. Mr. Dykeman was educated at the Delavan High School and then took up farming until his health failed. He and both his wives members of the Methodist Episcopal Church. Res., Darien, Wis.

Children, by second m., b. Fairfield:

  822. Iva Gertrude, b. June 17, 1892.

  823. Ruth Thressa, b. Nov. 28, 1893.

  824. Son, b. Nov. 16, 1896; d. Nov. 16, 1896.

  825. Helen Irene, b. Jan. 7, 1899.

  826. Archibald, b. Nov. 21, 1902.

  827. Charles, b. May 10, 1906.

Frank Main Kniffen (781), son of Lloyd S. and Louisa A. (Main 745) Kniffen, b., Rutland, Dane Co., Wis., Jan. 22, 1875; m., Chester, Howard Co., Ia., July 9, 1902, Edith Delephine Tibbals, b., Chester, Sept. 28, 1884; dau. of Edward and Effie (Phifer) Tibbals, of Chester. Mr. Kniffen is a farmer; in politics, a Republican; and both he and his wife attend the Methodist Episcopal Church. Res., Lime Springs, Howard Co., Ia.

Children, b. Lime Springs:

  828. Lloyd Florence, b. Sept. 14, 1903.

829. Gertrude Grace, b. Mar. 31, 1905.
830. Donald Main⎫
831. Dorothy May⎭ twins, b. Aug. 16, 1907.

Louisa Melinda Kniffen (784), sister of the preceding, b., Darien, Wis., Aug. 4, 1883; m., Columbia Falls, Mont., June 26, 1907, Chester H. Conlin, b., Pepeston, Minn., Mar. 3, 1883; son of J. Henry and Etta (Green) Conlin, of Columbia Falls. Mr. Conlin is a locomotive engineer. Res., Whitefish, Mont.

Here end the descendants of Rial Main (503).

Chandler Main (504), son of David (289) and Mrs. Esther (Palmer, née Dean) Main, b., Stonington, Conn., Oct. 29, 1791; m. Nancy Brown, b., Stonington, Dec. 8, 1789; d. Oct. 28, 1824, aged thirty-four years; dau. of Dea. Josiah Brown, b., Stonington, May 30, 1761, and Deborah Griffin, b. Oct. 6, 1763.

Children, b. No. Stonington, Conn.:
832. Chandler Dean, b. 1822.
833. Nancy Brown, b. Oct., 1824; d. Nov. 28, 1825.

Chandler Dean Main (832), b. 1822; d. May 16, 1859, aged thirty-seven years; m., No. Stonington, Conn., Jan. 25, 1852, Frances Almira Clapson, b. 1835; d., Brooklyn, N. Y., Sept. 28, 1908, aged seventy-three years; dau. of William and Fanny Clapson, of No. Stonington. She m. (2) Jerome F. Brown (B. G., p. 157). Mr. Main after the death of his parents lived until his marriage with his grandparents, at the old historic homestead of Elder Simeon Brown. His early schooling was in the same school with the compiler of these records. Mrs. Main had excellent literary abilities, and for a number of years was the No. Stonington correspondent of the *Narragansett Weekly*, now the *Westerly Daily Sun*. The last two years of her life she was nearly blind, and was lovingly cared for by her daughter, Mrs. Rogers, Brooklyn, where she died. She had poetic ability, and dictated to her daughter, only a short time before her death, the following lines, having a pathetic meaning and making them a farewell message:

> My life is drawing to a close;
> The night is coming on
> When I shall sleep in calm repose,
> With all my life-work done.
>
> I 've had the bitter with the sweet;
> I 've suffered all unseen;
> I 've fought the fight 'gainst wind and tide
> With brave and tireless mien.

113

But now the end is drawing nigh;
The time has almost come
When I shall bid you all good-by,
And sail away for home.

Dau.:

834. Frances Eva Main, b., No. Stonington, Jan. 9, 1855; m., No.
Stonington, July 9, 1884, Joshua P. Rogers, b., Salem, Conn.,
May 6, 1852; son of Henry C. and Maria (Palmer) Rogers,
of Salem. Mr. Rogers was shipping-clerk with the Standard
Oil Company for six years; he is now associated with the
Parkway Driving Club, Brooklyn, N. Y. Mrs. Rogers
completed her education at the East Greenwich Academy,
R. I.; afterwards taught twelve terms in the common schools,
until her marriage. She is a member of the Baptist Church.
No issue.

Fenner Main (505), son of David (289) and Mrs. Esther (Palmer, née
Dean) Main, b., Stonington, Conn., Oct. 29, 1791; d., Windham, Conn.,
Sept. 24, 1869; m., No. Stonington, Conn., Feb. 1, 1813, Lucretia Main, b.,
Stonington, Dec. 10, 1788; d., Windham, Sept. 23, 1865. They turned
their steps toward Windham, where they made their home. He was a
successful farmer, a man highly esteemed, endowed with a genial nature,
finding enjoyment in social life, and was always a pleasant friend to meet.
They were Baptists.

Children, doubtless b. Windham:

835. Harriet L., b. Aug. 16, 1814; m. Samuel Stanton (844a–844d).
836. Jonathan W., b. Sept. 15, 1817; m. Lydia C. Robinson (845–
847).
837. Avery, b. Aug. 8, 1819; m. Almira Holmes (853).
838. Sumner B., b. Dec. 9, 1822; m. Hannah M. Sprague (850, 851).
839. Laura, b. Nov. 17, 1825; d., Iowa, Nov., 1859; m. Peter
Meyers. They had two children.
840. Albert, b. Apr. 8, 1827; d., Windham, Sept. 30, 1836.
841. Hannah, b. Apr. 4, 1829; m. Joseph Porter. They have two
children. Res., Willimantic, Conn.
842. Ann, b. Sept. 15, 1831; d. Sept. 20, 1855; m., Albany, N. Y.,
Benjamin Meyers. They had one child.
843. M. Elizabeth, b. Aug. 16, 1833. Res., 1909, Windham, Conn.
844. Jane, b. Apr. 8, 1836; d., Windham, Sept. 15, 1844.

Harriet L. Main (835), dau. of Fenner and Lucretia (Main) Main, b. Aug. 16, 1814; d., Windham, Conn., Feb. 21, 1895; m., Windham, Dec. 19, 1830, Samuel Stanton.

Children, b. Windham:

    844a. Mary Ann, b. Jan. 27, 1833; d. Jan. 19, 1867; m. Rev. J. M. Coley. No children living.

    844b. Louisa, b. Jan. 11, 1841; d. Dec. 7, 1873; unm.

    844c. Robert Fenner, b. Oct. 31, 1844; m., Mar. 4, 1880, Lucy A. Larkin. No issue.

    844d. Adelaide, b. Mar. 4, 1851; d. Dec. 5, 1859.

Jonathan W. Main (836), son of Fenner (505) and Lucretia (Main) Main, b., Windham, Conn., Sept. 15, 1817; d., Scotland, Conn., Mar. 20, 1894; m. Lydia C. Robinson, dau. of Andrew Robinson, who served in the War of the Revolution.

Children, b. Scotland:

    845. Albert Walker, b. June 11, 1843; m. Lois P. Palmer.

    846. Agustus, b.——; d., Scotland, Dec. 27, 1862; unm.

    847. Andrew Henry, b. Feb. 6, 1850; m., Scotland, May 14, 1874, Estella N. Parkhurst, b., Scotland, Mar. 12, 1854; dau. of Anthony and Nancy (Cleveland) Parkhurst. Mr. Maine spent his early life at the old Robinson homestead in Windham, erected in 1800, which is still held by the family. He engaged in farming and the lumber business in Scotland until 1902, when he removed with his family to Groton, Conn., where he is engaged in the real-estate business. Mrs. Maine was educated at the Willimantic High School.

Children, b. Scotland:

    848. Clarence Agustus Maine, b. Nov. 27, 1879; m., Groton, May 10, 1904, Louie Anderson. Mr. Maine was educated in the public schools of Scotland, in business college, and at Effingham College of Photo-engraving in Illinois. Res., Boston, Mass.

    849. Eva P. Maine, b. Mar. 14, 1883. She was educated at Norwich Academy and New London Business College.

Albert Walker Maine (845), son of the preceding, b. June 11, 1843; d., Nebraska, 1889; m., Scotland, Conn., Apr. 30, 1872, Lois P. Palmer, b., Scotland, Dec. 3, 1846; dau. of Alfred and Caroline (Parkhurst) Palmer, of Scotland. Mr. Main moved from Connecticut to Ulysses, Butler

Co., Ia., and for a time was a farmer; afterwards was in the banking business. Res., 2919 Q St., Lincoln, Neb.

Children, b. Ulysses:

> 849a. Flora E. Maine, b. Mar. 4, 1877; m., Lincoln, Oct. 6, 1908, Dr. George Herbert Hanson.
>
> 849b. Beulah C. Maine, b. Mar. 20, 1880.
>
> 849c. Ida P. Maine, b. Apr. 27, 1886.

Sumner B. Main (838), son of Fenner (505) and Lucretia (Main) Main, b., Windham, Conn., Dec. 9, 1822; d., Windham, Dec. 16, 1877; m., Killingly, Conn., May 12, 1853, Hannah M. Sprague, b., Scotland, Conn., Apr. 8, 1827; d., Danielson, Conn., Mar. 21, 1889; dau. of William B. and Hannah (Fuller) Sprague, of Scotland. Mr. Main was a farmer and brick manufacturer. They attended the Congregational Church, and his wife was a member.

Children, b. Windham:

> 850. M. Angie, b. Aug. 3, 1858. Res., Willimantic, Conn.
>
> 851. William Fenner, b. Feb. 10, 1864; m., Oct. 31, 1884, Kate Brown, b., Sprague, Conn., May 7, 1862; dau. of Charles Ames Brown and Delia Hyde, of Lisbon, Conn. Son: Harold Steven, b. July 23, 1886. Res., Windham, Conn. (See B. G., p. 482.)

Rhoda Main (506), dau. of David (289) and Mrs. Esther (Palmer, née Dean) Main, b., Stonington, Conn., May 16, 1794; d. Feb. 14, 1851; m. Joseph Holmes.

Children, probably b. No. Stonington, Conn.:

> 852. Rhoda Ann Holmes, b.——; m. Capt. John Leland Stanton. He was in the Civil War; killed at Port Hudson.
>
> 853. Almira Holmes, b.——; m. Avory Main (837), her cousin. They lived in Windham, Conn. Mrs. Main had a remarkable gift in religious services, and when Elder John Green heard her exhortation he said, " I better give up preaching."
>
> 854. Phebe Esther, b.——; m. Oliver Crandall. They lived on Cussaddoc Hill, No. Stonington, and she d. there. Children: Josephene and Mary Jane.
>
> 855. Lucinda, b.——; m. Joseph Worden. They lived in New York State.
>
> 856. Joseph, b.——; m. in Albany, N. Y., and lived in New York State.

Saxton Main (507), son of David (289) and Mrs. Esther (Palmer, née Dean) Main, b., Stonington, Conn., Aug. 27, 1796; m., No. Stonington, Conn., Sophronia Stanton, b. June, 1801; d. June 10, 1863; dau. of Amos and Amelia (Babcock) Stanton.

Children, b. No. Stonington:

    857. Stanton Babcock, b. Sept. 8, 1819; m. Mary Ann Main (860-862).

    858. Philena S., b.——; m. William Bailey.

    859. Emily E., b. June 7, 1833 (863, 864).

Stanton Babcock Main (857), son of Saxton (507) and Sophronia (Stanton) Main, b. Sept. 8, 1819; d., Voluntown, Conn., Aug. 25, 1876; m., Voluntown (at Lewis Main homestead), Nov. 28, 1844, Mary Ann Main (371), b., Voluntown, June 27, 1825; dau. of Lewis (315) and Hannah (Ray) Main, of Voluntown.

Children, b. Griswold, Conn.:

    860. De Witt Clinton, b. Mar. 8, 1847; d. ——, aged three years.

    861. George Burrows, b. Sept. 6, 1850 (865-869).

    862. Isabelle V., b. Jan. 15, 1852; d.——, aged two years.

Mrs. Mary A. (Main) Main m. (2), West Walworth, N. Y., May, 1883, Philetus Miller, b.——; d. 1883. No issue. Res., Dea. Zebulon Brown homestead, known later as the Mathew Brown homestead of No. Stonington. Mrs. Miller rendered valuable assistance in collecting data.

Emily E. Main (859), dau. of Saxton (507) and Sophronia (Stanton) Main, b. June 7, 1833; m. (1) John H. Hiscox, of Brooklyn, N. Y.; son of John S. and Amelia (Stanton) Hiscox. They were divorced. Mrs. Hiscox, née Main, m. (2), No. Stonington, Conn., William Henry Palmer, b. Aug. 3, 1839.

Son by first m.:

    863. William Edwin Hiscox, b., No. Stonington, Mar. 17, 1855; m., Griswold, Conn., Nov. 12, 1889, Hannah Worden, b., Russia, N. Y., May 31, 1856. Mr. Hiscox is a farmer at Jewett City, Conn. No issue.

Dau. by second m.:

    864. Bertha Etta Palmer, b., No. Stonington, Jan. 2, 1868; m., Voluntown, Conn., June 8, 1904, Nathaniel Culver, b. May 11, 1878. No issue. Res., No. Stonington. Conn.

THE EZEKIEL MAIN FAMILY

George Burrows Main (861), son of Stanton B. (857) and Mary A. (Main) Main, b. Sept. 6, 1850; m., Voluntown, Conn., Oct. 11, 1874, Minnie A. Young, b., Voluntown, Nov. 19, 1856; dau. of Orren Young and Sarah C. ——. Miss Young before her marriage was a school-teacher in Voluntown. Mr. Main taught school when he was seventeen years old. He was with W. H. Hillard in his store in No. Stonington, Conn., for four years; then with Babcock & Moss as bookkeeper in Westerly, R. I.; then was in business for three years under the firm name of Sheffield & Main, in Westerly. He was four years as head clerk and bookkeeper with E. D. Hall in Voluntown; after that he became manager of B. B. and R. Knight's store at Dodgeville, Mass.; promoted as manager of a larger business for them at Pontiac, R. I. In 1881 he was with the Nashua Lock Co. as bookkeeper at their store on Pearl St., Boston, Mass., and at the end of one year was manager and went all over New England to make the acquaintance of the different customers, with unprecedented success in selling goods. He was transferred to New York when that company opened a store in that city, and was sent all through the Middle, Southern, and Western States, introducing their goods successfully, and then was given an interest in the business and made vice-president. With increasing success with other companies in the hardware business, he formed The George B. Main Hardware Company, in 1908, at 70 Warren St., New York City.

Children:

865. George Clinton Clarence, b., Griswold, Conn., July 10, 1875; d., No. Stonington, Dec. 11, 1878.

866. Lillian Isabelle, b., Griswold, Sept. 25, 1876; d., Pontiac, R. I., May 26, 1880.

867. Lewis Stanton, b., Dodgeville, Feb. 3, 1879; d. Feb. 25, 1879.

868. Angie Frances Josephine, b., Pontiac, Sept. 29, 1880. Miss Main after her graduation from the Waltham, Mass., High School, took two and one half years' course at the Boston University. Since 1903 she has been a teacher in the Waltham schools.

869. Herbert Alonzo, b., Somerville, Mass., Sept. 16, 1882; m., Havana, Cuba, Sept. 21, 1908, Mae B. Hazletine, b., Digby, Nova Scotia, Feb. 9, 1889; dau. of Mr. and Mrs. William Hazletine, of Nova Scotia. Mr. Main was educated in the public schools of Waltham, and was a graduate of the High School and of a business college of Boston. He was for three years in the collection business for himself in Boston,

and two years as treasurer and president of the Mann Mercantile Agency. One year, 1907–08, in the employ of the Charles River Basin Commission, Boston and Cambridge, Mass. This commission engaged in building a dam across Charles River, forming a fresh-water basin. Now [1909] he has a civil-service position, in the War Department, U. S. A., Adjt.-General's office for the pacification of Cuba, at Havana, until the government is turned over to Cuban control.

Here end the records of the descendants of David Main (289).

Nathaniel Main (290), son of Jeremiah Main (269) and Thankful Brown, dau. of James Brown and Elizabeth Randall (B. G., pp. 14, 15), b. July 12, 1754; m. (1), Aug. 7, 1780, Abigail Thurston, of Hopkinton, R. I.; d. 1823. The Thurston family of Hopkinton more than one hundred years ago were among the most progressive and prominent citizens of the town. Their tombstones and monuments near Hopkinton City attest their excellent worth. Mr. Main was a wheelwright, and both he and his wife were church-members. Their descendants may well look backward to their ancestry with pride. Nathaniel Main m. (2) Abby Brown. No issue by last m.

Children by first m.

870. Job, b. May 17, 1781; m. Comfort Billings (880–885).
871. Gardner, b. Nov. 20, 1782; m. Hannah Hakes. He was a farmer and lived in Brooklyn, Conn. Children: Elias, James, Charles, and Caroline. All m. and had families.
872. Betsey, b. Feb. 10, 1785; m. Gersham Ray. They settled in New York State and had three children. She came back once, on horseback, to visit her people.
873. Adah, b. Feb. 14, 1787; m. Israel Palmer Park (1331–1338).
874. Russel, b. May 31, 1789; m. Keturah Chapman, sister of Andrew Chapman. Children: (1) Eliza, b.——, m.——, had a family; (2) Lois, b.——, unm.; (3) Lucy, b.——, unm.; (4) Hannah, b.——, unm.; (5) Russel, b.——.; unm.
875. Nabby, or Abigail, b. July 11, 1791; m. Thomas Thompson (886–895).
876. Ezra (twin), b. Oct. 3, 1793; m. Duffy Davis, and had children.
877. Clarissa (twin), b. Oct. 3, 1793; m. Ichabod Eggleston (896–899).
878. Hannah, b. Oct. 30, 1795; m.—— Wheeler and lived in Brook-

lyn. They had no children, but assisted in the care of her sister Ruby's children.

879. Ruby, b. Dec. 13, 1800; m. Jonathan Chapman. They lived in Brooklyn, and had sixteen children.

[The names and births of the preceding ten children are taken from town records.]

Job Main (870), son of Nathaniel (290) and Abigail (Thurston) Main, b., Stonington, Conn., May 17, 1781; m. Comfort Billings.

Children, b. No. Stonington, Conn.:

880. Palmer, b.——; unm.
881. Charles, b.——; m., Sept. 12, 1848, Frances Hewitt, b. Mar. 15, 1820; dau. of Benjamin and Desire (Babcock) Hewitt.
882. William, b.——; m. (1) Frances ——; m. (2) her sister Louise.
883. Daniel, b.——; m. and had children.
884. Betsey, b.——; m. —— Webb. They had two boys.
885. Mary, b.——; unm.

Nabby, or Abigail, Main (875), dau. of Nathaniel (290) and Abigail (Thurston) Main, b., Stonington, Conn., July 11, 1791; m., No. Stonington, Conn., Oct. 30, 1813, Thomas Thompson, b. July 9, 1789; d., No. Stonington, Oct. 10, 1849. He was vivacious, quick, and active. When, at work on the road, the men were removing a big rock with handspike and fence-rails, he came and put his ox-goad under and said, "Now, all together."

Children, b. No. Stonington:

886. Betsey, b. Nov. 27, 1814; m. Simeon Perry Slocum (900–906).
887. Sally Bishop, b. Sept. 5, 1815; unm.
888. Lucy Emeline, b. Oct. 6, 1817; m. Joseph Allen Douglas (907–909).
889. Frances Almira, b. Apr. 23, 1820; m., July 26, 1851, Thomas M. Stevens. [Wrote granddaughter, Three Oaks, Mich., who did not answer queries.]
890. Mary Esther, b. Nov. 17, 1823; d. Sept. 21, 1849; unm.
891. James Dixon, b. June 15, 1825; m. Eliza Swan (915).
892. Thomas, b. Nov. 20, 1827; d. Sept. 3, 1866; unm.
893. Abby Calista, b. Feb. 20, 1830; m. Dwight Bromley (927).
894. Charles Dwight, b. June 30, 1834; m. Mary A. Billings (933, 934).
895. Harriet W., b. Sept. 13, 1836; m. Robert P. Palmer (935–937).

Clarissa Main (877), dau. of Nathaniel (290) and Abigail (Thurston) Main, b., Stonington, Conn., 1795; d. Apr. 19, 1848; m. Ichabod Eggleston, b., Groton, Conn., May 13, 1800; d., No. Stonington, Jan. 29, 1875. He was a farmer, a Republican, and attended the First Baptist Church of Pendleton Hill, Conn. His wife was a member.

Children, b. No. Stonington:

896. Thankful, b. Apr. 4, 1830; m. Lester Main (938-945).
897. Stiles Park, b. June 13, 1834; m. Louisa A. Main (955, 956).
898. Angeline, b. Apr. 5, 1836; m. Calvin H. Burdick (959-964).
899. Latham M., b. Sept. 9, 1842; d., Washington, D. C., Jan., 1864. He was a soldier in the Civil War.

Betsey Thompson (886), dau. of Thomas and Abigail (Main) Thompson, b., No. Stonington, Conn., Nov. 27, 1814; m., No. Stonington, Jan. 29, 1843, Simeon Perry Slocum, b., No. Stonington, Oct. 22, 1819; d. Aug. 15, 1902. Interment, River Bend. Mr. Slocum was a farmer, frugal and industrious. He bought and sold farms.

Children, all b. No. Stonington:

900. Elizabeth, b. Nov. 28, 1843; d. in infancy.
901. Texanna, b. June 12, 1845; m., Sept. 29, 1870, Rev. J. Wesley Holman, b. June 3, 1844; d. Sept. 29, 1902. Mr. Holman was a Baptist minister, having pastorates in New Jersey, Connecticut, and Rhode Island. He was the son of Rev. J. W. Holman, who was pastor of the Third No. Stonington Church in 1870, a man of superior ability, having rich stores of Biblical knowledge. Son: George Arthur, b. June 27, 1872. Res., with his mother, Ashaway, R. I.
902. William Spencer, b. May 4, 1847; d. Oct. 10, 1849.
903. Josephine May, b. Dec. 13, 1848; d. ——, aged twelve years.
904. Simeon Thompson, b. Oct. 20, 1850; m. Addie Darrow.
905. Peleg Abram, b. Apr. 3, 1853; unm. He was a farmer, but later was superintendent of streets of Westerly. Res., with his mother, Westerly, R. I.
906. Ida Abby, b. Aug. 3, 1855; d. ——, aged five years.

Lucy Emeline Thompson (888), dau. of Thomas and Abigail (Main 872) Thompson, b., No. Stonington, Conn., Oct. 6, 1818; d. Niantic, R. I.; m., No. Stonington, July 3, 1844, Joseph Allen Douglass, b., Exeter, R. I., Jan. 22, 1833; d. Niantic; son of Daniel McMain and Mary (Stanton) Douglass, of Exeter. He was educated in the schools of Ashaway, Niantic, and Westerly, R. I. He was superintendent of a textile mill. Both he and his wife were members of the Baptist Church, Niantic, where they resided.

Children, b. Niantic:

907. Henry D., b. Nov. 6, 1845; d. Apr. 22, 1868.
908. Mary Frances, b. July 29, 1848 (910-914).
909. Ella Thompson, b. May 29, 1859.

Mary Frances Douglass (908), dau. of the preceding, m., Westerly, R. I., Dec. 31, 1873, Benjamin Barber, b., Hopkinton, R. I., June 19, 1849; d., Niantic, R. I., Sept. 6, 1906. Mr. Barber was a merchant in Niantic; in politics, a Republican. Mrs. Barber is a member of the Baptist Church. Res., Niantic, R. I.

Children, b. Niantic:

910. Elnora D., b. June 20, ——
911. Lulu G., b. Aug. 20, 1881; d., Niantic, Dec. 25, 1887.
912. Birdie C. C., b. Mar. 29, 1886.
913. Lona M., b. May 27, 1889; d. Apr. 19, 1890.
914. Willis R., b. Aug. 29, 1891.

James Dixson Thompson (891), son of Thomas and Abigail (Main) Thompson, b., No. Stonington, Conn., June 15, 1825; m., Nov. 25, 1852, Eliza Swan.

Son:

915. George Dixson Thompson, b., Stonington, Conn., Oct. 27, 1853; m., Potter Hill, R. I., May 3, 1877, Agnes McDonald, b., Willimantic, Conn., Aug. 2, 1854; dau. of William and Elizabeth (Wilson) McDonald, of Potter Hill. Mr. Thompson is an active, industrious farmer and dairyman. His wife is a member of the Baptist Church. Res., No. Stonington, Conn.

Children, b. No. Stonington, except the first:

916. James William, b., Stonington, Conn., Mar. 16, 1879 (921, 922).
917. George Dixson, Jr., b. July 23, 1880 (923-925a).
918. Elizabeth Agnes, b. Dec. 25, 1882 (926).
919. Carrie Eliza, b. June 14, 1884.
920. Harrison M., b. Dec. 12, 1888; d. Feb. 24, 1909. He was a young man of much promise, a member of the Baptist Church, and an earnest worker in the Sunday school.

James William Thompson (916), son of George D. and Agnes (McDonald) Thompson, b., Stonington, Conn., Mar. 16, 1879; d., No. Stonington, Conn., May 12, 1905; m., Boston, Mass., July 5, 1903, Elizabeth Catherine Boyce, b., New Jersey, Dec. 6, 1881. Mr. Thompson was a machinist at Mystic, Conn. Her res., No. Stonington, Conn.

Children:

921. Edith Agnes, b., Mystic, May 2, 1904.

922. James William, Jr., b., No. Stonington, May 21, 1905.

George Dixson Thompson, Jr. (917), brother of the preceding, b., No. Stonington, Conn., July 23, 1880; m., Moosup, Conn., Aug. 28, 1901, Florence E. Harris, b., Moosup, Apr. 11, 1874; dau. of Hiram and Cynthia (Lyon) Harris, of Moosup. Mr. Thompson is a Republican, and he and his wife attend the Methodist Episcopal Church. His education was secured in public schools. They lived in Providence, R. I., five years; now, at Hope, R. I. He is a machinist. Mrs. Thompson's education was secured in the public schools of Moosup and in Killingly High School. She taught in Plainfield, Conn. She held a position in the office of *Munsey's Magazine* at New London, Conn., and was compositor in the *Journal* office at Moosup. She is a member of the Methodist Episcopal Church, Providence.

Children, first three b. Providence:

923. Janette Lyon, b. Dec. 19, 1902.

924. Lesley George, b. Feb. 12, 1904.

925. Winthrop Eugene, b. May 11, 1905.

925a. Louise Elizabeth, b., Hope, Dec. 12, 1908.

Elizabeth Agnes Thompson (918), sister of the preceding, b. Dec. 25, 1881; m., No. Stonington, Conn., Aug. 5, 1903, Julius B. Gavitt, b., Charlestown, R. I., Apr. 18, 1879; son of John E. and Francina H. (Pendleton) Gavitt, of Westerly, R. I. Mr. Gavitt is a machinist, a Republican, and both he and his wife are members of Calvary Baptist Church, Westerly. Mr. Gavitt is unassuming and thoughtful, giving strict attention to his duties. Mrs. Gavitt before marriage taught school for three years. She is a willing worker in the church and Bible school, and was superintendent of the Primary Department. Res., Stonington, Conn.

Son:

926. Roland Duane, b., Westerly, Nov. 27, 1905.

Carrie Eliza Thompson (919), sister of the preceding, b. June 12, 1884; m., No. Stonington, Conn., June 17, 1908, Louis Osmos Palmiter, of Albion,

Wis. He is a farmer. She is a church-member. Res., Holmes St., Janes-ville, Wis.

Abby Calista Thompson (893), dau. of Thomas and Abigail (Main 872) Thompson, b., No. Stonington, Conn., Feb. 20, 1830; d., Stonington (Pawcatuck), Conn., Apr. 20, 1899; m., Voluntown, Conn., Oct. 29, 1868, Dwight Bromley, b., Griswold, Conn., Sept. 29, 1840; son of Orren P. and Mary Ann (Burdick) Bromley, of Griswold. Mr. Bromley is a farmer and a Republican. Res., Westerly, R. I.

Son:

927. Henry Thomas Bromley, b., No. Stonington, Aug. 19, 1869; m., Westerly, July 4, 1894, Hattie M. Barnes, b., Hopkinton, R. I., Jan. 18, 1875; dau. of Robert T. and Annie A. (Thomas) Barnes, of Westerly. Mr. Bromley is a farmer, a Republican, and both he and his wife are members of the Methodist Church. Res., Westerly, R. I.

Children, b. Stonington:

928. Henry Dwight, b. May 14, 1895.
929. Hollis Thompson, b. Dec. 16, 1896.
930. Abbie Calista, b. July 9, 1898.
931. Maud Alice, b. Aug. 23, 1903.
932. George Robert, b. Jan. 21, 1906.

Charles Dwight Thompson (894), son of Thomas and Abigail (Main 872) Thompson, b., No. Stonington, Conn., June 30, 1834; m., No. Stonington, Nov. 29, 1868, Mary Adelaide Billings, b. Apr. 23, 1849; dau. of Gilbert and Mary A. (Fish) Billings. Mr. Thompson is a farmer, a Republican, a school trustee, and a Justice of the Peace. Res., No. Stonington, Conn.

Children, b. No. Stonington:

933. Lucille Billings (twin), b. June 5, 1873; m., No. Stonington, Oct. 20, 1897, George Asher Wheeler, son of Nelson Wheeler, of Stonington, Conn. Children: (1) Nelson Thompson, b. May 15, 1903; (2) Louise Billings, b. Feb. 17, 1908.

934. Louise Billings (twin), b. June 5, 1873; unm. She attended the Wheeler High School at No. Stonington and the State Normal School, and is now a teacher at Stonington, Conn.

Harriet Wealthia Thompson (895), dau. of Thomas and Abigail (Main) Thompson, b., No. Stonington, Conn., Sept. 13, 1836; d. Feb. 18, 1901; m., No. Stonington, Jan. 16, 1865, Robert Potter Palmer, b., No. Stoning-

ton (Pendleton Hill), July 6, 1830; d. Apr. 24, 1908; son of Luther Palmer
and Sarah, dau. of Thomas and Mary (Robinson) Wells, of Hopkinton,
R. I. Mr. Palmer spent his whole life at the homestead of his father, and
was a man that was endeared to everybody, and his wife as well, free and
social, given to much hospitality. The home was full of sunshine, friendship, and real love. Both were active members and strong supporters of
the Baptist Church, of which the whole family were members. The children rise up to call them blessed.

Children, b. Pendleton Hill, Conn.:

935. Sarah Thompson Palmer, b. Feb. 15, 1867; unm.
936. Julia Robinson Palmer, b. Aug. 30, 1869; m., No. Stonington,
July 22, 1907, Harris Boardman, who is superintendent of
electric railroad. Son: Harris, Jr., b., Lancaster, Penn., Apr.
22, 1908. Res., Lancaster, Penn.
937. Amelia Potter Palmer, b. Apr. 13, 1873; m., No. Stonington,
Dec. 25, 1904, Dr. Charles E. North. Dau.: Anna Palmer,
b. Apr. 22, 1908. Res., Montclair, N. J.

Thankful Eggleston (896), dau. of Ichabod and Clarissa (Main 877)
Eggleston, b., No. Stonington, Conn., Apr., 1830; m., Mar. 31, 1856,
Lester Main (1234), b., Griswold, Conn., Oct. 10, 1830; d., No. Stonington,
Mar. 12, 1895; son of John Main (1174) and Hannah Palmer. Mr. Main
was a farmer, and both he and his wife members of the Baptist Church,
Hopkinton, R. I. Interment in Union Cemetery, No. Stonington, Her res.,
17 Avery Court, New London, Conn.

Children, b. No. Stonington (Laurel Glen), except the first:

938. William Lester, b., No. Stonington (Ashwillet), Dec. 1, 1857
(946, 947).
939. Dwight, b. Jan. 21, 1859; m. H. Ella Eccleston (948–951).
940. Clara Jane, b. Apr. 5, 1863; d. Jan. 28, 1880.
941. Hannah Mary, b. Aug. 17, 1864; m., May 5, 1889, Orsmus
Stillman Barnes, b., Westerly, R. I., 1864. Mr. Barnes is
steward at the Crocker House, New London, and has been
for many years. Both he and his wife are members of the
Baptist Church. Son: Arthur Orsmus, b. June 16, 1895.
942. Fred, b. May 27, 1866; m., No. Stonington, July 3, 1891, Annie
Whipple. He is a carpenter. Children: (1) Lester Denison,
(2) Charles, (3) Louisa. Res., Wakefield, R. I.
943. Ruth Etta, b. Jan. 21, 1868; m., Jan. 1, 1883, Myron Holdredge,

b. 1866. Occupation, carpenter. Mrs. Holdredge is a member of the Baptist Church. Children: Harold and Russell. Res., Pittsfield, Mass.

944. Sarah Edith, b. Feb. 13, 1870; m. Elmer E. Miller (952-954).
945. Ursula Maria, b. Sept. 3, 1872. Res., 6 Burrows Place, Boston, Mass.

William Lester Maine (938), son of Lester and Thankful (Eggleston 896) Main, m., June 13, 1880, Mary Elizabeth Maine, b., Bolton, Conn., Oct. 18, 1858; dau. of Carey E. Maine (972). Mr. Maine owns the old Zebulon York farm, where he resides, in No. Stonington, Conn. (See B. G., p. 505.) Both are members of the Pendleton Hill Church.

Children, b. No. Stonington:

946. Clara Imogene, b. July 10, 1881; m., Feb. 20, 1904, John H. Geer, of No. Stonington. Son: Bourdon Everett, b. Mar. 4, 1905.
947. Emma Josephine, b. July 5, 1884.

Dwight Main (939), brother of the preceding, b., No. Stonington, Conn., Jan. 21, 1859; m., Rockville, R. I., Nov. 26, 1884, H. Ellen Eccleston, dau. of Gardner W. Eccleston, of Voluntown, Conn. Both were educated in the common schools. They have lived in No. Stonington and in Woodville, R. I., seventeen years. Res., Laurel Glen, Conn.

Children, b. Woodville:

948. Howard E., b. Feb. 20, 1891.
949. Walter G., b. Aug. 7, 1899.
950. Alice F., b. Apr. 10, 1901.
951. Ruth V., b. Apr. 11, 1904.

Sarah Edith Main (944), sister of the preceding, b., No. Stonington, Conn., Feb. 13, 1870; m., Laurel Glen, Jan. 1, 1895. Elmer E. Miller, b. Ashwillet, Conn.; son of Oliver S. and Sarah A. (Eccleston) Miller. He is a farmer, a Republican, and he and his wife attend the Congregational Church. Mrs. Miller is a member. Res., Jewett City, Conn.

Children:

952. Everett Avery ⎱ twins, b., Ashwillet, 1897.
953. Ruth Ethel ⎰
954. Herbert Lester, b., Preston, Conn., 1906.

Stiles Park Eggleston (897), son of Ichabod and Clarissa (Main 877) Eggleston, b., No. Stonington, Conn., June 13, 1834; m. Louisa Almira Main, b. Apr. 4, 1839; d., No. Stonington, Oct. 31, 1908; dau. of Charles H. and Almira B. (Eggleston) Main. Mr. Eggleston is a large landholder, farmer, and merchant. He has held public offices in town, county, state, and was postmaster for a number of years.

Children, b. No. Stonington (Ashwillet):

955. Ida L., b. Mar. 19, 1859; m. Henry E. Randall (957, 958).

956. Stiles Curtis, b. Oct. 29, 1865; m. Nellie M. Miner. (See p. 46, No. 238; also 1381.)

Ida L. Eggleston (955), dau. of Stiles P. and Louisa A. (Main) Eggleston, b. Mar. 19, 1859; m., No. Stonington, Conn., Mar. 25, 1880, Henry E. Randall, of Hopkinton, R. I.; b. July 13, 1858; son of Joseph Allen Randall, son of Reuben Randall, of Voluntown, Conn.; his mother was Martha Chapman, dau. of Prentice and Martha (Church) Chapman. Mr. Randall is a Republican and a farmer. Both he and his wife are members of the Baptist Church. He has taken deep interest in supporting the meetings at Ashwillet Chapel, near his home, assisted by his wife. For a number of years he has been the correspondent of the *Westerly Daily Sun.*

Children, b. No. Stonington:

957. Louisa Belle, b. Aug. 19, 1883.

958. Clifford Eggleston, b. May 21, 1900; d. June 2, 1900.

Angeline Eggleston (898), dau. of Ichabod and Clarissa (Main 877) Eggleston, b., No. Stonington, Conn., Apr. 5, 1836; m., No. Stonington, 1856, Calvin H. Burdick, b., No. Stonington, 1834. He is a farmer and a Republican. Res., Charlestown, R. I.

Children, the first four b. No. Stonington:

959. Thomas C., b. Oct. 21, 1857; m. Sarah Sisson.

960. Oscar J., b. Dec. 28, 1859; unm.

961. Charles E., b. Sept., 1865; unm.

962. Alice A., b. Jan. 23, 1868; m. Henry J. Cassidy.

963. Marion G., b., Westerly, R. I., July 13, 1874; m. Edgar E. Burdick.

964. Mabel E., b., Charlestown, June 13, 1879; m. Robert L. Noyes.

Here end the records of Nathaniel Main and Abigail Thurston (290).

Jabish* (or Jabez) Maine (554), son of Jabish (483) and Freelove

*Usage, in this case, has adopted the latter spelling, which will be employed hereafter with *these* descendants.

(Edwards) Maine, b., No. Stonington, Conn., Apr. 20, 1796; d., Bolton, Conn., Apr. 8, 1843; m. Lydia Edwards, b. May 6, 1792; d. Sept. 10, 1847. Mr. Maine was a farmer by occupation and lived for several years in Bolton, where he died, but forty-seven years of age, at what was known as the "Gate House" (Bolton Hill). He was a soldier in the War of 1812, and served at the Defense of Stonington.

Children, b. No. Stonington, excepting the last:

965. Lydia Angeline, b. Sept. 30, 1816; m. Perry Popple (974-977).
966. Hiram Leonard, b. Dec. 9, 1818; m. (1) Mary Elizabeth Coleman; m. (2) Julia Ann Simons (978-988).
967. Lyman Franklin, b. May 7, 1821; m. (1) Mary Spofford; m. (2) Mrs. Delia (Spofford) Forbes (989-999).
968. Erastus Lester, b. July 19, 1823; m. Eliza Mise Pierce (1000-1009).
969. Phebe Esther, b. Jan. 14, 1825; d., an old lady, Mansfield, Conn.; unm.
970. John Henry, b. Dec. 24, 1826; m. Mary C. Adams (1010).
971. Christopher Ira, b. Feb. 13, 1829; d., Groton, Conn., Feb. 10, 1906; m. Mary Phillips. No issue. Interments in Voluntown, Conn.
972. Cary Edwards, b. July 30, 1831; m. (1) Mary McNeil; m. (2) Emma A. Chapman (1011-1016).
973. Freelove Margaret, b., Bozrah, Conn., Mar. 6, 1835; m. (1) Charles Risley; m. (2) Milo M. Maine (1084, 1085).

Lydia Angeline Maine (965), dau. of Jabez (554) and Lydia (Edwards) Maine, b., No. Stonington, Conn., Sept. 30, 1816; d., Mansfield, Conn., June 3, 1898; m. Perry Popple, b. Dec. 22, 1821; d. June 10, 1898. Children:

974. Charlotte Augusta, m. Simeon A. Easterbrooks.
975. Mary Louise, m. Stephen Clark Gurley.
976. Charles Alonzo, m. Sarah Hunt.
977. Caroline Melissa, m. James L. Palmer.

Hiram Leonard Maine (966), brother of the preceding, b., No. Stonington, Conn., Dec. 9, 1818; d., Faribault, Minn., Sept. 9, 1902; m. (1), Mar. 11, 1838, Mary Elizabeth Coleman, b. Jan. 19, 1820; d. Feb. 27, 1854; m. (2), May 11, 1854, Julia Ann Simons, b. Sept. 22, 1824. Res., Faribault, Minn.

Children by first m.:

978. Adelaide Rosalie, b. and d. 1840.

979. Fernando Delorain, b. and d. 1842.
980. Ninette, b. July 29, 1844; m., Sept. 9, 1865, Harrison Lowater. Mrs. Lowater is a poetess of note. Children: Charles, Ninette, and Frank. Res., 1909, Rock Elm, Wis.
981. Eugene Adelbert, b. and d. 1846.
982. Eugene Herbert, b. and d. 1848.
983. Effie Imogene, b. Oct. 11, 1853; d. Sept., 1864.
Children by second m.:
984. William Leonard, b. Sept., 1855; d. Mar., 1856.
985. Ida Elizabeth, b. July 14, 1857; d. 189–; m. a Curtis. They had three children.
986. Olin Hiram, b. Jan., 1860; d. Sept., 1864.
987. Arthur Hiram, b. 1864; m. Mina Maine. They had three children.
988. Lillie R., b. 1867; m. Daniel Morrow. They had three children.

Lyman Franklin Maine (967), brother of the preceding, b., No. Stonington, Conn., May 17, 1821; d. Willimantic, Conn.; m. (1) Mary Spofford; m. (2) Mrs. Delia (Spofford) Forbes, widowed sister of first wife.
Children by first m.:
989. Ellen Louisa, m. Emery Pierce.
990. Nautella, d. ——
991. Mary Ann, m. Jerome Lewis.
992. Lyman, m. Dette Snow.
993. Jabez, m. ——
994. George, d. ——
995. Edwin, m. Josephine Lillibridge.
996. Fred (twin), d. ——
997. Ferd (twin), m. ——; d. ——.
998. Frank, d. ——; unm.
999. William, m. Mrs. Hattie (Goodrich) Howes.

Erastus Lester Maine (968), brother of the preceding, b., No. Stonington, Conn., July 19, 1823; d., Winnebago, Minn., May 20, 1895; m., 1854, Eliza Mise Pierce.
Children:
1000. Jessie (Hooser), d., Canada, July, 1908, aged fifty-two years.
1001. Irving C., aged fifty years. Res., 1909, Amboy, Minn.
1002. Spencer T., aged forty-eight years. Res., 1909, Winnebago, Minn.

1003. Selwyn A., aged forty-six years. Res., 1909, Bertha, Minn.
1004. Harriet (McLearen), aged forty-four years. Res., 1909, Porcupine Hills, Alta, Canada.
1005. Ossian L., aged forty-two years. Res., 1909, Pequoit, Minn.
1006. Olive A., aged forty years. Res., 1909, Truman, Minn.
1007. Ralph C., aged thirty-eight years. Res., 1909, Winnebago, Minn.
1008. Mina, d., Faribault, Minn., Sept. 9, 1898, aged twenty-two years.
1009. Chrissie (Beeson), aged thirty years. Res., 1909, Neosho, Mo.

John Henry Maine (970), brother of the preceding, b., No. Stonington, Conn., Dec. 24, 1826; m., Faribault, Minn., May 9, 1858, Mary C. Adams, of Prince Edwards Island, deceased. Mr. Maine's res., 1909, Newport, Ore. Son:

1010. John Henry, Jr., b., Faribault, Feb. 25, 1859; m., Aug. 19, 1898, Sarah F. Hamilton, b. June 17, 1873. Dau.: Mary M., b. Aug. 10, 1899.

Cary Edwards Maine (972), brother of the preceding, b., No. Stonington, Conn., July 30, 1831; m. (1) Mary McNeil, d. 1869; m. (2) Emma A. Chapman. Mr. Maine was a drummer in the Civil War, member of Co. B., 11th Regt., Conn. Vol. Infantry. Enlisted 1861; discharged 1865. He is a farmer by occupation. Res., 1909, No. Stonington, Conn.
Children by first m.:

1011. Josephine Louise, b., Bolton, Conn., May 18, 1856; m. Alden F. Miner. Children: Winnifred Estelle, Walter Adelbert, and Ethel Mary. Res., 1909, Ashaway, R. I.
1012. Joseph Montzumi, b., Bolton, 1857; d. ——, aged seven months.
1013. Mary Elizabeth, b., Bolton, Oct. 18, 1858; m. William L. Maine (946, 947).
1014. Emily Margaret, b., Ellington, Conn., Apr. 17, 1861; d. Aug. 4, 1883; unm.

Children, by second m.:

1015. Clarence Edward, b., No. Stonington, Jan. 24, 1877.
1016. Cary Edwards, b., Coventry, Conn., Aug. 12, 1880.

Collins Maine (555) (sometimes spelled "Collings"), son of Jabish (483) and Freelove (Edwards) Maine, b., No. Stonington, Conn., Dec. 16, 1797; d., Bolton, Conn., June 16, 1875; m. Susan Peabody, dau. of John

Peabody, of No. Stonington; b. Feb. 21, 1800; d., Bolton, Aug. 20, 1878. Interments in Quarryville Cemetery. Mr. Maine was a farmer by occupation. In politics he was a strong Abolitionist, taking an active part as a campaign speaker in his State. He was a soldier in the War of 1812 at the Defense of Stonington, going as a substitute for Jesse Chapman, of No. Stonington. Res., Bolton, from about 1830.

Children, first five b. No. Stonington; last five b. Bolton; others uncertain:

1017. Fanny Mary, b. Dec. 16, 1817; d., Bolton, Dec. 2, 1850; m., Mar. 12, 1837, Dexter Clark.

1018. Daniel Harrison, b. Jan. 22, 1820; d., Chelsea, Mass., July 29, 1859; m. (1), Aug. 28, 1842, Elizabeth M. Roberts; m. (2) Parmelia Jennings.

1019. Albert Noyes, b. Jan. 16, 1822; d. Oct. 8, 1845; buried in Quarryville Cemetery; m. Aug. 21, 1843, Susan E. Harvey.

1020. Susan Elizabeth, b. Mar. 9, 1824; d., Bolton, Feb. 16, 1864; m., Aug. 17, 1845, Gilbert G. Rose, d., Bolton, Jan. 10, 1897. Interments in Quarryville.

1021. Nathan Sands, b. Oct. 13, 1825; d., Bolton, June 2, 1902; m. (1), June 4, 1851, Cornelia E. Carver, dau. of Wm. Carver, d., Bolton, Nov. 1, 1853; m. (2), Sept. 28, 1854, Sarah M. Jennings, d. Bolton; m. (3) Sophia Moser. Child by first m.: Nathan Collins, b., Bolton, Dec. 25, 1852; m., Chelsea, July 26, 1875, Elizabeth B., dau. of Joseph Everdeen. Has in his possession the Collins Maine Bible, from which these family records are taken. Res., 1909, Bolton, Conn., in the house built by his grandfather about 1835.

1022. Jonas Chapman, b. Jan. 26, 1828; d. Aug. 30, 1828.

1023. Jonas Chapman, b. Nov. 30, 1829; drowned, Quarryville, July 4, 1873; buried in Quarryville; m., Nov. 25, 1852, Ellen M. Brown.

1024. Jeanette Laura, b. Jan. 31, 1832; d., Wapping, Conn., Sept. 14, 1893; buried in Wapping; m., Jan. 30, 1851, J. Frank Strong.

1025. Melinda Jane, b. Mar. 26, 1834; d., Bolton, July 23, 1894; buried in Quarryville Cemetery; m., Feb. 25, 1855, Albert Wesley Cowles.

1026. Lorin Smith, b. Feb. 25, 1836; m. (1), June 28, 1858, Susan L. Royce, d. Feb. 15, 1887; m. (2), Jan. 2, 1888, Margaret Jane Jennings, d. Mar. 14, 1903; m. (3) Mrs. Amelia (Pardee) Davis. Res., 1909, Bolton Notch, Conn.

1027. Rhoda Ann, b. May 2, 1838; d., Bolton, Sept. 25, 1871; buried in Quarryville Cemetery; m. Austin M. Tullar.

1028. Juliette, b. Feb. 22, 1840: d., Leeds, Me., Feb. 13, 1907; m. Howard Jennings.

1029. Ida Ellen, b. Sept. 6, 1843; d., Torrington, Conn., Mar. 3, 1906; m. George Crippen.

1030. Albert Noyes, b. July 27, 1845; m., Dec. 16, 1868, Mary Warner.

Cynthia Louesa Maine (558), dau. of Jabish (483) and Freelove (Edwards) Maine, b., No. Stonington, Conn., June 23, 1804; d., Manchester, Conn., June 6, 1891; m., Columbia, Conn., Oct. 1, 1829, Alfred Turner, of Groton, Conn.; d. Bolton, Conn. Interments in Bolton Hill. Mrs. Turner was a woman of strong character and sterling worth, and was very much devoted to her family. After Mr. Turner's death she lived with her daughters in So. Manchester, Conn., where she died.

Children:

1031. Cynthia Azelia, b. May 26, 1832; m. Rufus Austin Russell, of Rocky Hill, Conn. Both buried in (Quarryville), Bolton, where they lived for many years.

1032. Clarinda Mary, b. June 27, 1833; d. Feb. 4, 1842.

1033. Amy Edwards, b. Jan. 12, 1835; m. Ezra House, of Eastbury, Conn. He d. Bolton; buried in Manchester, where they lived for many years. She res., 1909, Springfield, Mass.

1034. William Orrin, b. Nov. 3, 1835; unm. Instructor in vocal and instrumental music. Res., 1909, Willimantic, Conn.

1035. Henry Edwin, b. Dec. 29, 1838; m. Abbie Jane Dart, of Waterford, Conn., Both d.; buried in Colchester, Conn., their home for many years.

1036. Eliza Adelaide, b. Nov. 26, 1841; m. Joel Edwards Hawley, of Watertown, Conn. Res., 1909, Manchester, Conn.

1037. Mary Jane, b. Nov. 25, 1843; d. Nov. 2, 1856; buried at Bolton Hill.

1038. Charlotte Louise, b. Oct. 7, 1847; d. Feb. 9, 1870; buried at Bolton Hill.

Dr. Jonas Chapman Maine (559), son of Jabish (483) and Freelove (Edwards) Maine, b., No. Stonington, Conn., Mar. 7, 1806; d., Colchester, Conn., July 17, 1877; m. (1), Groton, Conn., Feb. 1, 1835, Melinda Turner, b., Groton, Oct. 24, 1801; d., Cromwell, Conn., Aug. 20, 1875;

The home of Edgar W. Comstock and wife,
Anna Maria (Main)
(749)
Oregon, Wis.
Page 108

Mary Emeline (Brownell), Sarah Clarinda (Hale)
(1045)   (1047)

Daughters of Clarinda (Maine) Hunt (560), who was born
and twice married in the homestead below

Page 133

Homestead of Jabish B. (483) and Freelove (Edwards) Maine

North Stonington, Conn.

Now owned and used as a summer residence by a great-grandson,
Dr. C. Wesley Hale (1067), of Springfield, Mass.

m. (2) Mrs. Julia Wells, of Troy, N. Y. Dr. Maine graduated from Castleton (Vt.) College in 1830, receiving the M.D. degree. He also studied law at Yale, and combined an occasional legal case with his medical practice. He was a man of varied talents and much natural ability. His Tax List of 1850, which he made out in detail and in rhyme, was quite widely circulated. He lived many years at his "Music Vale" farm in Bolton, Conn., but his last days were spent in Colchester, where he died.

Children, by first m.:

1039. Fidelia Melinda, b., Bolton, Feb. 17, 1837; d., So. Coventry, Conn., Aug. 23, 1909; m. Charles Clark, a grandson of Collins Maine (555). No issue.

1040. Jonas Chapman, Jr., b., Bolton, Jan. 24, 1841; d., Bolton, Jan. 15, 1847.

Clarinda Wells Maine (560), dau. of Jabish (483) and Freelove (Edwards) Maine, b., No. Stonington, Conn., Mar. 30, 1808; d., Bolton, Conn., June 10, 1888; buried in Quarryville Cemetery; m. (1), No. Stonington, Dec. 20, 1831, Elias Sprague, of So. Coventry, Conn.; b. Jan. 26, 1793; d., So. Coventry, July 23, 1838; m. (2), No. Stonington, May 6, 1839, Capt. William Hunt, a widower of (Quarryville) Bolton (see Hunt Genealogy, p. 200), b., Bolton, Sept. 5, 1792; d., Bolton, Sept. 29, 1876; buried in Quarryville. Mrs. Hunt inherited her mother's ability as a nurse, and was much sought after in cases of sickness or accident. She was always cheerful and possessed a rare quality of unselfish devotion to the happiness of others.

Dau. by first m. (Sprague), b. So. Coventry:

1041. Elizabeth Freelove, b. July 8, 1833; m. Guilford D. Young (1048–1056).

Children by second m. (Hunt), b. Bolton:

1042. William Harrison, b. Mar. 17, 1840; m. Emma S. Wetherby (1057).

1043. Mary Clarinda, b. Feb. 12, 1842; d. June 21, 1842; buried in Quarryville Cemetery.

1044. Chauncey Tyler, b. June 3, 1843; m. Martha Ann Hodge (1058–1064).

1045. Mary Emeline, b. Oct. 2, 1845; m. Edgar A. Brownell (1065, 1066).

1046. Ralph Ira, b. Aug. 26, 1848; d. Oct. 1, 1849; buried in Quarryville.

1047. Sarah Clarinda, b. Dec. 10, 1849; m. Charles W. Hale (1067).

Elizabeth Freelove Sprague (1041), dau. of Elias Sprague and Clarinda Wells Maine (560), b., So. Coventry, Conn., July 8, 1833; m., Bolton, Conn., Dec. 19, 1853, Guilford D. Young, of Tolland, Conn. Res., 1909, Rosalia, Kan.

Children:

    1048. Ella Elizabeth, b. Sept. 18, 1854.
    1049. George Alfred, b. Oct. 31, 1856.
    1050. Emma Sarah, b. Dec. 3, 1858.
    1051. Charles Sprague, b. July 19, 1861.
    1052. William Lorenzo, b. Feb. 13, 1863.
    1053. Frederick Hunt, b. July 29, 1866.
    1054. Arthur Guilford, b. Jan. 8, 1869.
    1055. Mary Clarinda, b. Aug. 14, 1871.
    1056. Carrie Rebecca, b. Sept. 4, 1874.

William Harrison Hunt (1042), son of Capt. William Hunt and Clarinda Wells Maine (560), b., Bolton, Conn., Mar. 17, 1840; d., Bolton, July 24, 1902; m., New York City, 1862, Emma S. Wetherby. Both are buried in Quarryville Cemetery.

Dau., b. Bolton:

    1057. Lulu Emma, b. July 24, 1872; m. Andrew Rudolph. Children: (1) Emma Marion, (2) Selma Valentine, (3) Louis Andrew. Res., 1909, Hartford, Conn.

Chauncey Tyler Hunt (1044), brother of the preceding, b., Bolton, Conn., June 3, 1843; m., Dec. 29, 1864, Martha Ann Hodge, of Glastonbury, Conn. Res., 1909, Rockville, Conn.

Children, b. Bolton:

    1058. Olin Elijah, b. Dec. 31, 1866; m. Sarah A. Hughes. Children: (1) George, (2) Vera, (3) Mabel. Res., 1909, Hartford, Conn.
    1059. Charles Clinton, b. May 29, 1868; m. Vienna S. Rose. Son: Gilbert Guy. Res., 1909, Brooklyn, N. Y.
    1060. Lena May, b. July 9, 1873; m. George Bartlett. Children: (1) Wallace Earle, (2) Inez, (3) Charles Addison, (4) Rena Arlene, (5) Dorothy, (6) Lindsley Hunt, d. young, (7) Lois May, (8) Mortimer Olin. Res., 1909, Addison, Conn.
    1061. Edith Eola, b. May 29, 1876; m. Harry L. Symonds. Dau.: Doris Eulalia. Res., 1909, Rockville, Conn.
    1062. Eva Belle, b. Sept. 28, 1881; m. William J. Boutelle. Res., 1909, Hartford, Conn.

Dr. C. Wesley Hale
(1067)
Springfield, Mass.
Page 135

Della May (Presbrey), wife of Dr. C. Wesley Hale
(1067)
and daughter, Fiona Presbrey Hale
(1068)
Taken in 1901
Pages 134 and 135

1063. Daisy Viola, b. May 10, 1883. Res., Rockville, Conn.

1064. Raymond Earl, b. Apr. 11, 1888. Res., Rockville, Conn.

Mary Emeline Hunt (1045), sister of the preceding, b., Bolton, Conn., Oct. 2, 1845; m., Bolton, Oct. 7, 1865, Edgar Alonzo Brownell, of Royalston, Vt., who d., Bolton, Mar. 15, 1875, aged thirty-eight years, and is buried in Quarryville Cemetery. Mrs. Brownell res., 1909, at the Hunt homestead, Bolton (Notch), Conn.

Children, b. Bolton:

1065. Mary Estella, b. Jan. 5, 1871; d. Apr. 6, 1871; buried in Quarryville.

1066. Rev. Edgar Alonzo, b. May 16, 1875; d., Granville, Mass., Nov. 28, 1908; buried in Quarryville; m. Ellen Sumner Clark. Children: (1) Laura Sumner, (2) Edgar Clark, (3) Mary Hunt, (4) Amos Chadbourne.

Sarah Clarinda Hunt (1047), sister of the preceding, b., Bolton, Conn., Dec. 10, 1849; m., Bolton, Apr. 21, 1870, Charles Wesley Hale, of West Windsor, Vt., b., Hartland, Vt., Jan. 2, 1838; d., Springfield, Mass., Jan. 4, 1905; buried in Oak Grove Cemetery, Springfield. Mrs. Hale is actively interested in work of the Woman's Christian Temperance Union. Res., 1909, Springfield, Mass.

Son, b. Bolton:

1067. Charles Wesley, b. Feb. 13, 1872; m. Della M. Presbrey (1068, 1069).

Dr. C. Wesley Hale (1067), son of Charles W. Hale and Sarah C. Hunt (1047), b., Bolton, Conn., Feb. 13, 1872; m., Rockville, Conn., July 25, 1894, Della May Presbrey, b., Willington, Conn., May 30, 1873; dau. of Frederick Hunt Presbrey, of Rockville. Dr. Hale was educated at Rockville (Conn.) High School, Wesleyan University, Middletown, Conn., and in 1902 graduated with honors from Harvard University Dental School, receiving the degree of D.M.D. Resides [1909] and has successful dental practice in Springfield, Mass. He has shown a very loyal interest in his ancestry and is the present owner of the homestead of his great-grandparents, Jabish B. (483) and Freelove (Edwards) Maine, of No. Stonington. To him is the compiler indebted for the collection of records and illustrations of Jabish B. Maine (483) and descendants.

Children, b. Springfield:

1068. Fiona Presbrey, b. Jan. 19, 1899.

1069. Charles Wesley, b. and d. Jan. 2, 1904.

Dr. Christopher Ira Maine (561), son of Jabish (483) and Freelove (Edwards) Maine, b., No. Stonington, Conn., Nov. 5, 1810; d., Spencer, N. Y., Nov. 15, 1881; m., 1831, Electa M. Randall, b. Feb. 6, 1807; d. Nov. 9, 1867. Interments in Spencer. Dr. Maine attended Castleton (Vt.) Medical College, from which he graduated, receiving the degree of M.D. He was a skilful physician and built up a very successful practice at Spencer, becoming quite well-to-do. Like his brother, Dr. Jonas C., he possessed some knowledge of law and occasionally defended a case in court.

Children:

 1070. Henry Randall, b. June 27, 1832; d. 1891; m. Lucy Wheeler. Children: (1) Freelove, (2) Ida, (3) Hattie.

 1071. Frances Eliza, b. Feb. 13, 1834; d., Ithaca, N. Y., Sept. 30, 1907; buried in Spencer; m., Dec. 31, 1851, Jesse B. Van Kleeck. Children: (1) Ira, (2) Electa Louisa, (3) Hattie, (4) Charles, (5) Irene Belle.

 1072. Elmina Electa, b. Apr. 1, 1836; m. Jackson Montgomery. Son: George. Res., 1909, Spencer, N. Y.

 1073. Ira Leonard, b. June 5, 1838; m. Mary Woodruff. Children: (1) Luella, (2) Ira, (3) Charles Elmer, (4) Cora Belle. Res., 1909, Van Etten, N. Y.

 1074. Harriet Elizabeth, b. Feb. 12, 1840; d. 1896; m. Elmer Brown. Son: Ira.

 1075. William, b. 1842; m. Susie ——. Children: (1) Nettie, (2) Nellie, (3) Charles Oscar, (4) Jonah Duane.

Judge Sebeus Colver Maine (562), son of Jabish (483) and Freelove (Edwards) Maine, b., No. Stonington, Conn., June 22, 1812; d., Stoughton, Mass., Nov. 25, 1887; buried in Stoughton; m., Sept. 18, 1843, Julia Octavia Stevens, dau. of Caleb Stevens, of Pittston, Kennebec Co., Me. She was b., Pittston, Feb. 27, 1806; d., Boston, Mass., May 2, 1881; buried in Pittston (now Randolph), Maine, Cemetery. Mr. Maine was a prominent lawyer, was judge of the Boston (Mass.) Police Court for many years, and was a member of the Massachusetts Senate in 1855.

Children, b. in Chelsea, Mass.:

 1076. Annie Evans; unm. She lives with her brother at Melrose Highlands, Mass.

 1077. William Studley Bartlett; unm. Mr. Maine is a well-known landscape artist. Res., 1909, Melrose Highlands, Mass.

Dr. Charles O. Maine
(1078)
Stonington, Conn.
Page 137

Dr. Myron M. Maine

(1081)

Office, South Manchester, Conn.

Residence, Bolton, Conn.

Page 138

Sidney Orrison Maine (565), son of Jabish (483) and Freelove (Edwards) Maine, b., No. Stonington, Conn., May 6, 1818; d., No. Stonington, Aug. 20, 1894; m., Nov. 28, 1841, Eliza Lucinda Wentworth, b., Hinsdale, Mass., Apr. 12, 1818; d., No. Stonington, Dec. 2, 1899; dau. of Daniel and Mary (Haradon) Wentworth, who lived at Hinsdale, Mass., and subsequently at Barkhamstead and New Hartford, Conn. Mr. and Mrs. Maine are both buried in the Union Cemetery, No. Stonington. Mr. Maine spent most of his life in No. Stonington, and lived just south of his former home and birthplace. He was a farmer and stone-mason by occupation, also taught successfully many terms in the public schools. In literary taste he was not lacking, and is well remembered as a "spicy" newspaper correspondent.

Children:

1078. Charles Orrison, b., New Hartford, Conn., Apr. 10, 1843; m. Phebe Sarah Main (1083).

1079. Milo Milton, b., Norwich, Conn., Oct. 10, 1845; m. Freelove Margaret Maine (1084, 1085).

1080. Albert Stanley, b., Salem, Conn., Sept. 3, 1848; m. (1) Mrs. Sarah (Kenyon) Partelo; m. (2) Mrs. Ella (Roode) Merritt.

1081. Myron M., b., Salem, Sept. 12, 1850; m. Mary E. Butler.

1082. Oreanna Maria, b., No. Stonington, Feb. 18, 1861; m. (1) Henry M. Newton; m. (2) John Merriss (1086-1089).

Dr. Charles O. Maine (1078), son of Sidney (565) and Eliza (Wentworth) Maine, b., New Hartford, Conn., Apr. 10, 1843; m., Dec. 18, 1866, Phebe Sarah Main (1400), b. June 16, 1845; dau. of Robert P. Main (1394), of Voluntown, Conn. Dr. Maine graduated from Dartmouth College in 1870 with the degree of M.D. and is a popular and successful physician at Stonington, Conn. He has served on the Board of Burgesses and held other important offices in the borough.

Son:

1083. Dr. Charles Everett Maine, b., Voluntown, Nov. 6, 1867; m., June 5, 1889, Susan Marion Miller, of Stonington. Dr. Maine graduated from New York Dental College in 1888, receiving the degree of D.D.S. Res., 1909, and has office in same building with his father, at Stonington, Conn.

Milo Milton Maine (1079), brother of the preceding, b., Norwich, Conn., Oct. 10, 1845; m. Freelove Margaret Maine, b., Bozrah, Conn., Mar. 6, 1835; dau. of Jabez Maine (554). She d., Niantic, R. I., Feb. 17, 1908;

buried in Union Cemetery, No. Stonington, Conn. Mr. Maine is a stone-
mason and blacksmith by trade. Res., 1909, Stonington, Conn.
Children:
    1084. Minnie May.
    1085. Maurice Manning.

Dr. Albert Stanley Maine (1080), brother of the preceding, b., Salem,
Conn., Sept. 3, 1848; m. (1) Mrs. Sarah (Kenyon) Partelo; m. (2) Mrs.
Ella (Roode) Merritt. Dr. Maine is a specialist in the treatment and re-
moval of cancer without the use of the knife. No issue. Res., 1909, West
Mystic, Conn.

Dr. Myron M. Maine (1081), brother of the preceding, b., Salem, Conn.,
Sept. 12, 1850; m., Jan. 5, 1891, Mary E. Butler, dau. of James Butler, of
Ipswich, Mass. Dr. Maine graduated from Baltimore Dental College in
1881 with the degree of D.D.S., taking the first prize for operative skill
demonstrated in competitive examination. No issue. Res., 1909, Bolton,
Conn., and continues successful dental practice at So. Manchester, Conn.

Oreanna Maria Maine (1082), sister of the preceding, b., No. Stonington,
Conn., Feb. 18, 1861; m. (1), No. Stonington, Oct. 26, 1879, Henry M.
Newton, of Voluntown, Conn.; d., No. Stonington, Feb. 11, 1898; m. (2),
Stonington, Conn., Dec. 25, 1904, John Merriss, of Niantic, R. I. Mr.
Merriss has been in the employ of the N. Y., N. H. and H. Railroad Company and its predecessors since 1870. Mrs. Merriss was formerly a school-
teacher. At present, in addition to the duties of home, she is actively interested in the work of the Woman's Christian Temperance Union. Res.,
1909, Niantic, R. I.
    Children, by first m., b. No. Stonington:
        1086. Louis Edwin, b. Nov. 5, 1885.
        1087. Charles Orrison, b. May 5, 1889.
        1088. Clifford Butler, b. Dec. 5, 1891.
        1089. Frank Duane, b. Oct. 30, 1893.

Amos C. Main (494), son of Amos (284d) and Abigail Brown, b., Stonington, Conn., July 3, 1779; m., Stonington, Mar. 29, 1804, Susan Wheeler, b.
May 14, 1783; dau. of Hosea and Bridget (Grant) Wheeler. Mr. Main's
residence was east of the town house in No. Stonington and near the residence of Ephraim Wheeler, for whom the oldest son was named. The
only recollection the compiler has of Mr. Main was of going, when a lad,

with his father to a cottage prayer meeting led by Mr. Main. He remembers all the children, except Nancy B.

Children, b. No. Stonington:

1095. Susan, b. May 24, 1806; m. Capt. David Coats, Jr. (1102–1104).

1096. Bridget Wheeler, b. July 25, 1807; m. Leland D. Miner (1113–1115).

1097. Ephraim Wheeler, b. Oct. 31, 1812; m. Catherine Thompson (1122–1128).

1098. Nancy B., b.——; m. Nathan York, Jr. (1140, 1141).

1099. Ralph H., b. Apr. 13, 1816; m. Elizabeth Irving (1142a).

1100. Cyrus Wheeler, b. May 23, 1822; m. Julia Edgecomb (1143–1145).

1101. Amos, b.——; d. young.

Susan Maine (1095), dau. of the preceding, b. May 24, 1806; d. Jan. 28, 1892; m., No. Stonington, Conn., Oct. 14, 1824, Capt. David Coats, Jr., son of David Coats and Molly Brown. Interment in Wheeler Cemetery, No. Stonington.

Children, b. No. Stonington (see B. G., pp. 99, 100):

1102. Mary Ann, b. Mar. 24, 1826; d. May 14, 1906; m., No. Stonington, Dec. 15, 1846, Allen Wheeler, Jr., b. Aug. 8, 1823; son of Dea. Allen and Jemima A. Wheeler, both of No. Stonington. No issue. Res., 1909, No. Stonington, Conn.

1103. Ralph Coats, b. Apr. 30, 1828; d., Tuckahoe, N. Y., Sept. 23, 1897; m., Norwich, Conn., May 18, 1856, Sarah Miner, née Crandall, dau. of Beriah Crandall; b. Apr. 30, 1823. Mr. Coats removed to Tuckahoe, and was superintendent of the farm of A. T. Stewart, the merchant prince of New York City. Children, b. No. Stonington: (1) Walter Arnold, b. July 15, 1857, d. Mar. 4, 1874; (2) Maria May, b. Apr. 1, 1859; m., Tuckahoe, Feb. 26, 1884, W. R. S. Bates; they have five children. Res., 1909, So. Norwalk, Conn.

1104. Elizabeth Coats, b. July 28, 1832; d. Jan. 28, 1886; m., No. Stonington, Dec. 29, 1852, Ephraim Wheeler, b. Jan. 3, 1831; d. Sept. 23, 1897; son of Ephraim and Bridget (Ayer) Wheeler.

Children, b. No. Stonington:

1105. Mary Elizabeth, b. Aug. 21, 1854; m. Nathan G. Wheeler (1109, 1110).

1106. Martha Hull, b. Oct. 8, 1856; m. Chas. E. Williams (1111, 1112).

1107. Ephraim, 3d, b. Apr. 1, 1861; d. Feb. 20, 1862.

1108. Delia A., b. Oct. 8, 1865; unm. Res., No. Stonington, Conn.

Mary Elizabeth Wheeler (1105), dau. of Ephraim and Elizabeth (Coats) Wheeler, b. Aug. 21, 1854; d. Feb. 3, 1877; m., June 18, 1872, Nathan G. Wheeler, d. Mar. 22, 1882.

Children, b. Stonington, Conn.:

1109. Lucy M. Wheeler, b., Stonington, May 29, 1874; graduated from Smith College 1898; m. James F. Brown, Jr., Nov. 29, 1899; son of Colonel James F. Brown, of No. Stonington. Children: Dorothy W., b. Nov. 23, 1900; Elizabeth, b. Sept. 24, 1902.

1110. Perez Wheeler, b. Feb. 11, 1876; d., Stonington, Dec. 10, 1901; m. Hattie Brown, b., Savannah, Ga., Dec. 9, 1874; sister of James F. Brown, Jr. Son: Ralph Perez, b., Stonington, Feb. 16, 1897. Mrs. Hattie Wheeler, née Brown, m. (2) Isaac Becket. Res., 1909, Savannah, Ga.

Martha Hull Wheeler (1106), dau. of Ephraim and Elizabeth (Coats) Wheeler, b. Oct. 8, 1856; m., No. Stonington, Conn., Jan. 5, 1876, Charles Edwin Williams, b., Stonington, Conn., Jan. 26, 1850. Res., Northampton, Mass.

Children, b. Stonington:

1111. Harriet Atwood, b. May 30, 1877; graduated from Smith College 1898; m., Northampton, July 23, 1904, Charles Anthony De Rose, b., Amherst, Mass., Feb. 17, 1878. Res., 1909, Northampton, Mass.

1112. Nathan, b. Nov. 16, 1878; unm. He is a dentist; graduated from the University of Pennsylvania, May, 1903. Res., 1909, Northampton, Mass.

Bridget Wheeler Maine (1096), dau. of Amos C. (494) and Susan (Wheeler) Main, granddau. of Amos (294d) and Abigail (Brown) Main, b., No. Stonington, Conn., July 25, 1807; d. Oct. 16, 1836; m., No. Stonington, Apr. 15, 1829, Leland Daniel Miner, b., No. Stonington, 1806; son of Saxton and Content (York) Miner, son of Henry and Desire (Brown) Miner.

Children, b. No. Stonington:

1113. Henry Leland, b. Sept. 24, 1832 (1116).

1114. George Hermon, b. Sept. 15, 1834 (1117–1121).

1115. Bridget Wheeler, b. July 18, 1836; d. Sept. 6, 1848.

Ephraim W. Maine Family in 1887

(1097)

Read from left to right: Susan F., Mary T., Nancy W., Herbert E., Elmina C.,
Bessie B., Father and Mother, Grandmother Thompson
(Elmina York), Eldora T.

Page 141

Zebulon York House

North Stonington, Conn.

In this house Elmina York was born, May 4, 1809, who
married Aaron Thompson. It is now [1910]
owned by William Lester Maine (938)

Page 126

Homestead of David Main

(289)

North Stonington, Conn.

Page 74

Henry Leland Miner (1113), son of the preceding, b. Sept. 24, 1832; d., Westerly, R. I., Apr. 6, 1907; m., No. Stonington, Conn., Jan. 5, 1858, Mary Jane Bentley, b., No. Stonington, Sept. 10, 1833; d., Westerly, Mar. 14, 1901; dau. of Russell and Susan (Stanton) Bentley. He was a farmer, a merchant in Westerly, and a Republican. Both were members of the Baptist Church of Westerly. (See B. G., p. 515.)

Dau.:

1116. Jennie Bentley Miner, b., No. Stonington, Oct. 17, 1865; unm.

Rev. George Herman Miner (1114), son of Leland D. and Bridget W. (Main) Miner, b. Sept. 15, 1834; m., Providence, R. I., Aug. 12, 1864, Abby Frances Butts, b., Providence, Aug. 12, 1846; dau. of Edward Perry and Marianne (Bailey) Butts, of New Bedford, Mass. He is a Baptist clergyman, but has now retired from active pastoral service. He graduated from Brown University in 1863; ordained at Central Falls, R. I., in 1864. He held pastorates at Central Falls, Cambridge, and Newburyport, Mass., and New Britain and Mystic, Conn. He went abroad with his family in 1905 and 1906. Res., Mystic, Conn. (See B. G., p. 515.)

Children:

1117. Lillian Burleigh, b., Central Falls, Mar. 14, 1867.
1118. Grace Childs, b., Cambridge, Mar. 18, 1869; d., Newburyport, Jan., 1874.
1119. Bertha, b., Cambridge, Mar. 8, 1871.
1120. Ella Chapman, b., Newburyport, 1873; d., Newburyport, Jan., 1874.
1121. George Leland, b., Newburyport, Nov. 11, 1875.

Ephraim Wheeler Maine (1097), son of Amos C. (494) and Susan (Wheeler) Main, b., No. Stonington, Conn., Oct. 31, 1812; d., No. Stonington, June 29, 1894; m., No. Stonington, Nov. 5, 1845, Catherine Thompson, dau. of Aaron and Elmina (York) Thompson, b., No. Stonington, Mar. 3, 1826; d. Apr. 20, 1909. Mr. Maine owned the farm that formerly belonged to Ephraim Wheeler, where he resided with his family for twenty-two years. It is one of the most beautiful and picturesque locations in No. Stonington, where the compiler of this book lived from 1845 to 1848, and he finds it a pleasure to look backward to those happy days. Mr. Maine lived a good, clean, quiet, and unassuming life, and exerted a good and lasting influence on the community. Mrs. Maine ably sustained her part in the home, both living devout Christian lives. They were, with their children, valuable members of the Third Baptist Church. (See B. G., pp. 517, 518.)

Children, b. No. Stonington:

1122. Elmina Catherine, b. Oct. 1, 1846; m. Rev. B. F. Arnold (1129, 1130).

1123. Herbert Ephraim, b. Mar. 9, 1849; m. Clara E. Horton (1131).

1124. Nancy Wheeler Maine, b. Jan. 19, 1856; m., No. Stonington, May 12, 1891, Rev. Benjamin Allen Green, b., Harrison-ville, R. I., Nov. 6, 1846; son of Alvin and Maria (Arnold) Green, of Westerly, R. I. He was a graduate of Brown University and Newton Theological Institution. He has had pastorates at Westboro and Lynn, Mass. At the latter place he remained sixteen years. He commenced his third pastorate at Evanston, Ill., Mar., 1897. No issue.

1125. Susan Florence, b. Feb. 8, 1858; m. Edgar O. Silver (1132–1138).

1126. Eldora Thompson Maine, b. Oct. 17, 1862; unm. She is a school-teacher, having taught in Brookline, Mass., Buffalo, N. Y., and Bryn Mawr, Tenn. In 1905 she was associated with her sister, Mary Talulah, in their College Preparatory School at Brentwood Hall, So. Orange, N. J. Later they located at Lawrence Park, Bronxville, N. Y.

1127. Bessie B. Chapman Maine, b. June 30, 1866 (1139).

1128. Mary Talulah Maine, b. Oct. 6, 1869; unm. She is a graduate of Wellesley College, and has taught in Stamford, Conn., and Chelsea High School, Chelsea, Mass.

Elmina Catherine Maine (1122), dau. of Ephraim W. (1097) and Catherine (Thompson) Maine, b., No. Stonington, Conn., Oct. 1, 1846; m., No. Stonington, Jan. 1, 1868, Benjamin Franklin Arnold, b., So. Kingstown, R. I., Apr. 8, 1834; son of George and Charlotte (Gardner) Arnold. In connection with his brother-in-law, Herbert E. Maine, they conducted a wholesale grocery and tea house, under the firm name of Arnold & Maine, at Providence, established in 1860, with branches at Pawtucket, R. I., and Worcester, Mass. Mr. Arnold is a deacon of the Cranston St. Baptist Church. (See B. G., p. 520.) Res., Providence, R. I.

Children:

1129. Kate Arnold, b., No. Stonington, May 27, 1871; d., Button-woods, R. I., Aug. 31, 1906.

1130. Margaret Arnold, b., Providence, Oct. 29, 1875; m., Providence, Apr. 10, 1901, John Davis Edmands Jones, b.,

Worcester, Feb. 4, 1872; son of Preston and Ella (Johns) Jones. Mr. Jones is an insurance agent. He and his wife are members of the Baptist Church. Children: (1) John Davis Edmands Jones, Jr., b., Providence, Mar. 22, 1902; (2) Arnold Wheeler Jones, b., Providence, Mar. 2, 1904; (3) Meredith Wharton Jones, b., Buttonwoods, Aug. 4, 1906. Res., Providence, R. I.

1130a. Franklin Herbert Arnold, b., Providence, Apr. 23, 1878.

Herbert Ephraim Maine (1123), son of Ephraim W. (1097) and Catherine (Thompson) Maine, b., No. Stonington, Conn., Mar. 9, 1849; m., Providence, R. I., Jan. 29, 1879, Clara Eldora Horton, b., Dover, N. H., Feb. 19, 1858; dau. of Alfred Ziba and Mary Ann (Goodwin) Horton. In his young manhood he was a school-teacher at No. Stonington, and superintendent of the Sunday school. After his removal to Providence he was deacon of the Cranston St. Baptist Church, and superintendent of its Sunday school for many years. He is a merchant. (See above.) Res., Parade St., Providence, R. I.

Dau.:

1131. Bertha Maine, b. Aug. 29, 1880; d. Mar. 12, 1881.

Susan Florence Maine (1125), sister of the preceding, b., No. Stonington, Conn., Feb. 8, 1858; m., Providence, R. I., Jan. 4, 1888, Edgar Oscar Silver. He is a graduate of Brown University, and a member of the publishing-firm of Silver, Burdett & Co., of New York, Boston, and Chicago. Mrs. Silver is a graduate of Wellesley College. Res., East Orange, N. J.

Children:

1132. Katherine Silver, b. Aug. 5, 1890.
1133. Anne Louise Silver, b. June 25, 1892.
1134. Edgar Oscar Silver, Jr., b.——
1135. Helen Florence Silver, b.——
1136. Priscilla Warren Silver, b.——
1137. Geraldine Silver, b.——
1138. Blanche Silver, b.——

Bessie B. Chapman Maine (1127), sister of the preceding, b., No. Stonington, Conn., June 30, 1866; m., No. Stonington, Aug. 6, 1890, Rev. Freeman Tupper Whitman, b. Milton, Nova Scotia; son of Nathan T. and Matilda (Freeman) Whitman, of Milton. He graduated from Worcester Academy, from Brown University, and from Newton Theological Institution. He was pastor of the Baptist Church at Newton Upper Falls, Mass.; seven years at Brighton Ave. Baptist Church, Boston; four years at English Church, Rangoon, Burmah; five years at Framingham, Mass.; his last pastorate at Valley Falls, R. I.

Dau.:

1139. Elizabeth Wave Whitman, b., No. Stonington, Dec. 26, 1891.

Nancy B. Main (1098), dau. of Amos C. (494) and Susan (Wheeler) Main; granddau. of Amos and Abigail (Brown) Main; b. No. Stonington, Conn.; d., No. Stonington, Feb. 20, 1841; m., No. Stonington, Nathan York, Jr., b., No. Stonington, Sept. 16, 1811; d. Nov. 13, 1855. Mr. York was a farmer and a school-teacher; in politics, a Whig. Both he and his wife were members of the Baptist Church.

Children, b. No. Stonington:

1140. Charles Caisus, b.——

1141. Calvin, b.——

Nathan York, Jr., m. (2) Harriet Brown, of No. Stonington.

Dau.:

1142. Martha B. York, m. Edwin White.

Ralph H. Maine (1099), brother of the preceding, b., No. Stonington, Conn., Apr. 13, 1816; d., Vineland, N. J., July 5, 1886; m., Hartford, Conn., Dec. 24, 1846, Elizabeth C. Erving. Rev. Ralph H. Maine commenced his preparatory course for college in 1840, at the Connecticut Literary Institution at Suffield, and entered Trinity College in 1842, graduating in the class of 1846, receiving the degree of A.B. He accepted a call to the Baptist Church at Tariffville, Conn., where he was ordained May, 1846. He was chaplain at the State Reform School at Meriden for three and one-half years. In 1857 he accepted a recall to Tariffville church. He was pastor at Bloomfield and Plainville, Conn. He was pastor at Sandisfield for eight years. He served as pastor for two churches, No. and So. Colebrook, for three years. All his pastorates and other labors were attended with blessed revivals, and converts were gathered into the churches. For the last seven years of his life he lived at Vineland, N. J., much encumbered with bodily infirmities. His last days were full of peace and hope. He calmly made all his arrangements for the expected change, even selecting the hymns to be sung at his funeral. Interment in Cedar Hill Cemetery, Hartford, Conn.

Dau.:

1142a. Flora, b.——; d. 1856, aged seven years.

Cyrus Wheeler Maine (1100), son of Amos C. Main (494) and Susan Wheeler; grandson of Amos (284d) and Abigail (Brown) Main; b., No.

Stonington, Conn., May 23, 1822; d., Providence, R. I., July 14, 1894; m., No. Stonington, Oct. 28, 1847, Julia Edgecomb, b., No. Stonington, Dec. 22, 1825; d., Providence, Oct. 23, 1870; dau. of Nathan Edgecomb. Interments in No. Stonington (Yaubux). Mr. Maine and his wife, as the compiler remembers them in the "forties," were among the highly esteemed young people of our town; but with later years, and removals into sterner active life, he has no further recollection. Both were active Christian young people in their home life.

Children:

    1143. Henry M. Maine, b., No. Stonington, July 27, 1849.

    1144. Ella Maine, b., Stonington, Conn., Dec. 9, 1858 (1146).

    1145. William E. Maine, b., Providence, Jan. 31, 1870 (1147-1150).

Henry Miller Maine (1143), son of Cyrus W. and Julia (Edgecomb) Maine, b. July 27, 1849; m. (1), Providence, R. I., Jan. 25, 1870, Ellen M. Williams, b. Providence; d., Providence, Feb. 12, 1871; dau. of Joshua and Abby Williams, of Providence. Both were members of the Roger Williams Church. He m. (2), Hartford, Conn., Apr. 6, 1872, Lavinia N. Wyant, b. New York City; d., Providence, Oct. 15, 1904. He m. (3), New Bedford, Mass., Nov. 11, 1905, Jennie Richardson, b. New Bedford; dau. of Marcus and Abby (Reed) Richardson. Mr. Maine was a member of the City Council. He is engaged in the Steam Carpet Cleaning and Rug Weaving Works at New Bedford. No issue.

Ella Maine (1144), sister of the preceding, b., Stonington, Conn., Dec. 9, 1858; before her marriage she lived in Stonington and No. Stonington; m., Providence, R. I., June 15, 1881, William D. Walker, b., Providence, Aug. 8, 1859; son of Ezra Ide and Margaret (Lambert) Walker, of Providence. Mr. Walker in politics is a Democrat. Both he and his wife are members of the Calvary Baptist Church of Providence. He secured his education in the public schools of Providence. He was in the carriage business from 1877 to 1890; then private secretary to Mayor Potter of Providence for two years; clerk of the Committee on Finance of Rhode Island Legislature, House of Representatives, 1893, 1894; Assistant Postmaster at Providence from 1895 to 1901; bookkeeper for L. Candee, New Haven, Conn., from 1904 to the present time. He is Past Grand of Crescent Lodge No. 24, I. O. O. F. of Providence. Res., 285 York St., New Haven, Conn.

Son:

    1146. Ralph E., b., Providence, June 28, 1883.

William E. Maine (1145), son of Cyrus W. and Julia (Edgecomb) Maine, b., Providence, R. I., Jan. 31, 1870; m., No. Attleboro, Mass., June 25, 1895, Harriet F. Horton, b., No. Attleboro, Feb. 10, 1872; dau. of Francis E. and Lydia M. (Leming) Horton. Mr. Maine in politics is an Independent. Both he and his wife are members of the Baptist Church. In his boyhood days he lived with his parents in No. Stonington, Conn.; later, in Providence, where he received his education. At the age of eighteen he entered the employ of Arnold & Maine, his cousins, and was with them a number of years; now [1909] in the employ of Shepard and Co., Providence. Mrs. Maine received her education in No. Attleboro, where she lived until her marriage. She graduated from the grammar and high schools. Res., Wendell St., Providence, R. I.

Children, b. Providence, except the second:

    1147. Herbert Francis, b. May 10, 1896.
    1148. Henry Cyrus Leming, b., No. Attleboro, Apr. 24, 1898.
    1149. Lydia Harriet, b. Dec. 3, 1903.
    1150. Meredith Julia, b. May 19, 1908.

John Main (273), son of Jeremiah (260) and Mrs. Ruth (Brown) Main, b., Stonington, Conn., May 20, 1716; m., Nov. 8, 1738, Sarah Morgan.

Children:

    1151. Judith, b. July 31, 1739.
    1152. John, b. Feb. 12, 1741.
    1153. Jonathan, b. Feb. 12, 1743.
    1154. Caleb, b. Apr. 18, 1745.
    1155. Sarah, b. Oct. 5, 1750.

Peter Main (274), son of Jeremiah (260) and Mrs. Ruth (Brown) Main, b., Stonington, Conn., Aug. 5, 1718; m., Sept. 17, 1740, Mary Eggleston.

Children:

    1156. Peter, b. July 9, 1741; d. young.
    1157. Peter, b. July 9, 1742 (1167–1177).
    1158. Joseph, b. Feb. 14, 1744; d. young.
    1159. Mary, b. Jan. 16, 1746.
    1160. Asa, b. June 17, 1748.
    1161. Lucy, b. Nov. 4, 1750; d. young.
    1162. Joseph, b. Apr. 4, 1753.
    1163. Sands, b. Feb. 5, 1756.
    1164. David, b. Aug. 21, 1761.
    1165. Lucy, b. Mar. 18, 1764.
    1166. Prudence, b. Mar. 7, 1768.

Peter Main (1157), son of Peter (274) and Mary Eggleston, b., Stonington, Conn., July 9, 1742; m. Patience Eggleston, b. June 6, 1744.
Children, b. Stonington:

    1167. Peter, b. Dec. 4, 1765.

    1168. Agnes, b. Aug. 4, 1767.

    1169. Joseph, b. Sept. 21, 1769.

    1170. Philena, b. May 12, 1771.

    1171. Polly, b. May 9, 1774.

    1172. Amos, b. Aug. 16, 1776; m. Abigail Slocum (1178-1191).

    1173. Jared, b. Jan. 22, 1778; m. Patience Eggleston (1403-1409).

    1174. John, b. Apr. 6, 1780; m. (1) Ellen Lewis; m. (2) Maria Geer; m. (3) Hannah Palmer.

    1175. Deborah, b. May 6, 1782.

    1176. David, b. Aug. 20, 1784 (1392-1399).

    1177. Prudence, b. May 3, 1789.

Amos Main (1172), son of Peter Main (1157) and Patience Eggleston, b., Stonington, Conn., Aug. 16, 1776; d. June 9, 1855; m. (1), Dec. 25, 1797, Abigail Slocum, b. May 9, 1776; d. Sept. 4, 1837. He m. (2), Sept. 24, 1843, Mary A. Burton, b.——; d. Apr. 3, 1892. This family lived the most of their days at the old homestead near Laurel Glen, Conn., just over the line in Hopkinton, R. I. [Dates from Azariah Main's Bible.]
Children by first m.:

    1178. Amos S., b. Nov. 25, 1798; d. Nov. 27, 1852.

    1179. Carey C., b. Dec. 6, 1799. In early life went West.

    1180. William, b. May 9, 1801. He also went West.

    1181. Azariah, b. Aug. 29, 1802; m. Philura Slocum (1192-1202).

    1182. Prudence, b. Jan. 28, 1804.

    1183. John, b. June 16, 1805; m. Charlott Main (1203-1210).

    1184. Eunice, b. Apr. 10, 1807.

    1185. Mary (twin), b. July 4, 1808.

    1186. Silence (twin), b. July 4, 1808; m. Alfred Rounds. They went West.

    1187. Henry, b. Sept. 3, 1811; d. Jan. 25, 1869.

    1188. Samuel, b. Aug. 29, 1814.

    1189. Hannah, b. Oct. 14, 1817.

Children by second m.:

    1190. Stephen A., b. June 18, 1844; d. Feb. 8, 1863.

    1191. Thomas Dorr, b. Dec. 19, 1845, the only survivor in 1909.
          [Dates of children from Amos Main's Bible.]

Azariah Main (1181), son of Amos (1172) and Abigail (Slocum) Main,
b., Stonington, Conn., Aug. 29, 1802; d. Oct. 23, 1872; m. Philura Slocum,
b. Aug. 23, 1805. [Records from Azariah Main's Bible.]
Children:

1192. Charles Cranston, b. Nov. 9, 1826; d. Aug. 17, 1865; unm.
1193. Emily Maria, b. Jan. 29, 1828; d. June 25, 1853; m. Henry C. Geer (1210a–1210c).
1194. Frances Elizabeth, b. May 9, 1830; m. Abram Coon (1211–1213).
1195. William Tyler, b. Mar. 11, 1832; d.——, aged two years.
1196. Ebenezer Franklin, b. Feb. 4, 1834; d.——, aged forty; unm.
1197. Susan Jane, b. July 22, 1837; unm. Miss Main gave the compiler all the links to this family tree. Res., Westerly, R. I.
1198. Lydia Abby, b. Jan. 9, 1839; m. James Sheffield (1214).
1199. James Monroe, b. Jan. 4, 1842; m. Sarah A. Smith (1217–1219).
1200. Jesse Babcock, b. Mar. 8, 1844; m. Maggie Livingstone (1224, 1225).
1201. Phydelia Catharine, b. Aug. 8, 1846; d. Providence, R. I.; m. Feb. 28, 1876, John R. Holberton. No issue.
1202. William Diton, b. Dec. 8, 1856; d. Dec. 12, 1869.

John Main (1183), son of Amos (1172) and Abigail (Slocum) Main, b·
June 16, 1805; m. Charlott Main, his cousin, dau. of John and Ellen
(Lewis) Main.
Children:

1203. Ellen, b.——
1204. Martha Ann, b.——
1205. Abby, b.——
1206. Hannah Frances, b.——
1207. Lorinda, b.——
1208. Melvina, b.——
1209. Curtis J., b.——; d. Jan. 27, 1908.
1210. Carey A., b., Westerly, R. I., Mar. 9, 1845; m., Hopkinton, R. I., May 12, 1866, Margaret Maria Kenyon, b. June 16, 1849; dau. of Benjamin F. and Mary Catherine (Langworthy) Kenyon. Mr. Maine is the only survivor of his brothers and sisters. He is employed at the Cotterell Machine-shops for the manufacture of printing-presses. He is a Seventh-Day Baptist, and is constant in church work.

Mrs. Maine is an excellent singer and has had a long experience in training children in singing and arranging for Sabbath-school concerts. Both are members of the Seventh-Day Baptist Church, Westerly, R. I. No issue.

Emily Maria Main (1193), dau. of Azariah (1181) and Philura (Slocum) Main, b. Jan. 29, 1828; d. June 25, 1853; m. Henry C. Geer, b. 1826; d., No. Stonington, Conn., 1908. He was an active member of the Third Baptist Church.

Children, b. No. Stonington (Laurel Glen):

    1210a. Fanny Emily Geer, b. Mar. 14, 1850; m., No. Stonington. Sept. 26, 1887, George W. Stone, b., Marlboro, Mass., 1862. Divorced. Son: George H., b., No. Stonington. Aug. 6, 1888. Res., No. Stonington, Conn.

    1210b. Mary L. Geer, b. Jan. 12, 1851; d., Westerly, R. I., Apr. 5, 1905; m., Voluntown, Conn., Jan. 11, 1873, Frank H. Brown, b., Voluntown, Sept. 14, 1851; son of Smith and Rebecca (Miner) Brown. They had two children that d. young. Res., No. Stonington, Conn. (See B. G., p. 155.)

    1210c. David S. Geer, b. Feb. 1, 1853; unm. He is a mariner.

Frances Elizabeth Main (1194), dau. of Azariah (1181) and Philura (Slocum) Main, b., No. Stonington, Conn., May 9, 1831; d. Apr. 6, 1892; m., Stonington, Conn., Sept. 2, 1849, Abram Coon, b. Feb. 22, 1824; d.——- Mr. Coon was a mariner and spent his last days on Beach St., Westerly, R. I. He had in his yard — and they are still there — a boat, capstan, wheel, and other marine paraphernalia. He was accustomed to sit on the piazza and think of his seafaring life, as hale and hearty as if he would last for many years; but suddenly he was gone from his accustomed seat.

Children:

    1211. Edward Oliver, b., No. Stonington, Nov. 9, 1850; m., Providence, R. I., Sept. 27, 1875, Melissa Card. No issue.

    1212. Charles Franklin, b., Westerly, July 21, 1853; unm. Mr. Coon is superintendent of Wilcox Park, the munificent gift of Mrs. Stephen Wilcox to the town of Westerly, with perpetual care.

    1213. Eugene Willard, b., Westerly, Oct. 9, 1857; m., June 11, 1882, Julia Etta Miller. Mr. Coon was Chief of Police in Westerly for ten years. He is now Deputy Sheriff of Washington Co., R. I. Children, b. Westerly: (1) Julia Ethel, b. Feb. 7,

1885, d. Dec. 15, 1885; (2) Charles Eugene, b. May 12, 1887; (3) Daisy Elizabeth, b. Mar. 17, 1891. Res., Westerly, R. I.

Lydia Abby Main (1198), dau. of Azariah (1181) and Philura (Slocum) Main, b., No. Stonington, Conn., Jan. 9, 1839; m., Hopkinton, R. I., May 9, 1858, James Sheffield, b., Richmond, R. I., Jan. 18, 1838; son of Samuel and Amy (Browning) Sheffield. He is a farmer, a Republican, and a member of the Friend Society. They attend the First Day Church of Hopkinton.

Son:

    1214. George F. Sheffield, b., No. Stonington, Mar. 18, 1859; m., Locustville, R. I., Dec. 24, 1882, Annie Martha Palmer, b., Hopkinton, Dec. 6, 1864; dau. of Peter P. and Caroline (Chappell) Palmer. Mr. Sheffield is a Republican. His wife is a member of the Baptist Church. Res., Westerly, R. I.

Children:

    1215. Elizabeth Adella, b., Richmond, Oct. 30, 1888.

    1216. James Palmer, b., Hopkinton, Mar. 12, 1891.

James Monroe Maine (1199), son of Azariah and Philura (Slocum) Main, b., Hopkinton, R. I., Jan. 4, 1842; m., No. Stonington (Clark's Falls), Conn., Aug. 11, 1866, Sarah Ann Smith, b., Voluntown, Conn., Mar. 21, 1844; dau. of David Smith, of Chesham, England, and Eunice Palmer. Mr. Maine is a farmer. His wife is a member of the First Baptist Church. Both were educated in the public schools, and Mrs. Maine took a course at the East Greenwich Academy, R. I. They lived after marriage at Minneapolis, Waltham, Mower Co., and Austin, Minn., for seventeen years, returning to No. Stonington, where they now reside.

Children:

    1217. Ida Bell, b., Minneapolis, Minn., Oct. 28, 1872 (1220, 1221).

    1218. Edna Violet, b., Waltham, Minn., Sept. 13, 1876; m. Reuben D. Cook. (See 400.)

    1219. Jesse James, b., Waltham, Feb. 21, 1879 (1222, 1223).

Ida Bell Maine (1217), dau. of the preceding, m., Laurel Glen, Conn., June 5, 1894, Elnathan Burdick, b., Stonington (Pawcatuck), Conn., June 18, 1865; son of Benjamin F. and Rozanna (Mitchel) Burdick. Mr. Burdick was educated in the public schools of his native town, and for sixteen years was a member of the life-saving station at Watch Hill, R. I. Mrs.

Burdick was educated in the public schools of Mower Co., Minn., and No. Stonington, Conn. She also took a business college course at Norwich, Conn. Both are members of the Baptist Church. Res., Westerly, R. I.

Children, b. Westerly (Watch Hill):

    1220. Harry Elnathan, b. Jan. 14, 1896.

    1221. Lloyd Erwin, b. Dec. 25, 1898.

Edna Violet Maine (1218), sister of the preceding, b., Waltham, Minn., Sept. 13, 1876; m., Hopkinton, R. I., May 10, 1903, Reuben D. Cook (400), b., No. Stonington (Pendleton Hill), Conn., Sept. 21, 1881; son of James M. and Annie (Ryder) Cook, of Pendleton Hill. Mrs. Cook is a member of the Pendleton Hill Baptist Church. No issue. Res., Westerly, R. I.

Jesse James Maine (1219), brother of the preceding, b., Waltham, Minn., Feb. 21, 1879; m. (1), Westerly, R. I., May 30, 1900, Margaret F. Farrell, b., Westerly, Feb. 16, 1880; d., Stonington (Lower Pawcatuck), Conn., Apr. 26, 1901. He m. (2), Stonington, Conn., June 21, 1903, Maggie May Cahoon, dau. of Stephen and Matilda (Abbey) Cahoon. Mr. Maine is an iron-moulder and a farmer. Res., Hopkinton, R. I.

Children, by second m., b. Stonington:

    1222. Lawrence E., b. Sept. 16, 1904.

    1223. Dorothy Marguerite, b. Mar. 8, 1906.

Jesse Babcock Maine (1200), son of Azariah and Philura Slocum, b., No. Stonington, Conn., Mar. 8, 1844; d., Westerly, R. I., Oct. 5, 1887; m., No. Stonington, Oct. 25, 1866, Margaret Livingstone, b., Scotland, May, 1846; d., Hopkinton, R. I., Apr. 19, 1895. He was a blacksmith at the quarries in Westerly, and a Republican.

Children:

    1224. Charles Fredrick, b., Ashaway, R. I., Jan. 19, 1869; unm. In young manhood he worked for James S. Brown (71), and went with him to France and Austria in the interest of racing-horses. He is now in the public market, Providence, R. I.

    1225. Jennie Elizabeth, b., Westerly, Oct. 6, 1879; m., Westerly, Dec. 19, 1900, Charles G. Turner, b., New London, Conn., Mar. 15, 1874; son of Charles R. and Helen A. (Champlin) Turner, of Westerly. He is a motorman on the electric cars. Both he and his wife were educated in the public schools of Westerly, and practically lived there all their lives. Mr. Turner is a member of the Baptist Church. No issue.

John Main (1174), son of Peter (1157) and Patience (Eggleston) Main, b., Stonington, Conn., Apr. 6, 1780; m. (1) Ellen Lewis; m. (2) Maria Geer; m. (3) Hannah Palmer, b., No. Stonington, Conn., July 26, 1806; d., No. Stonington, May, 1867; dau. of Oliver Palmer and Nancy Crandall Utter. Children by first m., b. No. Stonington:

> 1226. John Main, Jr., b.——; m. Mrs. Philura (Palmer) Hood.
>
> 1227. Charlott Main, b.——; m. John Main (1183), son of Amos Main (1172), her cousin (1203-1210).
>
> 1228. George Main, b.——; m. Julia Slocum (1263-1270).
>
> 1229. William Main, b.——; m. Ann Main. Children: Elizabeth and Ellen. All deceased.
>
> 1230. Lewis Main, b.——
>
> 1231. Mary A. Main, b. June 16, 1815; m. Benjamin F. Newton (1271-1278).
>
> 1232. Dorcas Main, b.——; m. Wilbur Eccleston. Children: (1) Emily, b.——, m. Oliver Maine, a cousin; (2) Sarah, b.——; m. David Johnson, of Ashaway, R. I.

Dau. by second m.:

> Mary, b.——; d.——, aged nine years.

Children by third m., b. No. Stonington (Laurel Glen), except the first two:

> 1233. Charles Main, b. Aug. 14, 1829; m. Catherine Urguhard (1293-1297).
>
> 1234. Lester Main, b., Griswold, Conn., Oct. 19, 1831; m. Thankful Eggleston (938-945).
>
> 1235. Ruth C. Main, b. 1833; m. Enoch Burrows Eccleston (1298-1303).
>
> 1236. Thomas T. Main, b. July 26, 1835; m. Susan Harris (1321-1326).
>
> 1237. Abram B. Main, b. May 20, 1837; d. Sept. 23, 1895; m., Voluntown, Conn., Frances A. Chesbro, b. Nov. 16, 1844. No issue. Interment in Union Cemetery.
>
> 1238. N. Peter Main, b.——; m. Sarah Stillman, of Ashaway, R. I. Both are deceased. They were members of the M. E. Church.
>
> 1239. Joseph Main, b.——; d. a young man; unm.

John Main, Jr. (1226), son of John (1174) and Ellen (Lewis) Main, b. 1808; d., No. Stonington, Conn., Apr. 16, 1865; m. Mrs. Philena (Palmer) Hood, twin sister to John Main's (1174) third wife, Hannah

Palmer; b., No. Stonington, July 26, 1806; d., No. Stonington, June 12, 1875; dau. of Oliver and Nancy Crandall (Utter) Palmer. Interments in Union Cemetery, No. Stonington. Philena Palmer m. (1) John Hood. By this marriage there were three children: Leonard, John, and James Hood. They lived in Bridgeport, Conn.

Children:

1240. Nancy P. Maine, b., No. Stonington, Jan. 25, 1837; d. Apr. 17, 1879; m. Simeon P. White, of No. Stonington. Son: Clark P., b. Nov. 13, 1857.

1241. Oliver P. Maine, b., No. Stonington, Oct. 6, 1838; d. Apr. 9, 1900; m. Emily Ecclestone, b. Mar. 19, 1840. Children: (1) Sarah Leona, b. June 30, 1865, m., Jan. 30, 1884, Everett Brown, of Ashaway, R. I.; (2) Mertie Olive, b. Aug. 7, 1880; m., Sept. 20, 1906, William Pickering, of Clarks Falls, Conn.

1242. Ellen Maine, b., Voluntown, Conn., Sept. 10, 1840; unm. Res., Laurel Glen, Conn.

1243. Hannah Maine, b., No. Stonington, Apr. 17, 1843; d. July 25, 1875; m. Henry F. Geer, of No. Stonington. Children: (1) Herbert F., b. Nov. 12, 1861, d., aged three years; (2) Lena E., b. July 13, 1865, m. William Jordan; she d. soon after her marriage; (3) John H., b. Nov. 7, 1873. Res., No. Stonington, Conn. (4) Henrietta, b. June 7, 1875; m. William Avory, of Westerly, R. I.

1244. Lois Maine, b., Richmond, R. I., Dec. 17, 1846; m. (1) Gilbert Holdredge, of No. Stonington; m. (2) Perry Maine, of No. Stonington. No issue.

1245. Nathan T. Maine, b., Exeter, R. I., Apr. 11, 1848; m. Oceana B. Smith (1247–1254).

1246. Andrew J. Maine, b., Exeter, Oct. 24, 1849; m. Loansa Foster, dau. of Lawton and Nancy (Worden) Foster. Children: (1) Welcome Maine, of Hope Valley, R. I.; (2) Nancy Maine; unm. Res., Conanchet, R. I.

Nathan T. Maine (1245), son of John Maine, Jr., and Mrs. Philura (Palmer) Hood, b. Apr. 11, 1848; m. Oceana B. Smith, b., No. Stonington, Conn., May 29, 1853; dau. of David and Eunice (Palmer) Smith, of No. Stonington. Mr. Maine is a Republican, and both he and his wife are members of the Laurel Glen Baptist Church. Mrs. Maine rendered valuable assistance in furnishing the records of John Main (1174) and his descendants.

Children, all b. No. Stonington (Laurel Glen):

   1247. Attaway T., b. June 19, 1872; m. Wealthea Holdredge (1255-1257).

   1248. Jessie E., b. Nov. 17, 1874; d. Jan. 9, 1875.

   1249. Charlie R., b. Sept. 7, 1876; d. Aug. 16, 1896.

   1250. Idella C., b. June 12, 1878; d. July 31, 1891.

   1251. Leonard W., b. June 27, 1880; m. Jessie Bliven (1258, 1259).

   1252. Stella M., b. Mar. 17, 1883; m. F. Howard Martin (1260-1262).

   1253. Nathan Frank, b. Oct. 10, 1885; m., Westerly, R. I., Dec. 14, 1907, Alice James. Mr. Maine is a machinist, and both he and his wife are members of the Baptist Church. Res., Hope Valley, R. I.

   1254. H. Clyde, b. Mar. 23, 1892.

Attaway T. Maine (1247), son of Nathan T. Maine (1245), b., Laurel Glen, Conn., June 19, 1872; m., Laurel Glen, Sept. 27, 1896, Wealthea Holdredge, b. No. Stonington, Conn.; dau. of Charles P. and Lydia (Lewis) Holdredge. Mr. Maine is a farmer, and both he and his wife are members of the Baptist Church, Laurel Glen.

Children:

   1255. Charles A., b., La Fayette, R. I., Mar. 6, 1898.

   1256. Paul M., b., La Fayette, Oct. 16, 1899.

   1257. Gilbert C., b. Clarks Falls, Conn., June 29, 1903.

Leonard W. Maine (1251), brother of the preceding, b., Laurel Glen, Conn., June 27, 1880; m., Wood River Junction, R. I., May 17, 1904, Jessie Bliven, b. Charlestown, R. I.; dau. of Frank and Minnie (Crandall) Bliven, of Charlestown. He is an operator in a textile mill, and a member of the Baptist Church. Res., Sawyer St., New Bedford, Mass.

Children, b. Potter Hill, R. I.:

   1258. Leonard LeRoy, b. Mar. 16, 1905.

   1259. Vernon Winfield, b. May 24, 1907.

Stella M. Maine (1252), sister of the preceding, b. Mar. 17, 1883; m., Laurel Glen, Conn., Apr. 6, 1902, F. Howard Martin, son of Frank Martin, of Potter Hill, R. I.

Children:

   1260. Vera Irene, b. Aug. 9, 1903.

   1261. Helen Julia, b. Sept. 22, 1904.

   1262. Harry Alfred, b. Aug. 8, 1908.

George Main (1228), son of John (1174) and Ellen (Lewis) Main, b.——; m. Julia Slocum.

Children, b. No. Stonington, Conn.:

    1263. Lovina, b.——; m. Edward Peckham.

    1264. Louisa, b.——; m. John P. Burdick, of Ashaway, R. I.

    1265. George L., b.——; m. Alace Matilda Hall.

    1266. Alonzo V., b.——; m. Alzada Baton. Res., Conanchet, R. I.

    1267. Calvin, b.——; d., aged twelve years.

    1268. Hannah E., b. Oct. 11, 1850; m. Henry F. Babcock (1270a, 1270b).

    1269. Stephen, b.——; deceased.

    1270. Emma, b.——; m. Ralph Kenyon.

Hannah Ellen Maine (1268), dau. of George (1228) and Julia (Slocum) Main, b., No. Stonington, Conn., Oct. 11, 1850; m., Aug. 12, 1871, Henry F. Babcock, b., No. Stonington, Aug. 18, 1846; son of Hoxie and Elizabeth (White) Babcock.

Children, b. No. Stonington:

    1270a. Arthur, b. Dec. 14, 1872; m. Daisy Burdick.

    1270b. Pearl, b. Apr. 30, 1880; d., No. Stonington, Sept. 13, 1898.

Mary A. Main (1231), dau. of John Main (1174) and Ellen Lewis, b., No. Stonington, Conn., June 16, 1815; d. May 8, 1855; m., No. Stonington, Benjamin F. Newton, b. June 14, 1816; d., Hopkinton, R. I., Nov. 24, 1856. He was a farmer, and both he and his wife were members of the Baptist Church of Hopkinton. His death was accidental. He was drawing a cart through a gateway with the tongue on his shoulder when one wheel struck the gate-post, throwing him down, and the cart-pin at the end of the tongue penetrated his skull.

Children, b. Hopkinton:

    1271. Nathan F., b. Nov. 13, 1839; m. Mary Jane Chappell (1279, 1280).

    1272. Elijah Palmer, b. Jan. 19, 1841; m. Emma Morris Edwards (1281).

    1273. Mary M., b. Mar. 24, 1842; d. Jan. 13, 1844.

    1274. Mary E., b. Dec. 2, 1843; m. Samuel Thomas Merritt (1282, 1283).

    1275. Susan Jane, b. Aug. 16, 1847; d. Mar. 6, 1850.

    1276. Sarah Ann, b. June 27, 1848; m. (1) George Gray; m. (2) John Lee. Res., Potter Hill, R. I.

1277. Jane Frances, b. Mar. 11, 1852; m. Mark Bennett. Son: Mark
Newton Bennett.

1278. George S., b. Aug. 7, 1853 (1284-1286).

Nathan Franklin Newton (1271), son of Benjamin F. Newton and Mary
A. Main (1231), b. Nov. 13, 1839; m., Richmond, R. I., Nov. 10, 1861,
Mary Jane Chappell. Mr. Chappell is a farmer in So. Canterbury, Conn.
Children:

1279. Eva Mary, b., Hopkinton, R. I., Sept. 6, 1863 (1287–1289).

1280. Frank Henry, b., Mystic, Conn., July 31, 1866 (1290–1292).

Elijah Palmer Newton (1272), brother of the preceding, b., Hopkinton,
R. I., Jan. 19, 1841; d. in the Civil War unknown (the last known of him his
regiment was ordered to the front); m., Westerly, R. I., Mar. 11, 1860,
Emma Morris Edwards, b., Charlestown, R. I., Sept. 4, 1842; dau. of John
and Mary A. (Salvastor) Edwards. He was a farmer and a Republican,
and both he and his wife members of the Baptist Church.

Son:

1281. William Francis Newton, b., Hopkinton, May 6, 1862; m.,
Orange, Mass., Sept. 15, 1890, Fanny Ellen Morse, b.,
Winchendon, Mass., Aug. 22, 1867. Rev. Mr. Newton was
among the first students at Mount Hermon, Mass., the
school founded by Rev. Dwight L. Moody. He was ordained
at Charlemont, Mass., Sept. 17, 1890, and the same month
and year they went as missionaries and teachers to the
Indian Territory, at the Dower Academy. But under the
hardships in this country, living on coarse food (hoe-cake
and salt pork three times a day, and nothing else) Mrs.
Newton's health broke down. His salary for the year
amounted to four dollars and seventy-five cents. In 1891
they went to Nebraska for the American Baptist Home
Missionary Society, having charge of five churches, driving
more than five thousand miles the first year. His field was
larger than the State of Rhode Island. In 1894 they went
to Oklahoma and built up a strong church among the
Indians. Later they were engaged in evangelistic work in
the West and East.

In 1905 Mr. Newton went as singer to California with
Rev. Howard W. Pope, secretary of the Northfield Extension
Movement. In 1906 they began work at New London,

William Francis Newton
(1281)
The Evangelist
Page 156

The set of china, of which this cup and saucer were originally a part, consisted of twelve cups and saucers, twelve custard-cups, a tea-pot, sugar-bowl, cream-jug, slop-bowl, two cake-plates, and a tray.

It was bought in Baltimore, about the year 1820, by Nathan Stewart, who, with his daughter Elizabeth, stopped in the city for some time. They lodged in the house of an Irishwoman of the " reduced gentlewoman " type, who owned this and a quantity of other china. She sold the set to Nathan Stewart for fifty dollars. In 1824 the china was billed to Arnold R., Daniel B., and Elizabeth Stewart, who lived together at Middlebury, Ohio. In 1902 this bill was still in existence, and in the possession of Frances Hinkley, of Ripon, Wisconsin, a niece of Elizabeth Stewart.

Upon Elizabeth Stewart's death, in 1878, the china was bought by her sister Abby Stewart Perry, who kept one-half of the pieces, giving the remainder to the third sister, Eunice Hinkley, excepting only one piece, which was given to Anna Maria Wright, of Cleveland, a half-sister.

The daughters of Eunice Hinkley, Elizabeth Burdick and Frances Hinkley, inherited their mother's share of the china; and in November, 1902, they gave the cup and saucer illustrated to Jennie Stewart Briggs, of Los Gatos, California. The photograph of this china was made in December, 1902, at West Union, Iowa, by Bertha Stewart Quigley.

At the time of the purchase by Nathan Stewart, in 1820, the seller declared the china to be sixty years old. This was probably not true, as the decoration marks it as of the period of the Empire. The ware is exquisite — fine and thin. The color is an intense cobalt blue, traced all over with grapes, leaves, and tendrils in burnished gold. The medallions have each a different subject, but all represent the use of some musical instrument. The color on the checks of the figures is so vivid that it appears black in the photograph. The ware is not marked, but is probably Sèvres.

Conn., in the old Second Baptist Church, which was sold. He then organized a Sunday school in a tent, with fourteen scholars. During the year the school enrolled 272 scholars. From this beginning was founded the Montauk Avenue Baptist Church, which enrolls one of the largest Sunday schools in the State. They are still in evangelistic work in New England, under the direction of Rev. A. B. Coats, D.D. No issue. Res., New London, Conn.

Mary Elizabeth Newton (1274), dau. of Benjamin F. Newton and Mary A. Main (1231), b., Hopkinton, R. I., Dec. 2, 1843; m., Hopkinton, Oct. 24, 1861, Samuel Thomas Merritt, b., No. Stonington, Conn., Feb. 12, 1839; divorced. Son of Samuel Merritt, b. Apr. 12, 1804, d. Sept. 19, 1889, and Sarah G. Thomas, b. Apr. 12, 1807; d. Aug. 28, 1903. He was a farmer, and both he and his wife members of the Seventh-Day Baptist Church.

Children, b. No. Stonington, Conn.:

Twin sons, b. June 9, 1862; d. in infancy.

1282. Lillian Malena, b. Aug. 25, 1863; m. Dexter R. Porter.

1283. Edwin Thomas, b. May 13, 1867; d., Stonington, Sept. 21, 1879.

Mrs. Mary E. Merritt, née Newton (1274), m. (2), Westerly, R. I., Sept. 22, 1877, Charles Stebbins, b., East Lyme, Conn., Aug. 15, 1839. He was in the Civil War; enlisted in Co. G, 8th Regt. Conn. Vol., Sept. 19, 1861; discharged Dec. 20, 1863, by reason of reënlistment in Veteran Volunteers in same company and regiment, and was discharged from the service of the United States Aug. 20, 1865, at New Haven, Conn. Res., Westerly, R. I.

George Sheffield Newton (1278), son of B. F. Newton and Mary A. Main (1231), b., Hopkinton, R. I., Aug. 7, 1852; m., Westerly, R. I., Mar. 25, 1876, Fannie Maria Lewis, b., Hopkinton, May 3, 1857; d., Wakefield, R. I., Mar. 18, 1900; dau. of Maxson and Clara (Gates) Lewis, of Hopkinton. Mr. Newton is a Republican; by occupation a carriage-maker. Both he and his wife are members of the Seventh-Day Baptist Church. Res., Manton, R. I.

Children, b. Hopkinton:

1284. William Benjamin Newton, b. Apr. 4, 1881; m., Providence, R. I., Sept. 14, 1903, Florence Hortense Kenyon, b., Cranston, R. I., Dec. 30, 1881. He is a machinist. Children: (1) Barbara Fannie, b., Providence, June 14, 1904; (2) George Kenyon, b. Dec. 11, 1905; d., Wakefield, Sept. 6, 1908.

1285. Earl Maxson Newton, b. Aug. 13, 1884.
1286. Clara Lewis Newton, b. May 29, 1887; m., Providence, June 6,
1908, Thomas Carroll Rodman, b., Wakefield, Aug. 27,
1883.

Eva Mary Newton (1279), dau. of Nathan Franklin (1271) and Mary J.
(Chappell) Newton, b., Hopkinton, R. I., Sept. 6, 1863; m., Hopkinton,
July 3, 1883, Frank Hoxsie, b., Richmond, R. I., son of Enoch F. and Susan
T. (Johnson) Hoxsie. He is a merchant, a Republican, and was Judge of
Probate for eight years. He was elected town clerk and treasurer in 1897,
and still holds those offices in 1909. Both he and his wife are members of
the Congregational Church. Res., Canterbury, Conn.
Children:
1287. Ruby Geneva, b., Hopkinton, Aug. 20, 1887; d., Canterbury,
July 3, 1889.
1288. Howard Franklin, b., Stonington, Conn., May 12, 1891.
1289. Paul Henry, b., Canterbury, Sept. 13, 1897.

Frank Henry Newton (1280), brother of the preceding, b., Mystic, Conn.,
July 31, 1866; m., July 31, 1886, Ida J. Palmer. Mr. Newton is a farmer
in So. Canterbury, Conn.
Children:
1290. Richard Emery, b. Apr. 19, 1888.
1291. Frank Ellwood, b. Sept. 21, 1893.
1292. Harold Leslie, b. Aug. 19, 1895.

Lillian Malena Merritt (1282), dau. of Samuel T. and Mary E. (Newton
1274) Merritt, b., No. Stonington, Conn., Aug. 25, 1863; m., Stonington,
Conn., May 20, 1891, Dexter Rupert Porter, b., Kentville, Nova Scotia,
May 20, 1864; son of Truman A. and Harriet R. (Strong) Porter, of Saugus,
Mass. He is engaged in the dry-goods business. He was manager of Boston
Store, Westerly, R. I., for the J. H. Thorpe estate, from 1895 to 1901; then
of the firm of Walcott & Porter, Boston Store Co., from 1901 to 1903,
when stock was burned Dec. 23, 1903. He was proprietor of Boston Store
from 1904 to 1907. Member of Stonington Board of Education, 1903–1908;
and Board of Relief, 1904. He was ordained deacon of the First Baptist
Church, Westerly, Mar. 14, 1905, and was prominent in church work.
His wife was an able coadjutor in all church work. No issue.

Charles Main (1233), son of John (1174) and Hannah (Palmer) Main,
b., No. Stonington, Conn., Apr. 14, 1829; m., Stonington, Conn., 1859,

Catherine Urguhard, b., Edinburgh, Scotland, Sept. 22, 1832; d., Waltham, Minn., June 14, 1901; dau. of Alexander Urguhard, of Scotland. Mr. Main lived in No. Stonington until 1861; then removed to Wisconsin, where he lived until 1874; then removed to Minnesota, and lived there till 1901; then to Liberty, Mo., where he now resides.

Children, b. Wisconsin:

1293. Charles A. Main, b. May 10, 1862; m., Grand Meadow, Minn., Carrie Orwick, b. Sept. 13, 1865. Children: (1) E. Carl, b.——; d. Dec. 15, 1908, aged twenty years; (2) Ella, b. Oct. 4, 1887; m.——; lives in Minneapolis, Minn. Her husband is a policeman.

1294. Edgar Main (twin), b. Sept. 13, 1865; m. Lilly Bailey, b., Winterset, Ia., May 22, 1871. Mr. Main is a civil engineer. Children: (1) Roland, b. Apr. 21, 1893; (2) Sibyl, b. July 29, 1896; (3) Edgar, b. Apr. 11, 1899. Res., Liberty, Mo.

1295. Edwin Main (twin), b. Sept. 13, 1865; m. Minnie Lurvey, b., Sumner, Mo., Sept. 14, 1872. He is a civil engineer. Son: Howard, b. Dec. 8, 1896. Res., Rockford, Ill.

1296. Frank Main, b. Mar. 27, 1868; m. A. Mary Tilton, b., Brownsdale, Minn., July 16, 1869. Mr. Main is in the insurance business. No issue. Res., Minneapolis, Minn.

1297. Mary E. Main, b. Dec. 12, 1870; unm.

Ruth C. Main (1235), dau. of John (1174) and Hannah (Palmer) Main, b., No. Stonington, Conn., 1833; d. 1894; m. Enoch Burrows Eccleston. He was a farmer; in politics, a Republican. His wife was a member of the Baptist Church. Interment in Union Cemetery.

Children:

1298. Hannah Frances, b., No. Stonington, 1851; d. 1875.

1299. Charles Henry, b., No. Stonington, Nov. 15, 1855 (1304-1314).

1300. Abby Louanza, b., No. Stonington (1315, 1316).

1301. Latham Hull (twin), b., Columbia Co., Wis., Sept. 21, 1862 (1317-1320).

1302. William Jesse (twin), b., Columbia Co., Sept. 21, 1862; d. in infancy.

1303. William Clark, b., 1869; d. in infancy.

Charles Henry Eccleston (1299), son of Enoch B. and Ruth C. (Main 1235) Eccleston, b., No. Stonington, Conn., Nov. 15, 1855; drowned, Wickford, R. I., Sept. 1, 1898; m., Viana, Dane Co., Wis., Mar. 25, 1875,

Lillie Victoria Welch, b., Wisconsin, June 5, 1856; dau. of William and Eliza Welch.

Children, the first four b. Waltham, Mower Co., Minn.; the last six b. So. Kingston, R. I.:

    1304. William Burrows, b. Mar. 21, 1876.
    1305. Jessie Maud, b. Dec. 4, 1877.
    1306. Edwin Wallace, b. Oct. 19, 1879.
    1307. Estelle Geneva, b. Oct. 27, 1881.
    1308. Alice Victoria, b. Oct. 7, 1884.
    1309. Charles Latham, b. July 14, 1888.
    1310. George Ellsworth, b. Jan. 16, 1893.
    1311. Lois Angeline, b. Sept. 16, 1894.
    1312. Eveline Francis } twins, b. Oct. 7, 1897.
    1314. Ethel Gladys }

Abby Louanza Eccleston (1300), sister of the preceding, b. No. Stonington, Conn.; d., No. Stonington, Dec. 30, 1902; m., Oct. 9, 1879, George Washington Edwards. Res., Ashaway, R. I.

Children:

    1315. Fannie E., b. Oct. 5, 1880.
    1316. Ruth M., b. Apr. 21, 1882.

Latham Hull Eccleston (1301), son of Enoch B. and Ruth C. (Main) Eccleston, b., Columbia Co., Wis., Sept. 21, 1862; m., No. Stonington, Conn., Dec. 25, 1879, Ella Evangeline Lewis, b., Sterling, Conn., Jan. 28, 1859; dau. of Charles H. and Hannah B. (Locke) Lewis. He is an engineer. Res., Wakefield, R. I.

Children:

    1317. Charles Latham, b., Laurel Glen, Conn., Aug. 8, 1881; d. Oct. 19, 1882.
    1318. Dencie Frances, b., Woodville, R. I., June 5, 1887.
    1319. George Harrison, b., Lafayette, R. I., Feb. 17, 1890.
    1320. Hazel Dean, b., Rocky Brook, R. I., Oct. 6, 1898.

Thomas T. Maine (1236), son of John (1174) and Hannah Palmer Main, b., No. Stonington, Conn., July 26, 1835; m., Hopkinton, R. I., Dec. 31, 1856, Susan Harris, b. Oct. 4, 1837. Mr. Maine was a farmer, a Democrat, and both he and his wife members of the Baptist Church, No. Stonington. Res., Laurel Glen, Conn.

Children, first three and sixth b. No. Stonington (Laurel Glen):

    1321. David T., b. Apr. 29, 1858; m. Phebe E. Davis (1327–1330).

1322. Elmer E., b. July 17, 1861; m. Nellie Kilkenney. Son: John E., b. Mar. 17, 1882. Res., Clarks Falls, Conn.

1323. Sarah L., b. July 30, 1864; m. Edward Larkin; deceased. Children: (1) Bernice; (2) Son, b.——; d. in infancy.

1324. Ida M., b., Charlestown, R. I, July 16, 1868; m. George Barber, Jr., of So. Coventry, Conn. Children: Ida, Ethel, and Charley Barber.

1325. Mary E., b., Hopkinton, Aug. 6, 1870; d., Laurel Glen, 1879.

1326. Susie B., b. Mar. 17, 1873; d., Laurel Glen, 1879.

David T. Maine (1321), son of Thomas T. and Susan Harris Maine, b. Apr. 29, 1858; d., Noank, Conn., Dec. 13, 1907; m., Westerly, R. I., Sept. 4, 1881, Phebe E. Davis, b., Old Mystic, Conn., May 8, 1863; dau. of Phineas and Annie A. (Carpenter) Davis. Both secured common-school educations, and after marriage lived in different places, worked in mills, and later had charge of farms. The past eleven years he worked in the shipyard at Noank. He was held in high respect by all who knew him. He was a member of the Junior Order of American Mechanics. Her res., Noank, Conn.

Children:

1327. George Edgar, b., No. Stonington, Conn., Dec. 4, 1882; m., Groton, Conn., Sept. 4, 1904, Martha May Chapman. Children: (1) George Edgar, Jr., b. Dec. 31, 1905; (2) David E., b. Nov. 11, 1908.

1328. Ida May, b., Old Mystic, May 6, 1888.

1329. Lewis Curtis, b., Noank, Sept. 9, 1891.

1330. Gertrude Estelle, b., Noank, Sept. 22, 1904.

Ada Main (873), dau. of Nathaniel Main (290) and Abigail Thurston, b., Stonington, Conn., 1790; m., Stonington, Oct. 28, 1810, Israel Palmer Park, b. July 20, 1774; d., No. Stonington, Conn., Mar. 2, 1858; son of Melvin Park, son of Peter Park, who m., Nov. 24, 1771, Margaret Palmer; d. Sept. 5, 1804. This was Israel P. Park's second marriage. His home was west of the "Ash Schoolhouse." He is remembered as " Esq. Parks."

Children, b. No. Stonington:

1331. Alvin Hart, b. Aug. 12, 1811; m., May, 1835, Martha A. Perry. They went West; had four children.

1332. Bielby Porteus, b. May 6, 1813; m. Nancy W. Main (1339-1345).

1333. Clarissa Maria, b. Dec. 13, 1814; m. Denison W. Miner. (See Miner family, 203–207, p. 41.)

1334. Dewitte Ripley, b. Nov. 12, 1816; m. Harriet O. Chapman (1346-1348).

1335. Elbert Orrin, b. Jan. 2, 1819; m. Fanny E. Park (1349-1352).

1336. Faxon Burrows, b. Nov. 11, 1822; m. Cynthia A. Smith (1353-1357).

1337. Lucy Caroline, b. July 14, 1824; m. Jesse B. Slocum (1358-1360).

1338. Leroy, b. July 11, 1826; m. Harriet A. Stanton (1361-1367).

Bielby Porteus Park (1332), son of Israel Palmer Park and Ada Main (871), b., No. Stonington, Conn., May 6, 1813; d. July 19, 1873; m., Jan. 22, 1843, Nancy W. Main.

Children:

1339. William F., b. Nov. 3, 1843.

1340. George I., b. Oct. 29, 1845.

1341. Theodore Orrin, b. Jan. 24, 1848; m. Mary W. Wolfe (1368-1371).

1342. Israel P. Park, b. Sept. 8, 1850; m., Apr. 8, 1877, Emma Brown. Dau.: Nettie B., b. June 6, 1878.

1343. Bielby P. Park, b. May 19, 1853.

1344. Ada N., b. Apr. 22, 1855.

1345. Cora A., b. Apr. 10, 1860.

Clarissa Maria Park (1333), sister of the preceding, b., No. Stonington, Conn., Dec. 13, 1814; d. Dec. 29, 1897; m., May 20, 1832, Denison W. Miner (177), b. Dec. 13, 1809; d., No. Stonington, May 27, 1886; son of Isaac Miner (p. 39) and Katurah Brown. (See Miner family, p. 41.)

Dewitte Ripley Park (1334), brother of the preceding, b. Nov. 12, 1816; d. June 26, 1866; m., Sept. 22, 1847, Harriet O. Chapman. They lived near Wyassup Pond.

Children, b. No. Stonington, Conn.:

1346. John Palmer, b. Feb. 18, 1851; d. Jan. 31, 1854.

1347. Amos Ripley, b. Nov. 26, 1858.

1348. Georgie Belle, b. Aug. 25, 1864.

Elbert Orrin Park (1335), brother of the preceding, b. Jan. 2, 1819; m., Feb. 19, 1843, Fanny E. Park. He was tax-collector for No. Stonington a number of years.

Children:

1349. William Williams, b. Apr. 15, 1845; m., Mar., 1869, Martha W.

Swan. Children: (1) H. Lina, b. Jan. 2, 1871; (2) Elbert Orrin, b. July 15, 1875.

1350. Ann Elizabeth, b. Oct. 29, 1849; m., Oct. 29, 1867, Silas H. Browning. Children: (1) Esther Jane, b. May 17, 1869, d. Apr., 1880; (2) Daniel Lewis, b. Mar. 11, 1874; (3) Elbert Orrin, b. July 17, 1875; d. Aug. 28, 1875.

1351. Emogene, b. Sept. 3, 1857.

1352. Orrin Ray, b. Feb. 18, 1861.

Faxon Burrows Park (1336), brother of the preceding, b., No. Stonington, Conn., Nov. 12, 1822; d. Mar. 26, 1893; m., Nov. 5, 1851, Cynthia A. Smith, b. Apr. 22, 1832. Mr. Park was a farmer, a blacksmith, and a wood-worker; and, with the exception of a few years passed in New York prior to his marriage, always made his home in Stonington and No. Stonington. They lived at the Isaac Miner farm for fifteen years. (See Miner family, p. 39.)

Children:

1353. Eliza Ann, b. Nov. 5, 1852; m. Albert Badeau Gallandet (1372).

1354. Burrows Ripley, b. Oct. 31, 1855; m. Aurelia Eunice Perry (1373, 1374).

1355. Leander Faxon, b. Aug. 11, 1857; m., Nov. 7, 1900, Harriet Eliza Pendleton.

1356. Charles Alvin, b. Oct. 13, 1863; d. Sept. 21, 1877.

1357. Ella Louise, b. Dec. 14, 1867; m. Andrew Wheaton Perry (1375-1377).

Lucy Caroline Park (1337), dau. of Israel P. Park and Ada Main (871), b., No. Stonington, Conn., July 14, 1824; m. Jesse B. Slocum.

Children:

1358. Lucy Ursula, b. May 1, 1846; m. Courtland P. Miner. (See Miner family, p. 46, and 1378-1381b.)

1359. Ann Elizabeth, b. Dec. 31, 1847.

1360. William Israel, b. Mar. 15, 1853.

Leroy Park (1338), son of Israel P. Park and Ada Main (871), b., No. Stonington, Conn., July 11, 1826; d., Ashaway, R. I., Aug., 1900; m., Nov. 15, 1852, Harriet A. Stanton, dau. of Joshua C. and Harriet (Hewitt) Stanton. He was given the old homestead of his father in No. Stonington.

He was a farmer, a Republican, and both he and his wife were members of the Baptist Church.

Children, b. No. Stonington:

1361. Harriet Ada, b. Feb. 3, 1854; m. Henry B. Kenyon (1382–1387).

1362. George Palmer, b. May 12, 1857; unm.

1363. Benjamin F., b. Jan. 29, 1860; d. Dec. 11, 1876.

1364. Mary Emily, b. Oct. 10, 1862; m. Calvin A. Snyder (1391, 1392).

1365. James Alfred, b. Nov. 3, 1865; m. Res., Ashaway, R. I.

1366. Carrie Ida, b. July 16, 1868; m.

1367. Fred Walter, b. Oct. 2, 1871; m., 1902, Grace Manwaring, b., Van Buren, N. Y., Oct. 28, 1881. Children: Bertha L., b., Ashaway, R. I., Dec. 20, 1904; Ella, b. Feb. 22, 1907; d. in infancy.

Theodore Orrin Park (1341), son of Bielby P. (1332) and Nancy W. (Main) Park, b. Jan. 24, 1848; m., June 20, 1872, Mary W. Wolf.
Children:

1368. Reuben Palmer, b. Oct. 21, 1873; d. June 8, 1874.

1369. Elizabeth Nancy, b. Aug. 28, 1875; m., May 31, 1905, Arthur W. Kesler.

1370. Emma Leona, b. Dec. 22, 1877.

1371. Theodore Orrin, Jr., b. Nov. 22, 1879.

Eliza Ann Park (1353), dau. of Faxon Burrows (1336) and Cynthia A. (Smith) Park, b. Nov. 5, 1852; m., Mar. 2, 1877, Albert Badeau Gallandet.
Dau.:

1372. Alice Louise, b. July 5, 1881; m., Dec. 5, 1900, Frederick W. Hewitt. Son: Reginald G., b. Mar. 20, 1903.

Burrows Ripley Park (1354), son of Faxon Burrows (1336) and Cynthia A. (Smith) Park, b., No. Stonington, Conn., Oct. 31, 1855; m., Waterford, Conn., Apr. 12, 1894, Aurelia Eunice Perry, dau. of Almond F. Perry, of Waterford. Mr. Park received his education in his native town, at the Westerly High School, and at the East Greenwich Academy, R. I. He learned the wheelwright and blacksmith trades of his father, and for a while lived in New York City. In 1888 he bought the Stephen Main saw and grist mill in No. Stonington, in partnership with his father; and later, for three years, his brother Leander F. Park was associated with him in business. He gives his undivided attention to furnishing ship timber, railroad timber, shingles, telegraph-poles, etc. He gives employment to from ten to fifty men, as the business demands, and by systematic business methods has met with encouraging success, and has before him a bright future.

Children, b. No. Stonington:

1373. Ruby Rillie, b. Sept. 27, 1896.
1374. Burrows Ripley, b. Mar. 27, 1903.

Ella Louise Park (1357), sister of the preceding, b. Dec. 14, 1867; m., Oct. 19, 1892, Andrew Wheaton Perry.

Children:

1375. Burrows Bertie, b. Nov. 15, 1897.
1376. Mildred Louise, b. Aug. 31, 1902.
1377. Annie Phelps, b. Oct. 26, 1903.

Lucy Ursula Slocum (1358), dau. of Jesse B. and Lucy C. (Park) Slocum, b., No. Stonington, Conn., May 1, 1846; m., May 20, 1866, Courtland P. Miner, son of Palmer N. and Martha P. (York) Miner.

Children, b. No. Stonington (see Miner Records, p. 46):

1378. George P., b. Feb. 20, 1867; unm.
1379. Charles E., b. Aug. 31, 1868; m. Maria Gore (248-250).
1380. Willie J., b. Aug. 4, 1872; m. Addie R. Pierce (251-253).
1381. Nellie May, b. May 16, 1875; m. S. Curtis Eggleston (254, 255).
1381a. Anna Grace, b. Jan. 3, 1880; m. Charles H. C. Miner (256).
1381b. Arthur Courtland, b. Oct. 26, 1885; m. Anna M. Chapman (257).

Harriet Ada Park (1361), dau. of Leroy Park (1338) and Harriet A. Stanton, b., No. Stonington, Conn., Feb. 3, 1854; m., Hopkinton, R. I., Nov. 21, 1874, Henry B. Kenyon, b., Canonchet, R. I., Jan. 17, 1847; son of Augustus R. and Fidelia (Burdick) Kenyon. They resided in No. Stonington after marriage, except four years in Voluntown, Conn.; then removing, Mar., 1890, to So. Canterbury, Conn., where they now reside. He is a farmer, a Republican, and both he and his wife are members of the Congregational Church. The twenty-fifth anniversary of their marriage was a memorable and interesting occasion. (See Babcock Records, p. 31.)

Children, the first three and sixth b. No. Stonington:

1382. Jennie Ada, b. Nov. 23, 1875; m., Jan. 1, 1902, Walter Lincoln Burdick, of Rockville, R. I. Mrs. Burdick is a member of the Congregational Church. Son: Perle Lincoln, b., Canterbury, Conn., June 5, 1904. Res., New London, Conn.

1383. Charles Henry, b. June 10, 1878; m., Apr. 16, 1902, Bertha Christiana Kempel, of New York City. No issue. Res., Groton, Conn.

1384. Birdie May, b. Dec. 29, 1879; m. Stephen R. Babcock (1388–1390).

1385. Son, b., Voluntown, Oct. 27, 1884; d. Jan. 31, 1885.

1386. Clyde Wallace, b., Voluntown, Oct. 4, 1886.

1387. Vinnie Maud, b. June 27, 1888.

Birdie May Kenyon (1384), b. Dec. 29, 1879; m., Canterbury, Conn., Apr. 6, 1898, Stephen Richard Babcock, b., Plainfield, Conn., Feb. 6, 1870; son of William S. (53, p. 27) and Frances E. (Maine) Babcock. Mrs. Babcock is a member of the Congregational Church. Res., Plainfield, Conn.

Children, b. Plainfield:

1388. Ella May, b. Jan. 25, 1899.

1389. Ruby Ada, b. July 22, 1903.

1390. Richard Stewart, b. Oct. 31, 1906.

Mary Emily Park (1364), dau. of Leroy (1338) and Harriet A. (Stanton) Park, b., No. Stonington, Conn., Oct. 10, 1862; m., No. Stonington, Nov. 5, 1885, Calvin A. Snyder, b., Reading, Penn., Jan. 1, 1858; son of Reuben and Rebecca (Rhodes) Snyder, of Reading. He is a Republican, and both he and his wife are church-members. The first ten years of his life he lived in Philadelphia, Penn. He received a common-school education and attended the Westerly High School. After finishing his school course he faithfully performed the duties of grocery-clerk for twenty-one years, his genial manner making for him many friends. He represented his town in the State Legislature two consecutive terms, 1905–1907. He has successfully filled the offices of Town Clerk and Town Treasurer for nineteen years, and Judge of Probate for twelve years. He is an active member of the Congregational Church, and assistant superintendent of the Sunday school. He is a member of the Narragansett Lodge I. O. O. F. of Westerly, and of the No. Stonington Grange No. 138.

Children, b. No. Stonington:

1391. Carlton A., b. Oct. 25, 1886.

1392. Grace Louise, b. Jan. 26, 1891.

Here end the records of Ada Main (871) and the Park family.

Note.— The David Main family (1176) should have followed No. 1330, or preceded the Park family; but for convenience it is placed after No. 1392. In all cases follow the numbers.

David Main (1176), son of Peter Main (1157) and Patience Eggleston, b., Stonington, Conn., Aug. 20, 1784; m. (1), Nov. 21, 1811, Dorcas Palmer, b. Aug. 20, 1785; dau. of Stephen and Dorcas (Burdick) Palmer, m. Dec. 12, 1784. David Main m. (2), July 16, 1843, Sally Newton.

Children by first m.:

    1392a. Matilda, b. Apr. 3, 1812; m. Nathan Edwards.

    1393. Lucy, b., June 15, 1813; m. Isaac Edwards.

    1394. Robert Palmer, b. Aug. 16, 1814; m. Phebe Esther Edwards (1400, 1401).

    1395. David, b. July 11, 1819; m. Sarah Palmer.

    1396. Sands, b. Oct. 6, 1821; m. Maria Perry.

    1397. Stephen, b. Dec. 4, 1822; unm.

    1398. Dorcas, b. Dec. 17, 1825; m. (1) Wm. Main; m. (2) Frank Main.

    1399. Elijah, b. Oct. 12, 1827; unm.

Children by second m.:

      Silas.

      Moses.

Robert Palmer Main (1394), son of David Main (1176) and Patience Eggleston, b. Aug. 16, 1814; d., Voluntown, Conn., June 9, 1897; m., Oct. 15, 1843, Phebe Esther Edwards, b. Aug. 26, 1824; d., Stonington, Conn., Jan. 24, 1902; dau. of Nathan Edwards and Sarah Main; granddau. of Phineas Edwards and wife Mary; great-granddau. of Christopher Edwards and Phebe Wells.

Children:

    1400. Phebe Sarah, b. June 16, 1845; m. Dr. Charles O. Maine (1078).

    1401. Crawford Reynolds, b. Feb. 25, 1847; d. Oct. 8, 1877; m. (1), Nov. 7, 1869, Hattie Maria Tucker, d. Sept. 21, 1875; m. (2), Sept. 25, 1876, Abby Saunders, d. June 7, 1885.

Dau., by first m.:

    1402. Gertrude Louise Maine, b. Mar. 7, 1873; m., June 29, 1898, Hiram Justin Latham. Dau.: Muriel, b. June 6, 1900. Res., Stonington, Conn.

Jared Main (1173), son of Peter Main (1157) and Patience Eggleston, b., Stonington, Conn., Jan. 22, 1778; m., Stonington, by Joshua Babcock, Esq., Sept. 10, 1801, Abigail Eccleston.

THE EZEKIEL MAIN FAMILY

Children, b. Stonington:
1403. Jared, Jr., b. Mar. 18, 1802; m.——; d. Interment, Laurel
Glenn, Conn. Dau.: Nancy Main, m. Charles Harrington.
He was a very large man. Children, lived in Nebraska:
Charles, b.——, was in the Civil War and d. in the service;
William, b.——, lived in David City, Neb.; Olney, b.——,
lives in David City; dau., b.——; d. Through her influence her father became a minister in Nebraska. [The
family did not answer queries.]
1404. John Van Rensselaer, b. Jan. 12, 1806.
1405. Filena, b. June 13, 1807.
1406. Ira, b. Mar. 11, 1810; m. Martha A. Harvey (1505–1511).
1407. Almina, b. Mar. 8, 1811; m. Ira Winsor (1540–1542).
1408. Gersham, b. Mar. 11, 1814.
1409. Peter Nelson, b. Mar. 23, 1816.
Other children, Nancy, William, and David.

Lewis Main, Jr. (364), son of Lewis (315) and Hannah (Ray) Main, b.,
No. Stonington, Conn., June 9, 1804; d., Griswold, Conn., Sept. 16, 1880;
m., Preston, Conn., May 29, 1836, Cynthia Hewitt Stewart, b., New York
State, Oct. 12, 1812; d., East Berlin, Conn., Mar. 20, 1891; dau. of George P.
and Mary (Hewitt) Stewart, of No. Stonington. She is sister to Elizabeth
Stewart, m. Stephen Main (324). They lived in No. Stonington until 1861;
then moved to Plainfield, Conn.; in Apr., 1878, moved to Griswold. They
were at one time, with all their children, members of the Union Baptist
Church, Plainfield, Conn. He was much esteemed in all the relations of
life, and his moral and social endowments won for him the sincere respect
of all his acquaintances. In front of his father's house he set out two pop-
lar trees, which made the place conspicuous for miles around; but they have
long since disappeared. Interments in Moosup, Conn.
Children, b. No. Stonington, or just over the line, in Voluntown, Conn.:
1410. Cynthia Ann Maine, b. July 6, 1837; m. Isaac E. Avery, b.,
Montville, Conn., May 2, 1839; d., No. Stonington, Dec. 31,
1897. His death was accidental, he being thrown from a
wagon at Laurel Glen, Conn. He was the son of Isaac B.
and Mary (Hyde) Avery, of Montville. Mr. Avery's mother
had passed away the day before his sudden death. She was
ninety-seven years old. Mr. Avery was a farmer. He and
his wife members of the Baptist Church. No issue. Res.,
Middletown, Conn.

168

Hermon Clinton Maine
(1443)
Page 169

Lewis Avery Main
(1429)
Cedar Rapids, Ia.
Page 171

1411. George Lewis Maine, b. Dec. 21, 1839; d. Sept. 23, 1842.
1412. Ellen Winthrop Maine, b. Aug. 16, 1843; unm. Miss Maine
   completed her education at the Plainfield Academy, and began teaching when fifteen years of age, teaching in No.
   Stonington, Plainfield, Sterling, and Middletown, Conn.,
   and continued for thirty years. She furnished all the records
   of her father's family. Res. with her sister Cynthia, 228
   Main St., Middletown, Conn.
1413. Hermon Clinton Maine, b. Oct. 28, 1846 (1416-1418).
1414. Alice Leonora Maine, b. July 21, 1851; m. Albert McBay
   (1419, 1420).
1415. Emily Augusta Maine, b. June 10, 1853; m. Judson Davis
   (1421-1424).

Hermon Clinton Maine (1413), son of Lewis Main, Jr. (364), and Cynthia
Hewitt Stewart, b., No. Stonington, Conn., Oct. 28, 1846; d., Middletown,
Conn., Oct. 9, 1906; m. (1), Putnam, Conn., Oct. 21, 1874, Esther A. Cole,
b., Plainfield, Conn., Dec., 1843; d., Moosup, Conn., Apr. 9, 1877; dau. of
Warren Cole, of Moosup. He m. (2), East Berlin, Conn., Sept. 13, 1883,
Clara Augusta Bowers, b., East Berlin, Aug. 19, 1855; dau. of Newell and
Julia (Wilcox) Bowers. Mr. Maine completed his education at the Plainfield Academy. He was of a genial disposition and had a large circle of
friends. He was a member of the Knights of Pythias, and he and both his
wives were members of the Baptist Church. Before his marriage he lived in
No. Stonington and Plainfield; but after the death of his first wife he lived
in East Berlin, until 1902; then removed to Middletown. He was in a
grocery-store a portion of his time. His death was caused by a fall from a
stone wall, while on a vacation in No. Stonington. He was going through
the fields and over the walls when a stone fell and crushed his leg, causing
his death.
   Children, by second m., b. East Berlin:
      1416. Edson Lewis Maine, b. May 27, 1884; m., Rock Falls, Conn.,
         Aug. 12, 1908, Lizzie Levis. He received his education in
         the schools of East Berlin and the business college at Mid-
         dletown. He is a plumber and painter.
      1417. Alice Augusta Maine, b. Aug. 17, 1886; m., Aug. 19, 1907,
         Charles Armstrong, son of George Armstrong, of Middle-
         town. Dau.: Dorothy Alice, b. May 11, 1908.
      1418. Clara Maria Maine, b. May 9, 1896.

Alice Leonora Maine (1414), dau. of Lewis Main, Jr. (364), and Cynthia Hewitt Stewart, b., No. Stonington, Conn., July 21, 1851; d., Providence, R. I., Feb. 1, 1890; m., Plainfield, Conn., Dec. 24, 1874, William Albert McBay, b. Chicopee, Mass. He was in early life in a grocery-store, and after his marriage had stores at Moosup, Voluntown, and East Berlin, Conn., where he remained several years; but on account of the health of his wife he removed to Providence. Mrs. McBay before her marriage taught school for twelve terms at Plainfield and Lisbon, Conn. She was a member of the Baptist Church. Mr. McBay is a merchant at Providence.

Children, b. Voluntown:

1419. Lewis Albert, b. July, 1877; d. Mar., 1878.
1420. Eva May, b. Aug., 1879; d. in infancy.

Emily Augusta Maine (1415), sister of the preceding, b., No. Stonington, Conn., June 10, 1853; d., Providence, R. I., July 13, 1889; m., Plainfield, Conn., Apr. 11, 1872, Judson Davis, b. June 8, 1852; son of Richard and Freelove (Kenney) Davis. Mrs. Davis before her marriage taught school in Voluntown and Griswold, Conn. Mr. Davis is the engineer at the pumping-station in Providence, and has been for a number of years. Both are members of the Baptist Church, Providence.

Children:

1421. Nellie Stewart, b., Providence, Nov. 22, 1873 (1425).
1422. Grace Mary, b., Providence, Nov. 30, 1881 (1426–1428).
1423. James, b. Moosup; d. in infancy.
1424. George, b. Providence; d. in infancy.

Nellie Stewart Davis (1421), dau. of the preceding, b., Providence, R. I., Nov. 22, 1873; m. (1), Providence, Jan. 15, 1890, Edward B. Gardner, of Providence; divorced. She m. (2), Natick, R. I., July 24, 1897, William H. H. Hutchins, b., Danielson, Conn., Mar. 24, 1865; son of Erastus Dwight Hutchins, of Danielson. This also is Mr. Hutchins's second marriage. Mr. Hutchins is overseer of cloth-room at Moosup, Conn. Both are members of the Baptist Church at Moosup. Res., Moosup, Conn.

Son, by first m., b. Providence:

1425. Lewis Thomas Gardner, b. Apr. 27, 1891.

Grace Mary Davis (1422), dau. of Judson Davis and Emily Augusta Maine (1415), b., Providence, R. I., Nov. 30, 1881; m., Westfield, Conn., May 24, 1906, Clarence Ellsworth Boardman, b., Westfield, Mar. 18, 1869; son of George F. and Ann Elizabeth (Knowles) Boardman, of Westfield.

He is engaged in farming and is a Republican. His wife is a member of the Congregational Church. Res., Westfield, Conn.

Children, b. Westfield:

1426. George Davis, b. Jan. 7, 1907.

1427. Grace Mary (twin), b. Sept. 1, 1908; d. Oct. 30, 1908.

1428. Judson Ellsworth (twin), b. Sept. 1, 1908.

Avery Main (365), son of Lewis Main (315) and Hannah Ray, b., Voluntown, Conn., Aug. 29, 1806; d. West Walworth, N. Y.; m., Fenner, N. Y., Laura Ann Baldwin, b., Fenner, Nov. 12, 1816; d., West Walworth, May 24, 1894; dau. of John and Ruby (King) Baldwin, of Fenner. Mr. Main went West before his marriage. He learned the mason business at Syracuse, N. Y., and lived there several years; and in the fall of 1837 he returned with his wife and three boys to No. Stonington, Conn. In the spring of 1848 he moved with his family, in a " prairie schooner," to Norwich, N. Y., on a farm owned by Dudley R. Wheeler, of No. Stonington. Later he bought a farm at Fenner. This he sold, and bought near Oneida, N. Y.; from here he removed to West Walworth, where he made a permanent settlement and was again elected deacon of the Baptist Church. His whole term of service was forty years. He was a man highly respected, honest from principle, and his strong faith and splendid Christian character endeared him to all who knew him. His wife was a true helpmeet, full of good deeds, and her children rise up to call her blessed.

Children:

1429. Lewis Avery, b., Lenox, N. Y., Dec. 10, 1832; m. Fannie L. Loomis (1437–1441).

1430. Marquis Sardius, b., Lenox, Sept. 15, 1834; m. Janette Ten Eyck (1446–1452).

1431. John White, b., Naples, N. Y., July 17, 1836; m. Hannah Morris (1453–1457).

1432. Emily, b., No. Stonington, Apr. 9, 1838; d., aged two years.

1433. Susan Wattles, b., No. Stonington, 1841; m. A. M. Lynch (1458, 1459).

1434. Helen Augusta, b. No. Stonington; d. young, at Fenner.

1435. Frances Laura, b., Norwich, Jan. 11, 1853; m. M. E. Williams (1460–1462).

1436. Alice Perlina, b., Fenner, Dec. 4, 1855; m. Herbert Smith (1463–1466).

Lewis Avery Main (1429), son of Avery Main (365) and Laura Ann

Baldwin, b., Lenox, N. Y., Dec. 10, 1832; m., Nelson, N. Y., Dec. 10, 1856, Fannie Lucretia Loomis, b., Cazenovia, N. Y., Feb. 14, 1833; d., Independence, Ia., Nov. 20, 1899; dau. of Lewis Terrell Loomis and Mary Ann Loomis, of Cazenovia. Mr. Main was educated in Norwich (N. Y.) Academy, and in the Academic Department of Madison University, N. Y. Soon after his marriage he went West, where, with the exception of a few years, he has lived ever since. He served in the Civil War, being a member of Co. C, 27th Iowa Infantry, 1862–1865. Soon after his return home to Independence he was elected treasurer of his county, and served in that capacity six years, after which he held other important offices of responsibility and trust. Mr. Main is a Republican, a member of the Baptist Church, and a farmer by occupation. He was deacon at Independence, Ia., over forty years.

Fannie L. (Loomis) Main was educated in Cazenovia (N. Y.) Seminary, and subsequently taught school. She was a member of the Presbyterian Church, patriotic, and of strong religious convictions. She was a descendant of Jerusha Brewster Loomis (see Brewster Genealogy); also of Governor Bradford of the Mayflower Colony and the early Boston Puritans. Res., 1909, Cedar Rapids, Ia.

Children, b. Independence, except first, b. Nelson:

  1437. Helen Augusta, b. Dec. 26, 1859; unm.
  1438. Lewis Palmer, b. Sept. 1, 1862; m. Edith E. Borst (1442).
  1439. Willis Elderkin, b. July 31, 1868; m. Bertha E. Curtis (1443–1445).
  1440. Maurice Avery, b. Oct. 15, 1870; unm.
  1441. Merton Loomis, b. Nov. 4, 1874; unm.

Helen Augusta Main (1437), dau. of the preceding, b., Nelson, N. Y., Dec. 26, 1859; unm. She wrote for publication in different papers, but in later years has given herself to church and missionary work. Res. with her father at Cedar Rapids, Ia.

Lewis Palmer Main (1438), son of Lewis Avery Main (1429) and Fannie Lucretia Loomis, b. Sept. 1, 1862; m., Independence, Ia., Mar. 31, 1887, Edith E. Borst, b., Janesville, Wis., Sept. 23, 1863; d., Cedar Rapids, Ia., May 17, 1902; dau. of David and Malinda (Willsie) Borst, of Independence. Mr. Main is a graduate of Knox College, Galesburg, Ill., class of 1884. He taught school four years after his graduation, and has practised law since 1888, for the first ten years at Kearney, Neb., and eight years at Cedar Rapids; now [1909] at Durango, Col., having a large and successful practice. He was school director in Nebraska, and for over twenty years an elder in the Presbyterian Church.

Dau.:

1442. Grace Helen, b., Kearney, July 15, 1893.

Willis Elderkin Main (1439), brother of the preceding, b., Independence, Ia., July 31, 1868; m., Independence, Oct. 5, 1892, Bertha E. Curtis, b., Independence, May 7, 1875; dau. of Wilbur and Rosetta (Dillingham) Curtis, of Independence. He received his education in the public schools, and is a progressive farmer. He is serving the fifth term on the Board of Assessors. He and his wife are members of the Baptist Church. Res., Independence, Ia.

Children, b. Independence.

1443. Laura J., b. Aug. 29, 1893.
1444. Lewis W., b. May 22, 1896.
1445. Maurice S., b. Oct. 20, 1899.

Marquis Sardis Main (1430), son of Avery Main (365) and Laura A Baldwin, b., No. Stonington, Conn., Sept. 15, 1834; m., Clockville, Madison Co., N. Y., Sept. 22, 1858, Janette Ten Eyck, b., Norwich, Chenango Co., N. Y., June 17, 1840; dau. of Jacob A. and Sarah (Duncan) Ten Eyck, of Clockville. He is a farmer, a Republican, and a deacon of the Baptist Church. His wife is also a member. Mr. Main's childhood was spent in No. Stonington. He removed with his parents to New York, attending district school winters and the Cazenovia Seminary and the Oneida Castle one term each, then teaching school in Lenox, N. Y. He then turned his attention to farming on two hundred acres of productive land, combining with it other industries, and for fifteen years was an extensive dealer in commercial fertilizer. His farm being located in a good fruit-belt, he turned his attention to evaporating apples, with a yearly product of five to twelve thousand pounds, which has been a financial success. He continued in that branch of business over thirty years. He also raises a variety of small fruits. In one year he produced twenty-two thousand quarts of raspberries. Although his life has been full of business activities, he has been assessor for twenty-two years and has borne a conspicuous part in all work of morality, education, and religion. Res., West Walworth, N. Y.

Children, the last five b. West Walworth.

1446. Florence, b., Oneida, N. Y., Apr. 13, 1860
1447. Luella, b., Oneida, Nov. 18, 1861.
1448. Edith, b. Aug. 22, 1863; d., West Walworth, Nov. 1, 1881.

1449. Jennie, b. Aug. 13, 1865.
1450. Marquis Avery, b. June 1, 1869.
1451. Willis Jacob, b. Aug. 6, 1874.
1452. Edward Everett, b. June 10, 1876.
These children are married and have children and grandchildren.

Edward Everett Main (1452), last preceding, m., Charlotte, Mich., Dec. 5, 1899, Jennie C. Shaw, b., Chester, Mich., Feb. 23, 1878. He was educated at West Walworth and Macedon Academy, N. Y.; afterwards taught school four years. Mrs. Main was educated at Lansing and the Charlotte High School, Mich., and taught school before her marriage. They have lived in West Walworth, N. Y., and in California; but now are at South Haven, Mich., where he is employed as letter-carrier. Both are members of the Baptist Church. Mrs. Main is the daughter of Noble A. and Celia N. (McConnell) Shaw, who now reside at Fairbanks, Alaska. Mrs. Main visited her parents in Alaska, starting from Redlands, Cal., and returning to her home in South Haven, travelling 14,000 miles. No issue.

John White Main (1431), son of Avery Main (365) and Laura A. Baldwin, b., Naples, N. Y., July 17, 1836; m., Oneida, N. Y., Dec. 11, 1856, Hannah Morris, b., Oneida, 1839; dau. of John and Mary (Adle) Morris, of Oneida. Mr. Main is a farmer; in politics, a Republican. His wife is a member of the Methodist Episcopal Church. He has served two terms as Justice of the Peace, and was one of the commissioners appointed for the division of the old town of Lenox, N. Y. They celebrated their golden wedding Dec. 11, 1906. Res., Canastota, N. Y.

Children, the last three b. Oneida:
1453. Avery Morris, b., Fenner, N. Y., 1863.
1454. Fannie Lewis, b., Stockbridge, N. Y., 1866.
1455. Lillie Mary, b. 1868.
1456. Helen Frances, b. 1873.
1457. Prescott Dodge, b. 1877.

Susan Wattles Main (1433), sister of the preceding, b., No. Stonington, Conn., 1841; d., Amsterdam, N. Y., 1906; m., West Walworth, N. Y., 1863, A. M. Lynk, b., Lenox, N. Y., 1843; deceased; son of Jacob and Christina (Shorts) Lynk, of Lenox. He was a farmer at Wampsville, N. Y. She m. (2), Amsterdam, 1895, James Marcellas. Res., 13 Union St., Schenectady, N. Y.

Children, by first m.:
1458. Cora, b. 1865; d., Lenox, 1878.
1459. Jacob A., b. 1872; d., Sullivan, N. Y., 1897.

Frances Laura Main (1435), sister of the preceding, b., Norwich, N. Y., Jan. 11, 1853; d., Fairport, N. Y., July 6, 1898; m., West Walworth, N. Y., Nov. 30, 1869, Milton E. Williams, b., Penfield, N. Y., Aug. 14, 1846; son of Thomas and Sarah (Heath) Williams, of West Walworth. Mrs. Williams was educated at West Walworth and the Macedon Academy. She was a school-teacher until her marriage, and was always active in church work. Mr. Main owned a farm at Lincoln, N. Y., but removed to Fairport, where he and his son Irving carry on the blacksmithing business. He is a Republican, and both he and his wife are members of the Free Baptist Church. Res., Fairport, N. Y.

Children, b. West Walworth:

    1460. Millie D. Williams, b. Dec. 11, 1870; m., West Walworth, Dec. 14, 1887, Albert E. Eckler, b., Penfield, Jan. 29, 1864; son of James H. Eckler, of Penfield. Children: (1) Ella E., b., Lincoln, N. Y., July 2, 1890; (2) Albert B., b., Lincoln, July 12, 1892; (3) Emerson T., b., Penfield, Oct. 29, 1898; (4) Oneita T., b., Penfield, Feb. 14, 1905. Res., Webster, N.Y.

    1461. Irving J. Williams, b. Mar. 8, 1875.

    1462. Cora E. Williams, b. Feb. 4, 1881.

Alice Perlina Main (1436), dau. of Avery Main (365) and Laura A. Baldwin, b., Fenner, N. Y., Dec. 4, 1855; m., Brighton, N. Y., 1883, Herbert Smith, b., Castile, Canada, May 12, 1858; son of Elias and Catherine D. (Defoe) Smith, of Rochester, N. Y. Mr. Smith is a dairyman at Fairport, Monroe Co., N. Y.

Children, the last three b. West Walworth, N. Y.:

    1463. Laura A. Smith, b., Lincoln, N. Y., Sept. 24, 1883; m., Penfield, N. Y., Nov. 26, 1903, Frank Greenfield. Children: (1) Iona, b. Sept. 14, 1904; (2) Lee, b. Feb. 26, 1905, d. Sept. 10, 1905; (3) Avery, b. Sept. 24, 1907, d. July 18, 1908; (4) Floyd, b. Dec. 2, 1908.

    1464. Avery A. Smith, b. Dec. 11, 1885; m., Webster, N. Y., Feb. 13, 1908, Eva D. Hurley, b., Webster, Oct. 21, 1888; dau. of Frank and Jeanette (Luitweller) Hurley, of Webster. Mr. Smith is a casket-maker, a Republican, and both he and his wife are members of the Methodist Church. Res., Webster, N. Y.

    1465. Frances L. Smith, b. Mar. 29, 1887; m., Fairport, N. Y., July 23, 1906, Francis Morris. Dau.: Levern, b. May 18, 1907.

    1466. Ruth E. Smith, b. Aug. 19, 1892.

Charles Henry Main (367), son of Lewis Main (315) and Hannah Ray, b., Voluntown, Conn., Feb. 4, 1811; m., Dec. 18, 1833, Almira B. Eccleston, dau. of William and Lucy (Geer) Eccleston.

Children:

 1467. Charles Henry, Jr., b., No. Stonington, Conn., Nov. 1, 1834; d., Stonington, Conn. (Wequetequock), Feb. 10, 1900; interment in Ashwillet; m. Mary A. Varley. No issue. Her res., Utica, N. Y.

 1468. Louise Almira, b. Apr. 4, 1839; m. Stiles P. Eggleston (955, 956).

 1469. Irtis, b.——; m. Harriet Main, his cousin, dau. of Jesse Palmer and Abby (Benjamin) Main. He lived and d. at Wequetequock.

 1470. Avery Alonzo, b., Franklin, Conn., Apr. 19, 1844 (1473-1480).

 1471. Mary E., b. May 12, 1847; d. Oct. 19, 1873; m. Theodore Main (380). Buried at River Bend.

 1472. Lucy Emeline, b., No. Stonington, July 26, 1850; m. Sanford N. Billings (1481-1488).

Note.— After the names of parents at the end of a line, the children with corresponding numbers are often found backward as well as forward. Follow the numbers.

Avery Alonzo Main (1470), son of the preceding, b., Franklin, Conn., Apr. 19, 1844; d., No. Stonington, Conn., Dec. 13, 1908; m. (1), Aug., 1867, Mary J. Brown, b. Sept. 16, 1847; d. 1873; dau. of Palmer A. and Sarah (Perry) Brown, of So. Kingstown, R. I.

Children by first m.:

 1473. Austin A., b., Glasgo, Conn., Dec. 20, 1868; m., No. Stonington, Mar. 30, 1890, Eva A. Burdick, b., Norwich, Conn., Mar. 9, 1868; dau. of Horace F. and Mary Frances (Sherley) Burdick. Mr. Main is in the grocery business, a Republican in politics, and both he and his wife are members of the Baptist Church. No issue. Res., Voluntown, Conn.

 1474. Elmer E., b., No. Stonington, May 15, 1872; m., No. Stonington, Mar. 26, 1893, Minnie Jane Davis, b., Stonington, Conn., Feb. 11, 1872; dau. of Charles H. and Jane (Saunders) Davis, of Stonington. His occupation is farming on the same land that was first settled by John Brown (8) in 1688 (B. G., p. 12), the ancestor of the compiler of this book. He and his wife are members of the Baptist Church.

Son:

1475. Clarence Raymond, b., Stonington, June 4, 1903.

Avery Alonzo Main (1470) m. (2), Westerly, R. I., Nov. 18, 1877, Mary
Adeline Ayers, b., Westerly, Oct. 9, 1860. Address, Westerly, R. I.

Children by second m., b. Stonington, except the second:

1476. Mary A. Main, b. Nov. 3, 1878; d. July 3, 1903.

1477. Irving Randall Main, b., No. Stonington, May 20, 1880; m.,
Stonington, Sept. 14, 1896, Bertha Merton Stone, b., Plainfield, Conn., Sept. 6, 1876; dau. of Charles and Emma Jane
(Young) Stone. Children: (1) Gladys Emma, b. Sept. 14,
1897; (2) Ralph Irving, b. Feb. 12, 1900.

1478. Herbert Lewis Main, b. Sept. 11, 1882; m., Stonington, Sept.
10, 1902, Annie May Davis. Res., Westerly, R. I., R. F. D.
Children: (1) Mildred Annie, b. Apr. 3, 1904; (2) Raymond
Davis, b. Aug. 11, 1905.

1479. William Rhodes Main, b. Sept. 5, 1884; m., Apr. 2, 1902,
Bertha May Kinnie, b., Stonington, June 20, 1882. No issue.

1480. Frances Claud Main, b. Apr. 8, 1897; d. Sept. 16, 1897.

Lucy Emeline Main (1472), dau. of Charles Henry (367) and Almira R.
(Eccleston) Main, b., No. Stonington, Conn., July 26, 1850; m., Worcester,
Mass., Oct. 28, 1867, Sanford N. Billings, b., No. Stonington, May 18,
1841; son of Horatio Nelson and Mary Ann (Fish) Billings, of No. Stonington. Mr. Billings is an agriculturist of the progressive type; a Republican,
attending the Congregational Church, of which his wife is a member. He
came to Stonington, Conn., in 1873. He was a private in the Civil War,
enlisting in Co. G, 21st Conn. Vol. Infantry, Aug. 20, 1862, and was discharged at the close of the war, at Baltimore, Md., May 15, 1865. Res.,
Stonington, Conn.

Children, the last six b. Stonington:

1481. Byron Billings, b., No. Stonington, Jan. 4, 1869; m., Aug. 18,
1900, Geneva Newbury Rogers. Children: (1) Priscilla
Alden, b. July 11, 1901; (2) Esther Marion, b. Mar. 10, 1903.

1482. Mary Billings, b., No. Stonington, May 15, 1871; m., June 7,
1893, Arthur G. Wheeler. Children: (1) Nelson Farnsworth,
b. Feb. 25, 1894; (2) Mary Starr, b. Sept. 14, 1895; (3)
Arthur G., Jr., b. Apr. 13, 1897; (4) Donald and (5)
Dorothy (twins), b. June 28, 1900.

1483. William W. Billings, b. Sept. 19, 1873; m., Apr., 1897, Mary

Clark. Children: (1) Jennie D., b. Mar. 31, 1898; (2) Gilbert, b.——

1484. Lucy Billings, b. June 20, 1881.

1485. Grace Wheeler Billings, b. Dec. 18, 1882; m., Stonington, Sept. 16, 1903, Horace D. Miner, b. Sept. 17, 1855; son of Elias H. and Clarissa (Miner) Miner. (See B. G., p. 162.) Children: (1) Elias Billings, b. July 2, 1904; (2) Muriel H., b. Nov. 29, 1905; (3) Latham H., b. May 29, 1907; (4) Grace D., b. Apr. 5, 1909; d. Apr. 30, 1909.

1486. Lilla M. Billings, b. July 6, 1886; d., Griswold, Conn., Jan. 31, 1907.

1487. Priscilla Alden Billings, b. May 29, 1892.

1488. Sanford Nelson Billings, Jr., b. Aug. 17, 1895.

Jesse Palmer Main (368), son of Lewis Main (315) and Hannah Ray, b., Voluntown, Conn., Feb. 15, 1813; m., 1838, Abby Benjamin, dau. of Elam Benjamin.

Children:

1489. Lydia, b.——; m. Frank Pierce.

1490. Celesta, b.——; m. Frank Eggleston.

1491. Edgar Palmer, b.——; m.——; both deceased. Dau.: Sadie Main, legally adopted by Irtis Main.

1492. Harriet, b.——; m. Irtis Main. (See 1469.)

1493. Hannah, b.——; m. Avery Miller. Dau.: Leonora Miller, m. Ernest Rose. No issue. Mrs. Rose has been for many years, and still is, a school-teacher at Westerly, R. I. Res., Norwich, Conn.

Gersham Albert Main (369), son of Lewis Main (315) and Hannah Ray, b., Voluntown, Conn., Dec. 23, 1815; d., Norwich, Conn., Apr. 13, 1903; m., by Rev. Charles A. Weaver, No. Stonington, Conn., Dec. 7, 1840, Susan A. Billings, b., No. Stonington, Jan. 4, 1822; d., Norwich, Oct. 6, 1906; dau. of Joseph and Phebe (Brown) Billings. Mr. Main was a farmer, and both he and his wife were church-members.

Children:

1494. Susan Emma, b. July 28, 1843 (1497, 1498).

1495. Albert Billings, b. July 29, 1845 (1499, 1500).

1496. Harriet A., b. Jan. 18, 1859; unm. She is a school-teacher. Res., Norwich, Conn.

Susan Emma Maine (1494), dau. of the preceding, b. July 28, 1843; d.,

Webster, Mass., Aug. 14, 1884; m., Lisbon, Conn., Mar. 18, 1874, David A. Witter.

Children, b. Webster:

1497. Myron David Witter, b. Mar. 20, 1879; m., Los Angeles, Cal., Oct. 3, 1907, M. Ethel Welcome. Mr. Witter is editor of the *Branbey News*. Res., Branbey, Cal.

1498. Grace Emma Witter, b. Dec. 12, 1881; unm. She is a teacher in the public schools. Res., Danielson, Conn.

Albert Billings Maine (1495), son of Gersham Albert Main (369) and Susan A. Billings, b., Griswold, Conn., July 29, 1845; m. (1), Stonington, Conn., May 11, 1869, Maria W. Beebe, b., Stonington, Oct. 24, 1846; d., Norwich, Conn., Jan. 17, 1896; dau. of Austin G. Beebe, of Stonington. He m. (2), Waterford, Conn., Sept. 4, 1905, Sabrina Hillard, b., No. Stonington, Conn., Mar. 11, 1849; dau. of William M. and Lucy Morella (Dewey) Hillard. (See B. G., p. 456.) Mr. Maine is a merchant at Norwich, and a member of the Baptist Church.

Children, by first m., b. Norwich:

1499. William Austin, b. Jan. 6, 1873; unm.

1500. Mary Ella, b. Dec. 22, 1874; m. William H. Covey, Jr. Children, b. Norwich: (1) Henry Albert, b. Dec. 22, 1898; (2) William Benjamin, b. Mar. 15, 1902; (3) Lewis Maine, b. June 7, 1904.

Esther Stafford Main (370), dau. of Lewis Main (315) and Hannah Ray, b., Voluntown, Conn., June 14, 1821; d., Stonington, Conn., Oct., 1864; m., Voluntown, Nov. 25, 1847, William Chapman, b., No. Stonington, Conn., Dec. 7, 1818; d., Stonington, Aug. 8, 1892; son of Elias Chapman. Mr. Chapman worked on the farm for the compiler's father for one year, 1846-47; then after his marriage began for himself. He soon after purchased a fine farm in Stonington at the beginning of the Civil War and built a fine house and barn on a beautiful elevation, where his son Charles lived after him. By his industry and frugality he acquired considerable property. He also bought, near by, another smaller farm, where he lived until his death. In all his thrift and hurry he was an active church-member, attending to his religious duties. His wife also was active in church work from early youth until her death. Their acts of beneficence stand in grateful remembrance by the members of the Third Baptist Church, of which both were members. The last letter Mrs. Chapman wrote to her youngest sister,

Mary A., May 2, 1864, breathes forth the true state of her heart,— that it
was fixed by faith on things above and not on the earth.
Children:

  1501. Lydia Esther, b., No. Stonington, Apr. 28, 1849; d. Jan. 9, 1850.
  1502. Mary Ella, b., No. Stonington, July 17, 1851; d. Sept. 12, 1852.
  1503. Henrietta, b., Stonington, Dec. 18, 1853; m., Stonington, Dec.
        25, 1877, Frank W. Main, b. Apr. 3, 1855; son of Clark B.
        and Abby E. (Mitchell) Main, of No. Stonington. Children:
        (1) Florence Edith, b. Dec. 27, 1886, m. and has two chil-
        dren; (2) Maurice Eleanor, b. Apr. 26, 1889; unm.
  1504. Charles William, b., Stonington, Apr. 20, 1859; d. Apr. 19,
        1901; unm. Mr. Chapman conducted his father's farm for
        a few years very successfully, but he was not in good health.
        He was highly respected by all who knew him.

Ira Main (1406), son of Jared Main (1173) and Abigail Eccleston, b.,
No. Stonington, Conn., Mar. 11, 1810; d. Apr. 26, 1885; m., Green River,
N. Y., Feb. 22, 1834, Martha A. Harvey, of Willimantic, Conn.; b. Mar. 22,
1818; d. Apr. 20, 1906. Interments, Wood River, R. I.
Children:

  1505. Ira Monroe, b., Willimantic, July 11, 1835; m. Sarah Bills
        (1524, 1525).
  1506. Gersham Philetus, b., East Haddam, Conn., July 20, 1839; m.
        Mary Jane Underwood (1512-1515).
  1507. Charles Henry, b., Uncasville, Conn., Nov. 10, 1843 (1516-
        1520).
  1508. Ambrose L., b., Almyville, Conn., July 24, 1846; d. July 27,
        1847.
  1509. George Riley, b., Plainfield, Conn., June 25, 1848; m. Hannah
        Francis Richmond (1521, 1522).
  1510. Amasa Franklin, b., Housatonic, Mass., Mar. 4, 1851; m.
        Eunice Belinda Earl. Son: Arthur, b.——; m.; has three
        children.
  1511. Matilda, b., Van Deusenville, Mass., Apr. 9, 1853 (1523).

Gersham Philetus Main (1506), son of Ira Main (1406) and Martha A.
Harvey, b., East Haddam, Conn., July 20, 1839; d., Boston, Mass., Feb. 15,
1908; buried in Central Village, Conn.; m. (1), Willimantic, Conn., Feb. 26,
1860, Mary Jane Underwood; divorced; m. (2), Moosup, Conn., June 2,
1871, Lydia E. Boss; d. July 1, 1876, aged thirty-two years; m. (3), Volun-

town, Conn., Feb. 10, 1878, Elizabeth Abigail Finan, b., Baltimore, Md.,
Aug. 31, 1855. Mrs. Main is one a compiler is pleased to meet, being able
from memory to give complete and accurate records. The family Bible of
Ira Main (1406) is in her possession, of which she is the careful custodian.
She noticed what the older people had to say of their ancestry, and her
memory is wonderful. After the death of the mother of Frank E. Main
(1514) she cared for him several years. Her res., Westerly, R. I.

Children by first m.:

1512. William Gersham, b., Willimantic, June 2, 1861; m. Emma F.
Whitman (1526–1531).

1513. Annie Louisa, b., Wickford, R. I., Jan. 19, 1864; m., Apponaug,
R. I., Dec. 22, 1896, Albert James Dawley, b. July 22, 1837.
No issue. Res., Danielson, Conn.

Son by second m.:

1514. Frank Edgar, b., Willimantic, Mar. 15, 1874; m. Susie A.
Huntington (1532).

Son by third m.:

1515. Harold Lester, b., Fitchburg, Mass., Jan. 17, 1882; m., Webster,
Mass., June 15, 1903, Doretta May Rafter. They had four
children who d. in infancy.

Charles Henry Main (1507), son of Ira Main (1406) and Martha A.
Harvey, b., Uncasville, Conn., Nov. 10, 1843; m. (1), about Oct. 1, 1867,
Julia Tabor, deceased; dau. of Henry Tabor, of Rockville, R. I. He m. (2),
Sept. 30, 1876, Susan A. Lillabridge, of Exeter, R. I. Res., Mansfield, Mass.

Children by first m.:

1516. Genevieve Main, b. Oct. 1, 1868; m. George Babbington. He
is in the jewelry business, Providence, R. I. Children:
Flora, Vernon, and Persey.

1517. Charles Henry Main, Jr., b., Wyoming, R. I., Oct. 1, 1869;
m. Clara Bell Ball, b., Bristol, R. I., May 17, 1869. Children, b. Hills Grove, R. I.: (1) Fred Joseph, b. Dec. 11,
1888; (2) Irving Chester, b. Nov. 23, 1897. Res., Apponaug,
R. I.

1518. Harriet Main, b. Nov., 1871; m. Edwin Holden, deceased, of
East Greenwich, R. I. Dau.: Mildred, b. 1894.

Children by second m.:

1519. Wallace Main, b., Voluntown, Conn., June 18, 1880. Res.,
Providence, R. I.

1520. Ernest Ransom Main, b., Hills Grove, Jan. 9, 1884; m., June 27, 1904, Agnes Lillian Barr, b. Oct. 18, 1884; dau. of Alexander W. Barr. Res., Mansfield, Mass.

George Riley Main (1509), son of Ira Main (1406) and Martha A. Harvey, b., Plainfield, Conn., Jan. 25, 1848; d., No. Stonington, Conn., Feb. 3, 1905; m., Exeter, R. I., Jan. 9, 1870, Hannah Frances Richmond, b., Exeter, Oct. 28, 1851; dau. of Stephen and Eliza Ann (Corey) Richmond, of Exeter. Res., Escoheag, R. I.
Children, b. Exeter:
1521. Henry Monroe, b. 1870; m. Mary Etta Waite (1532a-1536).
1522. Martha Ann, b. Mar. 28, 1873; m. Byron D. Wilcox (1537-1539).

Matilda Main (1511), dau. of Ira (1406) and Martha A. Harvey, b., Van Deusenville, Mass., Apr. 9, 1853; m., Hopkinton, R. I., Mar. 22, 1871, William Jason Clark, b., Windham, Conn., Oct. 6, 1849.
Dau.:
1523. Lulu Bell Clark, b., Exeter, R. I., Apr. 25, 1872; m., No. Kingstown, R. I., Mar. 22, 1890, Ambrose B. Taylor, of No. Kingstown. Children: (1) Ethel M., b. July 29, 1892; (2) Hazel L., b. Feb. 6, 1894.

Ira Monroe Main (1505), son of Ira (1406) and Martha A. Harvey, b., Willimantic, Conn., July 11, 1835; d., Wickford, R. I., Oct. 9, 1900; m., Stockbridge, Mass., Jan. 1, 1855, Sarah M. Bills, b., Great Barrington, Mass., June 7, 1834.
Children:
1524. Ida M., b., Narragansett, R. I., Oct. 30, 1863; m., Apr. 22, 1900, Henry Phillips. No issue. Res., Hope Valley, R. I.
1525. Ora M., b., Voluntown, Conn., Dec. 20, 1869; m., Feb. 23, 1895, Edwin G. Crandall, b., Hope Valley, Feb. 25, 1870. No issue. Res., Hope Valley, R. I.

William Gersham Main (1512), son of Gersham P. Main (1506) and Mary Jane Underwood, b., Willimantic, Conn., June 2, 1861; m., Exeter, R. I., Dec. 25, 1879, Emma F. Whitman, b., Allenton, R. I., Mar. 16, 1862; dau. of Caleb and Margaret W. (Harvey) Whitman. Mr. Main is in the wholesale ice-cream business. He started business at the bottom rung of the ladder, at Arcadia, R. I., in 1884, with a wheelbarrow. Through his dau., Emma Varon, he conducts business at Wakefield, R. I., giving [in 1909] his personal attention to his plant in Westerly, R. I. He is the oldest ice-cream manufacturer in Washington Co. He is full of energy and push, taking in a wide circle of business in Westerly, Watch Hill, and surrounding towns. He takes a deep interest in family records, and through him was opened the family tree from his great-grandfather Jared Main (1173) down to the present time.

Children:

1526. Lillian Grace, b., Wyoming, R. I., Oct. 20, 1880.

1527. Mary Luella, b., Arcadia, R. I., Nov. 5, 1881; d. Feb. 6, 1891.

1528. Emma Varon, b., Voluntown, Conn., July 26, 1884.

1529. William Ira, b., Arcadia, July 20, 1887.

1530. Ambrose Burnside, b., Hope Valley, R. I., Apr. 5, 1890.

1531. Mamie Susan, b., Wakefield, Nov. 4, 1894.

Frank Edgar Main (1514), son of Gersham P. Main (1506) and Lydia E. Boss, b., Willimantic, Conn., Mar. 15, 1874; m., Boston, Mass., Nov. 15, 1905, Susan A. Huntington, dau. of John and Susan (Ashmore) Huntington, of Willimantic. Mr. Main was educated in the public schools of Providence, R. I., graduating from the grammar school at the age of fifteen. He then entered the service of the Providence and Worcester R. R., as the treasurer's clerk, from 1890 to 1896; then for three years as travelling salesman for Jones & Primley, of Elkhart, Ind.; then until 1902 with the N. Y., N. H. & H. R. R. Co. Now [1909] with Pullman Co., with office at Boston.

Mrs. Main was adopted by her husband's parents at the age of six months, and remained in the family five years. She was then adopted by Charles A. Rix, of Dunlap, Ia., where she remained until twenty years of age, returning then to New Haven, Conn., in 1899, and residing with her brother until her marriage.

Son:

1532. Edgar Huntington, b., So. Boston, Mass., Sept. 4, 1907.

Henry Monroe Main (1521), son of George Riley (1509) and Hannah F. (Richmond) Main, b., Exeter, R. I., July 4, 1870; m., Hopkinton, R. I., Mary Etta Waite, b., Coventry, R. I., Nov. 18, 1869. Res., Arcadia, R. I.

Children, b. Hopkinton:

1532a. Ira, b. 1892; drowned, aged nine years.

1533. Arthur Edwin, b. June 27, 1894.

1534. Mary Francis, b. Jan. 16, 1897.

1535. George Albert, b. June, 1899.

1536. Stephen Henry, b. June 3, 1901.

Martha Ann Main (1522), dau. of George Riley (1509) and Hannah F. (Richmond) Main, b., Exeter, R. I., Mar. 28, 1873; d. Sept. 19, 1896; m., Hopkinton, R. I., July 27, 1887, Byron Damond Wilcox, b., Hopkinton, Apr. 25, 1868.

Children, b. Hopkinton:

    1537. George Henry, b. Feb. 25, 1889.

    1538. Maurice Lester, b. June 24, 1891.

    1539. Harold Clyde, b. Apr. 29, 1894.

Almina Main (1407), dau. of Jared Main (1173) and Abigail Eccleston, b., Stonington, Conn., Mar. 8, 1811; m. Ira Winsor, of Stonington.

Children:

    1540. John Winsor, b.——; m. three times; d. in 1905. No issue. He was a celebrated physician at Quidnick, R. I.

    1541. Curtis Winsor, b.——; d. in Connecticut. The latter part of his life he spent in the West. He was twice m., and had two sons by the first m.

    1542. Frances Winsor, b. Sterling, Conn.; m. John Turner, of Sterling. Children: (1) Minnie, (2) Maud, (3) son, drowned at Quidnick. He was studying medicine, and was a young man of much promise.

NOTE.— Always follow the numbers as given, to connect with families.

Sanford Main (316), son of Rufus Main (296) and Sarah York, b. Stonington, Conn.; d., Westerly, R. I., Oct. 27, 1860, aged sixty-five years; m. Rebecca Billings, b.——; d., No. Stonington, Conn., Dec. 31, 1858, aged sixty-five years. Dea. Sanford Main lived in Ashwillet, Conn., and at one time owned and lived at the Nathan Pendleton house on Pendleton Hill. His wife died there. He was an active member of the First Baptist Church, Pendleton Hill, and served the church as deacon faithfully and well, and his name lives to-day in that old church. He died at the home of his daughter Mrs. Lucy B. (Main) Sheffield, at Westerly, and the funeral was at the Pendleton Hill Church. Interment in Rixtown, Griswold, Conn. Most of these records were taken from tombstones. In this cemetery are buried his parents, Rufus and Sarah (York) Main.

Children:

    1543. Sanford B., b.——; d. July 12, 1819.

    1544. Rebecca B., b. Jan. 21, 1819; d. Oct. 4, 1840.

    1545. Infant son, b.——; d. Dec. 1, 1822.

    1546. Lucy B., b. Aug. 7, 1822; m., Mar. 8, 1854, Wm. F. Sheffield.

1547. Sanford Austin, b. May 9, 1828; m. Harriet P. Hewitt (1549, 1550).
1548. Calvin K., b.——; d. Mar. 17, 1860, aged twenty-nine years.

Sanford Austin Main (1547), son of Dea. Sanford (316) and Rebecca (Billings) Main, b., No. Stonington, Conn., May 9, 1828; d. Jan. 17, 1866; m. Harriet P. Hewitt, b. Mar. 26, 1829; d. Mar. 29, 1868. Mr. Main was a young man of excellent qualities, a student at the Connecticut Literary Institution at Suffield, Conn., in 1850, taking a partial course of study. It was then the compiler of these records met him, and he is remembered as a worthy young man of fine Christian character. After leaving school he kept the store on Pendleton Hill; later, at Greenville, now Norwich, Conn. The whole family have passed away. Interments in River Bend, Westerly, R. I.
    Children, b. No. Stonington:

1549. Gertrude, b. Sept. 15, 1860; d. in infancy.
1550. Minnie E., b. Aug. 9, 1863; d. Nov. 26, 1892.

Benajah Main was first heard from as a soldier of the Revolutionary War; and he came to Ledyard, Conn., or Stonington, and made a permanent settlement. He m. Mary Woodward. Their descendants follow:
    Son:

1551. John Main, b. No. Stonington, Conn.; d. No. Stonington; m., Ledyard, Conn., Matilda Brown, b. Ledyard; d., No. Stonington, Sept., 1844; dau. of Nathaniel Brown and Deborah Morgan, of Ledyard. Mr. Main was a farmer and was in the War of 1812. He served in the 7th Company in the defence of Stonington Borough when that place was attacked by the British, Aug. 9 and 10, 1814.

    Children, b. No. Stonington:

1552. David Morgan, b.——; m. Martha Burdick, of Mystic, Conn. She m. (2) Rathbun. Res., near Noyes Beach, R. I.
1553. Jesse M., b. 1816; m. Hannah Partelo (1561–1563).
1554. Son, b.——; d. in infancy.
1555. Nathaniel N., b. Feb., 1819; m. Mary Frink (1564–1567).
1556. Sabrina, b.——; m. Clark L. Brown (1568, 1569).
1557. Deborah, b. Sept. 18, 1825; m. Horace F. York (1570–1572).
1558. Hannah Elizabeth, b. June 11, 1828; m. John E. Clark (1579).
1559. Mary Matilda, b. 1829; d. Aug., 1854; unm.
1560. John S., b. May 7, 1832; m. Frances Abby Wheeler (1580–1583).

Jesse Morgan Main (1553), son of John Main and Matilda Brown, b. 1816; m., No. Stonington, Conn., Nov. 26, 1837, Hannah M. Partelo, b. Feb. 10, 1821; dau. of John and Mary Main Partelo. (See B. G., p. 117.) Mr. Main was a farmer. He was a soldier in the Civil War, enlisting at Norwich, Conn., Sept., 1862, in Co. G, 21st Regt. Conn. Vol. He d. in the Ninth Army Corps Hospital, Knoxville, Ind., Nov. 20, 1862. Interment in Union Cemetery, No. Stonington.

Children, b. No. Stonington:

> 1561. Mallory O., b. Sept. 10, 1848; m., No. Stonington, Dec. 31, 1868, Mary L. Clark, b. May 25, 1850. Children: (1) Wilfred A., b. Nov. 6, 1878; (2) Harold E., b. Mar. 10, 1888. Res., Cononchet, R. I.
>
> 1562. Eddie, b. Apr. 10, 1851; d. Sept., 1868.
>
> 1563. Mary Alice, b. Feb. 14, 1857; m. Charles H. Brown. Children: (1) Lillian Alice, b. No. Stonington, m. Wm. H. Avery; (2) Charles H., Jr., b. June 27, 1882, d. May 22, 1901; (3) Margaret Hannah, b. Mar. 15, 1886. (See B. G., p. 67.)

Nathaniel N. Main (1555), son of John and Matilda (Brown) Main, b., No. Stonington, Conn., Feb., 1819; m. Mary Ann Frink, b. 1823; dau. of Zechariah and Phebe (Holmes) Frink. Mr. Main was in the Civil War, a member of 26th Conn. Vol.; d. in the army at Baton Rouge, La., Apr. 17, 1863. She m. (2) Robert Avery, deceased. Mrs. Avery, née Frink, res., 1909, Swantown Hill, No. Stonington, Conn.

Children:

> 1564. Harriet E., b., No. Stonington, Sept. 10, 1842; m. Jacob D. Benjamin (1586–1588).
>
> 1565. Mary M., b., Ledyard, Conn., Sept. 6, 1848; m. Thos. G. Maine (1589–1591).
>
> 1566. Nathan N., b., No. Stonington, Aug. 27, 1851; m. Mary E. Rathbun (1592–1596).
>
> 1567. John L., b., Preston, Conn., Mar. 18, 1855; m., Lebanon, Conn., June 12, 1890, Emma A. Williams, b. New York. He is a farmer, a Republican, and both he and his wife are church-members.

Sabrina Main (1556), dau. of John and Matilda (Brown) Main, b.——; m. Clark L. Brown. She was his second wife. He was a farmer, a devoted Christian, and a member of the Second Baptist Church. He was of robust stature and great physical strength. Descendant of Elder Simeon Brown (B. G., p. 153).

Children, b. No Stonington, Conn :

> 1568. George C. Brown, b. July 30, 1864; m., No. Stonington, June
> 29, 1886, Nellie A. Maine, b. Jan. 8, 1864; dau. of Adam and
> Lucy M (Main) Main. Res., No Stonington, Conn

> 1569. John J. Brown, b.——; unm. (See Simeon Main family, p 35.)

Deborah Main (1557), dau. of John Main (1551) and Matilda Brown,
b., No. Stonington, Conn., Sept. 25, 1825; d , No. Stonington, July 5, 1890,
m., Groton, Conn , Dec. 1, 1850, Horace Franklin York, b., No. Stonington,
Nov. 14, 1828; son of Nathan and Martha (Breed) York. Mr York has
spent his whole life in his native town, and is one of its respected citizens.
He and his wife are members of the Second Baptist Church, and he for
many years has been an active deacon

Children, b No. Stonington:

> 1570. Anna Deborah, b. Sept. 7, 1851 (1573-1575).

> 1571 Mary Matilda, b. Feb 26, 1853 (1576, 1577)

> 1572. Horace Franklin, Jr., b Apr. 2, 1854 (1578).

Anna Deborah York (1570), dau of Horace F. and Deborah (Main)
York, b Sept. 7, 1851; d., Hope, R. I , Aug. 31, 1906; m., No Stonington,
Conn., Nov 23, 1875, Wm. Henry Latham, b Sept 1, 1850, d , Hope, Oct
15, 1906. He was overseer of a weave shop, a Republican, and both he
and his wife members of the Methodist Church.

Children:

> 1573 Mary Ethel, b., Pontiac, R. I., Dec. 3, 1877.

> 1574. Anna Mabel, b , Pontiac, Feb. 18, 1879; m., Sept. 13, 1904,
> Harvey E. Mason, of Hope.

> 1575. Arthur Henry, b., East Greenwich, R I , Aug. 30, 1888, d.
> Sept. 1, 1890.

Mary Matilda York (1571), sister of the preceding, b. Feb 26, 1853;
m., No. Stonington, Conn , June 27, 1876, Rev Archibald McCord. He
is a Congregational clergyman at Taunton, Mass

Children:

> 1576. Beatrice, b., Cohasset, Mass., Aug. 31, 1877.

> 1577. Horace Maxwell, b , Chatham, Mass., June 12, 1884.

Horace Franklin York, Jr. (1572), son of Horace F. and Deborah (Main)
York, b Apr. 2, 1854, m , Providence, R I , Aug 8, 1876, Callie Davis
Pullin, b , So Kingstown, R I., 1855; dau. of William and Abby (Holly)
Pullin. Mr York is a Republican Both he and his wife are members of the
Congregational Church, Tenafly, N J.

Son:

1578. Ernest W. York, b., Stonington, Conn., July 17, 1883; d., Tenafly, June, 1899.

Hannah Elizabeth Main (1558), dau. of John and Matilda (Brown) Main, b. June 11, 1828; m., No. Stonington, Conn., Nov. 19, 1862, John E. Clark, b., No. Stonington, Mar. 31, 1814; d., No. Stonington, Aug. 17, 1895. Mr. Clark was early left an orphan, and was brought up by his maternal grandfather, John Burdick, in No. Stonington. He was proprietor of the saw and grist mills at Clark's Falls, Conn., for thirty-seven years, retiring from active service about 1875. He was a member of the Second Baptist Church. Mrs. Clark is somewhat enfeebled in health, but is of excellent memory and good reputation. Res., Clark's Falls, Conn.

Dau.:

1579. Jessie F. Clark, b., No. Stonington, Apr. 27, 1869; m., No. Stonington, Mar. 13, 1890, John B. Perry, b., Matunuc, R. I., Nov. 14, 1867; son of Wm. H. and Sarah A. (Nichols) Perry, of Matunuc. Sarah A. Nichols was the dau. of George and Annie Nichols of Henniker, N. H. Mr. Perry is a farmer, a Republican (not rabid), and a member of the Friends Church. His wife is a member of the Baptist Church. Children, b. No. Stonington: (1) Maurice C., b. Nov. 6, 1891; (2) Oscar E., b. July 22, 1896. Res., Clark's Falls, Conn.

John S. Main (1560), son of John and Matilda (Brown) Main, b., No. Stonington, Conn., May 7, 1832; d., No. Stonington, Mar. 25, 1881; m., No. Stonington, Mar. 18, 1860, Frances Abby Wheeler, b., No. Stonington, Apr. 14, 1839; dau. of Dea. Allen and Jemima A. (Wheeler) Wheeler. The descendants look backward with pride to their noble parentage. The very name Dea. Allen Wheeler is a synonym of goodness and brotherly love. His name shall be in everlasting remembrance.

Children, b. No. Stonington:

1580. Chester Sands, b. Dec. 16, 1860; m. Abby M. Newton (1584).
1581. Clinton Ulysses, b. Sept. 8, 1864; d. Aug. 17, 1866.
1582. Fannie Wheeler, b. Sept. 29, 1867; m. George D. Coats (1585).
1583. Annie May, b. May 9, 1872; unm. Res. with her sister, Mrs. G. D. Coats.

Chester Sands Maine (1580), son of John S. (1560) and Frances Abby (Wheeler) Main, b., No. Stonington, Conn., Dec. 16, 1860; m., No. Stonington, July 7, 1886, Abby M. Newton, b , Hartford, Conn , Aug 7, 1866, dau. of William A and Mary J. (Manion) Newton, both deceased. Miss Newton was brought up by her uncle and aunt, who resided in Washington, D C , to whom she always looked as her guides during her early life She was educated in the public and high schools of Hartford, and graduated from the State Normal School in New Britain, Conn , in 1885. She was a teacher in the public schools at No Stonington; was a member of the School Board for nine years. She is a member of the Third Baptist Church, and an efficient leader in all church work.

Mr. Maine received a public-school education and attended the Ashaway, R. I., High School. He is giving attention to farming and other important industries. He has served his town as selectman, and in 1909 is a member of the State Legislature. Resident and owner of the farm known as "The Rufus Williams Farm," No Stonington; the buildings can be seen for miles around.

Son:

 1584. Carrol Chester, b. Mar. 23, 1888 He resides with his parents, and is chief manager and farmer, thus relieving his father of care and responsibility.

Fannie Wheeler Maine (1582), dau. of John S. (1560) and Frances Abby (Wheeler) Main, b. Sept. 9, 1867; m , No. Stonington, Conn , Mar 16, 1886, George D. Coats, b July 14, 1864; son of George F. and Freddie M. (Koopman) Coats. Mr. Coats makes farming his occupation on the beautifully located farm, known as "The Ephraim Wheeler Farm," later, as "The Ephraim Main Farm." On this farm the compiler of these records spent three pleasant years of his life, 1845-48. Mr. Coats has held important town offices.

Son:

 1585. Allen Ansel Coats, b Dec 19, 1889. (See B. G , p. 102.)

Harriet E. Maine (1564), dau. of Nathaniel N. (1555) and Mary A. (Frink) Maine, b., No. Stonington, Conn., Sept 10, 1842, m , Preston, Conn , 1859, Jacob D. Benjamin, b , Preston, July 2, 1838, d., Preston, Oct 20, 1906 His occupation was farming Both he and his wife church-members.

Children, b. Preston:

 1586. Charles H , b. Nov. 26, 1859.
 1586a. Mary E , b. Mar 4, 1865, d., Preston, Nov 20, 1886.
 1587. Everett D., b. Oct. 25, 1870.
 1588. Nettie B , b. June 17, 1882.

Mary M. Maine (1565), sister of the preceding, b., Ledyard, Conn., Sept. 6, 1848; d., Voluntown, Conn., Feb. 22, 1871; m., Preston, Oct. 10, 1865, Thomas G. Maine, of Ledyard.

Children:

    1589. Annie B. Maine, b. Oct. 16, 1866.

    1590. Julia E. Maine, b. Apr. 21, 1868; m. Wm. H. Johnson.

    1591. Mary M. Maine, b. Feb. 8, 1871; d. Aug. 8, 1871.

Nathan N. Maine (1566), son of Nathaniel N. Main (1555) and Mary A. Frink, b., No. Stonington, Conn., Aug. 27, 1851; m., Norwich, Conn., Mar. 3, 1875, Mary E. Rathbun, b., Norwich, 1854; dau. of Asher and Betsey M. (Pierce) Rathbun. Mr. Maine is a farmer; in politics, a Democrat. He furnished the records of his father's family. Res., No. Stonington (Ashwillet), Conn. Address, Norwich, Conn., R. F. D.

Children:

    1592. Ella M. Maine, b. Nov. 25, 1875; m., No. Stonington, Dec. 12, 1900, Charles A. Palmer, son of James Palmer. No issue.

    1593. N. Elmer Maine, b., Preston, Conn., Feb. 17, 1877; d. June 7, 1884.

    1594. Addie E. Maine, b., Preston, Sept. 26, 1878; m., July 27, 1901, Clarence E. Palmer, b., Mansfield, Conn., Apr. 30, 1878, brother of Charles A. Palmer. Children: (1) James N., b. Nov. 7, 1902; (2) Edith M., b. Feb. 20, 1904.

    1595. Grover Cleveland Maine, b., Preston, Nov. 25, 1885; m., Griswold, Conn., July 27, 1905, Lena M. Johnson, b. Sept. 13, 1887; dau. of Wm. H. and Julia E. (Maine) Johnson.

    1596. Frances M. Maine, b. May 27, 1889.

Laban Main (298), son of Timothy Main (277) and Elizabeth Brown, son of Dea. Thomas Main (264) and Annah Brown, b. Jan. 27, 1764; d. 1842; m., Stonington, Conn., Oct. 19, 1794, Mary Brown, b., Stonington, Feb. 28, 1771; d. 1855; dau. of Elder Eleazer Brown and Ann Green. (See B. G., p. 115.)

Children, b. Stonington:

    1597. Mary, or Polly, b. Jan. 12, 1795; m. John Partelo (1602–1606).

    1598. Harry, b. 1797; unm.

    1599. Maranda, b. 1799; unm.

    1600. Alfred, b. Apr. 26, 1804; m. Samantha Stillman (1607–1611)

    1601. Erastus, b. 1806; m. Dorcas Perry.

        These children are also given under numbers 318–322.

Mary, or Polly, Main (1597), dau. of Laban and Mary (Brown) Main, b. Jan. 12, 1795; m., Stonington, Conn., 1820, John Partelo, b., Stonington, Aug. 29, 1796; d., No. Stonington, Conn., Mar. 31, 1891; son of Ezeriah and Nabby (Main) Partelo. Interments in Brown Cemetery, No. Stonington.

Children, b. No. Stonington:

    1602. Hannah M., b. Feb. 10, 1821; m. Jesse M. Main (1561–1563).

    1603. Nancy, b. June 18, 1825; m. Amos H. Allen (1612–1614).

    1604. John Hamilton, b. Aug. 29, 1829; m. Hannah H. Bailey (1615–1619).

    1605. Rebecca, b. Oct. 13, 1834; m. Joseph Woolhiser (1620–1624).

    1606. Eleazer Brown, b. May 17, 1839; m. Phebe R. Bailey (1625–1630).

    These children are all living in 1909. (See B. G., pp. 117–119.)

Alfred Main (1600), son of Laban (298) and Mary, or Polly, (Brown) Main, b., Stonington, Conn., Apr. 26, 1804; d. Oct., 1882; m. Samantha Stillman.

Children, first three b. Edmeston, N. Y.:

    1607. Alexander Hamilton, b. June 22, 1824; m. (1) Mary Cottrell; m. (2) Emma Cottrell (1631–1637).

    1608. Willett Stillman, b. Aug. 15, 1828; m. (1) Eliza Anne Jenison; m. (2) Sophia L. Smith (1638–1644).

    1609. Amelia Angeline, b. Oct. 30, 1832; m. James Hopkins (1645–1650).

    1610. Frances Alma, b., Clarksville, N. Y., May 9, 1839; m. (1) Russell Ashman Vilas; m. (2) T. L. Haecker (1651–1653).

    1611. Ann Elizabeth, b. Clarksville; m. John Coit Spooner (1654–1657).

Nancy Partelo (1603), dau. of John and Mary, or Polly, (Main) Partelo, b., No. Stonington, Conn., June 18, 1825; m., No. Stonington, Dec. 22, 1852, Amos H. Allen, b. Jan. 15, 1825. Both are members of the Second Baptist Church. He was leader of the church music for many years, as early as 1850. Res., No. Stonington, Conn.

Children, b. No. Stonington:

    1612. Henry L., b. July 29, 1853; m., Hopkinton, R. I., Apr. 12, 1879, Elizabeth Champlin, b., Hopkinton, June 6, 1860; dau. of Elijah and Fally A. (Lewis) Champlin. Both are members of the Second Baptist Church. He is a good

THE EZEKIEL MAIN FAMILY

singer. Son: (1) Charles Henry, b. Apr. 27, 1881; m.,
Westerly, R. I., Oct. 18, 1906, Annie Noyes Pendleton, b.
Jan. 4, 1883; dau. of Chas. Henry and Harriet Elizabeth
(Noyes) Pendleton, of Westerly. (2) Devere Allen.

1613. Frances Adelaide, b. Mar. 9, 1855; m., Westerly, Dec. 24,
1873, Nelson J. Lyon, b., New London, Conn., July 19,
1853. Res., Waterford, Conn. Children: (1) Robert Allen,
b., New London, June 25, 1877, m., Waterford, Nov. 4,
1899, Mary Ann Gates, b., Waterford, Aug. 5, 1880; (2)
Everett Nelson, b., Waterford, Sept. 30, 1892; (3) Nancy
Allen, b., Waterford, Jan. 26, 1895.

1614. E. Gertrude, b., No. Stonington, Mar. 11, 1858; m., Stonington, Jan. 7, 1879, E. Everett Watrous, b., Stonington, May 6,
1856. No issue.

John Hamilton Partelo (1604), son of John and Mary, or Polly, (Main)
Partelo, b., No. Stonington, Conn., Aug. 29, 1829; m., Exeter, R. I., Nov.
27, 1851, Hannah H. Bailey, b., Warwick, R. I., Oct. 1, 1835. She was a
pupil of the compiler of these records in 1848–49, in Exeter. Her husband
afterwards taught the same school, and in the public schools of Connecticut
and Iowa forty-nine terms; also several terms in grammar schools. Res.,
Boone, Boone Co., Ia.

Children:

1615. Ella J., b., Westerly, R. I., July 24, 1854; m. James Lewellen.
They have seven children: Edgar, Hattie, Elsie, Laura,
Harry, Ernest, Ray. Res., Myrtle Point, Coos Co., Ore.

1616. Hannah E., b., No. Stonington, Oct. 10, 1857; d. Nov. 29,
1897; m. Samuel F. Barger. Children: (1) Pearl, m. Frank
Voas; (2) Grace, m. Will Sherley; (3) Ernest. Res., Min-
burn, Dallas Co., Ia.

1617. Joseph H., b., No. Stonington, Aug. 29, 1861; m. Lenora
Nicholas. They have six children: Lloyd, Holmes H.,
Arthur, Hattie, Dewey, Pearl. Res., Boone, Ia.

1618. Charles A., b., Ledyard, Conn., May 4, 1867; m. Nellie
Huttonhow. They have three children: Alfred, William,
and Tressie. Res., Boone, Ia.

1619. Lillie B., b., Boone, Feb. 5, 1873; m. Frank C. Little. Son:
George Little. Res., Boone, Ia.

Rebecca Partelo (1605), dau. of John and Mary, or Polly, (Main) Partelo, b., No. Stonington, Conn., Oct. 18, 1834; m., No. Stonington, Nov. 13, 1855, Joseph Woolhiser, b., New York, Sept. 17, 1833. Res., Boone, Ia.

Children, first four b. No. Stonington:

    1620. Mary E., m. H. A. Barger.

    1621. Frederica, m. G. M. Weston.

    1622. Kate I., m. L. L. Springer.

    1623. Carrie T., m. A. Turner.

    1624. Joseph H., b. Boone, Ia.; m. Jessie Bailey.

           These four daus. and one son have twenty-seven children.

Eleazer Brown Partelo (1606), son of John and Mary, or Polly, (Main) Partelo, b., No. Stonington, Conn., May 17, 1839; m., Ashaway, R. I., Sept. 28, 1861, Phebe R. Bailey, b., Warwick, R. I., Oct. 9, 1841; sister of the wife of J. H. Partelo; dau. of Joseph and Hannah (Tibbetts) Bailey.

Children:

    1625. Minnie F., b. Apr. 5, 1863; m. James E. Sheffield. Children: Phebe Bailey, b. Jan. 25, 1890; Grace, b. Dec. 22, 1891.

    1626. Lillie Lenora, b. July 17, 1865; unm.

    1627. William Henry, b. June 22, 1868; m., Hope Valley, R. I., Mar. 30, 1909, Harriet Maud Nye, b. July 31, 1885; dau. of Lewis Edwin and Jane (Collins) Nye.

    1628. Anna Lena, b. June 18, 1870; m. Herbert B. Vincent, son of Charles W. and Angeline (Brown) Vincent. Res., No. Stonington, Conn.

    1629. Phebe Adelaide, b. Apr. 7, 1872.

    1630. Frank Mason, b. Aug. 4, 1874; m. Olive Merrell. Res., No. Stonington, Conn.

Alexander Hamilton Main (1607), son of Alfred (1600) and Samantha (Stillman) Main, b., Edmeston, N. Y., June 22, 1824; d., Madison, Wis., Jan. 9, 1896; m. (1), Wirt, N. Y., Sept. 7, 1852, Mary Cottrell, b., Scott, N. Y., July 7, 1831; d., Sun Prairie, Wis., Feb. 18, 1862; m. (2), Richburg, N. Y., Sept. 16, 1863, Emma Cottrell, sister of first wife; b., Scott, Jan. 21, 1863; daus. of John B. Cottrell and Eunice Babcock. Mr. Main was an insurance agent, a Republican, and a member of the Baptist Church.

Children by first m.:

    1631. Willet Eugene, b. Mar. 14, 1855 (1658).

    1632. Ernest Alfred, b. Jan. 8, 1859; d., Cincinnati, O., Oct. 8, 1888.

Children by second m., b. Madison:

1633. George Carpenter, b. Mar. 21, 1865; m., Winnipeg, Manitoba, Canada, Mar. 15, 1898, Camille Cleaveland. He is in the insurance business; is a Republican. His wife is a Catholic. No issue.

1634. Edward Stillman, b. June 27, 1869; m. Janette Doyon (1659-1661).

1635. Mary Hamilton, b. Sept. 15, 1871.

1636. Royal Cottrell, b. Feb. 23, 1875; m. Maude Kinsley (1662-1664).

1637. Frances Cecelia, b. Nov. 1, 1879.

Willet Stillman Main (1608), son of Alfred (1600) and Samantha (Stillman) Main, b., Edmeston, N. Y., Aug. 15, 1828; d., Madison, Wis., July 5, 1902; m. (1), Indianapolis, Ind., June 3, 1855, Eliza Anne Jenison, b., Indianapolis, Aug. 21, 1834; d., Cleveland, O., Jan. 15, 1866. He m. (2), Madison, June 18, 1867, Sophia L. Smith, b. Rochester, Vt.; dau. of Samuel N. and Lois (Williams) Smith, of Middleton, Wis. Mr. Main is a Republican. Both he and his wife are members of the Baptist Church.

Children by first m.:

1638. Hamilton Wingate, b. May 3, 1858; m., Madison, Nov. 10, 1885, Lillie E. Correll, b., Madison, Mar. 6, 1864. Dau.: Elyda, b., Hastings, Neb., Nov. 20, 1893.

1639. Frank Jenison, b. Apr. 21, 1864; m. (1) Delia Gilman Lyman; m. (2) Henrietta Phillips.

Children by second m., b. Madison:

1640. Elyda, b. Oct., 1869; d., Madison, Mar., 1877.

1641. Susan, b. Dec. 21, 1870; m. Charles P. Spooner (1665, 1666).

1642. Anne Elizabeth, b. Feb. 6, 1874; m. A. J. Kempton (1667-1669).

1643. John Smith, b. Nov. 23, 1875; unm. He is a real-estate agent, a Republican, and a member of the Baptist Church. Res., Madison, Wis.

Dau.:

1644. Lois Williams, b. Oct. 8, 1882.

Amelia Angeline Main (1609), dau. of Alfred (1600) and Samantha (Stillman) Main, b., Edmeston, N. Y., Oct. 30, 1832; m., Madison, Wis., Oct. 30, 1850, James Hopkins, b. Springville, N. Y.; d., Chicago, Ill.,

1899. He was a builder; in politics, a Republican. Both he and his wife were members of the Baptist Church.

Children, b. Madison:

1645. Frances Ellen Hopkins, b. Aug. 29, 1851; d., Hudson, Wis., 1879; m., Madison, John K. Wetherly. He is a lawyer at Minneapolis, Minn.; in politics is a Democrat. His wife was a member of the Baptist Church. No issue.

1646. Annie Louise Hopkins, b. June 22, 1854; m., Madison, W. R. B. Smythe (1670-1672).

1647. Edward Dayton Hopkins, b. Oct. 25, 1856; d. young.

1648. Alfred Ashman Hopkins, b. May 15, 1859; m., Hudson, Wis., Jessie Koons, b. Madison, Wis. Res., St. Paul, Minn. Children, b. Hudson: (1) Robert, b. July, 1894; (2) Alfred Ashman, b. 1896.

1649. Arthur Hamilton Hopkins, b. Aug. 9, 1861; m., Eau Claire, Wis., Jan. 30, 1890, Elizabeth Clarke, b., Eureka, Wis., Jan. 23, 1863; dau. of Ellery C. Clark and Emily J. Priest, of Little Rock, Ark. Children, b. Minneapolis, Minn.: (1) Clarke, b. Aug. 11, 1905; (2) Arthur, b. Sept. 13, 1907.

1650. Charles Henry Hopkins, b. May 26, 1865; unm. He is a post-office clerk.

Frances Alma Main (1610), dau. of Alfred (1600) and Samantha (Stillman) Main, b., Clarksville, N. Y., May 9, 1839; m. (1), Madison, Wis., Feb. 15, 1860, Russell Ashman Vilas, b., Ogdensburgh, N. Y., Oct. 12, 1833; d., Ogdensburgh, 1884; son of Royal Vilas and Mary Ashman, of Ogdensburgh. He was an accountant; in politics, a Republican. His wife is a member of the Baptist Church. Both well educated. He was assistant paymaster in the navy during the last years of the Civil War, afterwards going into the land office in California and into copper-mines, etc. Mrs. Vilas was in the office of the Secretary of State of Wisconsin for eleven years.

Children by first m., b. Madison:

1651. Anne Ashman Vilas, b. Mar. 22, 1861.

1652. George Stillman Vilas, b. Apr. 19, 1862; d. Oct. 12, 1864.

1653. Percival Madden Vilas, b. Aug. 23, 1869; m., Concord, Mass., Dec. 20, 1897, Katharine M. Garland, b. Mar. 24, 1875. Mr. Vilas is a railroad man. Mrs. Vilas is a fine musician, a Smith College graduate in music. Son: William Howard, b. May 19, 1900.

Mrs. Frances Alma Vilas, née Main (1610), m. (2), Madison, Oct. 23, 1888, Theophilus L. Haecker, b. Liverpool, O. Professor Haecker entered the University of Wisconsin in 1863; left to join the army, Mar. 11, 1864; enlisted in Co. A, 37th Infantry; was at Cold Harbor, Va. Later he was placed in charge of the 9th Corps Hospital supplies at City Point. He rejoined his regiment at the close of the war, and was given charge of the drum corps, participating in the great review in Washington; discharged with his regiment in Madison, July 27, 1865. In 1867 he again entered the university. In his third year his health failed and he was compelled to return home. He then established the *Ackley Independent*, Iowa, in 1873. He sold his paper and settled on a farm in Cottage Grove, Wis. Soon after, he was offered and accepted a position in the executive office of Wm. R. Taylor, then Governor of Wisconsin, holding this position through five administrations, covering a period of seventeen years.

All this did not cause him to lose interest in his farm and stock-raising. He spent much of his time out of office looking after his stock,— no small matter with the farm ten miles away. Relieved from office in 1890, he joined the first class in the Wisconsin Dairy School; later he was appointed assistant in butter-making in the Minnesota Agricultural School. In June, 1893, he was made full professor in the College of Agriculture. His remarkable works in animal nutrition led the Regents to make a new division of animal nutrition, with Mr. Haecker professor and head, in addition to his other professorships. His services to the state and country are of incalculable benefit. His feeding standards, replacing those of the German authorities, are received as authorized standards all over this country, being taken with many years of records and experiments with close study. Res., 1205 Raymond Ave., St. Paul, Minn.

Ann Elizabeth Main (1611), dau. of Alfred (1600) and Samantha (Stillman) Main, b., Clarksville, N. Y., Nov. 9, 1842; m., Madison, Wis., 1868, John Coit Spooner, b., Indiana, Jan., 1841; son of Phelps L. Spooner, of Madison. Mr. Spooner is a lawyer in New York City. He is a Republican. His wife is a member of the Baptist Church. Mrs. Spooner was educated in the Albany Academy, Albany, N. Y., being valedictorian of her class. She is a fine vocalist. John Coit Spooner was U. S. Senator for sixteen years, being held in high esteem by three Presidents, and was attorney for West Wisconsin. He left college, where he later graduated, to enter the army. He resigned from the Senate, at the height of his power, to recoup his fortunes and to provide for his family. He resided in Hudson, Wis., for some years, all the children but the oldest being born there; later in Madison, where they own a beautiful home.

Children:

1654. Charles Philip Spooner, b., Madison, June 5, 1869; m. Susan Main, 1641 (1665, 1666).

1655. Willet Main Spooner, b., Hudson, Dec., 1870; m., Oshkosh, Wis., Kate Noyes, b. June 8, 1876; dau. of Dr. J. Noyes, of Oshkosh. Both are graduates of Wisconsin University. Mr. Spooner graduated from the Law School of the University. Res., Milwaukee, Wis.

1656. John Coit Spooner, b. Hudson; d. young.

1657. Philip Loring, b., Hudson, 1879. He is a graduate of Wisconsin University, and is a fine vocalist and artist. Res. at home.

Willet Eugene Main (1631), son of Alexander H. (1607) and Mary (Cottrell) Main, b., Little Genesee, N. Y., Mar. 14, 1855; m., Madison, Wis., Sept. 10, 1880, Mrs. Jennie (Harnden) Noble, b. Rome, Wis.; dau. of Gen. Henry Harnden, of Madison. He is an insurance agent, and a Republican. General Harnden was the officer in command of the forces that captured Jefferson Davis, the president of the Southern Confederacy, May 15, 1865. At the time of his death he was Department Commander of the Wisconsin G. A. R. Res., Madison, Wis.

Dau.:

1658. Laura Harnden, b., Madison, Oct. 1, 1882; d., Madison, Aug., 1886.

Edward Stillman Main (1634), son of Alexander H. (1607) and Emma Cottrell, b., Madison, Wis., June 27, 1869; m., Madison, Jan. 24, 1900, Janette Doyon, dau. of Moses R. Doyon, of Kokomo, Ind., and Amelia Herrick. His occupation, Western Roofing Co. He is a Republican. His wife is a Congregationalist. Res., Chicago, Ill.

Children, b. Chicago:

1659. Elizabeth Herrick, b. July 11, 1901.

1660. Janette Strowbridge, b. June 29, 1904.

1661. Edward Stillman, Jr., b. Mar. 10, 1907.

Royal Cottrell Main (1636), brother of the preceding, b., Madison, Wis., Feb. 23, 1875; m., St. Louis, Mo., Jan., 1902, Maude Kinsley. He is in the insurance business; in politics is a Republican. His wife is a member of the Catholic Church.

Children:

 1662. Helen Marie, b., Milwaukee, Wis., Oct. 19, 1903; d., Milwaukee, Oct. 21, 1903.

 1663. Alexander Hamilton, b., Chicago, Ill., Aug. 7, 1905.

 1664. Mary Ellen, b., Chicago, Mar. 13, 1908.

Susan Main (1641), dau. of Willet Stillman Main (1608) and Sophia L. Smith, b., Madison, Wis., Dec. 21, 1870; m., Madison, June 11, 1896, Charles Philip Spooner (1654), b., Madison, June 5, 1869; son of John C. Spooner and Ann Elizabeth Main (1611). He is a lawyer, practising first in Milwaukee, Wis., and later in Seattle, Wash., where he now resides. He is a graduate of Princeton University and the Wisconsin University Law School. He and his wife are members of the Baptist Church.

Children:

 1665. Dorothy, b., Milwaukee, Nov. 1, 1897.

 1666. Annie, b., Seattle, June 1, 1906.

Anne Elizabeth Main (1642), sister of the preceding, b., Madison, Wis., Feb. 6, 1874; m., Madison, Feb. 14, 1899, Rev. A. J. Kempton, b., Margaree, Cape Breton, Dec. 31, 1866; d., Madison, Aug. 30, 1908; son of Rev. Joseph F. and Pamelia (Bigalow) Kempton, of Nova Scotia. He was a Baptist clergyman; his wife was a member of the Baptist Church.

Children:

 1667. Willet Main, b., Mt. Carroll, Ill., Feb. 4, 1900.

 1668. Elizabeth, b., Mt. Carroll, Nov. 16, 1901.

 1669. Judson, b., Muscatine, Ia., Feb. 5, 1907.

Annie Louise Hopkins (1646), dau. of James Hopkins and Amelia Angeline Main (1609), b., Madison, Wis., June 22, 1854; m., Madison, Oct. 30, 1876, W. R. B. Smythe, b., Otsego, Wis., Sept. 3, 1852. Mr. Smythe was for thirty years the resident agent for McCormick machines, located at first at Freeport, Ill.; then at Mankato, Minn. He is now a banker at Park Rapids, Minn. In politics he is a Republican. Both he and his wife are members of the Baptist Church.

Children:

 1670. Fanny Rebecca, b., Freeport, Sept. 17, 1877 (1673, 1674).

 1671. Angeline Main, b., Mankato, Jan. 18, 1885.

 1672. William Ralph, b., Mankato, July 8, 1891.

Fanny Rebecca Smythe (1670), dau. of W. R. B. Smythe and Annie Louise Hopkins Smythe (1646), b., Freeport, Ill., Sept. 17, 1877; m.,

Wichita, Kan., Sept. 3, 1900, Herbert C. Snow, b., New York, Apr. 4, 1876; son of Seward R. Snow and Florence G. ———, of Little Falls, Minn. He is a hotel keeper. Mrs. Snow is a member of the Baptist Church.
Children, b. Mankato, Minn.:

    1673. Louise Aileen, b. June 24, 1901.

    1674. Florence Irene, b. Sept. 27, 1905.

Zebulon Brown (304), son of Dea. Zebulon Brown and Anne Main (279), b., Stonington, Conn., May 20, 1756; m., Stonington, Theda York, b. Oct. 4, 1758; d., Brookfield, N. Y., July 6, 1839; dau. of Bell and Ruth (Main) York. (See B. G., pp. 168, 171.)
Children:

    1675. Eunice, b., Stonington, Jan. 6, 1780; m. Robert Randall (1677–1687).

    1676. Zebulon, b., Stonington, June 30, 1781; m. Sarah Lewis (1688–1696).

Eunice Brown (1675), dau. of Zebulon (304) and Theda (York) Brown, b., Stonington, Conn., Jan. 6, 1780; d., Brookfield, N. Y., Dec. 27, 1872; m., Brookfield, May 4, 1797, Robert Randall, b., Stonington, Feb. 6, 1774; d., Brookfield, Dec. 15, 1859; son of Robert and Lucy (Pendleton) Randall.
Children, b. Brookfield:

    1677. Robert Brown Randall, b. July 15, 1798; m., Pittsfield, N. Y., Dec. 25, 1844, Ruth Briggs, b., Pittsfield, Oct. 7, 1798; dau. of John and Patience Briggs. No issue.

    1678. Eunice Randall, b. Oct. 4, 1800; m. Clark Nichols (1697–1708).

    1679. Ella Babcock Randall, b. Apr. 19, 1803; d., Cortland, N. Y., Jan. 8, 1824; unm.

    1680. Alvin Randall, b. May 10, 1805; d., Leonardsville, N. Y., Sept. 29, 1896; m. (1), Brookfield, Sept. 26, 1831, Lucy Hinkley, b., Brookfield, Sept. 20, 1812; d., Brookfield, Jan. 26, 1873; dau. of Luther Hinkley. He m. (2), Dec. 22, 1875, Mrs. Elizabeth M. Chesebrough, née Dutcher, b. Edmeston, N. Y.; d. Apr. 28, 1902. No issue.

    1681. Maria Randall, b. June 4, 1807; m. Thomas Rogers (1709, 1710).

    1682. Marcus Delazon Randall, b. Dec. 4, 1809 (1711).

    1683. Harriet Stevens Randall, b. Feb. 27, 1812; d. Nov. 25, 1891;

m. (1), Brookfield, Dec. 25, 1843, Thomas Rogers, b., Brookfield, Aug. 26, 1808; d., Brookfield, Apr. 12, 1847. She m. (2), Brookfield, Oct. 14, 1855, Justus R. Brown, b., Brookfield, Oct. 25, 1807 (990). (See B. G., p. 137.)

1684. Amelia Louise Randall, b. Sept. 16, 1813; d., Brookfield, Jan. 28, 1815.

1685. Roswell Randall, b. Jan. 11, 1816; d., Brookfield, Nov. 13, 1844; m., Canton, N. Y., Sept. 29, 1843, Letitia, dau. of Isaac and Mary J. Hill, b., Elbridge, N. Y., Sept. 1, 1820. He was a teacher. No issue.

1686. Hannah Brown Randall, b. Dec. 29, 1818; d., Brookfield, N. Y., Sept. 19, 1884; unm.

1687. Roxie F. Randall, b. Apr. 29, 1822; unm. She has taken great interest in family records, and has supplied much of the information of the descendants of her grandmother, Theda (York) Brown (304). In 1909 she is the only one living of eleven children. (See B. G., p. 184.) Res., Olean, N. Y.

Zebulon Brown (1676), son of Zebulon Brown (304) and Theda York, son of Dea. Zebulon Brown and Anne Main (279), dau. of Dea. Thomas Main (264) and Annah Brown, dau. of Eleazer Brown and Ann Pendleton. Eleazer Brown was the son of Thomas Brown and Mary Newhall, of Lynn, Mass., b., Stonington, Conn., June 30, 1781; m., 1807, Sarah Lewis, b., Petersburg, N. Y., Mar. 12, 1781; dau. of Zebulon Lewis and Mary York; dau. of Bell York and Ruth Main. His nine children mostly resided on farms in and near Brookfield, to old age.

Children:

1688. Sarah, b. Dec. 28, 1809; m. Jared Chesbro (1712, 1713).

1689. Zebulon Lewis, b. May 17, 1812; d., Columbus, N. Y., Dec. 5, 1897; m., Nov. 19, 1833, Lois D. Palmer, b. Nov. 7, 1815; d. 1891.

1690. Horace B., b. July 1, 1814; m. (1) Mary A. Gorton; m. (2) Esther Crandall (1714-1722).

1691. Alonzo H., b. Apr. 4, 1817; m. Emeline Mason (1723-1725).

1692. Sabrina, b. Feb. 10, 1819; m. Elliott G. Fitch (1726-1729).

1693. Mary L., b. Feb. 24, 1823; m. Lelan C. York (1730-1735).

1694. Alvin, b. Apr. 14, 1826; d. Apr. 6, 1834.

1695. John F., b. Aug. 9, 1829; m. Sophia Dresser (1736-1740).

1696. Eunice A., b. Sept. 24, 1834; m. Jacob A. Dresser (1741-1745).

Roxie F. Randall
(1687)
Olean, N. Y.
Page 200

Mrs. Maria Elvira Norton
(1704)
Olean, N. Y.
Page 213

Eunice Randall (1678), dau. of Eunice Brown (1675) and Robert Randall, b., Brookfield, N. Y., Oct. 4, 1800; d., Clarksville, Allegany Co., N. Y., Feb. 28, 1868; m., Brookfield, Feb. 7, 1820, Clark Nichols, b., Brookfield, Mar. 11, 1787; d., Clarksville, Sept. 19, 1854; son of Jonathan and Phœbe Nichols. Both were members of the Baptist Church, but became Methodists later.

Children, first eight b. Brookfield; the others, Clarksville:

1697. Elvira Nichols, b. Dec. 22, 1820; d., Brookfield, 1824.

1698. Jabish Brown Nichols, b. Feb. 9, 1821; d., Clarksville, Jan. 4, 1894; m., Brookfield, June 12, 1855, Lusalla Allice, b., Brookfield, Sept., 1830; dau. of Hannah Allice. No issue. He was a farmer, and a Republican. He and his wife were members of the Baptist Church. Her res., Cuba, N. Y.

1699. William Henry Nichols, b. Dec. 7, 1822; d. 1824.

1700. Ela Randall Nichols (twin), b. Jan. 29, 1824; m. Mary Jacobs (1824, 1825).

1701. Abigail Nichols (twin), b. Jan. 29, 1824; m. John F. Adams (1826, 1827).

1702. Henry Webb Nichols, b. Jan. 30, 1828; m. Lucinda M. Ellwood (1828–1831).

1703. William Randall Nichols, b. Feb. 26, 1830; m. Mary J. Labar (1832, 1833).

1704. Maria Elvira Nichols, b. Jan. 30, 1832; m. Lavosier D. Norton (1834–1836).

1705. Robert C. Nichols, b. July 10, 1834; m. Elizabeth Helmer (1837–1841).

1706. Louise A. Nichols, b. Nov. 4, 1837; m. Henry J. Norton (1842–1845).

1707. Clarke J. Nichols, b. Oct. 22, 1839; d., Clarksville, Aug. 19, 1849.

1708. James Albert Nichols, b. July 15, 1842; m. Charlotte Peckham (1846–1849).

Maria Randall (1681), dau. of Eunice Brown (1675) and Robert Randall, b., Brookfield, N. Y., June 4, 1807; d. Sept. 13, 1842; m. Thomas Rogers, b. Aug. 26, 1808; d. Apr. 2, 1847; son of James Rogers and Thankful Brown. (See B. G., p. 125.) They had five children, three of whom d. in childhood.

Children:

1709. John T. Rogers, b., Brookfield, Sept. 29, 1832; d., Norfolk,

Va., May 6, 1901; m., Dec. 25, 1853, Belinda R. Talbot, b. June 5, 1833; her father was akin to Lord Talbot of England, and her mother a sister of Stephen W. Taylor, founder of Hamilton University of New York. Children: (1) L. De Forest, b. Sept. 5, 1854, d., Brookfield, Jan. 28, 1863; (2) Delia D., b. Oct. 10, 1855, d., Brookfield, Jan. 8, 1863; (3) Birdie May, b. July 15, 1860; m., Oct. 12, 1880, L. Edmond Shepherd, M.D., of Toronto, Canada. Children: (1) L. Van Norman, b., Richburg, N. Y., Aug. 26, 1882; (2) Ethel M., b., Detroit, Mich., Sept. 19, 1886; d., Norfolk, July 13, 1893.

    1710. James Robert Rogers, b. Mar. 9, 1839; d. Nov. 4, 1839.

Marcus Delazon Randall (1682), son of Robert Randall and Eunice Brown (1675), b., Brookfield, N. Y., Dec. 4, 1809; d., Milton Junction, Wis., Sept. 4, 1891; m. (1), Clarksville, N. Y., Sept. 3, 1837, Adeline D. Worden, b., Brookfield, Aug. 14, 1820; d., Brookfield, May 15, 1842; m. (2), Albion, Wis., Nov. 4, 1854, Deborah, dau. of Asa and Dorcas Odell; b., Allegany, N. Y., Oct. 14, 1821.

Dau. by second m., b. Albion:

    1711. Adaline Deborah Randall, b. June 14, 1858; d., Milton Junction, Aug. 19, 1879; unm. (See B. G., p. 205.)

Sarah Brown (1688), dau. of Zebulon (1676) and Sarah (Lewis) Brown, b., Brookfield, N. Y., Dec. 28, 1809; d. June 5, 1896; m., Feb. 29, 1832, Jared Chesebro, b. Feb. 29, 1808; d., Brookfield, Mar. 18, 1895.

Children:

    1712. J. Hiram Chesebro, b. Apr. 3, 1833; m. Harriet Williams (1746-1748).

    1713. Rhoda L. Chesebro, b. Jan. 1, 1836; d. Aug. 11, 1838.

Horace B. Brown (1690), son of Zebulon (1676) and Sarah (Lewis) Brown, b., Brookfield, N. Y., July 1, 1814; d., Prairieburg, Ia., 1882; m. (1), Brookfield, 1834, Mary A. Gorton, dau. of Wanton Gorton, of Brookfield. His father, Samuel A. Gorton, came to Brookfield from Westerly, R. I., about 1795, and settled on what was called Gorton Hill. She was b. in Baltimore, Md., in 1816; d., Brookfield, 1846. In 1848 he removed to Columbus, N. Y., and in 1855 removed to Prairieburg, Linn Co., Ia., where he resided to the time of his death. He was a farmer, a Republican, and he and his wife were members of the Baptist Church. Mr. Brown m. (2), Columbus, 1848, Esther Crandall, b., Columbus, Aug. 14, 1808; d., Prairieburg, 1876; dau. of Freeman Crandall, of Columbus, and Rhoda, his wife.

Children by first m., b. Brookfield:

1714. Henry H., b. Dec. 18, 1835 (1749–1754).

1715. Alvin H., b. Aug. 22, 1837 (1755–1761).

1716. Lois M., b. May 12, 1839 (1762–1767).

1717. Jared Fitch, b. 1841; d. 1842.

1718. Catherine R., b. Mar. 8, 1843 (1768–1773).

1719. Sarah W., b. 1844; d. 1845.

Children by second m., b. Columbus:

1720. Perry O., b. Feb. 14, 1849 (1774–1778).

1721. Freeman E., b. Oct. 30, 1851 (1779–1782).

1722. Lewis C., b. Feb. 22, 1853 (1783–1792).

Alonzo H. Brown (1691), son of Zebulon (1676) and Sarah (Lewis) Brown, b., Brookfield, N. Y., Apr. 4, 1817; d. Jan. 18, 1894; m., July 13, 1843, Emeline Mason, b. Aug. 10, 1824. Res., 1905, Columbus, N. Y.

Children:

1723. Flora L., b. Apr. 23, 1844; d. July 20, 1884.

1724. Viola M., b. Jan. 26, 1847 (1793, 1794).

1725. Zebulon L., b. Feb. 12, 1849; m. Julia A. Cook (1795–1797).

Sabrina Brown (1692), sister of the preceding, b., Brookfield, N. Y., Feb. 10, 1819; d., Brookfield, Dec. 2, 1901; m., Brookfield, Oct. 13, 1839, Elliott G. Fitch, b., Brookfield, May 4, 1817; d., Brookfield, Jan. 22, 1901; son of Patten and Lois (Babcock) Fitch, of Brookfield. He was a wagonmaker and lived in No. Brookfield. He was a Republican from the organization of that party, and he and his wife were members of the Baptist Church. Lived all his life in Brookfield, except three years when he resided in Morrisville, N. Y. He was a Justice of the Peace for years; was president of the Board of Education of No. Brookfield Union School four years or more. Was public-spirited and very successful in business. He retired from business with what was then considered a competency.

Children:

1726. Sorannus A. Fitch, b., Brookfield, Apr. 22, 1844; m., New York City, Dec. 19, 1866, Sarah M. Van Wagenen, b., Kingston, N. Y., Apr. 17, 1846; dau. of William and Margaret (Deyo) Van Wagenen, of Kingston. He studied law; was Deputy Clerk of Madison Co., N. Y., in 1866 and 1867; merchant at No. Brookfield from 1868 to 1886; was Postmaster, Justice of the Peace, and Supervisor of the town of Brookfield. Since 1886 he has been in the insurance business and has been secretary of the Hamilton Mutual Fire Insurance Co. of Hamilton, N. Y., where he resides. He is a Republican, and he and his wife are members of the Baptist Church, of which he is a deacon.

1727. L. Sherwood Fitch, b. Mar. 26, 1846 (1798).

1728. Sarah L. Fitch, b. Aug. 10, 1849 (1799–1801).

1729. Luella Fitch, b. Sept. 7, 1863 (1802–1804).

Mary L. Brown (1693), dau. of Zebulon (1676) and Sarah (Lewis) Brown, b., Brookfield, N. Y., Feb. 24, 1823; m. Lelan C. York, b., Brookfield, Jan. 31, 1815; d. Sept. 16, 1897; son of Yeomans and Catherine (Collins) York, son of Bell and Ruth (Main) York. He was a cheese-maker and a farmer. His widow res. with her son in the old homestead. They belong to the Society of Friends.

Children, b. Brookfield:

1730. Alonzo L. York, b. Feb. 13, 1846. (See B. G., p. 209.)

1731. Mary York, b. Dec. 15, 1847. (See B. G., p. 210.)

1732. Florinda E. York, b. Mar. 22, 1852. (See B. G., p. 210.)

1733. Mahlon York, b. Jan. 27, 1858; m., West Laurens, N. Y., Apr. 10, 1891, Ruth E. De Forest, b., Unadilla, N. Y., Oct. 18, 1861; dau. of John N. and Charlotte A. De Forest, of Unadilla. He is a Prohibitionist. Res., Unadilla, where he is a cheese manufacturer.

1734. Jared F. York, b. Feb. 23, 1860. (See B. G., p. 210.)

1735. Eveline F. York, b. Jan. 23, 1864 (See B. G., p. 210.)

John F. Brown (1695), brother of the preceding, b., Brookfield, N. Y., Aug. 9, 1829; m., May 9, 1851, Sophia Dresser, b. Aug. 29, 1829; d. June 27, 1893. Res., Brookfield, N. Y.

Children:

1736. De Ette, b. Nov. 19, 1854 (1805–1807).

1737. A. Duane, b. Sept. 8, 1860 (1808, 1809).

1738. William H., b. May 8, 1866 (1810–1812).

1739. Mary J., b. Aug. 11, 1868 (1813, 1814).

1740. Iva J., b. Sept. 22, 1874 (1815).

Eunice A. Brown (1696), sister of the preceding, b., Brookfield, N. Y., Sept. 24, 1834; m., Unadilla Forks, N. Y., Oct. 10, 1858, Jacob A. Dresser, b., Edmeston, N. Y., May 12, 1832; son of Samuel and Betsey (Burdick) Dresser. He is a farmer at Poolville, N. Y.; is a Republican in politics, and he and his wife are members of the Society of Friends. Both were educated in the common schools and in Brookfield Academy. Both taught school before their marriage, and all of their children have been teachers, the youngest teaching for thirteen consecutive years. They moved to the farm now occupied by them the next day after their marriage.

Children, b. Brookfield:

1741. Hazel S. Dresser, b. Apr. 9, 1860 (1816, 1817).

1742. Cora M. Dresser, b. Aug. 25, 1862 (1818–1820).

1743. Almer H. Dresser, b. July 3, 1867 (1821, 1822).

1744. Daisy Dresser, b. Sept. 19, 1871 (1823).

1745. Angie Dresser, b. July 12, 1874; m., Brookfield, June 28, 1905, Arthur Brand, b., Brookfield, Oct. 20, 1882, son of Nathan and Edah (Talbot) Brand, of Brookfield. He is a farmer, a Republican, and he and his wife belong to the Society of Friends. Res., Poolville, N. Y.

J. Hiram Chesbro (1712), son of Jared and Sarah (Brown) Chesbro (1688), dau. of Zebulon (1676) and Sarah (Lewis) Brown, son of Zebulon (304) and Theda (York) Brown, son of Dea. Zebulon and Anne Main (279), b. Apr. 3, 1833; m., Dec. 20, 1853, Harriet Williams, b. Dec. 19, 1835.

Children:

1746. Alvin D. Chesbro, b. Mar. 3, 1855; m., Jan. 1, 1874, Hattie A. Hinckley. No issue.

1747. Orra Chesbro, b. Apr. 27, 1862 (1850, 1851).

1748. Ida L. Chesbro, b. Oct. 1, 1866; m., Jan. 3, 1895, Fred H. White, b. July 22, 1871. No issue.

Henry H. Brown (1714), son of Horace B. (1690) and Mary A. (Gorton) Brown, son of Zebulon (1676) and Sarah (Lewis) Brown, son of Zebulon (304) and Theda (York) Brown, son of Dea. Zebulon Brown and Anne Main (279), dau. of Dea. Thomas Main (264) and Annah Brown, dau. of Eleazer Brown and Ann Pendleton, son of Thomas Brown and Mary Newhall, of Lynn, Mass., b., Brookfield, N. Y., Dec. 18, 1835; m., Prairieburg, Ia., May 26, 1861, Mary J. Wagner, dau. of Henry Wagner, of Prairieburg; b. Nov. 4, 1843; d., Cottage Grove, Ia., Mar. 13, 1905. He was a farmer at Cottage Grove; was a Republican.

Children, first four b. Prairieburg; last two, Park Rapids, Ia.:

1749. Ada, b. Oct. 3, 1862; d., Prairieburg, Aug. 16, 1863.

1750. William, b. Jan. 4, 1866 (1852–1854).

1751. Grace (twin), b. Nov. 16, 1868 (1855).

1752. Grant (twin), b. Nov. 16, 1868 (1856, 1857).

1753. Alice, b. Sept. 9, 1872 (1858).

1754. George Wagner, b. Feb. 28, 1875; m., Portland, Ore., Dec. 25, 1904, Nora Vanfleet.

Alvin H. Brown (1715), brother of the preceding, b., Brookfield, N. Y., Aug. 22, 1837; m., Columbus, N. Y., Feb. 10, 1867, Mary A. Sisson, b., Sherburn, N. Y., Nov. 24, 1842; d., Newaukum, Wash., Sept. 6, 1893; dau. of George and Clara (Church) Sisson, of Sherburn. During the war he was a member of the 44th Regt. Iowa Vol. Inf. He was chairman of the Board of Supervisors of Osceola Co., Ia., in 1877. He removed to Prairieburg, Ia., in 1855; to Osceola Co. in 1872; to Cottage Grove, Ore., in 1877; and to Napavine, Wash., in 1878. He is a farmer at Newaukum, Lewis Co., Wash., and a Republican. His wife is a member of the Methodist Church.

Children, first three b. Prairieburg:

1755. Clara B., b. Nov. 7, 1867 (1859–1864).

1756. Blanche M., b. July 12, 1869; m., Chehalis, Wash., Aug. 21, 1898, Henry A. Romerman, b., Nasel, Wash., Apr. 7, 1873. He is a logger, and a Republican. Res., Napavine, Wash.

1757. Sarah L., b. Jan. 29, 1871 (1865, 1866).

1758. Cora E., b., Ashton, Ia., July 10, 1873 (1867, 1868).

1759. Clarence A., b., Newaukum, May 8, 1881.

1760. Mary E., b., Newaukum, Jan. 18, 1884.

1761. Edna, b. Oct. 5, 1886; d., Newaukum, Feb. 4, 1890.

Lois M. Brown (1716), sister of the preceding, b., Brookfield, N. Y., May 12, 1839; m. (1), Prairieburg, Ia., Apr. 15, 1860, Allen F. McQueen, b. Indiana; d., Helena, Ark., 1863; son of William and Mary (Mosier) McQueen, of Prairieburg. He was a member of the 24th Regt. Iowa Vol. Inf. She m. (2), Prairieburg, Nov. 20, 1867, John T. Argubright, b., Illinois, July 3, 1838. He served as a soldier in an Illinois regiment during the War of the Rebellion. He is a mason and plasterer, and resides at Seattle, Wash. He is a Democrat. He and his wife are members of the Congregational Church.

Children by first m., b. and d. in Prairieburg:

1762. Alvin H. McQueen, b. Jan. 17, 1861; d. June, 1863.

1763. Cora A. McQueen, b. Feb. 24, 1862; d. June 25, 1863.

Children by second m.:

1764. Bertha M. Argubright, b., Prairieburg, Sept. 5, 1868 (1869–1871).

1765. Charles J. Argubright, b., Prairieburg, Nov. 2, 1871; m., Port

Byron, Ill., Dec. 22, 1896, Mary T. Dailey, b., Port Byron, July 12, 1875. Graduated from Business College at Davenport, Ia.; taught in public schools and business colleges; is now president of Battle Creek Business and Normal College at Battle Creek, Mich.

1766. Lulu Argubright, b., Doon, Ia., July 23, 1873; d. 1873.

1767. Edith Argubright, b., Doon, May 7, 1879; m., Everett, Wash., July 6, 1904, Robert Hoffman, b., Spring Valley, Ill., Dec. 16, 1876; son of Austin Hoffman and Julia A. (Throop) Hoffman, of Round Lake, Minn. She graduated from the Musical Department of Epworth Seminary at Epworth, Ia., June 8, 1897; taught music for two years in Hull Educational Institute at Hull, Ia.; she is now organist of the United Presbyterian Church of Everett. Her husband removed with his parents from Spring Valley to Round Lake in 1888, and in 1903 he removed to Everett; he is in the shipping department of a sash-and-door factory. He is a Republican, and he and his wife are members of the United Presbyterian Church.

Catherine R. Brown (1718), sister of the preceding, b., Brookfield, N. Y., Mar. 8, 1843; m., Marion, Ia., Jan. 28, 1864, George W. McQueen, b., Indiana, 1837; d., Lorane, Ore., Dec. 27, 1898; son of William and Mary (Mosier) McQueen, of Prairieburg, Ia. He was a member of the 8th Regt. Iowa Vol. Inf.; was taken prisoner at the battle of Shiloh, and after spending some time in Southern prisons was paroled and rejoined his regiment. He was a farmer at Elkton, Ore., and a Republican. Res., Cottage Grove, Ore.

Children, first four b. Prairieburg; last two, Doon, Ia.:

1768. Dora McQueen, b. Jan. 18, 1865; d., Prairieburg, Sept. 28, 1865.

1769. Ivan McQueen, b. Jan. 20, 1866. He was elected County Superintendent of Schools for Lyon Co., Ia., in 1888; reelected in 1890; was elected to the Legislature of Oregon from Lane Co. in 1898, and reëlected in 1900.

1770. Mary L. McQueen, b. Apr. 27, 1868; graduated at Hull Educational Institute, Hull, Ia.; studied music at Cornell College and at Epworth College, Ia.; gave music lessons and taught school; m., 1901, Cottage Grove, Ore., Solomon Davidson. He is a jeweler. Address, Boise, Idaho.

THE EZEKIEL MAIN FAMILY

1771. William McQueen, b. Apr. 11, 1870.
1772. George W. McQueen, b. Mar. 26, 1874 (1872).
1773. Zaida L. McQueen, b. Jan. 29, 1885.

Perry O. Brown (1720), son of Horace B. Brown (1690) and his second
wife, Esther Crandall, b., Columbus, N. Y., Feb. 14, 1849; m. (1), Prairieburg, Ia., Dec. 25, 1873, Emma A. Belknap, b. Linn Co., Ia.; d., Prairieburg, Nov. 24, 1874; m. (2), Linn Co., June 23, 1878, Irene E. Abbott. He
is a merchant in Portland, Ore., a Republican, and he and his wife are
members of the Methodist Church. Res., Portland, Ore.
  Son by first m.:
    1774. Guy, b., Prairieburg, Nov. 29, 1874.
  Children by second m., all b. Prairieburg:
    1775. Horace E., b. May 2, 1879; d., Prairieburg, Feb. 3, 1883.
    1776. Esther M., b. Apr. 10, 1880.
    1777. Linus P., b. July 29, 1884.
    1778. Lem L., b. July 8, 1886.

Freeman E. Brown (1721), brother of the preceding, b., Columbus,
N. Y., Oct. 30, 1851; m., Prairieburg, Ia., May 22, 1878, Nettie A. Fleming.
He is a mason by occupation, and a Republican. His eldest daughter died
some years ago. He is said to have had two other children, whose names
are not ascertained. Res., Prairieburg, Ia.
  Children:
    1779. M. Alverda, b. Feb. 28, 1880.
    1780. Mary E., b. Aug. 28, 1882.
    1781. Lewis E., b. June 9, 1885.
    1782. Albert, b. Apr. 5, 1887.

Lewis C. Brown (1722), brother of the preceding, b., Columbus, N. Y.,
Feb. 22, 1853; m., Prairieburg, Ia., Oct. 30, 1875, Emily M. Ary. He removed from Prairieburg to Winnebago Co., Ia., in 1890. In 1892 he was
elected County Superintendent of Schools, and was reëlected in 1894 and
1896; was again elected in 1903, and still holds the office. He is a Republican. Res., Forest City, Ia.
  Children, first seven b. Prairieburg; last three, Forest City:
    1783. Aurilla, b. Apr. 9, 1877.
    1784. Ethel, b. Apr. 3, 1879; d., Prairieburg, 1883.
    1785. Wesley, b. Jan. 29, 1881; d., Prairieburg, 1883.
    1786. C. Edgar, b. Feb. 4, 1883.
    1787. Marion L., b. Feb. 12, 1885.

1788. Arthur D., b. Feb. 6, 1887.

1789. Edna M., b. Apr. 18, 1889.

1790. Claire, b. Feb. 18, 1893.

1791. Reginald, b. Sept. 16, 1895.

1792. James, b. May 10, 1896.

Viola M. Brown (1724), dau. of Alonzo H. (1691) and Emeline (Mason) Brown, b. Jan. 26, 1847; m., Sept., 1870, Alonzo Adams, of Michigan.
Children:

1793. Calvin J. Adams, b. 1872 (1873, 1874).

1794. Ethel R. Adams, b. 1881 (1875).

Zebulon L. Brown (1725), brother of the preceding, b. Feb. 12, 1849; d. Dec. 12, 1896; m. (1), Jan. 1, 1871, Julia A. Cook, d. Nov. 28, 1871; m. (2), Mar. 21, 1878, Ida F. Sarle.
Children, by second m.:

1795. Adilla E., b. Dec. 12, 1878; d., Columbus, N. Y., May 8, 1898.

1796. Emma M., b. June 25, 1881; d., Columbus, Nov. 28, 1896.

1797. Sarl, b. 1893. Res., 1905, with his mother, in Columbus, O.

L. Sherwood Fitch (1727), son of Elliott G. and Sabrina (Brown) Fitch (1692), b., Brookfield, N. Y., Mar. 26, 1846; m. (1), No. Brookfield, Mar. 21, 1866, Alice M. Gorton, b. No. Brookfield; d., No. Brookfield, Feb. 4, 1886; dau. of Marsena Gorton, of No. Brookfield, and Westley (Morgan) Gorton; m. (2), June 27, 1888, Melida Vanderpoel, b., Paris, N. Y., May 3, 1856; dau. of Albert De Witt Clinton and Eliza (Randall) Vanderpoel.
Child, by first m.;

1798. Lynn Fitch, b., Brookfield, Oct. 16, 1869.

Sarah L. Fitch (1728), sister of the preceding, b., No. Brookfield, N. Y., Aug. 13, 1849; m., No. Brookfield, Jan. 7, 1868, Brownell Tompkins, b., Madison, N. Y., Aug. 21, 1845; son of Philip Tompkins, of Hamilton, N. Y., and Mary (Simmons) Tompkins. She was educated in the country schools and at Whitestown Seminary. He attended the country schools, the Union School at Hamilton, and Eastman's Business College at Poughkeepsie, N. Y. He entered the First National Bank at Morrisville, N. Y., soon after its organization, in 1864, and is now its cashier, having been elected to the latter position in 1882. He and his wife are members of the Congregational Church, of which he is an ardent supporter, being one of its deacons and superintendent of the Sunday school for many years. He is a Republican. Res., Morrisville, N. Y.

Children:

1799. S. Blanche Tompkins, b., Morrisville, Sept. 4, 1870 (1876–1879).

1800. B. Fitch Tompkins, b. Jan. 20, 1875; m., Syracuse, N. Y., June 30, 1897, Mae Louise Jenner, b., Clyde, N. Y., Mar. 6, 1874; dau. of John W. Jenner, of Clyde, and Harriet (Nichols) Jenner. He graduated from Olivet College, Mich., in 1896; clerk in First National Bank at Morrisville; studied law with Judge John C. Smith, of Morrisville; admitted to the bar at Albany, N. Y., Oct., 1898; has since practised law at Morrisville, first as a member of the firm of Smith & Tompkins, and later as a member of the firm of Coman & Tompkins; volunteer fireman since 1896, and foreman of H. & L. Co.; elected Justice of the Peace in 1903. His wife graduated from State Normal School at Geneseo, N. Y., in 1893; was a teacher in High Schools at Avon, Bath, and Morrisville, all in New York.

1801. Mary Elizabeth Tompkins, b. Feb. 2, 1880 (1880).

Luella Fitch (1729), sister of the preceding, b., No. Brookfield, N. Y., Sept. 7, 1863; m., No. Brookfield, Nov. 7, 1882, Lucius P. Burdick, b., Edgerton, Wis., Oct. 27, 1861; son of Joseph Burdick. He is a farmer, a Republican, and he and his wife are members of the Seventh-Day Baptist Church. Res., Brookfield, N. Y.

Children, all b. Brookfield:

1802. Iva Marina Burdick, b. Mar. 31, 1885.

1803. Dora Lucile Burdick, b. Jan. 31, 1899.

1804. Raymond Fitch Burdick, b. June 19, 1900.

De Ette Brown (1736), dau. of John F. (1695) and Sophia (Dresser) Brown, b. Nov. 19, 1854; d. Aug. 5, 1899; m., Feb. 18, 1875, Edgar Harris, b. 1850.

Children:

1805. Arthur Harris, b. Feb. 10, 1876.

1806. John B. Harris, b. Apr. 14, 1878. He is a school-teacher.

1807. Lewis H. Harris, b. Nov. 25, 1884; m., Mar. 28, 1905, Angie Mason.

A. Duane Brown (1737), brother of the preceding, b. Sept. 8, 1860; m., Oct. 3, 1887, Nettie Page, b. Jan. 4, 1863.

Children:

1808. Jennie, b. Aug. 18, 1890.

1809. Floy, b. Nov. 17, 1895.

William H. Brown (1738), brother of the preceding, b. May 8, 1866; m., Sept. 20, 1893, Nettie F. Babcock, b. Mar. 8, 1876.

Children:

1810. Harry L., b. May 18, 1896.

1811. Mary E., b. Sept. 13, 1897.

1812. Sarah, b. Jan. 8, 1899.

Mary J. Brown (1739), sister of the preceding, b. Aug. 11, 1868; m., Dec. 24, 1890, Jay Samson, b. May 22, 1866.

Children:

1813. Edith Samson, b. May 22, 1896.

1814. Elbert L. Samson, b. Sept. 3, 1902.

Iva J. Brown (1740), sister of the preceding, b. Sept. 22, 1874; m., Dec. 20, 1893, Claude Chesebro, b. 1874.

Son:

1815. C. Rupert Chesebro, b. Dec. 12, 1896.

Hazel S. Dresser (1741), dau. of Jacob A. Dresser and Eunice A. (Brown) Dresser (1696), b., Brookfield, N. Y., Apr. 9, 1860; m., Brookfield, Nov. 27, 1884, Cora Rollins, b., Brookfield, Apr. 20, 1867; dau. of William Rollins, of Brookfield, and Alice, his wife. He is a farmer, a Prohibitionist, and he and his wife are members of the Society of Friends. He taught school winters from 1879 to 1890, and made cheese summers from 1880 to 1890. They lived for three years in Sherburn, N. Y., and since then have lived in the town of Hamilton, N. Y. Address, Poolville, N. Y.

Children:

1816. Irving Dresser, b., Brookfield, Nov. 26, 1885.

1817. Lynn Dresser, b., Poolville, July 2, 1901.

Cora M. Dresser (1742), sister of the preceding, b., Brookfield, N. Y., Aug. 25, 1862; m., Brookfield, Feb. 20, 1889, Adelbert Harris, b., Brookfield, Mar. 19, 1855; son of Milton Harris, of Brookfield, and Louisa, his wife. He is a Republican, a farmer, and he and his wife are members of the Society of Friends. She taught school from 1879 to 1889. He worked on a farm, and later made cheese. He lived for a time in Sherburn, N. Y., after marriage, and made cheese; later moved to Brookfield. Address, Poolville, N. Y.

Children:

    1818. Lulu E. Harris, b. Dec. 19, 1890.

    1819. Mildred M. Harris, b. May 8, 1895.

    1820. Leon M. Harris, b. June 14, 1899.

Almer H. Dresser (1743), brother of the preceding, b., Brookfield, N. Y., July 3, 1867; m., Unadilla, Otsego Co., N. Y., Jan. 25, 1893, Blanch E. Mott, b., Unadilla, Nov. 3, 1869; dau. of Leroy Mott, of Unadilla, and Frances, his wife. He is a hardware merchant, and he and his wife are members of the Methodist Church. Worked on the farm until eighteen years of age; taught school winters and made cheese summers until his marriage. Res., Eaton, Madison Co., N. Y.

Children:

    1821. M. Floyd Dresser, b. Apr. 17, 1898.

    1822. A. Lawrence Dresser, b. Mar. 23, 1905.

Daisy Dresser (1744), sister of the preceding, b., Brookfield, N. Y., Sept. 19, 1871; m., Brookfield, Nov. 15, 1896, George Kleck, b., Russia, Apr. 23, 1869; son of Julian Kleck and Dorothy, his wife. He is a farmer and an immigrant agent, a Republican, and he and his wife are members of the Society of Friends. She taught school before her marriage. While in Russia he worked in a police-station as a clerk. He has been a farmer since coming to this country. About six years ago he bought the farm in Brookfield where they now reside. Address, Poolville, N. Y.

Dau.:

    1823. Eunice Kleck, b. Nov. 2, 1899.

Ela Randall Nichols (1700), son of Clark and Eunice (Randall) Nichols (1678), dau. of Robert and Eunice (Brown) Randall (1675), b., Brookfield, N. Y., Jan. 29, 1824; d., Rawson, N. Y., June 28, 1902; m., Genesee, N. Y., Feb. 20, 1853, Mary Jacobs, b., Lockport, Niagara Co., N. Y.; dau. of William Jacobs and Elizabeth McLaren. He was a farmer, and he and his wife were members of the Baptist Church.

Children:

    1824. Louise Josephine Nichols, b. Dec. 17, 1853; d., Rushford, N. Y., Mar. 3, 1857.

    1825. Robert Arthur Nichols, b., Rushford, Allegany Co., N. Y., 1868; unm. Res., Cuba, N. Y.

Abigail Nichols (1701), sister of the preceding, b., Brookfield, N. Y., Jan. 29, 1824; d., West Clarksville, Allegany Co., N. Y., Apr. 1, 1902; m.,

Clarksville, Sept. 3, 1849, John F. Adams, b. Allen, N. Y.; d., Clarksville, 1862; son of John Francis Adams and his wife, A. E. He was a farmer. His wife was a member of the Baptist Church.

Children:

    1826. Charles Frederick Adams, b., Allen, Aug. 19, 1851 (1881).

    1827. John Q. Adams, b., West Clarksville, Dec. 5, 1859 (1882, 1883).

Henry Webb Nichols (1702), brother of the preceding, b., Brookfield, N. Y., Jan. 30, 1828; d., St. Paul, Howard Co., Neb., Feb. 24, 1904; m., Hume, N. Y., Sept. 16, 1852, Lucinda M. Ellwood, b., Cortland, N. Y., Nov. 14, 1832; d., St. Paul, Feb. 22, 1904; dau. of William Ellwood, of Hume, Allegany Co., N. Y. He was a farmer and a stone-mason, a Republican, and he and his wife were members of the Methodist Church. He enlisted, Aug. 29, 1862, in Co. K, 136th N. Y. Vols., and served with credit three years; honorably discharged June 22, 1865.

Children, all except the last b. Clarksville, Allegany Co., N. Y.:

    1828. Letitia Nichols, b. Nov. 27, 1853 (1884).

    1829. Clark R. Nichols, b. July 1, 1856 (1885).

    1830. Charles H. Nichols, b. May 11, 1860 (1886-1890).

    1831. Alanson Nichols, b., Millington, Ill., Sept. 14, 1869 (1891).

William Randall Nichols (1703), brother of the preceding, b., Brookfield. N. Y., Feb. 26, 1830; d., Clarksville, Allegany Co., N. Y., Oct. 16, 1887; m., Wirt, Allegany Co., N. Y., Apr. 28, 1850, Mary J. Labar, dau. of Henry and Betsey Labar. He was a blacksmith, a Republican, and he and his wife were members of the Baptist Church.

Children, b. Clarksville:

    1832. Eunice Nichols, b. Feb. 7, 1851 (1892-1895).

    1833. William Henry Nichols, b. Aug. 22, 1855; d., Clarksville, Nov. 26, 1863.

Maria Elvira Nichols (1704), sister of the preceding, b., Brookfield. N. Y., Jan. 30, 1832; m., Friendship, Allegany Co., N. Y., Sept. 25, 1856. Lavosier D. Norton, b., Cortland, N. Y., Sept. 4, 1831; d., Olean, N. Y., Mar. 27, 1895; son of Harvey and Mary Norton, of Friendship, N. Y. He was a farmer, a Republican, and he and his wife were members of the Methodist Church. In 1877 she completed the Normal Course at Chautauqua prescribed for Normal Dept. M. E. S. S. Union; in 1882 she completed the four years' course in reading required by the C. L. S. C.; for the past twenty-seven years she has been superintendent of the Primary Dept. M. E. S. S. at Olean. Res., Olean, N. Y.

Children, first two b. Genesee, N. Y.; last, Clarksville, Allegany Co., N. Y.:

    1834. Infant son, b. June 28, 1857; d. July 3, 1857.

    1835. Lillia S. Norton, b. Feb. 22, 1859 (1896–1899).

    1836. Herman H. Norton, b. June 23, 1860; d., Clarksville, Feb. 14, 1869.

Robert C. Nichols (1705), brother of the preceding, b., Clarksville, Allegany Co., N. Y., July 10, 1834; d., Marion, Ind., Sept., 1904; m., Cuba, N. Y., July 11, 1858, Elizabeth Helmer, b. Cuba; d. Marion; dau. of John Helmer. He worked in a sawmill and later in a factory; was a Republican.

Children:

    1837. Frankie D. Nichols, b., Kansas Mills, Ill., Jan. 22, 1859.

    1838. Minnie E. Nichols, b., Kansas Mills, Mar. 17, 1861.

    1839. Frederick Nichols, b., Nettle Creek, Ill., Jan. 10, 1865.

    1840. Sprague L. Nichols, b., Nettle Creek, Feb. 17, 1871.

    1841. William M. Nichols, b., Goodland, Newton Co., Ind., Oct. 25, 1874.

Louise A. Nichols (1706), sister of the preceding, b., West Clarksville, Allegany Co., N. Y., Nov. 4, 1837; m., Rushford, N. Y., Sept. 7, 1861, Henry J. Norton, b., Cortland, N. Y., Oct. 28, 1832; brother of L. D. Norton, husband of Maria Elvira Norton (1704); d., Olean, N. Y., Aug. 13, 1896; son of Harvey and Mary Norton, of Friendship, N. Y. He was a farmer and resided at West Clarksville; was a Prohibitionist, and the family attended the Church of the United Brethren.

Children:

    1842. Hattie Eliza Norton, b., West Clarksville, June 20, 1862; d., West Clarksville, Mar. 13, 1863.

    1843. Rubie Estelle, b., West Clarksville, June 7, 1871; d., West Clarksville, Apr. 3, 1875.

    1844. Ruth Emma Norton, b., West Clarksville, July 8, 1878; m., Olean, Oct. 29, 1902, George D. Moore, of Olean. Res., Olean, N. Y.

    1845. Mattie A. (Champlin), an adopted dau., b. Oct. 28, 1861; m., Clarksville, N. Y., Jan. 12, 1878, Clarence Burdette Starkey. Res., Los Angeles, Cal.

James Albert Nichols (1708), brother of the preceding, b., West Clarksville, N. Y., July 15, 1842; m., West Clarksville, Dec. 22, 1867, Charlotte
Peckham, b., West Clarksville, July 11, 1847; dau. of Prentice Peckham,
of West Clarksville, and Polly (Murray) Peckham. He is a carriage-
maker at Olean, N. Y.; in politics, a Republican.

Children:

    1846. Robert Herman Nichols, b., Clarksville, N. Y., Oct. 9, 1868
         (1900).

    1847. Hattie Leon Nichols, b., Clarksville, Apr. 11, 1871; d., Clarks-
         ville, Nov. 27, 1874.

    1848. Mary De Ette Nichols, b., Clarksville, Sept. 22, 1873 (1901–
         1904).

    1849. Roy Nichols, b., Clarksville, July 25, 1878; m., Andover, N. Y.,
         Feb. 7, 1903, Florence Cochrane. He is a laborer; in politics,
         a Republican. No issue.

Orra Chesebro (1747), dau. of J. Hiram (1712) and Harriet (Williams)
Chesebro, son of Jared and Sarah (Brown) Chesebro (1688), b. Apr. 27,
1862; m., Nov. 13, 1883, Arthur D. Page, b. Sept. 11, 1862.

Children:

    1850. Alvin E. Page, b. Feb. 22, 1890.

    1851. Floyd W. Page, b. Nov. 9, 1894.

William Brown (1750), son of Henry H. (1714) and Mary J. (Wagner)
Brown, b., Prairieburg, Ia., Jan. 4, 1866; m., Cottage Grove, Ore., Jan. 13,
1889, Mattie Shortridge, b., Cottage Grove, Sept. 1, 1866; dau. of Wallace
Shortridge and E. J. (Keyes) Shortridge. He is a carpenter and a Republi-
can. His wife is a member of the Christian Church. Res., Cottage Grove,
Ore.

Children, all b. at or near Cottage Grove:

    1852. Aimee Z., b. Feb. 14, 1890.

    1853. Annie L., b. Jan. 9, 1897; d., Cottage Grove, Feb. 15, 1897.

    1854. Mary E., b. Apr. 16, 1898.

Grace Brown (1751), sister of the preceding, b., Prairieburg, Ia., Nov. 16,
1868; m., Cottage Grove, Ore., May 1, 1889, Charles Lewis, b. Springfield,
Ill.; son of Andy O. and Sarah (Tucker) Lewis. He is a farmer at Cottage
Grove.

Dau., b. Cottage Grove:

    1855. Elsie Lewis, b. May 25, 1891.

Grant Brown (1752), brother of the preceding, b., Prairieburg, Ia., Nov. 16, 1868; m., Cottage Grove, Ore., Oct. 13, 1900, Callistia J. Garoutte, b., Cottage Grove, Jan. 28, 1875; dau. of Howard N. Garoutte, of Cottage Grove, and Sophia J. (Taylor) Garoutte. He is a farmer at Cottage Grove.
Children:

  1856. Ralph, b., Cottage Grove, Aug. 7, 1901.
  1857. Son, unnamed, b., Springfield, Ore., Feb. 2, 1904.

Alice Brown (1753), sister of the preceding, b., Rock Rapids, Ia., Sept. 9, 1872; m., Cottage Grove, Ore., Charles Thornton, son of Jesse Thornton, of Cottage Grove, and Martha (Sprey) Thornton. He is a Republican. Res., Cottage Grove, Ore.
Son:

  1858. Frederick Thornton, b., Lebanon, Ore., Oct. 17, 1895.

Clara B. Brown (1755), dau. of Alvin H. (1715) and Mary A. (Sisson) Brown, b., Prairieburg, Ia., Nov. 7, 1867; m., Newaukum, Wash., Jan. 14, 1894, Lewis C. Easter, son of William and Alice Easter, of Chesley, Idaho. He is a farmer at Chesley, and a Republican.
Children, first two b. Lewis Co., Wash.; the others, Chesley:

  1859. Florence B. Easter, b. Sept., 1896.
  1860. Frances M. Easter, b. Oct. 20, 1897.
  1861. Dewey Easter, b. 1899.
  1862. Curtis Easter, b. 1901.
  1863. Clarence Easter, b. 1903.
  1864. Teddy Easter, b. 1904.

Sarah L. Brown (1757), sister of the preceding, b., Prairieburg, Ia., Jan. 29, 1871; m., Newaukum, Wash., Nov. 25, 1899, Charles L. Knapp, b., Michigan, 1855. He is a mason at Everett, Wash., and a Republican.
Children, b. in Olympia, Wash.:

  1865. Francis Earl Knapp, b. Apr., 1902.
  1866. Fanny May Knapp, b. May 1, 1904.

Cora E. Brown (1758), sister of the preceding, b., Ashton, Ia., July 10, 1873; m., Sheldon, Ia., June, 1897, Chester Linch, son of Robert Linch, of Sheldon. She graduated in 1892 from Hull Educational Institute at Hull, Ia., and subsequently taught school in Washington and in Sioux Co., Ia. Her husband is a farmer at Sheldon, and a Republican. She is a member of the Congregational Church.

Children, all b. Sheldon:
 1867. Robert Linch, b. 1899.
 1868. Alvin Linch, b. Apr., 1904.

Bertha M. Argubright (1764), dau. of John T. Argubright and Lois M. (Brown) Argubright (1716), dau. of Horace B. Brown (1690), son of Zebulon (1676), son of Zebulon (304), son of Dea. Zebulon and Anne Main (279), b., Prairieburg, Ia., Sept. 5, 1868; m., Hull, Ia., Jan. 26, 1898, Arthur D. Cross, b., Grove Creek, Ia., Feb. 13, 1869; son of Orlando and Mary Ann (Foster) Cross. She graduated from the classical course at Hull Academy and took one year of the scientific course and one year of the art course at Cornell, Ia.; taught in the country and graded schools of Iowa for eight years. Her husband is a bookkeeper and office manager. Res., 1818 Rucker Ave., Everett, Wash.
 Children:
  1869. Lois Cross, b., Minneapolis, Minn., Nov. 12, 1898.
  1870. Marian, b., Hull, May 10, 1901.
  1871. John Cross, b., Everett, Aug. 15, 1904.

George W. McQueen (1772), son of George W. and Catherine R. (Brown) McQueen (1718), dau. of Horace B. Brown (1690), son of Zebulon (1676), son of Zebulon (304), son of Dea. Zebulon and Anne Main (279), b., Doon, Ia., Mar. 26, 1874; m., Cottage Grove, Ia., 1899, Bertha Griffin, dau. of Robert Griffin, of Cottage Grove. He is a Republican. Res., Cottage Grove, Ia.
 Son:
  1872. George Robert McQueen, b., Cottage Grove, 1901.

Calvin J. Adams (1793), son of Alonzo and Viola M. (Brown) Adams (1724), dau. of Alonzo H. (1691), son of Zebulon (1676), son of Zebulon (304), son of Dea. Zebulon and Anne Main (279), b. 1872; m., Michigan, Mertie Halliday.
 Children:
  1873. Irena Hobart Adams, b. 1900.
  1874. Dorothy H. Adams, b. 1902.

Ethel R. Adams (1794), sister of the preceding, b. 1881; m. Joseph Maxwell.
 Dau.:
  1875. Robertia M. Maxwell, b. about 1903.

Sarah Blanche Tompkins (1799), dau. of Brownell and Sarah L. (Fitch) Tompkins (1728), dau. of Elliott G. and Sabrina (Brown) Fitch (1692), b., Morrisville, N. Y., Sept. 4, 1870; m., Morrisville, June 8, 1891, Nelson Landon Hoyt, b., Chicago, Ill., Oct. 28, 1869; son of William M. Hoyt, of Winnetka, Ill., and Emily J. Landon. He attended school at Lake Forest, Ill., and Hudson River Institute at Claverack, N. Y. He is a Republican, and the manager of a wholesale grocery department at Winnetka. His wife was educated at Morrisville Union School and Claverack College, graduating as A.B. and in music in 1889. She is a member of the Congregational Church.

Children.

    1876. William M. Hoyt, b., Winnetka, July 15, 1892.

    1877. Sarah E. Hoyt, b., Chicago, Mar. 25, 1894.

    1878. N. Landon Hoyt, Jr., b., Chicago, Dec. 10, 1897.

    1879. Josephine Hoyt, b., Winnetka, Nov. 2, 1902.

Mary Elizabeth Tompkins (1801), sister of the preceding, b., Morrisville, N. Y., Feb. 2, 1880; m., Morrisville, July 12, 1902, Percy Wentforth Penhallow Bradstreet, b., Boston, Mass., Aug. 24, 1878; son of Edwin Bradstreet and Carrie (Calroer) Bradstreet, of Winnetka, Ill. He is a Republican, and a cashier in a business house. He graduated at the Evanston High School. His wife graduated at the Morrisville High School and was one year at Elmira College, N. Y., and at Northwestern University, Evanston, Ill., one year. She is a member of the Second Congregational Church. Res., Evanston, Ill.

Son:

    1880. Brownell T. Bradstreet, b., Evanston, Oct. 1, 1904.

Charles Frederick Adams (1826), son of John F. Adams and Abigail (Nichols) Adams (1701), dau. of Clark and Eunice (Randall) Nichols (1678), dau. of Zebulon Brown (304), son of Dea. Zebulon and Anne Main (279), b., Allen, N. Y., Aug. 19, 1851; m., Cuba, N. Y., Dec. 14, 1872, Mary Ann Doty, b., Belfast, N. Y., Feb. 19, 1854. He is a Democrat, and a merchant at Belmont, N. Y. His wife is a member of the Baptist Church.

Dau.:

    1881. Jennie Adams, b., Clarksville, Allegany Co., N. Y., Mar. 12, 1874; d., Belmont, June 8, 1893 (1905).

John Quincy Adams (1827), brother of the preceding, b., Clarksville, Allegany Co., N. Y., Dec. 5, 1859; m., Nile, N. Y., Mar. 6, 1881, Mary Ann Harris, b., Pikeville, N. Y., Aug. 8, 1863. He is a Democrat, and a barber at Belmont, N. Y.

THE EZEKIEL MAIN FAMILY

Children:

    1882. Ellie Robert Adams, b., Belmont, Jan. 6, 1883; d., Belmont,
           July 8, 1903.
    1883. George Francis Adams, b., Belmont, Oct. 25, 1885.

Letitia Nichols (1828), dau. of Henry Webb Nichols (1702) and Lucinda
M. (Ellwood) Nichols, son of Clark and Eunice (Randall) Nichols (1678),
dau. of Eunice Brown (1675) and Robert Randall, b., Clarksville, Allegany
Co., N. Y., Nov. 27, 1853; m., Brookfield, N. Y., Feb. 26, 1877, William
Tompkins, b., Green Co., N. Y., July 18, 1844. They removed to Hast-
ings, Neb., in 1879.

    Dau.:

    1884. Rose L. Tompkins, b., Brookfield, Mar. 3, 1878 (1906).

Clark R. Nichols (1829), brother of the preceding, b., Clarksville, N. Y.,
July 1, 1856; m., Brookfield, N. Y., 1880, Emma Gage, b., Brookfield,
1857. He is a farmer at Lester, Lyon Co., Ia.

    Son:

    1885. Chester Nichols, b., Lester, 1895.

Charles H. Nichols (1830), brother of the preceding, b., Clarksville,
N. Y., May 11, 1860; m., Brookfield, N. Y., Feb. 12, 1885, Lizzie Gage, b.,
Brookfield, Nov. 25, 1862; dau. of Richard and Mary (Jennings) Gage.
He is a farmer at Woodbine, Ia., and a Republican. His wife is a member
of the Presbyterian Church.

    Children:

    1886. Jessie Nichols, b. Apr. 1, 1886.
    1887. John Nichols, b. Oct. 20, 1887.
    1888. Florence Nichols, b. Aug. 26, 1891.
    1889. Raymond Nichols, b. Dec. 17, 1893; d. Mar. 13, 1898.
    1890. Baby, b. Dec. 18, 1902; d. Dec. 28, 1902.

Alanson Nichols (1831), brother of the preceding, b., Millington, Ill.,
Sept. 14, 1869; m., Joliet, Ill., June 21, 1901, Ruth Kniver, b., Illinois,
1870. He is a photographer at Plainfield, Ill., a Republican, and he and his
wife are members of the Presbyterian Church.

    Dau.:

    1891. Elizabeth Nichols, b., Plainfield, Jan. 5, 1902.

Eunice Nichols (1832), dau. of William Randall Nichols (1703) and
Mary J. Labar, son of Clark Nichols and Eunice (Randall) Nichols (1678),

THE EZEKIEL MAIN FAMILY

dau. of Robert and Eunice (Brown) Randall (1675), b., Clarksville, Allegany Co., N. Y., Feb. 7, 1851; m., Clarksville, Jan. 25, 1871, Ithamer Ferrington, b., Clarksville, July 8, 1849; son of Jabish and Melvina Ferrington. He is a farmer and a Democrat.

Children:

    1892. William H. Ferrington, b., Clarksville, Oct. 21, 1872.

    1893. Martin Ferrington, b., Clarksville, May 8, 1875.

    1894. Carl Ferrington, b. Sept. 18, 1878 (1907–1909).

    1895. Miles L. Ferrington, b. Sept. 16, 1880; d., Clarksville, Aug. 29, 1881.

Lillia S. Norton (1835), dau. of Lavosier D. and Maria Elvira (Nichols) Norton (1704), dau. of Clark and Eunice (Randall) Nichols (1678), dau. of Robert and Eunice (Brown) Randall (1675), b., Little Genesee, N. Y., Feb. 22, 1859; m., Olean, N. Y., Oct. 12, 1881, Rev. J. P. Brushingham, b., New York, Feb. 16, 1855; son of Thomas Brushingham and Mary (O'Hern) Brushingham, of Olean. He graduated in 1881 from the Northwestern University, Evanston, Ill., and is now one of its Trustees. He is a Republican, and he and his wife are members of the First Methodist Church. They have resided in Chicago for the past twenty-five years. Res., 831 Millard Ave., Chicago, Ill.

Children:

    1896. Infant, b., Olean, Sept. 26, 1882.

    1897. Nellie Pearl Brushingham, b., Chicago, Feb. 22, 1885; m., Chicago, June 26, 1903, Carl W. Young, b., Chicago, June 1, 1865; son of William Young and Amanda, his wife. He is a voice teacher, Fine Arts Building, Chicago, and a Republican. His wife is a member of the Park Avenue Methodist Church.

    1898. Robert M. Brushingham, b., Chicago, Dec. 7, 1888.

    1899. John Norton Brushingham, b., Chicago, Nov. 3, 1898.

Robert Herman Nichols (1846), son of James Albert (1708) and Charlotte (Peckham) Nichols, son of Clark and Eunice (Randall) Nichols (1678), dau. of Robert and Eunice (Brown) Randall (1675), b., West Clarksville, Allegany Co., N. Y., Oct. 9, 1868; m., West Clarksville, Sept. 22, 1892, Margaret Ewart, d., Olean, N. Y., Sept. 22, 1904.

Son:

    1900. De Alton Nichols, b., Clarksville, N. Y., Apr. 20, 1893.

Mary De Ette Nichols (1848), sister of the preceding, b., West Clarksville, Allegany Co., N. Y., Sept. 22, 1873; m., Clarksville, N. Y., Jan. 1,
1891, Frank Healy. Res., West Clarksville, N. Y.

Children:

 1901. Noble Beatrice Nichols, b., Clarksville, Apr. 22, 1892; d.,
    Allentown, N. Y., Sept. 11, 1892.

 1902. John Nichols, b. July 1, 1893.

 1903. Basil Nichols, b. Oct., 1899.

 1904. Aileen Nichols, b. June 12, 1903.

Jennie Adams (1881), dau. of Charles Frederick Adams (1826) and Mary
Ann (Doty) Adams, son of John F. and Abigail (Nichols) Adams (1701),
dau. of Robert and Eunice (Brown) Randall (1675), dau. of Zebulon and
Theda (York) Brown (304), son of Dea. Zebulon and Anne (Main) Brown
(279), b., Clarksville, N. Y., Mar. 12, 1874; d., Belmont, N. Y., June 8,
1893; m., Clarksville, Fred Newcomb, b., Pike, N. Y., Oct. 25, 1867. Res.,
Belmont, N. Y.

Dau.:

 1905. Betsie Geraldine Newcomb, b., Clarksville, Mar. 17, 1891.

Rose L. Tompkins (1884), dau. of William Tompkins and Letitia
(Nichols) Tompkins (1828), dau. of Henry Webb (1702) and Lucinda M.
(Ellwood) Nichols, son of Clark and Eunice (Randall) Nichols (1678),
dau. of Robert and Eunice (Brown) Randall (1675), b., Brookfield, N. Y.,
Mar. 3, 1878; m., Hanson, Neb., Dec. 17, 1898, John W. Carriker, b.,
Missouri, 1872. He is a contractor and builder at Harvard, Neb.

Son:

 1906. Roy E. Carriker, b., Hanson, Apr. 6, 1902.

Carl Ferrington (1894), son of Ithamer Ferrington and Eunice (Nichols)
Ferrington (1832), dau. of William Randall Nichols (1703) and Mary J.
Labar, son of Clark and Eunice (Randall) Nichols (1678), dau. of Robert
and Eunice (Brown) Randall (1675), dau. of Zebulon Brown and Theda
(York) Brown (304), son of Dea. Zebulon and Anne (Main) Brown (279),
b., Clarksville, Allegany Co., N. Y., Sept. 18, 1878; m., Nov. 1, 1899,
Mildred Cushman.

Children:

 1907. Miles I. Ferrington, b. Oct. 29, 1900.

 1908. Mildred I. Ferrington, b. Oct. 17, 1903.

 1909. Lemur J. Ferrington, b. Feb. 9, 1905.

Mathew Brown (310), son of Dea. Zebulon Brown and Anne Main (279), b., Stonington, Conn., 1766; d. Apr. 9, 1800, of twelve days' quinsey; m., Stonington, by Elder Simeon Brown, his uncle, May 25, 1788, Elizabeth Brown, his cousin, b. Aug 5, 1766, d Nov 12, 1853; dau. of Elder Simeon and Dorothy (Hern) Brown. Interments, Brown Cemetery, No. Stonington, Conn.

Children, b. Stonington:

    1910. Betsey, b. Apr 10, 1789; m. Elias Miner (1919-1925).
    1911 Matilda, b. Mar. 10, 1791; m Luke Miner (1933-1941)
    1912. Mathew, b. Sept. 5, 1793, m. Lucy Ann Denison (1961-1964).

Phebe Brown (311), dau of Dea. Zebulon Brown and Anne Main (279), b , Stonington, Conn , 1770, d. June 27, 1817, aged forty-seven years; m. Elias Miner, son of Christopher and Mary (Randall) Miner, b , Stonington, Mar. 4, 1775; d. Jan 22, 1858, aged eighty-four years. He m. (2) Betsey Brown (1910), dau. of Mathew (310) and Elizabeth (Brown) Brown, b., Stonington, Apr. 10, 1789: d. Dec 1, 1883. Interments, Angwilla.

Children by first m.:

    1913. Christopher, b.——
    1914. Thomas, b.——
    19·5 Mary, b ——; m. Benj. Spaulding.
    1916. Phebe, b.——; m. (1) James Wheeler, m. (2) Clark Davis.
    1917. Alfred, b. Mar. 14, 1810; m Minerva Niles
    1918 Latham, b. Mar. 4, 1814, m. (1) Lydia Dodge, m. (2) Maria Johnson.

Children by second m. ·

    1919 Dudley, b. Sept. 28, 1818; d. Oct. 15, 1819.
    1920 Charles W , b. Apr. 19, 1821; d. Jan. 17, 1822.
    1921 Almira, b Mar 21, 1823; d. Apr. 16, 1867; m., Sept. 20, 1838, Rev. Ichabod B. Maryott.
    1922 Elias H., b. Nov. 23, 1825 (1926-1928).
    1923 Nelson B., b. Nov. 13, 1827; d Feb. 12, 1830.
    1924 Erastus D., b. Dec. 16, 1829; m. Jane P. Breed (1929-1932).
    1925 Martha E , b. Sept 7, 1832; m , July 4, 1852, Noyes S. Chapman.

Elias H. Miner (1922), son of Elias and Betsey (Brown) Miner (1910), b., Stonington, Conn., Nov. 23, 1825; m., No. Stonington, Mar. 22, 1853, Clarissa Miner, b., No. Stonington, July 26, 1836; dau. of Denison W. Miner (177 Miner family) and Clarissa M. Park (1333 Park family). Mr.

Miner and his sons are owners of large farms, rich and very productive, in Stonington (Angwilla). (See Miner family 204, p. 41.)

Children, b. Stonington:

1926. Horace D. Miner, b. Sept. 17, 1855; m. (1), Sept. 16, 1880, Lucy Chapman, b. Aug. 2. 1862; d. Sept. 16, 1884; dau. of W. R. and Lovinia (Sherman) Chapman, of Westerly, R. I. Dau.: Bessie Lucy Chapman Miner, b. Jan. 10, 1881; m., Somerville, Mass., Oct. 5, 1902, Geo. Albert Marshall, b., Lowell, Mass., Jan. 9, 1877. He is cashier and bookkeeper for Armour & Co., Westerly, in 1909. Child: Clara Angenette, b. Apr. 21, 1905. Mr. Miner m. (2) Grace Wheeler Billings. (For their children see 1485.)

1927. John R. Miner, b. Feb. 2, 1861; unm.

1928. Charles H. Miner, b. Nov. 13, 1862; d., aged ten years.

Deacon Erastus Denison Miner (1924), son of Elias and Betsey (Brown) Miner (1910), b., Stonington, Conn., Dec. 16, 1829; d. Apr. 23, 1907; m., Stonington, Aug. 15, 1852, Jane P. Breed, b. Nov. 15, 1831; dau. of Isaac Sheffield and Phebe Prentice (Hewett) Breed.

Children, b. Stonington:

1929. Hermon Erastus Miner, b. Aug. 9, 1853; m., Stonington, Conn., Mar. 12, 1884, Fanny M. Gavitt, b., Stonington, Sept. 9, 1855; d. Jan. 12, 1891; dau. of Timothy P. and Freelove V. (Thompson) Gavitt. He m. (2), Mystic, Conn., Dec. 8, 1897, Fanny F. Wilcox, b., Mystic, Oct. 22, 1857; d., Stonington (Angwilla), Oct. 30, 1904; dau. of Lodwick P. and Sarah A. (Davis) Wilcox, of Mystic. He m. (3), June 6, 1907, Annie Ethel Thorp, b., Leicester, England, July 17, 1880; dau. of Wm. Henry and Ada M. (Sargent) Thorp, of England. Mr. Miner is a farmer of ability, and he and his wife are members of the Christian Church of Westerly, R. I. He is a deacon. No issue.

1930. Sarah Jane Miner, b. Oct. 12, 1858; m. Hermon C. Brown. (See 1967.)

1931. Mary Emma Miner, b. Feb. 23, 1862; m. Frank E. Wilcox. No issue. Res., Westerly, R. I.

1932. Annie Elizabeth Miner, b. Feb. 27, 1864; m. John Seymore. No issue. Res., Westerly, R. I.

Matilda Brown (1911), dau. of Mathew (310) and Elizabeth (Brown) Brown, son of Dea. Zebulon and Anne (Main 279) Brown, b. Mar. 10, 1791; m., Stonington, Conn., Luke Miner, son of Christopher and Mary (Randall) Miner. Luke and Matilda soon after their marriage moved to Vermont, where three of their children were born. From there they moved to Pharsalia, N. Y., and later to Otselic, N. Y. Mrs. Miner was an ideal mother, a woman of rare Christian character, great courage, and good judgment. When moving from Pharsalia to Otselic she rode on a colt and carried her infant son Joshua in her arms. Then the country was new and wild; they travelled by blazed trees. What is now, 1909, the beautiful village of So. Otselic, N. Y., with city water and gas, then had nothing but log houses in the town.
Children:

1933. Luke Miner, m. Lucy Ann Miner, dau. of Joshua Miner. They lived at Galesburg, Ill.

1934. Eunice Miner, b.——; m. Samuel Messenger. Children: Rosanna, Frank, and Hannah.

1935. Mathew Brown Miner, b., Halifax, Vt., May 3, 1810 (1942–1944).

1936. Edson Miner, b.——; m., Brookfield, N. Y., Deborah York, dau. of Bell York. Children: Treat Y., b.——, res. George-town, N. Y.; Charles, b.——, res. Cortland, N. Y. [They did not answer queries.]

1937. Samuel Miner, b.——; m. Mary Brown, of Brookfield. No issue.

1938. Ezekiel Miner, b.——; m. Patience Myres. Children: Lovisa, John, Orcelia, and others living in different places West.

1939. Simeon Miner, b., Pharsalia, July 30, 1818; m. (1) Almira Bentley; m. (2) Harriette E. Burt (1945–1956).

1940. Joshua Miner, b. Pharsalia; d. Jan. 11, 1868; m. Elizabeth Main, of Brookfield. After his death his widow and children returned to So. Otselic, in 1869.

1941. Betsey Ann Miner, b., So. Otselic, July 17, 1825 (1957–1960).

Mathew Brown Miner (1935), son of Luke and Matilda (Brown) Miner (1911), b., Halifax, Vt., May 3, 1810; d., Brookfield, N. Y., May 31, 1896; m., Brookfield, Elizabeth Miner, dau. of Joshua Miner, son of Christopher.
Children, three d. in infancy, all b. Brookfield:

1942. Alfred, b. 1834; d. 1874; m.; both deceased.

1943. George Mathew, b. June 16, 1850; m., Brookfield, Sept. 15, 1870, Ellen M. Spohn, b. 1848. He is a farmer. Res., Leonardsville, N. Y.

Dau., b. Brookfield:

1944. Lela, b. July 16, 1879; m., Brookfield, Oct. 13, 1895, Elbert Henry Mott, b., Leonardsville, Sept. 2, 1875; son of Henry Samuel and Lucy (Dye) Mott. Both were educated in the public schools and high school of Leonardsville. He is a farmer. Dau.: Georgia L. Miner Mott, b. Feb. 27, 1901. Res., Unadilla Forks, N. Y.

Simeon Miner (1939), son of Luke Miner and Matilda (Brown) Miner (1911), b., Pharsalia, N. Y., July 30, 1818; d., So. Otselic, N. Y., July 2, 1900; m. (1) Almira Bentley; m. (2), De Ruyter, N. Y., Nov. 5, 1863, Harriette E. Burt, b., Linchlaen, N. Y., July 23, 1844; dau. of Francis and Susan E. (Stewart) Burt, of Linchlaen. She was educated in the public schools and the De Ruyter Seminary. He was a farmer and a Republican. Her res., So. Otselic, N. Y.

Children by first m.:

1945. Leslie, b.——. Res., Syracuse, N. Y.

1946. Philura, b.——; m. David Cross. Res., Linchlaen Center, N. Y.

1947. Rosetta, b., So. Otselic, May 5, 1843; m., So. Otselic, Oct. 19, 1859, George Hall, b., Chittenango, N. Y., 1834; d., Fort Plain, N. Y., May 14, 1896; son of Albro Hall and Carrie. Children, b. Little Falls, N. Y.: (1) Ernest E., b. May 19, 1865, d., Little Falls, June 16, 1872; (2) Jennie A., b. Feb. 5, 1867; m., Fort Plain, Oct., 1888, Joseph Fox; in 1905 she was divorced and resumed her maiden name. Dau.: Henrietta Rosetta, b., Fort Plain, Dec. 31, 1889; she was educated at the Academy of the Sacred Heart, Albany, N. Y. (3) Albro, b. Feb. 7, 1873, d., Little Falls, June 3, 1891; (4) Ernest Eugene; (5) Jennie Ann; (6) Albro W.

1948. Edgar, b.——; removed to a Western State.

1949. Philena, b.——; m. Albert Dellon; d. 1900.

1950. Emma, b.——; m. Martin Haven. Res., Syracuse, N. Y.

1951. Ethelyndia, b.——; m. Curtis Kenyon. Res., So. Otselic, N. Y.

1952. Everett, b.——. Res., East Homer, N. Y.

1953. Lida, b.——; m. Henry M. Peyser. Res., 1907, Brussels, Belgium.

Children by second m., b. So. Otselic, except one:

1954. Kittie A., b. Mar. 9, 1865; m., So. Otselic, Sept. 26, 1883,
Van Ness Peckham, of Georgetown, N. Y. Children:
Francis, Arlie, and Ivalou.

1955. Burt W., b. June 3, 1869; unm.

1956. Clayton L., b. Nov. 23, 1873; m., New Woodstock, N. Y.,
June 28, 1902, Linna Davis. Have one child. Res., So.
Otselic, N. Y.

Betsey Ann Miner (1941), dau. of Luke and Matilda (Brown) Miner
(1911), dau. of Mathew (310) and Elizabeth (Brown) Brown, b., So. Otselic,
N. Y., July 17, 1825; d., So. Otselic, Jan. 6, 1906; m., So. Otselic, John P.
Newton, b., So. Otselic, Oct. 2, 1825; son of Denny and Sally (Parker)
Newton. He is a retired merchant. Res., So. Otselic, N. Y.

Children, b. So. Otselic:

1957. Delia Newton, b. Oct. 23, 1850; m. Arthur R. Tucker.

1958. La Vette Newton, b. Sept. 25, 1852; m. Nettie Ufford. Son:
Channing L., b. 1881. Bookkeeper at Albany, N. Y.

1959. Ida De Ette Newton, b. Sept. 28, 1860; m. De Forest A.
Preston. Children: Niel D. Preston, a student at Cornell
University, N. Y., in 1906; Theodore Preston; Lona Adil
Preston; Paul, d. young.

1960. J. Floyd Newton, b. Jan. 28, 1865; m., Dec. 25, 1905, Minnie
Soule.

Mathew Brown (1912), son of Mathew Brown (310), son of Dea. Zebulon
Brown and Anne Main (279), b., Stonington, Conn., Sept. 5, 1793; d., No.
Stonington, Conn., Apr. 28, 1860; m., No. Stonington, July 4, 1816, Lucy
Ann Denison, b., Stonington, Feb. 18, 1799; d. July 20, 1848. He was
called "Esq. Mathew," and was a man of more than ordinary abilities; was
versed in matters of current events, and had good judgment. Mrs. Brown
was a woman of rare Christian character, and the choicest legacy left to
her children, grandchildren, and friends is the memory of her kind deeds
and loving acts. (See B. G., p. 44.)

Children, b. No. Stonington:

1961. Daniel, b. May 23, 1817; m. Jerusha A. Brown (1965-1972).

1962. Andrew Denison, b. Sept. 14, 1818; living (1973-1976).

1963. Lucy E., b. May 16, 1823; m. Reuben W. York (1985-1987).

1964. Hosmer A., b. Sept. 7, 1830; m., St. Paul, Minn., Jan. 1, 1869,
Mary L. Frink, b., No. Stonington, May, 1840; dau. of

Joseph Frink and Mrs. Lucy Coats, née Billings. Both received public-school education, and Miss Frink completed her education at the Connecticut Literary Institution, Suffield, Conn. She united with the Third Baptist Church, No. Stonington, at the age of sixteen, and never changed her membship. After their marriage they went to Browns-dale, Mower Co., Minn., to live, where she died, Aug. 1, 1900. Appended is a copy of one of her many poems.

Mr. Brown went with his brother Andrew to what is now known as Brownsdale, in 1855, and preëmpted a large tract of land, using in the payment a *Land Warrant* which was granted their father for services at Stonington, Conn., in the War of 1812. When they came to this wild country there were but two settlers for miles around. Putting in a saw-mill, they cut hundreds of acres of timber for lumber, and from this beginning sprang the beautiful village of Browns-dale. For two terms Mr. H. A. Brown has represented his district in the State Legislature of Minnesota. Res., 1909, Brownsdale, Mower Co., Minn. No issue.

MEMORIES

MRS. HOSMER A. BROWN

I 'm sitting to-night in my prairie home,
  And the purple twilight flings
Its dusky folds round the sadden'd soul
  Where Memory sits, and sings
Of the days of my sunny-hearted youth,
  That passed on downy wings.

She brings me dreams of my far-off home:
  The tree close up by the door;
I bend my ear to catch the sound
  Of the waterfall's muffled roar;
And watch, where the lilies at anchor ride,
  For the dip of the flashing oar.

I forget that beneath the homestead roof
  Stranger voices the echoes awake.
'T is a dream — the loved and the lost are there.
  With heart too full to speak,
Again I kiss the lines of care
  On brow and furrowed cheek.

My brother, with his golden hair
  Swept back from a brow like light;
How plain, across the mists of years,
  He rises to my sight!
His lips still wear their olden smile,
  His eye its sunny light.

227

One night his feet grew weary,
  He closed his earnest eyes;
And when morning walked the hilltops
  He was singing in Paradise.
And echoes roll round my haunted soul
  From out the starry skies.

And one — Oh! softly speak her name,
  And reverently, and low;
She walks upon eternal hills
  Where stainless lilies blow;
But just within the pearly gates
  She waits for me, I know.

Her saintly face shines on me still
  Through the twilight calm and clear;
I bend my ear to the sighing wind,
  Her voice I seem to hear;
It whispers " Peace ' to my waiting soul,
  And I know that she is near.

Ah well, I shall meet them all again
  When I reach that shore unknown,
With its wondrous city, pearly gates,
  And everlasting throne.

Daniel Brown (1961), son of Mathew (1912), son of Mathew (310), son of Dea. Zebulon Brown and Anne Main (279), b., No. Stonington, Conn., May 23, 1817; d., Stonington, Conn., Jan. 3, 1889; m., No. Stonington, Apr. 8, 1842, Jerusha A. Brown, b. Jan. 16, 1826; dau. of Dea. Josiah Brown, Jr., and Rebecca Blivin. He was a progressive farmer in Stonington, two miles west of Westerly, R. I. Mr. Brown took an active interest in genealogy and set the headstones to the graves of his great-great-great-grandfather Eleazer and wife Ann (Pendleton) Brown. Interments, Brown Cemetery, No. Stonington.

Children, all of whom are deceased:

 1965. Delos E., b. 1844; d. Apr. 10, 1870.

 1966. Arabella N., b. 1845; d. Aug. 2, 1877. (See Errata.)

 1967. Lucy A., b. 1847; d. Dec. 25, 1873; m. Hermon C. Brown.
  (See Babcock family, p. 25.)

 1968. Frank L., b. 1853; d. Mar. 6, 1875.

 1969. Mathew, b. 1857; d. Dec. 22, 1857.

 1970. John, b. 1862; d. Jan. 19, 1866.

 1971. Daniel, Jr., b. July 14, 1864; d. 1907; m., Stonington, Mar. 21,
  1894, Mary A. Taylor, b. Dec. 23, 1859. He lived and died
  on the homestead that was his father's, in Stonington. He
  took deep interest in the Brown Genealogy, but died before
  it was published.

Children:
> Two boys, d. in infancy.
> 1972. Mabel Irene Brown, b. Apr. 8, 1896

Andrew Denison Brown (1962), son of Mathew (1912) and Lucy A (Denison) Brown, b., No. Stonington, Conn., Sept. 14, 1818; m. (1), Greenfield, Mass., Sept., 1855, Adeline Partelo, d., Brownsdale, Minn., 1868; dau of Jonas and Phebe Partelo, of No. Stonington; m. (2) Melisse Bacon, 1872. His res., 1909, Brownsdale, Minn. Mr. Brown was a shrewd, calculating man, a school-teacher. In his young days he went on a whaling voyage with Chas. W. Austin. He also, with his brother, Hosmer A., went to California, returning in 1855, and soon after with his brother took up lands in Brownsdale, Minn., where he now resides.

Children by first m.:
> 1973. Lillian G., b. 1860 (1977–1981). .
> 1974. Florence E., b. Aug. 10, 1861 (1982–1984)

Children by second m., b. Brownsdale:
> · 1975. Winifred L., b. 1873, m. Louis Powers.
> 1976. Hosmer D., b. 1885.

Lillian G. Brown (1973), dau. of Andrew D and Adeline (Partelo) Brown, b. 1860; m., Dec. 17, 1884, Thomas E Doolittle, of Brownsdale, Minn. Res., 1907, No. Platte, Neb.

Children, b. Atkinson, Neb., except the first·
> 1977. Milton E., b., Illinois, Oct 7, 1885.
> 1978. Warren Andrew, b. Aug. 18, 1887.
> 1979. Thomas P., b. July 18, 1890.
> 1980. Florence Adeline, b. Dec. 2, 1892.
> 1981. Emily Jane, b. June 17, 1899.

Florence Evelyn Brown (1974), sister of the preceding, b Aug. 10, 1861; m., Aug. 14, 1889, Charles D. Holbrook. Res., So. Minneapolis, Minn.

Children, b. Minneapolis:
> 1982. DeWitt, b. Aug 21, 1891.
> 1983. Adeline Olive, b. Nov. 19, 1893.
> 1984. Howard Andrew, b. Aug. 30, 1898.

Lucy Elizabeth Brown (1963), dau. of Mathew (1912) and Lucy (Denison) Brown, son of Mathew (310) and Elizabeth (Brown) Brown, son of Dea. Zebulon and Anne (Main 279) Brown, b., No. Stonington, Conn., May 16, 1823; d. Dec. 16, 1885; m., No. Stonington, Oct. 8, 1840, Reu-

THE EZEKIEL MAIN FAMILY

ben W. York, b., No. Stonington, Jan. 22, 1819; d. June 9, 1897; son of
Nathan and Martha (Breed) York, of No. Stonington. Interments,
Union Cemetery, No. Stonington. The winter of their marriage Mr.
York taught the district school, and every morning read the Scriptures
and offered prayer. The compiler of these records was then a pupil of
his. Mr. and Mrs. York occupied, nearly all of their married life, the
Mathew Brown homestead, and were devoted members of the Second Bap-
tist Church, that was founded by her great-great-grandfather Elder Simeon
Brown. Mr. York was for many years its honored deacon.

Children, b. No. Stonington:

1985. Lucy E., b. Oct. 28, 1841; m. Geo. H. Blivin, who died soon
after marriage, and later Mrs. Blivin removed to Pasadena,
Cal., to live with her sister, Sarah Alice; d., Pasadena, Dec.
4, 1897. No issue.

1986. Reuben Oscar York, b. Apr. 21, 1843; m., Voluntown, Conn.,
Feb. 17, 1874, Sarah E. Stanton, b., Voluntown, Aug. 9,
1845; dau. of Gen. William C. Stanton, b., Voluntown, 1807,
and Mary A. Chesebro, b., Stonington, Sept. 29, 1811; d.,
Brownsdale, Nov. 30, 1905. Mr. York, after his two uncles
had established their homes in Mower Co., Minn., removed
from No. Stonington, and established himself in agricultural
pursuits in their immediate vicinity, where he still resides.
He has been prosperous in his business. Dau.: Jennie Alice
York, b., Brownsdale, Feb. 3, 1875; m., Oct. 14, 1903, James
H. Smith. Children: (1) Oscar Samuel, b., Udolpha, Minn.,
Sept. 13, 1906; (2) Eleanor Elizabeth, b., Udolpha, Apr.
14, 1908. Res., Lansing, Mower Co., Minn.

1987. Sarah Alice York, b., No. Stonington, July 22, 1845; d., Pasadena, Cal., June 27, 1908; m., No. Stonington, June 26,
1877, Rev. C. T. Douglass, pastor of the Second Baptist
Church, No. Stonington, who later removed to Pasadena,
Cal., and became corresponding secretary of the Southern
California Baptist Convention. He has held this position
for several years. Son: —— b., New Jersey, Feb. 13, 1884;
completed his education at the Leland Stanford University,
Cal. Res., Pasadena, Cal.

In the appendix of this book will be found additional records of the progenitors of the Main family.

THE EZEKIEL MAIN FAMILY

Joshua Main (278), son of Dea. Thomas Main (264) and Ann or Annah Pendleton. She was b., Stonington, Conn., Feb. 1, 1700; dau. of Eleazer Brown and Ann Pendleton. Eleazer Brown was son of Thomas Brown and Mary Newhall, of Lynn, Mass.

Joshua Main (278) [Dea. Thomas (264), Jeremiah (260), Ezekiel], b., Stonington, Apr. 1, 1729; d., Kent, N. Y., about 1788; m. (1), Nov. 2, 1752, Rachel Peckham, b. Sept. 5, 1731. (See Peckham family, after 553.) He m. (2), Nov. 4, 1775, Elizabeth Hovey. It is believed she was the dau. of Samuel Hovey and Elizabeth Perkins. Mr. Main moved from Stonington, Conn., to Frederickstown, afterwards called Franklin, now Patterson, Putnam Co., N. Y. He was a farmer and a most devout Presbyterian.

Children by first m.:

1988. Amos Main, b.——, 1768. The Mains of Cherry Creek, Chautauqua Co., N. Y., are probably in this line, but not included in this genealogy.

1989. Rachael Main, b.——, 1770; m. Samuel Burch, of Kent. Children: Alphonso, b. 1792; Ethel, b. 1794.

1990. Sebbeus* Main, b.——; m. Mary Hovey, of Mt. Carmel, N. Y. Children: Sebbeus, b. 1799; Joshua, b. 1801.

Son by second m.:

1991. Joshua Main, Jr., b., Patterson, Oct. 7, 1776; d., Liberty, Sullivan Co., N. Y., Aug. 13, 1830; m., Weston, Conn., Mar. 31, 1799, Hannah Gilbert, b., Weston, July 9, 1781; d., Georgetown, Conn., May 17, 1843; dau. of Ebenezer Gilbert and Ruth, his wife, of Weston. Hannah Gilbert was a direct descendant of Mathew Gilbert, who died and was buried in "New Haven Green;" his stone is still standing at New Haven, Conn. He was one of those who in 1639 framed the "Colonial Records of New Haven," better known in those days as the "Wethersfield Records," which included New Haven, Hartford, Windsor, and other localities. Mr. Main in politics was a Whig. Both he and his wife were members of the Congregational Church.

Children, b. Weston, except the first:

1992. Ebenezer Gilbert Main, b., Patterson, Nov. 13, 1800; d., Robertsonville, N. Y., Sept. 14, 1876 (2005–2009).

1993. Harriet, b. Jan. 1, 1802; m. Daniel Durfee Gilbert (2010, 2011).

1994. Sally, b. Sept. 3, 1804; d., Wilton, July 24, 1832; unm.

*This name "Sebbeus" appears on pages 73 and 84, with different spelling.

231

1995. William Pitt, b. Apr. 10, 1806; m. (1) Eliza Middlebrooks; m. (2) Mary Spencer; m. (3) Mary Parks (2012–2015).

1996. Bellinda Cordelia, b. Mar. 3, 1808; m. J. B. Nickerson (2016–2018).

1997. Zalmon Smith, b. Oct. 29, 1809; m. (1) Jerusha Harrington; m. (2) Martha Coleman; m. (3) Elizabeth Scott (2019-2031).

1998. Hester Ann, b. Mar. 4, 1811; m. Rollin Stoddard (2032, 2033).

1999. Samuel Merwin, b. Mar. 14, 1813; m. Maryette Foote (2045–2054).

2000. Asahel, b. Mar. 31, 1815; d., Weston, Conn., Oct. 16, 1818.

2001. Sylvester, b. Apr. 18, 1817; m. Susan Lobdell (2055–2058).

2002. Ruth, b. July 28, 1819; m. Rollin Stoddard for his second wife (2034-2044).

2003. Daniel Joshua, b. Sept. 29, 1821; d., Wilton, Conn., Nov. 7, 1844; unm.

2004. Hannah, b. May 4, 1825; m. Thomas Pardee (2059, 2060).

Ebenezer Gilbert Main (1992), son of Joshua Main, Jr. (1991), and Hannah Gilbert [son of Joshua Main (278) and Elizabeth Hovey, son of Dea. Thomas Main (264), son of Jeremiah (260), son of Ezekiel], b., Patterson, N. Y., Nov. 13, 1800; d., Liberty, N. Y., Sept. 14, 1876; m. (1), Weston, Conn., July 24, 1821, Lavinia Holmes; d., Liberty, Jan. 5, 1861. He m. (2), Apr. 6, 1862, Delia Carrie Benton, b. Mar. 6, 1808. He was a farmer.

Children, b. Liberty, except the first:

2005. Henry, b., Wilton, June 5, 1822; d., Liberty, March, 1886; m., Liberty, Betsey Ann Robinson. Children: (1) Sylvester, (2) Viola, (3) Jennie.

2006. Aaron, b. Sept. 13, 1823; d., Liberty, Mar. 3, 1868; m. Dau.: Lavinia.

2007. Caroline E., b. Apr. 29, 1826; d. Apr. 29, 1840.

2008. George, b. June 26, 1832; d., Ridgefield, Conn., Mar. 11, 1883; m., Ridgefield, Harriet Burr. Children, b. Ridgefield: (1) Oscar, b. Aug. 21, 1858; (2) Lillian, b. June 29 1862; (3) Harriet, b. Mar. 13, 1875.

2009. Maryette, b. Apr. 18, 1834; d. Apr. 15, 1855.

Harriet Main (1993), sister of the preceding, b., Weston, Conn., Jan. 1, 1802; d., Wilton, Conn., Aug. 22, 1835; m., Wilton, Mar. 3, 1826, Daniel Durfee Gilbert, b., Wilton, 1796; d. 1883.

Col Zalmon Smith Mann
(2011)
Page 233

Col. Zalmon Smith Main was born, at or near Liberty, N. Y., Aug. 2, 1833; died, at Hankins, N. Y., Oct. 13, 1867; married, at Hankins, N. Y., Mar. 29, 1864, Mary Hankins, who was born at Tusten, N. Y., Oct. 6, 1833, and died at Binghamton, N. Y., Oct. 17, 1907. Both are buried at Damascus, Penn.

One child, Florence Eliza, born Aug. 3, 1866, survives them.

Colonel Main received his early education in the district schools, and later at one of the academies of New York State. He began his business career as a bridge-builder, erecting several of the largest drawbridges in Ohio and Indiana. When the Civil War broke out he answered his country's call and helped organize the 52d Ind. Reg. of Vol. Infantry. He entered service as Capt. of Co. A, receiving his commission from Governor Morton of Indiana, Oct. 20, 1861. He was promoted to Major, May 14, 1862; Lieutenant-Colonel, June 5, 1862; and Colonel, Apr. 1, 1865. He took part in several important engagements, and acted as Brevet Brigadier-General for about four months, until the close of the war, when he was honorably discharged. He then returned to his former occupation as superintendent of bridge-building, which he followed until his death.

Children, b. Wilton:

    2010. Cyrus, b. June 8, 1828; m. Sarah Scribner (2351, 2352).

    2011. Hester Ann, b. June 27, 1831; m. John L. De Garmo (2060a-2060d).

William Pitt Main (1995), son of Joshua Main, Jr. (1991), and Hannah Gilbert, b., Wilton, Conn., Apr. 10, 1806; d., Santa Cruz, Cal., July, 1889; m. (1), Sept. 16, 1827, Eliza Middlebrooks, b. Feb. 25, 1805; she d. May 5, 1836; he m. (2), Jan. 10, 1838, Mary Spencer, b. Sept. 10, 1793; she d. Feb. 5, 1859; he m. (3) Mary Parks. Mr. Main early in life was a shoemaker, but later studied medicine and practised extensively, and in 1849 he went to California, where the children by the third marriage grew up.

Children by first m.:

    2012. William Wallace Main, b. Aug. 12, 1828; d., Rock Valley, N. Y., May 12, 1891; m. (1), 1852, Elizabeth Haight; m. (2), 1885, Frances Burroughs. Son, by second m.: Frank, b. 1888; d., Rock Valley, 1889.

    2013. Joshua Brooks Main, b. Apr. 12, 1830; d. Apr. 22, 1855; unm.

    2014. Zalmon Smith Main, b. Aug. 2, 1833; m., Mar. 29, 1864, Mary Hawkins. He was a Lieutenant-Colonel in the Civil War, in a New York regiment of volunteers and was in forty-one battles. Dau.: Florence Eliza, b. Aug. 3, 1866. (See 2380.)

    2015. Frederick Main, b. Sept. 3, 1835; d. Mar. 12, 1852.

Bellinda Cordelia Main (1996), sister of the preceding, b., Weston, Conn., Mar. 3, 1808; d., Wilton, Conn., Aug. 21, 1832; m., June 19, 1825, Joseph B. Nickerson.

Children:

    2016. Julia Ann, b. Mar. 27, 1827; d. Nov. 25, 1828.

    2017. Julia Ann, b. Feb. 4, 1830; d., Wilton, July 12, 1881; m., Ridgefield, Conn., Charles Cole, b. Aug. 22, 1829. Children: Mary and Charles.

    2018. Lorenzo Dow, b. Sept. 10, 1836; deceased.

Zalmon Smith Main (1997), son of Joshua, Jr. (1991), and Hannah (Gilbert) Main, b., Weston, Conn., Oct. 29, 1809; d., Ridgefield, Conn., Dec. 13, 1889; m. (1), Aug. 13, 1837, Jerusha Harrington; she d. Sept. 9, 1839; he m. (2), Mar. 22, 1840, Martha Coleman, b. Feb. 16, 1811; she d. Aug. 30, 1857; he m. (3), Aug. 11, 1859, Elizabeth Adeline Scott, b. June 27, 1828; she is living. He was a tinsmith, Ridgefield; as far as could be ascertained, this was his home, where all his children were born.

Children by first m.:

2019. Laura, b. Apr. 26, 1838; m. Allen Smith (2061-2065).

2020. Samantha, b. July 24, 1839; d. Oct. 3, 1839.

Children by second m.:

2021. Rollin, b. Apr. 12, 1841; d. May 8, 1847.

2022. James C., b. Feb. 6, 1843; m. Josephine C. Barnett (2066).

2023. Mary E., b. Sept. 12, 1846; m., Battle Creek, Mich., Dec. 19, 1867, Henry A. Chaydene.

2024. Almira F., b. May 19, 1848; m. Henry C. Beardsley (2067-2070).

2025. Sylvester Strong, b. May 20, 1850; m. Sarah A. Boones (2071-2074).

2026. Margaret, b. Aug. 19, 1853; d. June 13, 1855.

Children by third m.:

2027. Emma C., b. Dec. 28, 1861.

2028. David A., b. Sept. 9, 1863.

2029. Frances S., b. Sept. 28, 1864.

2030. Frederick B., b. Feb. 19, 1866.

2031. Bessie L., b. Sept. 8, 1870.

Hester Ann Main (1998), dau. of Joshua, Jr. (1991), and Hannah (Gilbert) Main, b., Weston, Conn., Mar. 4, 1811; d., Liberty, N. Y., Aug. 20, 1836; m., Oct. 10, 1830, Rollin Stoddard. After the death of his wife Mr. Stoddard m. (2), Apr. 22, 1837, Ruth Main (2002), sister of first wife; b., Weston, July 28, 1819; d., Callicoon, Sullivan Co., N. Y., Oct. 26, 1860.

Children by first m., b. Callicoon:

2032. Louise, b. Dec. 1, 1831; d., Callicoon, Dec. 14, 1831.

2033. John, b. Oct. 12, 1834; d., Callicoon, Oct. 22, 1861; unm.

Children by second m., b. Callicoon:

2034. Lucy, b. May 14, 1838; d. Mar. 12, 1860.

2035. Letitia, b. July 29, 1839; m. Isaac D. Mead (2111-2113).

2036. Phebe, b. June 1, 1841; m. George D. Bush (2114-2116).

2037. Hester Ann, b. Mar. 11, 1843; d., Callicoon, Apr. 12, 1867.

2038. Solon, b. Feb. 4, 1845; m., Sept. 28, 1870, Myra Gorton.

2039. Mary, b. Sept. 26, 1846; m. Heman B. Goodsell (2117-2123).

2040. Lavinia, b. Mar. 17, 1848; deceased; unm.

2041. Linda, b. July 8, 1850; d. 1906; unm.

2041a. Laura, b. Apr. 15, 1852.

2042. Main, b. Feb. 22, 1854.

Samuel M. Main
(1999)
Page 235

Eli Gilbert Main
(2054)
Page 244

2043. Kate, b. May 11, 1856; m. Alonzo Halsey (2124–2131).
2044. Rollin, Jr., b. May 18, 1858 (2132, 2133).

Samuel Merwin Main (1999), son of Joshua Main, Jr. (1991), and Hannah Gilbert [son of Joshua Main (278) and Elizabeth Hovey, son of Dea. Thomas Main (264) and Ann or Annah Brown, son of Jeremiah (260), son of Ezekiel], b., Weston, Conn., Mar. 14, 1813; d., Brooklyn, N. Y., May 5, 1892; m., Apr. 27, 1834, Maryette Foote, b. Mar. 10, 1815; d. Dec. 28, 1892. She was a direct descendant of Nathaniel Foote the emigrant, b. in England in 1593, who died at Wethersfield, Conn., in 1644. Mr. Main was a Methodist minister of marked ability for many years; but, having throat trouble, he spent his later years in mercantile pursuits. His son Eli Gilbert says, "I have in my early life listened to the words of my father, which found a lodgment in my heart, and I feel sure they shaped the future course of my life. He was one of the first Vice-Presidents of the Anti-Slavery Society in Connecticut, and labored and voted faithfully till he saw the fulfilment of his hopes and labors in the liberation of the slaves." He has left behind a precious heritage for the present and future generations, as one of the best of men. He enjoyed a happy old age in the bosom of his family, where he was greatly beloved by an affectionate household. He collected much valuable data of the Main family, which was a great help to his son Eli Gilbert in his many years of research.

NOTE.— The Post-office at Georgetown, Conn., is used by the abutting parts of Redding, Ridgefield, Weston, and Wilton.

Children, all b. Georgetown, Conn.:

2045. Samuel S., b. Apr. 5, 1836; d. Aug. 19, 1836.
2046. Annetta, b. June 14, 1837; d. Mar. 29, 1843.
2047. Samuel A., b. July 4, 1839; m. Edith E. Newman (2075–2079).
2048. John N., b. Mar. 22, 1841; m. Catharine A. Foley (2080, 2081).
2049. Amarissa A., b. Feb. 8, 1843; d., Redding, Jan. 15, 1845.
2050. Cornelia A., b. Feb. 14, 1845; m. Charles S. Gregory (2082–2086).
2051. Reuben F., b. Jan. 13, 1847; d., Redding, Feb. 20, 1847.
2052. Hulda F., b. July 13, 1849; m. (1) George H. Cole; m. (2) Albert S. Green (2087–2094).
2053. Antoinette C., b. Nov. 9, 1851; m. Orlando J. Williams (2095–2100).
2054. Eli Gilbert, b. Nov. 5, 1852; m. (1) Frances E. De Garmo; m. (2) Rose Rathbun Daniels (2101–2106).

Sylvester Main (2001), son of Joshua Main, Jr. (1991), and Hannah Gilbert [son of Joshua Main (278) and Elizabeth Hovey, son of Dea. Thomas Main (264) and Ann or Annah Brown, son of Jeremiah (260), son of Ezekiel], b., Weston, Conn., Apr. 18, 1817; d., So. Norwalk, Conn., Oct. 5, 1873; m., Ridgefield, Conn., May 27, 1838, Susan Lobdell, b., No. Salem, N. Y., Sept. 19, 1815; d., Ridgefield, Feb. 27, 1904; dau. of Philip and Temperance Titus (Smith) Lobdell. Sylvester Main was brought up on a farm; later he learned the harness-making business. He was also a hatter, when hats were made the old-fashioned way, by hand. He was a vocal teacher from 1833 to 1854. He then went to New York and was chorister in Allen St., Forsyth St., and 86th St. Methodist Episcopal Churches, up to 1860. In 1856, or earlier, he became acquainted with Prof. I. B. Woodbury and assisted him in compiling music-books. After Mr. Woodbury's death, in 1859, he connected himself with William B. Bradbury, continuing in the same business until Mr. Bradbury's death, in 1868, when the business was continued by Biglow & Main. At his death, in 1873, the firm name was continued till 1890, when the business name changed to Biglow & Main Company. The firm under its different names has sold more than *seventy million* copies of Sunday-school, Church, and Gospel Hymns music-books. The Gospel Hymns alone have reached over *fifty-seven million* copies since 1875. His son says of his father (2001) and Uncle Samuel (1999), "I would like to have their pictures in the book, for two better men never lived."

Children, b. Ridgefield:

2055. Hubert Platt, b. Aug. 17, 1839; m. Ophelia Louise De Groff (2107–2110).

2056. Julian Sylvester, b. Sept. 28, 1841; m. Sarah E. Smith (2360, 2361).

2057. Helen Ida, b. Oct. 21, 1844; m. John A. Pulling (2362-2365).

2058. Cynthia Isabella, b. Aug. 17, 1849; m. (1) J. S. Monroe; m. (2) F. E. Olmstead (2366-2368).

Hannah Main (2004), dau. of Joshua Main, Jr. (1991), and Hannah Gilbert, b., Weston, Conn., Mar. 4, 1825; d., Wilton, Conn., May 27, 1869; m., Wilton, Jan. 23, 1844, Thomas Pardee.

Children, b. Wilton:

2059. Frances A., b. Oct. 14, 1844; m. Charles Taylor.

2060. William F., b. Aug. 25, 1848.

Sylvester Main   and his son   Hubert Platt Main
(2001)   (2055)
Page 236   Page 242

Ira D. Sankey being associated with Mr. Hubert P. Main and composer of many of the Gospel hymns which were used in connection with the Moody and Sankey meetings in the United States and England, the compiler believes that a sketch of his life would be acceptable to the readers of this genealogy.

Ira David Sankey was born in Edinburg, Lawrence Co., Penn., Aug. 28, 1840. He was musical from his youth. Moved to Newcastle, Penn., in

1857. As early as 1860 he attended a Musical Convention held at Farmington, O., conducted by Wm. B. Bradbury. He enlisted in the army in the spring of 1861 at the call of President Lincoln. Married Miss Fanny V. Edwards, Sept. 9, 1863, by whom he had three sons, one of whom died some years ago. His son Ira Allan Sankey is now president of the Biglow & Main Co. In 1870 he was appointed a delegate to the International Sunday-School Convention at Indianapolis, Ind., where Mr. Moody found him and asked him to conduct the music; and at the close of the meeting invited him to come to Chicago and help him, which invitation he accepted in 1871, and removed to Chicago in 1872. In June, 1873, he sailed to England with Mr. Moody. Returned in August, 1875. He afterward made several visits to Europe. In the fall of 1875 Biglow & Main and John Church & Co., of Cincinnati, O., published "Gospel Hymns and Sacred Songs," by P. P. Bliss and Ira D. Sankey, since which time six numbers have been issued, and upwards of sixty million copies sold. In 1890 The Biglow & Main Co. was formed, and Mr. Sankey became connected with the house. He was the author of some 250 Gospel songs, among the most popular of which are "The Ninety and Nine," "I Am Praying for You," "Faith Is the Victory," "Under His Wings," "There'll Be No Dark Valley," and others, sung the world over. Mr. Sankey was stricken with blindness during the fall of 1903, and died at his home in Brooklyn, N. Y., Aug. 13, 1908.

Hester Ann Gilbert (2011), dau. of Daniel Durfee and Harriet (Main, 1993) Gilbert, b., Wilton, Conn., June 29, 1831; d, Easton, Conn., Apr. 29, 1868; m., Wilton, June 19, 1853, John L. De Garmo, b., Easton, Nov. 14, 1831.

Children:

    2060a. Lewis Sidney, b. May 1, 1854; d. Jan. 27, 1861.

    2060b. Sarah Louise, b. June 27, 1855; d. June 16, 1873.

    2060c. Frances Estelle, b. Oct. 8, 1856; d., Waterbury, Conn., Jan. 14, 1895; m. Eli Gilbert Main (2101-2106).

    2060d. William Fletcher, b. Sept. 16, 1860; d. Feb. 12, 1883; m., in 1881, Lucretia Beers, of Milford, Conn. No issue.

Laura Main (2019), dau. of Zalmon (1997) and Jerusha (Harrington) Main [Joshua, Jr. (1991), Joshua (278), Dea. Thomas (264), Jeremiah (260), Ezekiel], b., Ridgefield, Conn., Apr. 26, 1838; d. Mar. 10, 1870; m., Ridgefield, Nov. 25, 1855, Allen Smith.

Children:

    2061. Frank, b. Oct. 29, 1856.

    2062. Emma L., b. Mar. 19, 1860.

    ' 2063. Laura A., b. Dec. 9, 1862.

    2064. James A., b. Dec. 6, 1866.

    2065. Harry S., b. Apr. 6, 1869.

James C. Main (2022), son of Zalmon (1997) and Martha (Coleman) Main, b., Ridgefield, Conn., Feb. 6, 1843; m.,——, N. Y., Mar. 30, 1870, Josephine C. Burnett.

Son:

    2066. Henry Zalmon, b. Dec. 27, 1879.

Almira F. Main (2024), sister of the preceding, b., Ridgefield, Conn., May 19, 1848; m., Battle Creek, Mich., June 1, 1870, Henry C. Beardsley.

Children:

    2067. Howard, b. Apr. 2, 1873.

    2068. Henry C., b. July 6, 1874.

    2069. Leroy, b. 1876.

    2070. Bessie, b. 1879.

Sylvester S. Main (2025), brother of the preceding, b., Ridgefield, Conn., May 20, 1850; m., July 13, 1886, Sarah A. Boones.

Children:

    2071. Adah, b. May 26, 1887.

2072. Clifford B., b. July 13, 1888.
2073. Elmer R., b. Mar. 26, 1890.
2074. Laura, b. May 1, 1891.

Samuel A. Main (2047), son of Samuel M. Main (1999) and Maryette
Foote [Joshua, Jr. (1991), Joshua (278), Dea. Thomas (264), Jeremiah
(260), Ezekiel], b., Georgetown, Conn., July 4, 1839; d., Danbury, Conn.,
Aug. 23, 1900; m., Georgetown, Conn., June 1, 1865, Edith E. Newman, b.,
England, June 21, 1839; d., Danbury, Mar. 27, 1887; m. (2), July 11, 1888,
Caroline E. Goodwin, b. July 10, 1866. Mr. Main was in the Civil War.
He enlisted in the first three-months' call for volunteers, and reënlisted and
was under General Banks's command and was engaged in the various bat-
tles preceding the occupation of Port Hudson, La.

Children by first m., b. Danbury:

    2075. Frederick S., b. Nov. 2, 1869; d. Apr. 6, 1876.
    2076. Joshua Hubert, b. June 15, 1873; m., Danbury, Dec. 29, 1895,
        Nellie A. Knapp, b., Danbury, Dec. 29, 1872. He is a Re-
        publican, and he and his wife are members of the Episcopal
        Church. Children: (1) Roland H., b. Oct. 8, 1896; (2)
        Gladys E., b. May 29, 1898. Res., Danbury, Conn.
    2077. John N., b. July 11, 1876; m. (1) Anna G. Doyle; divorced.
        He m. (2), Bethel, Conn., Nov. 27, 1902, Mamie Hines, b.,
        Bethel, June 29, 1885; dau. of John S. and Bridget (Ma-
        lone) Hines, of Bethel. Mr. Main is a Republican, and a
        hatter by trade, and his wife is a member of the Methodist
        Church. Children, b. Bethel: (1) Florence Emeline, b. Sept.
        8, 1903; (2) Helen Ethel, b. June 19, 1905; (3) John Merwin,
        b. Feb. 24, 1907.
    2078. Minnie Edith, b. Nov. 25, 1877; m., Danbury, Nov. 26, 1903,
        Walter J. Stone, b., Milltown, N. Y., Feb. 21, 1862; son of
        William W. Stone, b., Danbury, Jan. 29, 1841, and Lydia J.
        Green, b., Milltown, July 3, 1843. Children, b. Bethel: (1)
        Walter Main, b. Sept. 16, 1904; (2) Edith Julia, b. Mar. 29,
        1908.

Son by second m., b. Danbury:

    2079. Samuel Merwin, b. Oct. 13, 1895.

John N. Main (2048), brother of the preceding, b., Georgetown, Conn.,
Mar. 22, 1841; d., Middleboro, Mass., Feb. 4, 1904; m., Brewsters, N. Y.,
May 8, 1859, Catharine A. Foley, b., Albany, N. Y., Apr. 4, 1839. Mr. Main

served in the Civil War. He first volunteered for three months and was in the first Bull Run battle, and afterwards reënlisted and was with Admiral Farragut in the expedition against Port Hudson as signal-corps officer.

Children, b. Georgetown:

2080. Julian A., b. May 8, 1860; d., Danbury, Conn., Apr. 8, 1869.

2081. Susan H., b. Aug. 30, 1865; m. Harry A. Witbeck. He is an electrician. Res., Middleboro, Mass. Children: (1) Chester M., b. July 4, 1891; (2) Julian H., b. July 11, 1894; (3) John A., b. Nov. 1, 1898.

Cornelia A. Main (2050), sister of the preceding, b., Georgetown, Conn. Feb. 14, 1845; m., Georgetown, May 28, 1865, Charles S. Gregory, b., Redding, Nov. 21, 1838; d., Bridgeport, Conn., Oct. 18, 1908; son of Mathew Gregory, of Georgetown:

Children, b. Georgetown:

2082. Mary E. Gregory, b. Apr. 20, 1866; m., Georgetown, May 5, 1883, Frank Haskell. He is a mechanic. Res., Worcester, Mass. Children: (1) Spencer H., b. Mar. 15, 1884; (2) Anna M., b. Aug. 9, 1889; (3) Hazel C., b. July 29, 1898.

2083. Reuben F., b. Mar. 9, 1868; d. July 3, 1875.

2084. Rebecca, b. Apr. 1, 1870; m., Georgetown, Oct. 1, 1889, Arthur P. Beers. Dau.: Blanche, b. Nov. 5, 1890. Res., Norwalk, Conn.

2085. Mabel, b. Jan. 1, 1872; d. May 7, 1875.

2086. Samuel M., b. Dec. 22, 1874; d. Sept. 13, 1875.

2086a. Helen Ida, b. Oct. 23, 1876; m., Norwalk, Aug. 29, 1895, Stoddard Grey Goodsell (2117), b., Weston, Conn., May 8, 1875; son of Rev. Heman B. Goodsell and Mary Stoddard (2039). Mr. Goodsell is a traveling salesman, and he and his wife are members of the Methodist Church. Children, b. Bridgeport: (1) Kenneth Gregory, b. Sept. 13, 1897; (2) Donald Grey, b. Jan. 2, 1900, d. Jan. 25, 1905; (3) Ralph Scott, b. May 15, 1905. Res., Bridgeport, Conn.

2086b. Matthew H. Gregory, b. Mar. 11, 1881; m., New York City, Sept. 7, 1904, Anna Letitia Phillips, b., Goshen, N. Y., June 20, 1880; dau. of Hudson and Ida May (Wilson) Phillips. Mr. Gregory was educated in the schools of Norwalk. He removed to Bridgeport at the age of fifteen, where he has since resided. Children: (1) Lois Muriel, b. Aug.

30, 1906; (2) Stanley Howard, b. Dec. 20, 1907. Res.,
98 Hazlewood Ave., Bridgeport, Conn.

Huldah F. Main (2052), dau. of Samuel M. (1999) and Maryette Foote,
b., Georgetown, Conn., July 13, 1849; m. (1), Georgetown, June 3, 1866,
George H. Cole, b., Webster, Conn., Dec., 1839; d., Webster, Nov. 24,
1870; son of Eben Cole, of Webster. She m. (2), Norwalk, Conn., Jan.
27, 1873, Albert S. Green, of Brooklyn, N. Y.
  Children by first m., b. Weston, Conn.:
    2087. John M. Cole, b. Aug. 21, 1868; d. June 1, 1869.
    2088. Maryette, b. June 12, 1870; m., Georgetown, Aug. 20, 1886,
           George C. Gilbert, b. Georgetown. Children: (1) Adleane
           J., b. Aug. 12, 1887; (2) Harriet H., b. Jan., 1889. Res., Dor-
           chester, Mass.
  Children by second m., b. Brooklyn, N. Y.:
    2089. Susan B. Green, b. Dec. 27, 1873; m., Brooklyn, Nov. 8, 1895,
           Phineas Hart. Children: (1) Gladys E., b. Jan. 7, 1897;
           (2) Charles A., b. Mar. 8, 1898. Res., Brooklyn, N. Y.
    2090. Charles A., b. Sept. 1, 1876; d. in infancy.
    2091. Bessie H., b. Sept. 13, 1877; m., Brooklyn, 1897, Charles M.
           Jeffreys; deceased. Dau.: Margaret, b. May 6, 1898. She
           m. (2) Charles K. Willetts. After her second marriage they
           removed to Chicago, Ill.
    2092. Emma F., b. Sept. 27, 1880; m., Michigan, Apr. 5, 1899,
           Stewart A. Shaw, b., Joliet, Ill., July 8, 1879; son of Alexan-
           der and Amelia (Brown) Shaw, of Joliet. Mrs. Shaw is a
           member of the Presbyterian Church, Brooklyn. Children:
           (1) Ella Louise, b. Dec. 25, 1900; (2) Stuart LeRoy, b. Nov.
           10, 1903; (3) Raymond Edgar, b. Nov. 12, 1907; d. May
           8, 1908.
    2093. Ella E., b. July 4, 1885; d. Mar. 27, 1899.
    2094. Hulda A., b. June 22, 1887; m., Joliet, Aug. 11, 1904, Burton
           D. Thompson, b., New York, Oct. 30, 1882. He is an elec-
           trician, Waukegan, Ill. Children: (1) Helen Marie, b. Apr.
           10, 1906; (2) Willard Albert, b. Oct. 23, 1908.

Antoinette C. Main (2053), dau. of Samuel M. (1999) and Maryette
(Foote) Main, b., Georgetown, Conn., Nov. 9, 1851; d., Danbury, Conn.,
Apr. 17, 1885; m., Brewster, N. Y., Mar. 26, 1871, Orlando J. Williams, b.
May 3, 1848; son of James Williams.

THE EZEKIEL MAIN FAMILY

Children:

2095. Clara Williams, b., Georgetown, May 2, 1872.

2096. Wallace M., b., Brooklyn, N. Y., July 12, 1873; m. (1), Brewster, Jan. 30, 1893, Effie Brown; divorced. He m. (2), Danbury, Dec. 24, 1903, Edith R. Hopkins, b., Danbury, Mar. 30, 1885; dau. of Ira C. and Sarah J. (Ferguson) Hopkins. Children, by first m.: (1) Stella R., b. Feb. 9, 1894; (2) Orlando H., b. Mar. 13, 1897. Res., Bethel, Conn.

2097. Julian O., b., Georgetown, Conn., Jan. 6, 1875; m., Danbury, June 17, 1896, Essie Watts, b. Carmel, N. Y.; dau. of Charles H. Watts and Mary E., his wife, of Danbury. He is a hatter by trade; now is assistant manager of Woolworth's Five and Ten Cent Store, Danbury. He and his wife are members of the Methodist Church. Children, b. Danbury: (1) Marie A., b. Jan. 28, 1897; (2) Louise C., b. Apr. 18, 1900; (3) Harold E., b. Aug. 16, 1901; (4) Dorothy A., b. Apr. 20, 1904; (5) Charles Kenneth, b. July 9, 1906; (6) Shelton A., b. Sept. 21, 1909.

2098. Antoinette Frances, b., Georgetown, July 12, 1877; m., Norwalk, Conn., Oct. 16, 1895, William Augustus Daniels, son of Henry and Elizabeth (Ray) Daniels, of Danbury. He is a hatter by occupation, and has taught dancing. Mrs. Daniels is a talented soprano concert singer and receives high commendation from the press. Children: (1) Marjorie G., b. July 23, 1899; (2) William Augustus, b. Nov. 1, 1901. Res., Danbury, Conn.

2099. Louis S., b., Danbury, Mar. 22, 1884; d. Feb. 12, 1889.

2100. Orlando, b., Danbury, Apr. 10, 1885; d. in infancy.

Eli Gilbert Main (2054), son of Samuel M. Main (1999) and Maryette Foote [Joshua, Jr. (1991), Joshua (278), Dea. Thomas (264), Jeremiah (260), Ezekiel], b., Georgetown, Conn., Nov. 5, 1852; m. (1), Milford, Conn., Mar. 26, 1878, Frances Estelle De Garmo, b., Wilton, Conn., Oct. 8, 1856; d., Waterbury, Conn., Jan. 14, 1895; dau. of John L. and Hester Ann (Gilbert) De Garmo, of Easton, Conn. He m. (2), Waterbury, Mrs. Rose Rathbun Daniels, b., Stockbridge, Mass., Oct. 20, 1854; dau. of Joseph and Ann (Martin) Rathbun, who are descendants of the Block Island Rathbuns. Mr. Main received his education in the public schools, and a business education at Cooper Institute, New York City. Mrs. Main's early education was in the common schools, and completed at the Easton Academy. Both he and his wife were members of the Congregational Church. His second wife was educated in Stockbridge and graduated from the High School. She is a church-member. Mr. Main is foreman of the Scovill Manufacturing Co., Waterbury. He is interested in genealogy and has furnished the direct lines of his ancestry from Joshua Main, Jr. (1991), and much other interesting data. Mr. Main's genealogical researches of the Main family cover a period of twenty years. Res., Waterbury, Conn.

Children, by first m.:

    2101. Willis D., b., Georgetown, Feb. 12, 1879; d. July 24, 1879.

    2102. Frances E., b., Milford, May 26, 1880.

    2103. Antoinette C., b., Waterbury, Aug. 27, 1882; m., Waterbury, Aug. 31, 1905, Louis A. Winchell. Son: Alfred M., b. June 14, 1906.

    2104. Bessie L., b., Danbury, Conn., Dec. 7, 1884; d., Brooklyn, N. Y., May 8, 1890.

    2105. Edith H., b., Brooklyn, Apr. 11, 1886; d., Brooklyn, Sept. 11, 1886.

    2106. Samuel J., b., Brooklyn, Dec. 17, 1888; d. there Aug. 5, 1889.

Hubert Platt Main (2055), son of Sylvester Main (2001) and Susan Lobdell [Joshua, Jr. (1991), Joshua (278), Dea. Thomas (264), Jeremiah (260), Ezekiel], b., Ridgefield, Conn., Aug. 17, 1839; m., New York City, Sept. 18, 1865, Ophelia Louise De Groff, b., Halfmoon, N. Y., Feb. 13, 1842; dau. of Lewis De Groff and Cornelia Caroline Best, of New York. Mr. Main is editor and compiler of music-books. In his young manhood he held several positions of trust till 1861, when he was postmaster's first assistant at Ridgefield; but returned to New York in 1862 and continued in Hazelton's pianoforte warerooms, where he had previously had a position, until 1864, when he went to Cincinnati, O., with Philip Phillips; later returned to New York and was bookkeeper for F. J. Huntington & Co., publishers of music-books. In 1866 he went again with Philip Phillips in his New York store. In February, 1868, with Biglow & Main [now, 1910, the Biglow and Main Company], of which he is treasurer, and has continued with that firm until the present time [1910]; and has compiled, with others, or for the firm, over five hundred publications of music. He has composed some fifteen hundred songs, etc., and held the position of organist in several churches for several years, up to 1895. In 1867 he joined the Masonic order; and he was a member of the Harmonic and Mendelssohn Societies. Res., Newark, N. J.

Children, the first three b. New York City:

2107. Carrie Virginia, b. Nov. 18, 1866.

2108. Lewis Arthur, b. July 24, 1868; d., New York, Sept. 14, 1868.

2109. Lucius Clark, b. Mar. 1, 1874; m., Newark, July 26, 1899, Ettie Stuart Burke, b., Bayonne, N. J., July 26, 1874; dau. of James T. Burke and Margaret Katherine Kennelieu. Mr. Main is an architect, also a church chorister. In politics he is a Republican. He and his wife are members of the Methodist Episcopal Church. Children: (1) Stuart De Groff, b., Newark, June 3, 1900; (2) Donald Gage, b., East Orange, N. J., Sept. 9, 1901. Res., Maplewood, N. J.

2110. Hubert De Groff, b., Newark, Dec. 2, 1884. He is an artist and bass soloist.

Letitia Stoddard (2035), dau. of Rollin Stoddard and Ruth Main (2002), b., Callicoon, N. Y., July 29, 1839; m., Youngsville, N. Y., Oct. 10, 1860, Isaac D. Mead, b. Jan. 16, 1830. Res., Liberty, N. Y.

Children, b. Callicoon:

2111. Florence Mead, b. July 17, 1862; d. Jan. 8, 1863.

2112. Henry W., b. Nov. 11, 1863; m., Dec. 30, 1890, Ida Craig.

2113. Frank S., b. Nov. 26, 1870; m., Feb. 1, 1893, Fannie Drennon. Dau.: Hilda M., b. Sept. 28, 1896.

Phebe Stoddard (2036), dau. of Rollin and Ruth (Main, 2002) Stoddard, b., Youngsville, N. Y., June 1, 1841; d., Rock Valley, N. Y., Jan. 24, 1896; m., Damascus, Wayne Co., Penn., Dec. 31, 1866, George D. Bush, b., Damascus, Aug. 13, 1830; son of George C. and Anna (Skinner) Bush, of Damascus, Mr. Bush in early life taught school in Indiana and Pennsylvania. He lived in Damascus until 1880, and for eight years in Cochecton Center, N. Y.; since 1889 at Rock Valley. Both he and his wife members of the Methodist Church.

Children, b. Damascus:

2114. Ruth Anna Bush, b. Oct. 13, 1867; m., East Branch, N. Y., May 26, 1898, William Wagner, b., Germany, Apr. 1, 1870; son of Conrad and Margaret Biedekapp, of Rock Valley. With his parents, Mr. Wagner, when he was one year old, came to this country, where he received common-school education. Mrs. Wagner was a school-teacher for several years before her marriage. She is a member of the Methodist Church. Children, b. Rock Valley: (1) Mabel, b. Feb. 26, 1899; (2) Carl, b. Apr. 15, 1903.

2115. Clark D. Bush, b. Aug. 8, 1872; unm.

2116. Cora Jane Bush, b. Oct. 16, 1877.

Mary Stoddard (2039), dau. of Rollin Stoddard and Ruth Main (2002), b., Callicoon, N. Y., Sept. 26, 1846; m., Weston, Conn., Feb. 17, 1874, Rev. Heman B. Goodsell, b. Oct. 15, 1848; son of Thomas and Mary (Grey) Goodsell, of Weston. Mr. Goodsell is a Baptist minister at No. Ashford, Conn.

Children, b. Weston:

2117. Stoddard Grey, b. May 8, 1875; m. Helen I. Gregory.

2118. Harry L., b. July 10, 1876; m. Anna Swartz.

2119. May M., b. Apr. 8, 1878; m. Alfred Gilbert.

2120. Bessie Frances, b. Nov. 29, 1879; m. William Wills.

2121. Grace S., b. July 27, 1881; m. Clyde Stearns.

2122. Edna Clara, b. May 19, 1883.

2123. Willis M., b. July 1, 1889; deceased.

2123a. Ruth.

Kate Stoddard (2043), dau. of Rollin Stoddard and Ruth Main (2002), b., Youngstown, N. Y., May 11, 1856; m., Hancock, N. Y. (Rock Valley), Oct. 28, 1877, Alonzo Halsey, b., Delhi, N. Y., May 18, 1846; son of James P. Halsey, of Rensselaerville, Albany Co., N. Y., and Anzolet Fish. Both he and his wife received common-school education. Mr. Halsey lived with his parents at Delhi until 1869, when he came to Rock Valley, N. Y., where he still lives, with his family. Kate Stoddard lived with her cousin William Main from 1860 until her marriage. She taught school two years. Mr. Halsey is a farmer and a Republican, and both he and his wife are members of the Methodist Church.

Children, b. Rock Valley:

2124. Anzolet Elizabeth Halsey, b. Oct. 28, 1878; d., Rock Valley, Jan. 14, 1882.

2125. Evelyn Evashta, b. Mar. 10, 1880; unm.

2126. William Zalamon, b. January, 1882; unm.

2127. James Peter, b. Jan. 17, 1884; m., Kingston, N. Y., Oct. 2, 1908, Ruby T. Storms, b., Franklin, N. Y., Apr. 15, 1889; dau. of Charles W. and Kate (Ellison) Storms, of Sussex, N. Y. Mr. Halsey is a farmer and in politics a Republican. His wife is a graduate of the High School, and a member of the Methodist Church. Res., Acidalia, Sullivan Co., N. Y.

2128. Lela Lavinia, b. Apr. 17, 1886; m., Rock Valley, Sept. 26, 1906, George S. Browne, b., Mileses, Sullivan Co., N. Y., Apr. 29, 1878; son of Melanchthon and Katherine (Brant) Browne, of Mileses. Mr. Browne is a farmer and a Republican. His wife is a member of the Methodist Church. Res., Rock Valley, N. Y. Son: Clifford A., b., Callicoon, N. Y., 1907.

2129. Leland Alonzo, b. Apr. 16, 1889.

2130. Mabel Elizabeth, b. Mar. 29, 1894.

2131. Nellie Mildred, b. Apr. 23, 1898.

Rollin Stoddard, Jr. (2044), son of Rollin and Ruth (Main) Stoddard, b., Youngsville, N. Y., May 18, 1858; m., Westport, Conn., Aug. 28, 1884, Marietta Brotherton, b., Westport, Jan. 23, 1865. Mr. Stoddard is a farmer and a Republican, and both he and his wife are members of the Congregational Church. Res., Westport, Conn.

Children, b. Westport:

2132. Howard Main, b. May 18, 1885; d. Feb. 2, 1904.

2133. Henry Solon, b. Jan. 18, 1888.

Keep in remembrance the good deeds of the fathers and mothers, and tell of them to the generations following.

Benajah Main (312d).) [son of Thomas (275) and Mary Pendleton, son of Dea. Thomas (264), son of Jeremiah (260), son of Ezekiel], b. Aug. 8, 1747, in Stonington, Conn., where he passed his whole life; m. Dolly Woodward, and by this union there were eight children.

Children, b. Stonington:

2134. Benajah, b.——

2135. Avel, b.——

2136. Samuel, b.——

2137. Thomas, b.—— 1781; d., Ledyard, Conn., Feb. 10, 1864; m. Lois Brown (2142–2157).

2138. John, b.——

2139. Dolly, b.——

2140. Sally, b.——

2141. Elizabeth, b.——

Thomas Main (2137), son of Benajah Main (312d), Thomas (275), Dea. Thomas (264), Jeremiah (260), Ezekiel], b., Ledyard, Conn., 1781; d., Ledyard, Feb. 10, 1864; m. Lois Brown, b. 1786; d., Ledyard, July 1,

1873, aged eighty-seven years. He lived in Ledyard and made farming his life-work. He was a man of large physique, of great muscular strength, and was able to do a vast amount of work. He affiliated with the Democrat party, and was always active in town affairs, holding at different times a number of offices in the gift of the people. The house where he lived has all gone, and a portion of the land has passed into other hands. He laid out the burying-ground and walled it with a heavy stone wall, where he and his wife are interred and a number of his descendants. It is on a high hill one mile west of Lantern Hill.

Children, all b. Ledyard:

2142. Thomas B. Main, b. 1804; d. Jan. 11, 1896; m. Lydia Hall, b. 1809; d. Sept. 15, 1864, aged sixty-four years. She was a woman beloved by everybody. They settled first in Stonington, Conn., later in Ledyard, where they died, without issue. Buried in the Thomas Main burying-ground.

2143. Aaron Main, b. May 14, 1806; m. Nancy Ashley (2158–2162).

2144. Timothy Main, b. 1810; m. Mary E. Gay (2163–2169).

2145. William Leeds Main, b. July 4, 1812; m. Sarah Arvilla Frink (2170–2180).

2146. John Main, b. ——; d. Dec. 8, 1839; m. Nancy Barns. They lived in Stonington. Children: (1) John L., b.——, d. Dec. 18, 1839, aged four years; (2) Nancy.

2147. Daniel Main, b.——; m. (1) Adelaide Roach; no issue. He m. (2) Emma Gay. Dau., Harriet, who when young became deaf, and after the death of her parents lived with her Uncle Amasa; now [1909] with Otis Chapman, in Stonington. He m. (3) Mary Main. Children: Delia, Catherine, and Ellen. Daniel and his three wives and dau. Catherine interred in the Thomas Main burying-ground in unmarked graves on the east side.

2148. Louisa Main, b. 1816; d., Ledyard, Sept. 26, 1888, aged seventy-two years; m. Coridon Main, b. 1812; d. May 1, 1884, aged seventy-three years. They had fourteen children, seven of whom died young. John, b. 1839, was accidentally killed by his gun, May 17, 1855. Interments in the center of the Thomas Main burying-ground. Those that came to maturity were: Lois, John and Jane (twins), Thomas, Mary, Sophia, and Amasa.

2149. Surviah Main, b. May 11, 1817; m. Albert Brown (2181–2192).

2150. Stanton Main, b. Feb. 5, 1820; m. Susan Gray (2193-2196).

2151. Mary Esther Main, b. ——; m. Miner A. Perkins (2197-2202).

2152. Nathaniel B. Main, b. 1823; d. Sept. 8, 1872. He remained on the old homestead in Ledyard all his life, where he died; unm.

2153. Seth Main, b. Sept. 13, 1824; m. Maryanna S. Woodward (2203-2208).

2154. Hannah Main, b. 1827; d. Aug. 3, 1860; m. Paul Burrows, of Mystic, Conn. Children: Fannie and Isabella.

2155. Fannie Main, b.——; m. George Parks, of Mystic, where she died. Children: Amasa, Georgianna, and Fannie.

2156. Amasa M. Main, b. Aug. 29, 1830; m. Lucy Orry Frink (2209-2218).

2157. Deborah Main, b.——; d. in Ledyard; m. Joseph Morgan. Children: (1) Joseph, d. young; (2) Amasa; (3) Mary; (4) William; (5) Nathan; (6) Hannah, deceased.

Aaron Main (2143), son of Thomas (2137) and Lois (Brown) Main [Benajah Main (312d). , Thomas (275), Dea. Thomas (264), Jeremiah (260), Ezekiel], b., Ledyard, Conn., May 14, 1806; d., Noank, Conn., Feb. 19, 1893; m. Nancy Ashley, b. Noank; d., Noank, Oct. 23, 1885. Mr. Main was a farmer in early life; later, and for several years, was in Washington Market, New York City, until his health failed, when he followed the seas and became a captain for a number of years. He returned to Noank, where he owned large tracts of land which is now built upon. They attended the Baptist Church.

Children, b. Noank:

2158. Andrew, b.——; d., Noank, July 25, 1878.

2159. Aaron, Jr., b. Mar. 25, 1837; m. Happy L. Brown (2219-2223).

2160. Benjamin, b.——; d. Dec. 24, 1840.

2161. John Tyler, b. Dec. 25, 1843; m. Katherine Williams, of New Jersey. Children: Ida L. and Walter.

2162. Annie, b. Mar. 24, 1845; m., Noank, Feb. 14, 1879, Frank Charlton, b., New Brunswick, Nov. 15, 1843; son of Francis Charlton and wife, Katherine, of New Brunswick. He is a ship-builder. His wife is a member of the Baptist Church of Noank. No issue.

Timothy Main (2144), son of Thomas (2137) and Lois (Brown) Main [Benajah Main (312d). Thomas (275), Dea. Thomas (264), Jeremiah

(260), Ezekiel], b., Ledyard, Conn., 1810; d. Sept. 13, 1889; m. Mary E. Gay, b. 1808; d. May 20, 1901. He made his home in Ledyard, and was a farmer. Interments in the Thomas Main burying-ground; also the children that are deceased.

Children, b. Ledyard:

2163. Mary Ann Main, b.——.
2164. Abby A. Main, b. 1838; d. Oct. 6, 1871; m. William D. Partelo. Children: (1) Phebe, (2) William, both of whom live in Ledyard; (3) Rebecca, b.——; lives in Mystic, Conn. Three other children, deceased.
2165. Timothy B. Main, b. 1843; d. May 22, 1871; m. Ann M. Crumb. Dau.: Ida E., d. in infancy in 1871.
2166. Thomas, b.——.
2167. George, b.——.
2168. Jedediah R., b. 1851; d. Mar. 1, 1879; m. His wife is interred by his side, in the Thomas Main burying-ground.
2169. Dwight, b.——.
Interments in the Thomas Main burying-ground.

William Leeds Main (2145), son of Thomas Main (2137) and Lois Brown [Benajah Main (312d).], Thomas (275), Dea. Thomas (264), Jeremiah (260), Ezekiel], b., Ledyard, Conn., July 4, 1812; d. June 22, 1890; m., No. Stonington, Conn., Feb. 26, 1837, Sarah A. Frink, b., No. Stonington, Apr. 11, 1818; d. Oct. 30, 1869; dau. of Zachariah and Phoebe E. (Holmes) Frink. Mr. Main during his active life conducted a store, a gristmill and a sawmill, and financially prospered in all of his undertakings. He was a man of energy and good judgment, and was a wise counsellor to those in need of advice. In his friendships he was staunch and true, and often lent a helping hand to those less fortunate. He was a conscientious official in public life and had a deep sense of the responsibility of those elected to do the will of the people. He represented the town of Ledyard for one term in the State Legislature. He was the largest landholder and the wealthiest man in Ledyard.

Children, b. Ledyard:

2170. Sarah Maria, b. Aug. 27, 1838; d. Sept. 18, 1858; m. David Boss, a farmer in No. Stonington.
2171. John Latham, b. Aug. 25, 1841; m. Phebe E. Frink. Children. William Oscar (deceased), John I., Sadie E., Calvin R., Nellie M., Melissa A., and Grace E. Res., Ledyard, Conn.

William Leeds Main

(2145)

Ledyard, Conn.

Page 248

Amasa M. Main
(2156)
Ledyard, Conn.
Page 252

2172. Leeds, b. Sept. 8, 1844; d. Nov. 9, 1895; m. Sarah Holdredge (2224-2231).

2173. Phebe E., b. July 4, 1846; d. Sept. 6, 1878; m. (1) John Finnegan; m. (2) William Harrington (2232-2234).

2174. Lura H., b. June 11, 1849; unm. Resides on the old homestead, with a beautiful meadow in front of the house; easterly is the beautiful foliage of Lantern Hill, which gives the home a picturesqueness like the White Mountains in summer.

2175. Iva D., b. Aug. 25, 1851; deceased; unm.

2176. Frances A., b. July 2, 1854; m. William Richmond (2243-2248).

2177. Alonzo (twin), b. Oct. 4, 1856; m. Ethel Main (2249, 2250).

2178. Melissa (twin), b. Oct. 4, 1856; m. Joseph E. Holdredge (2251-2256).

2179. Horace H., b. Aug. 9, 1859; m. Phebe Partelo (2257-2261).

2180. Amos, b. Nov. 3, 1862; m. Lucy A. Mathewson (2262, 2263).

Surviah B. Main (2149), dau. of Thomas (2137) and Lois (Brown) Main [Benajah Main (312d). . Thomas (275), Dea. Thomas (264), Jeremiah (260), Ezekiel], b. May 11, 1817; m., Sept. 6, 1835, Albert Brown, b. Sept. 1, 1811; d. Sept. 11, 1868; son of Nathaniel Brown; both were lifelong farmers and residents of Ledyard, Conn.

Children, b. Ledyard:

2181. Surviah L., b. Mar. 24, 1837; d. May 16, 1908; m., Nov. 7, 1858, John O. Peckham.

2182. Albert M., b. June 22, 1838; m., Jan. 5, 1862, Nancy A. Peckham.

2183. Happy L., b. Feb. 10, 1840; d. Aug. 21, 1867; m. Aaron Main, Jr., 2159 (2219-2221).

2184. Thomas M., b. Apr. 24, 1841; d. Jan. 11, 1859.

2185. Fannie E., b. Jan. 22, 1843; d. Oct. 4, 1846.

2186. Aaron A., b. Apr. 2, 1846; m., Feb. 1, 1872, Deborah B. Perkins, 2202 (2266-2269).

2187. Israel W., b. Feb. 15, 1848; m. Annette Whipple.

2188. Seth L., b. Mar. 24, 1850; m. Margaret Cantwell.

2189. Fannie E., b. Mar. 13, 1852; deceased; m., Oct. 11, 1868, Robert A. Peckham.

2190. Philetus W., b. May 1, 1854; d. Feb. 16, 1860.

2191. Nathaniel S., b. July 25, 1856; m., Dec. 20, 1877, Lydia Stoddard.

2192. Charles T., b. Feb. 12, 1862; d. May, 1878.

Stanton Main (2150), son of Thomas (2137) and Lois (Brown) Main [Benajah Main (312d). , Thomas (275), Dea. Thomas (264), Jeremiah (260), Ezekiel], b., Ledyard, Conn., Feb. 5, 1820; d. Feb. 5, 1864; m., Ledyard, Sept. 4, 1842, Susan Gray, b., Ledyard, Oct. 15, 1825; d., Ashaway, R. I., Jan. 1, 1909; dau. of Dr. Asa Gray, of Ledyard, and Louisanna Prosser, of Rhode Island. The Gray homestead in Ledyard is owned by George W. Gray, the youngest son and the only one living of the Gray family in 1909. The homestead has passed down to the fourth generation. Mr. Main is interred in the Thomas Main burying-ground; his wife, in the Union Cemetery, No. Stonington, Conn.

Children, b. Ledyard:

2193. Sarah Ann, b. June 17, 1843; d., Ledyard, July 19, 1878; m., Ledyard, Sept. 8, 1861, William A. Main, son of Abel Main. He was in the Civil War, and was buried at Mound City, Ill. Son: Walter; went West and was a stock-herder in Texas. For the past few years he has been a detective at Los Angeles, Cal.

2194. Stanton Francis, b. July 6, 1848; m., Norwich, Conn., Jan. 21, 1895, Julia S. Ayer, b., Ledyard, Apr. 19, 1854; dau. of Col. George and Julia A. (Stoddard) Ayer. He is a farmer. No. issue. Res., Norwich. R. F. D. 5.

2195. Walter A., b. Dec. 9, 1853; d., Ledyard, Nov. 24, 1861.

2196. Wilmot Holden, b. Mar. 20, 1860; m., Ashaway, Mar. 9, 1887, Hattie E. Park, b., No. Stonington, Apr. 19, 1861; dau. of Lafayette and Sarah (Lee) Park, of No. Stonington. Mr. Main in his early days was a farmer; later he was an operator in a woolen mill; still later he was in the dairy business and breeder of Ayrshire stock. He was postmaster at Woodville, R. I., and in the grocery business, until he was disabled by a fall; then he purchased a home in Ashaway, R. I., where he resides. Son: Clarence W., b., Ashaway, Feb. 16, 1893.

Mary Esther Main (2151), dau. of Thomas (2137) and Lois (Brown) Main [Benajah Main (312d). Thomas (275), Dea. Thomas (264), Jeremiah (260), Ezekiel], b. Ledyard, Conn.; d. Ledyard, Oct. 22, 1902, aged eighty-two years; m. Miner Perkins, b.——; d. Aug. 1, 1888, aged sixty-nine years. Interments, Thomas Main burying-ground.

Children:

2197. Lydia E. Perkins, b.——; d.——; m. Ishman Bromley. They lived in Preston, Conn. Children: Mary Esther, Miner, Henry, and Louisa.

2198. Hannah M. (twin), b., No. Stonington, Conn., Oct. 30, 1844; m. Dwight C. Brown (2264, 2265).

2199. Henry M. (twin), b. Oct. 30, 1844; m., No. Stonington, Oct. 24, 1875, Mary E. Brown, b. Sept. 4, 1855; dau. of Paul W. and Esther P. (Main) Brown. No issue. Res., 1909, No. Stonington, Conn.

2200. Stephen F., b. 1846; d. Sept. 21, 1878; unm. Buried, with his parents, in Thomas Main burying-ground.

2201. Eliza Ann, b.——; unm. Res. with her brother, Henry M. Perkins.

2202. Deborah Betsey, b., No. Stonington, Sept. 13, 1852; m. Aaron Alvah Brown (2266–2269).

Seth Main (2153), son of Thomas Main (2137) and Lois Brown, dau. of Nathaniel Brown [Benajah Main (312d). Thomas (275), Dea. Thomas (264), Jeremiah (260), Ezekiel], b., Ledyard, Conn., Sept. 13, 1824; d., Preston, Conn., Aug. 13, 1903; m., No. Stonington, Conn., Aug. 27, 1848, Maryanna Stanton Woodward, b., No. Stonington, July 6, 1816; d., Preston, May 18, 1907. They lived together to within fourteen days of fifty-five years of happy wedded life. Mr. Main was really a very successful business man. While farming was his principal business, he had other industries, conducting a gristmill a number of years. He owned a number of farms in Preston and No. Stonington, which he bought and sold. In 1894 he moved to the "Park Homestead Farm," in which he had for some time owned a half-interest. Three years later he became sole owner of this farm, which comprised in all about one hundred and fifty-four acres of excellent land. This beautiful farm became the care of his remaining days, and there he died. Politically he was a Democrat, and he took an active part in town affairs. In 1871 and again in 1884 he represented Preston in the State Legislature; among other offices, he was selectman for several years, member of the Board of Relief and Board of Assessors, and tax collector. He settled a number of estates in his time. He was a member and liberal supporter of Elder Peckham's Baptist Church in Ledyard.

Children, the first four b. No. Stonington:

2203. Seth Woodward, b. Aug. 3, 1849; m. (1) Ida Myers; m. (2) Hulda J. Gallup.

2204. Mary Rozilla, b. Apr. 14, 1851; m. Herbert H. Barlow (2270–2273).

2205. Cynthia Elvira, b. Jan. 22, 1853; m. Chauncey C. Pendleton (2274–2277).

2206. Appleton, b. Jan. 23, 1855; m. Isabelle Richardson (2278, 2279).

2207. Nathaniel, b., Preston, May 10, 1857; m. Nellie Holmes (2280).

2208. Leonard, b., Preston, Jan. 16, 1859; m. Annie E. Richardson (2281–2284).

Amasa M. Main (2156), son of Thomas (2137) and Lois (Brown) Main [Benajah Main (312d). Thomas (275), Dea. Thomas (264), Jeremiah (260), Ezekiel], b., Ledyard, Conn., Aug. 29, 1830; d., No. Stonington, Conn., June 16, 1908; m., Ledyard, Aug. 29, 1851, Lucy Orry Frink, b., No. Stonington, Feb. 11, 1836; d. Apr. 3, 1898; dau. of Zachariah and Phebe (Holmes) Frink. Mr. Main was a Republican, and held a number of offices in the gift of the people in the towns of Ledyard and No. Stonington. For four consecutive years he represented these towns in the State Legislature — from 1895 to 1898. He was selectman, game, and fish warden. In his life he accumulated considerable wealth.

Children, b. Ledyard:

2209. Lucy M., b. Jan. 1, 1854; d., Ledyard, June 2, 1863.

2210. Ellen E., b. Aug. 16, 1856; m. Harban O. Whitford (2285).

2211. Betsey Ann, b. Apr. 11, 1858 (twin); m. Isaac Maine (Simeon Main family, 142).

2212. Ada Ann, b. Apr. 11, 1858 (twin); d. Sept. 4, 1858.

2213. Amasa Everett, b. Aug. 27, 1859; m., Iowa City, Ia., Mar. 31, 1887, Kate L. Frye. He is a lawyer at Iowa City. No issue.

2214. Lillie A., b. July 20, 1861; m. Park B. Main (Simeon Main family, 150).

2215. Lafayette F., b. Nov. 25, 1867; m. Julia Emily Mather (2286–2288).

2216. Luther O., b. Feb. 14, 1870; m., Sept. 26, 1908, Edith Turpie. He is a farmer in Norwich, Conn. No issue.

2217. Fannie E., b. June 20, 1873; m. Otis Allen Chapman (2289–2292).

2218. Hattie B., b. Aug. 30, 1875; m. Edward Jerry Duro (2293-2297).

Aaron Main, Jr. (2159), son of Aaron (2143) and Nancy (Ashley) Main [Thomas Main (2137), ' Benajah Main (312d). , Thomas (275), Dea. Thomas (264), Jeremiah (260), Ezekiel], b., Noank, Conn., Mar. 25, 1837; m. (1), Ledyard, Conn., Oct. 30, 1859, Happy L. Brown (2183), b., Ledyard, Feb. 10, 1840; d., Ledyard, Aug. 21, 1869; dau. of Albert and Surviah (Main) Brown, of Ledyard. He m. (2), Ledyard, May 10, 1870, Lucy Frink, b., No. Stonington, Conn., Mar. 30, 1851; dau. of Thomas H. Frink and Sarah Hopkins; son of Zachariah Frink and Phebe Holmes. Thomas H. Frink was a soldier in the Civil War, and died in the service. Mr. Main was a seafaring man and spent the most of his life on the water. He and both his wives were members of the Baptist Church at Noank.

Children by first m.:

    2219. Ethel A. Main, b., Ledyard, Jan. 6, 1861; m., Norwich, Conn., July 30, 1879, Alonzo Main. Children: Mabel and James. Particularly mentioned further on.

    2220. Edgar A., b., Noank, Sept. 11, 1862; m., New London, Conn., Dec. 27, 1897, Alice C. Perron, b., Canada, 1868; dau. of Francis and Helen (Wilbur) Perron, of Mystic, Conn. Mr. Main is a fisherman. He and his wife attend the Noank Baptist Church. Children, b. Noank: (1) Helen A., b. Dec. 19, 1898; (2) Derwood E., b. Sept. 24, 1902; (3) Dorace H., b. June 28, 1904; (4) Charlotte E., b. Sept. 18, 1907.

    2221. Agnes P., b., Noank, Mar. 5, 1867; d., Brooklyn, N. Y., Jan. 26, 1895; m.; Noank, June 2, 1890, —— Peterson, b., Denmark, 1870; son of Andrew and Christina Peterson, of Denmark. Mr. Peterson is a machinist, and has a foundry at Noank. Politically he is a Republican; denominationally, a Methodist. Son: Harrie E., b. July 4, 1893.

Children by second m.:

    2222. Jennie L., b. Apr. 4, 1871; d., Noank, July 18, 1897.

    2223. George S., b. Jan. 3, 1876; m., New London, Sept. 30, 1902, Beezie Seery. Children: (1) Marguerite, b. July 30, 1903, d., Noank, Aug. 24, 1904; (2) Alice, b. Aug. 26, 1904.

Leeds Main (2172), son of William Leeds (2145) and Sarah A. (Frink) Main [Thomas (2137), Benajah Main (312d). , Thomas (275), Dea. Thomas (264), Jeremiah (260), Ezekiel], b., Ledyard, Conn., Sept. 8, 1844;

d., Ledyard, Nov. 9, 1895; m., Ledyard, Feb. 26, 1868, Sarah H. Holdredge, dau. of Daniel Holdredge. His home was in Ledyard, about two miles from the paternal homestead, which he purchased in 1876, where he successfully engaged in farming. Politically Mr. Main was a Democrat. He was an attendant of the Baptist Church. The farm is pleasantly located in Ledyard, where the widow and two daughters reside. Interment, Mystic, Conn. Address, No. Stonington, Conn., R. F. D.

Children, b. Ledyard:

2224. William Leeds, b. Mar. 6, 1869; m. Lizzie Amber Benjamin, b. Feb. 5, 1877; dau. of Nathan and Frances (Miner) Benjamin, of Preston, Conn. Mr. Main spent his early days in the vicinity of Old Mystic, Conn., where he received his early education. In his young manhood he engaged in teaching, spending three years in his native town, five years in Preston, two years in Voluntown, Conn., five years in Griswold, Conn., at that profession. In 1902 he bought the grocery-store of Isaac D. Miner, at Mystic, and the next year opened a store at Stonington borough. He also owns a store on Water Street, Mystic. As a business man he takes high rank, by fair dealing, and is in high esteem by the business community. In his fraternal relations he is identified with the Mistuxet Lodge and Knights of Pythias. No issue. (See p. 44, 221a.) Res., Mystic, Conn.

2225. Daniel H., b. Feb. 25, 1871; m. Olive Stimpson.

2226. James Stanton, b. Aug. 5, 1873; m. Lizzie Brown.

2227. Samuel Lewis, b. Feb. 14, 1876; m. Mary Chapman.

2228. Cora Ida, b. Aug. 16, 1878; unm. Res. with her mother.

2229. Julia Etta, b. Aug. 4, 1881; m. William R. Cromwell.

2230. Eliza Jane, b. Jan. 17, 1883; m., Old Mystic, Nov. 2, 1909, Clarence A. Davis, of Providence, R. I.

2231. Rose L., b. Mar. 19, 1886; m. Henry Mansfield.

Daniel H. Main (2225), son of Leeds (2172) and Sarah H. (Holdredge) Main, b., Ledyard, Conn., Feb. 25, 1871 ; m., Voluntown, Conn., Feb. 8, 1900, Olive Stimpson, b., Columbia, Conn., Apr. 27, 1883; dau. of Henry J. and Mary A. (Champlin) Stimpson, of Chaplin, Conn. He is a farmer, and his wife is a church-member. Children, b., No. Windham, Conn.: (1) Clarence Leeds, b. Feb. 16, 1901; (2) Daniel Arthur, b. Oct. 9, 1902. Res., Ledyard, Conn.

THE EZEKIEL MAIN FAMILY

James Stanton Main (2226), brother of the preceding, b., Ledyard, Conn. , Aug. 5, 1873; d., Mystic, Conn., Dec. 25, 1908; m., Mystic, Sept. 25, 1900, Lizzie Brown, dau. of Clark P. Brown and Mary Williams, of Mystic. He was a clerk in a store at Mystic. (See B. G., p. 157.) Children: (1) Harold Clark, b., Stonington, Conn., Sept. 25, 1902; (2) William Leeds, b., Noank, Conn., October, 1907; (3) James Stanton, b., Mystic, June 5, 1909.

Samuel Lewis Main (2227), brother of the preceding, b., Ledyard, Conn., Feb. 14, 1876; m., New London, Conn., Sept. 1, 1903, Mary A. Chapman, b., Stonington, Conn., Jan. 28, 1888; dau. of Reuben T. Chapman and Rosetta A. Main, of Mason's Island, Conn. He is a farmer, a Republican, and a member of the Old Mystic Church. Children: (1) Marshall Lewis, b., No. Stonington, Conn., Mar. 31, 1904; (2) Myrtle M., b., Groton, Conn., July 6, 1905; (3) Sarah Hannah, b., New London, Feb. 22, 1907. Res., Ledyard, Conn. Address, Old Mystic, Conn.

Julia Etta Main (2229), sister of the preceding, b., Ledyard, Conn., Aug. 4, 1881; m., Old Mystic, Conn., Jan. 2, 1901, William R. Cromwell, b., Mystic, Conn., Aug. 19, 1881; son of Ira Cromwell and Adie Brown, dau. of William Brown. Mr. Cromwell is supervisor of roads at Dolgeville, N. Y. His wife is a church-member. Son: Lewis Main Cromwell, b., Mystic, July 28, 1904.

Rose L. Main (2231), sister of the preceding, b., Ledyard, Conn., Mar. 19, 1886; m., No. Stonington, Conn., Nov. 1, 1905, Frank Mansfield, b. Poquetanuck, Conn.; son of Henry Mansfield. He is a teamster at Poquetanuck, and both he and his wife are church-members. Son: Charles Holdredge Mansfield, b. Nov. 1, 1906.

Phebe E. Main (2173), dau. of William Leeds (2145) and Sarah A. (Frink) Main [Thomas (2137), Benajah Main (312d). , Thomas (275), Dea. Thomas (264), Jeremiah (260), Ezekiel], b., Ledyard, Conn., July 4, 1846; d., Ledyard, Sept. 8, 1878; m. (1), 1865, John Finnegan, b. Dec. 25, 1810; d., Ledyard, Jan. 7, 1870. She m. (2), Mystic, Conn., 1877, William Harrington.

Children by first m., b. Ledyard:
  2232. Sarah Esther Finnegan, b. Aug. 26, 1866; m. James N. Holdredge (2235-2238).
  2233. John William Finnegan, b. Sept. 1, 1869; m. Henrietta A. Stoddard (2239-2242).

Son by second m., b. Ledyard:

    2234. James Leon Harrington, b. Aug. 29, 1878; unm. He graduated from the Jefferson Medical College of Philadelphia, Penn., in 1903, and is a practising physician at New London, Conn. Res. with his grandmother.

Sarah Esther Finnegan (2232), b. Aug. 26, 1866; d. Nov. 3, 1896; m., Norwich, Conn., Mar. 4, 1886, James N. Holdredge, b., Ledyard, Aug. 16, 1859; son of Randall and Nancy (Barnes) Holdredge.

    Children, b. Ledyard:

    2235. Phebe E. Holdredge, b. Aug. 14, 1888; m., Preston, Conn., Feb. 2, 1907, Frederick D. Clark, b. Aug. 8, 1886; son of Alfred J. and Mary (Cooley) Clark, of Ledyard. Children, b. Preston: (1) Frederick D., b. Sept. 19, 1907; (2) Edith May, b. Aug. 11, 1909.

    2236. Harry, b. Jan. 4, 1891.

    2237. Morris, b. Oct. 19, 1894.

    2238. Sarah, b. Nov. 2, 1896.

John William Finnegan (2233), b. Sept. 1, 1869; m., New York, Dec. 5, 1892, Henrietta A. Stoddard, b., Groton, Conn., Nov. 9, 1874; dau. of James A. and Anna Davidson Stoddard.

    Children, b. Ledyard:

    2239. Anna Alice, b. Oct. 24, 1893.

    2240. Grace Lillian, b. Jan. 4, 1896.

    2241. John William, Jr., b. Nov. 29, 1897.

    2242. Carrie Eldora, b. July 14, 1900.

Frances A. Main (2176), dau. of William Leeds Main (2145) and Sarah A. Frink [Thomas (2137), Benajah Main (312d). Thomas (275), Dea. Thomas (264), Jeremiah (260), Ezekiel], b., Ledyard, Conn., July 2, 1854; m., Westerly, R. I., Aug. 13, 1871, William J. Richmond. He has followed painting several years, but now is with his son in the ice-cream business in Westerly. Res., No. Stonington, Conn.

    Children:

    2243. Chauncey E. Richmond, b., Mystic, Conn., Dec. 16, 1872; m., Westerly, Mar. 16, 1898, Mattie S. Chapman, b., Westerly, June 12, 1872; dau. of Chester R. and Martha L. (Williams) Chapman. He is manager of Lincoln Park, near Norwich. Son: Leon Hadley, b., No. Stonington, Jan. 24, 1900.

2244. James E., b., Ledyard, Oct. 20, 1875; d., No. Stonington, Nov. 25, 1900.

2245. Charles William, b., Thomaston, Conn., June 25, 1880; m., Westerly, Oct. 13, 1909, Rachel Elizabeth Welch, b., Westerly, Mar. 8, 1884; dau. of Elmer E. and Mary Emogene (Main) Welch; granddau. of Nathaniel Peter and Sarah E. (Stillman) Main.

2246. Hattie Julia, b., Thomaston, Aug. 29, 1883; m., No. Stonington, Jan. 6, 1904, Chester T. Brown, b., No. Stonington, Feb. 6, 1877; son of Oliver G. and Frances L. (Collins) Brown, son of Denison W. and Julia (Brown) Brown. Son: Irving C., b. June 17, 1906. (See B. G., p. 536.)

2247. Dora Frances, b., No. Stonington, Oct. 23, 1886; m., Westerly, Oct. 25, 1905, John Milby, b., Dalbeattie, Scotland, June 13, 1881; son of Samuel Milby, drowned off Watch Hill, R. I., in 1889, and Ellen Scott. Mr. Milby is a granite cutter and member of the Congregational Church. Mrs. Milby, for a young woman, exhibits a remarkable knowledge and interest in her kindred. Children: (1) Samuel William, b. June 25, 1907; (2) Jennie Frances, b. Aug. 7, 1909.

2248. William Leeds, b., No. Stonington, Apr. 27, 1889.

Alonzo Main (twin) (2177), son of William Leeds (2145) and Sarah A. (Frink) Main [Thomas (2137), Benajah Main (312d). Thomas (275), Dea. Thomas (264), Jeremiah (260), Ezekiel], b., Ledyard, Conn., Oct. 4, 1856; m., July 30, 1879, Ethel Main, dau. of Aaron Main, Jr. (2159), son of Aaron Main (2143), son of Thomas Main and Lois Brown. Mr. Main since 1879 has lived at his present residence at the foot of Long Pond. For a number of years he has been boss of the silex mine at Lantern Hill. He is also interested and owner in mines in New Mexico, Colorado, and California. He combines with his many industries also farming. He, being a man of marked executive ability, has been often sought by his fellow-townsmen for public offices, but has always declined to serve. He has shown much interest in collecting family records. He places his father's picture in this genealogy. Address, Old Mystic, Conn.

Children, b. Ledyard:

2249. Mabel J., b. Sept. 7, 1880; m., Ledyard, Nov. 14, 1898, Courtland Stimpson, b., Willimantic, Conn., Nov. 30, 1875; son of Henry and Althea M. Stimpson, his wife. His occupation is teaming. Children: (1) Clifford A., b., Ledyard, Nov. 5,

1899; (2) Althea M., b. June 17, 1905, d., Ledyard, Oct. 26, 1905. Res., Ledyard, Conn.

2250. James F., b. July 23, 1882; m., No. Stonington, Conn., Dec. 10, 1902, Nellie White, b., Stonington, Conn., Apr. 19, 1874; dau. of Charles P. and Jane E. (Wheeler) White, of No. Stonington. His industries are farming and teaming. No issue. Res., Stonington, Conn.

Melissa Main (2178), dau. of William Leeds (2145) and Sarah A. (Frink) Main [Thomas (2137), Benajah Main (312d). , Thomas (275), Dea. Thomas (264), Jeremiah (260), Ezekiel], twin to Alonzo, b., Ledyard, Conn., Oct. 4, 1856; m., Norwich, Conn., 1877, Joseph Holdredge, b., Ledyard, Sept. 30, 1855; son of Randall and Nancy (Main) Holdredge, of Ledyard. Children, b. Ledyard:

2251. Randall L. Holdredge, b. Mar. 28, 1881; d., Ledyard, May 1, 1882.

2252. Marion M., b. Feb. 27, 1882; m., Ledyard, Dec. 5, 1906, Austin S. Lamb, son of Courtland and Jane (Lester) Lamb. Son: Earl Tyler, b., Ledyard, Jan. 27, 1908.

2253. J. Nelson, b. Sept. 18, 1883; m., Mar. 18, 1909, Fanny May Holdredge, dau. of Hiram and Mary (Rudock) Holdredge. Res., New London, Conn.

2254. Stella I., b. Jan. 28, 1887.

2255. William Leeds, b. Sept. 18, 1889.

2256. Gladys M., b. Apr. 10, 1895.

Horace H. Main (2179), son of William Leeds (2145) and Sarah A. (Frink) Main [Thomas (2137), Benajah Main (312d). Thomas (275), Dea. Thomas (264), Jeremiah (260), Ezekiel], b., Ledyard, Conn., Aug. 9, 1859; m., Westerly, R. I., Feb. 1, 1881, Phebe Partelo, b., Preston, Conn., Aug. 8, 1856; dau. of William Partelo, of Montville, Conn., and Abbie Main. Mr. Main is a farmer, and combines with it carpenter work and other industries. Mrs. Main is an expert in poultry-raising and gives much attention to that industry. Address, Norwich, Conn., R. F. D. 6.

Children, b. Ledyard:

2257. Florence B., b. Nov. 27, 1881; m., Dec. 21, 1898, Philetus Brown, b., Ledyard, Jan. 25, 1866; son of Albert M. and Nancy A. (Peckham) Brown, of Ledyard. Dau.: Iva Nancy, b. Nov. 30, 1901; d., Old Mystic, Conn., Sept. 23, 1907. Res., Old Mystic, Conn.

2258. Lura E., b. June 2, 1890.

2259. Phebe M., b. Nov. 11, 1894.

2260. Horace W. (twin), b. June 6, 1899.

2261. Harry W. C. (twin), b. June 6, 1899.

Amos Main (2180), brother of the preceding, b., Ledyard, Conn., Nov. 3, 1862; d., Norwich, Conn., July 7, 1901; m. (1), Norwich, Jan. 10, 1893, Lucy A. Mathewson, b., Norwich, Oct. 29, 1874; dau. of George W. and Georgianna (Morgan) Mathewson. He was a farmer, and his wife is a member of the Preston City Church. She m. (2) Paul Macy. Res., Preston, Conn.

Children, by first m.:

.2262. Lydia L., b. Apr. 6, 1894.

2263. Clifford M., b. Nov. 5, 1899.

Hannah M. Perkins (2198), dau. of Miner and Mary Esther (Main, 2151) Perkins, b., No. Stonington, Conn., Oct. 30, 1844; d. Apr. 23, 1908; m., No. Stonington, Feb. 15, 1876, Dwight C. Brown, b. Mar. 2, 1851; son of Paul W. and Esther P. (Main) Brown.

Children, b. No. Stonington:

2264. Stephen D., b. Dec. 27, 1877; unm.

2265. Mariette, b. Mar. 26, 1882; m., No. Stonington, Nov. 28, 1906, Thomas Edgar Brown, b. Oct. 24, 1859. This is his second m. He is a police officer, Westerly, R. I. Son: Dwight C., b. Feb. 27, 1908. (See B. G., pp. 157–160.)

Deborah Betsey Perkins (2202), dau. of Miner and Mary Esther (Main, 2151) Perkins, b., No. Stonington, Conn., Sept. 13, 1852; d., Mystic, Conn., Mar. 9, 1907; m. Aaron Alvah Brown, b., Ledyard, Conn., Apr. 2, 1846; son of Albert and Surviah (Main, 2149) Brown. He is a mechanic at Mystic. Albert Brown was the son of Nathaniel, longtime residents and farmers in Ledyard.

Children, b. Ledyard:

2266. Happy Louise Brown, b. Jan. 30, 1873; unm. She is a schoolteacher at Mystic.

2267. Wilfred E., b. Dec. 13, 1877; m. Bethia W. Spicer.

2268. May Hannah, b. Jan. 27, 1879; m., Stonington, Conn., Feb. 12, 1900, Albert L. Wheeler, b., Stonington, Jan. 28, 1876. Children: (1) Clarabelle, b. Sept. 19, 1903, d. Sept. 3, 1906; (2) Lester Brown, b. Nov. 13, 1907.

THE EZEKIEL MAIN FAMILY

2269. Albert Grover, b. Sept. 29, 1882; m., Oct. 23, 1908, Florence Leona Rankin, dau. of Augustus and Etta (Brewster) Rankin, of Rockland, Me. Mr. Brown is a boat-builder. Res., Mystic, Conn.

Wilfred Ernest Brown (2267), son of the preceding, b. Dec. 13, 1877; m., Mystic, Conn., June 24, 1901, Bethia Williams Spicer, b., Groton, Conn., Oct. 28, 1879; dau. of Edward E. Spicer and Sarah A. Griswold, of Groton. Mr. Brown was educated in the schools of Ledyard, Conn., and early in life became interested in the timber business. After marriage he settled in Mystic, where he was with the Holmes Shipbuilding Co., holding an important position with that firm, until January, 1906, when he purchased the ice business conducted by the late Elijah Morgan for more than forty years. Res., Old Mystic, Conn. Children: (1) Mildred Hope, b., West Mystic, Conn., Mar. 25, 1902; (2) Clare Spicer, b. Apr. 1, 1904; (3) Sophia Ernestine, b. May 9, 1906; (4) Milton Ayer, b., Old Mystic, Jan. 5, 1909.

Seth Woodward Main (2203), son of Seth (2153) and Marvanna Stanton (Woodward) Main [Thomas (2137), Benajah Main (312d). , Thomas (275), Dea. Thomas (264), Jeremiah (260), Ezekiel], b., No. Stonington, Conn., Aug. 3, 1849; d., Preston, Conn., Mar. 31, 1904; m. (1), Norwich, Conn., Apr. 5, 1881, Ida Frances Myers, d. Mar. 15, 1882. He m. (2), Preston, Nov. 21, 1883, Hulda Jane Gallup, of Preston, dau. of Dea. John D. Gallup, who held the office of deacon over forty years. His parents, when he was six years of age, removed to Preston, where he received his early education, supplemented by several terms in select school in Preston; he also attended the academy at East Greenwich, R. I., paying his own expenses from money he had saved from his own earnings. He taught school in East Greenwich one term, and one term in Preston, Poquetanuck district. Later he was a grocer's clerk at Norwich for a year and one half. He returned to Preston, engaging in farming for a short time; but the mercantile world proved too strong for him, and he again went to Norwich, clerking for two grocery firms for six years. He shortly afterwards purchased the general store of Daniel Brown, which he conducted successfully for about nine years; he then sold the store and began farming and gardening and the raising of small fruits, in which line of work he was engaged up to the time of his death. No children that survived. Interments, Preston City. Mrs. Main's res., 536 Main St., Norwich, Conn.

Mary Rozilla Main (2204), dau. of Seth Main (2153) and Maryanna S. Woodward [Thomas (2137), Benajah Main (312d), Thomas (275), Dea. Thomas (264), Jeremiah (260), Ezekiel], b., No. Stonington, Conn., Apr. 14, 1851; m., Preston, Conn., Sept. 27, 1877, Herbert H. Barlow, b., Belchertown, Mass., June 22, 1848; son of Henry W. Barlow, of Ware, Mass., and Emeline C. Hill. He is a retired farmer, a Republican, and both he and his wife are members of the Congregational Church. He was educated in the public schools of Ware and Belchertown. He is deacon and trustee of the church. He was collector of taxes for twelve years. His wife was educated in the schools of Preston and the Norwich Free Academy, and taught school for ten years before her marriage. She was on the School Committee of Enfield, Mass.; correspondent of *The Springfield Republican* and president of the Missionary Society of Enfield. Res., Enfield, Mass.

Children, b. Smith's, Mass.:

    2270. Seth H., b. May 17, 1880.
    2271. Alice R., b. June 14, 1883.
    2272. Henry M., b. Nov. 23, 1884.
    2273. M. Arline, b. Dec. 24, 1888.

Cynthia Elvira Main (2205), dau. of Seth (2153) and Maryanna S. (Woodward) Main, b., No. Stonington, Conn., Jan. 22, 1853; m., Preston, Conn., Chauncey Cleveland Pendleton, b., Preston, May 14, 1846; son of Ansel Pendleton, of Preston, and Ann Witter Button. Mr. Pendleton is engaged in farming, and a dealer in cattle. In politics he favors the Democrats. In young manhood he was a school-teacher. Both he and his wife are members of the Preston City Baptist Church. Res., Norwich, Conn. R. F. D. 1.

Children, b. Preston:

    2274. Maryanna Pendleton, b. June 9, 1875; m., Norwich, Feb. 27, 1895, Jesse Oakley Crary, b., Preston, May 26, 1873; son of Thomas Peabody Crary and Maria Stanton Ball. Miss Pendleton before her marriage was a school-teacher. Mr. Crary is a farmer, and both he and his wife are members of the Baptist Church. Res., Norwich, Conn. R. F. D. Dau.: Cynthia Lillian, b. Aug. 1, 1904.

    2275. George Ansel, b. Mar. 24, 1878; m., Preston, Aug. 12, 1903, Clara Belle Benjamin, b. No. Stonington, Dec. 5, 1884. Son: Charles Cleveland, b. Apr. 9, 1905.

    2276. Joseph Button, b. Jan. 26, 1886.
    2277. Mabel Cynthia, b. Dec. 9, 1892.

Appleton Main (2206), son of Seth (2153) and Maryanna S. (Woodward) Main, b., No. Stonington, Conn., Jan. 23, 1855; m., No. Stonington, June 22, 1892, Isabelle Richardson, b., No. Stonington, Apr. 29, 1870; dau. of William R. and Lucy (Dawley) Richardson, of No. Stonington. When he was three months old his parents removed to Preston, Conn. His common-school education was obtained in what was known as the "Plains District," and later he spent about three years in select schools in Preston City. After one term at East Greenwich, R. I., he began teaching, and continued for eight years; but it was not consecutive, for at the end of two years he was a clerk in a store at Norwich, Conn.; but on account of ill health he returned to his father's farm, where, with his brother Nathaniel, they engaged in farming until they dissolved partnership. He continued on his father's farm about eight years; then, in 1893, he purchased the "Ulysses Avery Farm" of one hundred sixty acres, where he is engaged in general farming. This beautiful farm, with its rows of maples, shading the avenue from the main road to the house, is remembered by the compiler, for he visited here with his sister for millinery work in 1846. Mr. Main has served his town for four years as selectman; also served on the Board of Relief and the Board of Assessors. In 1895 he represented his town in the Legislature of the State. All of these offices he filled with marked distinction. Mr. Main has been frequently called upon to frame deeds of property. He is a member of the Preston City Baptist Church, which he has served for several years as collector and superintendent of the Sunday school. His religion finds ex-pression not so much in words as in kind acts and deeds. His wife is a member of the church and active in church work.

Children, b. Preston:

2278. Gertrude Idell, b. Apr. 16, 1895.
2279. Lester Appleton, b. Oct. 1, 1896.

Nathaniel Main (2207), brother of the preceding, and son of Seth Main (2153) and Maryanna Woodward, b., Preston, Conn., May 7, 1857; d., Franklin, Conn., May 28, 1891; m., Preston, Sept. 4, 1884, Nellie M. Holmes, b., Mystic, Conn., Dec. 14, 1866; dau. of Shubael Holmes and B. Angeline Gray, of Preston. Mr. Main was a stock dealer and butcher. They lived in Ledyard, Lebanon, and Franklin, Conn. They attended the Preston City Baptist Church, and Mrs. Main is a member; also their son. Res., Norwich, Conn. R. F. D. 1.

Son:

2280. Ernest Nathaniel, b., Lebanon, Conn., Oct. 19, 1889. After the death of his father he went to live with his maternal grandfather, Shubael Holmes, where he attended common school and the Norwich Business College.

Leonard Main (2208), brother of the preceding, b., Preston, Conn., Jan. 16, 1859; m., No. Stonington, Conn., Mar. 27, 1884, Annie Elizabeth Richardson, sister of the wife of Appleton Main; b. Jan. 11, 1866; dau. of William Robinson Richardson and Lucy Ann Dawley, of Griswold, Conn. Mr. Main was educated in the public schools and at the Mystic Institute. He taught school for twenty winters before and after marriage, and farming during the summer. He is on the School Board, and has bought the store that was occupied by the late William H. Hillard in the village of No. Stonington. He and his wife and their oldest children are members of the Third Baptist Church.

Children, b. Preston:

2281. Leonard Richardson, b. Apr. 17, 1888.

2282. Allison Homer, b. June 8, 1892.

2283. Floyd Leslie, b. June 13, 1893.

2284. Evelyn Isabell, b. Jan. 27, 1901.

Ellen E. Main (2210), dau. of Amasa M. (2156) and Lucy O. (Frink) Main, b., Ledyard, Conn., Aug. 16, 1856; m., Stonington, Conn., Mar. 10, 1875, Harban O. Whitford, son of Clark Whitford.

Son:

2285. Harban C., b., No. Stonington, Conn., July 20, 1882; m., October, 1908, Phebe Wheeler.

Lafayette F. Main (2215), son of Amasa M. (2156) and Lucy Orry (Frink) Main, b., Ledyard, Conn., Nov. 25, 1867; m., No. Stonington, Conn., Aug. 1, 1900, Julia Emily Mather, b., Ledyard, Sept. 13, 1882; dau. of Frank J. and Lydia (Newton) Mather. Mr. Main is a man of considerable notoriety, and one of the best known of all these families. He is probably the largest landholder of any in the families. His house is located on Swantown Hill, No. Stonington, and is one of commanding appearance. His wife is a member of the Baptist Church.

Children, first two b. No. Stonington:

2286. Emily Pratt, b. July 10, 1901.

2287. Lucy Matilda, b. Feb. 22, 1903.

2288. Gladys Lydia, b., Pawtucket, R. I., Nov. 28, 1904.

Fannie Esther Main (2217), dau. of Amasa M. (2156) and Lucy O. (Frink) Main, b., Ledyard, Conn., June 20, 1873; m., Westerly, R. I., Nov. 7, 1890, Otis Allen Chapman, b., No. Stonington, Conn., Feb. 27, 1869; son of Kneeland and Abby (Main) Chapman, son of Dea. Reuben Chapman. Mr. Chapman owns the "Betsey Baldwin Farm" in Stonington, Conn. He is a Republican. His wife attended the Wheeler High School, No. Stonington. She is a member of the Baptist Church, Old Mystic, Conn.

Children, first three b. Mystic, Conn.:

2289. Ida May, b. Apr. 18, 1893; m., Stonington, Sept. 5, 1909, William Thayer Downing, b., Boston, Mass., 1890; son of Charles Downing. He is an electrician and has charge of eighteen miles of electric lines at Gardner, Mass.

2290. Oscar Barber, b. Aug. 26, 1896.

2291. Everett Amasa, b. Jan. 6, 1898.

2292. Harold Webster, b., Stonington, Oct. 15, 1905.

Hattie Bell Main (2218), sister of the preceding, b., Ledyard, Conn., Aug. 30, 1875; m., Stonington, Conn., Jan. 6, 1897, Edward Jerry Duro, b., Suncook, N. H., Mar. 22, 1868; son of Jerry and Delia (Huard) Duro. He is a carpenter by trade, painter, and fish-dealer. Mrs. Duro, before her marriage, was a school-teacher in Ledyard and Preston, Conn.: also superintendent of the Lantern Hill Sunday school and member of the Baptist Church. Res., Norwich, Conn. R. F. D. 1.

Children, b. Norwich:

2293. Child, b. June 2, 1900; d., unnamed.

2294. Gladys E., b. Aug. 17, 1901; d. Aug. 28, 1901.

2295. Edward H., b. Jan. 26, 1902.

2296. Frederic E., b. June 16, 1903.

2297. Theodore E., b. Aug. 20, 1904.

Here end the records of the Thomas Main family.

James Main (285), son of Jeremiah (269) and Thankful (Brown) Main, dau. of James Brown and Elizabeth Randall, b., Stonington, Conn., Jan. 27, 1743; d., Berlin, Rensselaer Co., N. Y., 1847, aged one hundred four years; m., Stonington, Mar. 4, 1763, Hannah Wallace.

Children, b. Stonington:

495. Hannah, b. Dec. 12, 1763.

496. James, Jr., b. Apr. 3, 1766; m. Miss Taylor.

497. ᵒGilbert, b. Jan. 10, 1768.

498. Lucinda, b. July 28, 1770.

To keep the connection, the above is a copy from pp. 73 and 74.

James Main, Jr. (496), son of James (285) and Hannah Wallace [Jeremiah (269), Jeremiah (260), Ezekiel], b., Stonington, Conn., Apr. 3, 1766. In his young manhood he removed to Stephentown, N. Y.; afterwards to Berlin, Rensselaer Co., N. Y.; m. (1) Miss Taylor; m. (2)——; name of second wife not ascertained.

Children by first m., b. Berlin:

 2298. James, b. Mar. 29, 1787 (2305-2314).

 2299. Daniel, b.——. Not further mentioned.

 2300. Polly, b.——; m. Stephen Wilcox (2315, 2316).

 2301. Mercy, b. ——; m. her cousin James, son of Gilbert Main.

Children, probably by second m.:

 2302. Keziah, b.——

 2303. Minerva N., b. June 18, 1821; m. Lyman Bennett, of Williams-town, Mass.

 2304. Hannah, b.——

James Main, 3d (2298), son of James Main, Jr. (496), and Miss Taylor, his wife [James (285), Jeremiah (269), Jeremiah (260), Ezekiel], b., Berlin, N. Y., Mar. 29, 1787; d., Adams, N. Y., Oct. 25, 1864; m., Berlin, Mar. 6, 1813, Susannah Sheldon, b. Oct. 11, 1796; d. May 30, 1879.

Children, b. Adams, except the first two:

 2305. Louisa Ann Main, b., Berlin, Nov. 4, 1814; d., Troy, N. Y., Jan. 5, 1892; m., Adams, Jan. 20, 1839, R. L. Thomas.

 2306. James Taylor, b., Berlin, June 8, 1816; d., Troy, Aug. 19, 1894; m. (1), Aug. 20, 1842, Arvilla Rhodes; m. (2), Feb. 9, 1854, Lucinda E. Horton; m. (3), 1863, ——

 2307. Survilla, b. Apr. 9, 1818; d., Adams, June 12, 1856; unm.

 2308. Elizabeth, b. Mar. 1, 1820; d., Adams, May 11, 1848; m., Adams, Oct. 4, 1845, H. Colfax. No issue.

 2309. Daniel C., b. June 9, 1822; d., Troy, Dec. 5, 1899; m., Adams, Oct. 31, 1844, Harriet Robbins.

 2310. Susan, b. June 27, 1824; m., Adams, Sept. 5, 1846, H. Robbins.

 2311. Isaac S., b. Jan. 12, 1827; m. (1) Lucy A. Holloway; m. (2) Mrs. Annah M. Hunt, née Van Hagen (2327, 2328).

 2312. Zurial D., b. Jan. 18, 1830; d., Troy, Feb. 1, 1909; m. (1),

Troy, Jan. 18, 1855, Caroline M. Holloway; m. (2), Troy, Dec. 16, 1896, Sarah A. Case. No issue by either m.

2313. Martha M., b. Jan. 20, 1834; m., Adams, Jan. 17, 1866, William D. Green.

2314. Orange H., b. Mar. 20, 1836; d., Adams, Jan. 29, 1875; m., Adams, Feb. 8, 1859, Jane Robbins.

Polly Main (2300), dau. of James Main, Jr. (496), and Miss Taylor, his wife [James (285), Jeremiah (269), Jeremiah (260), Ezekiel], b.——; m. Petersburg, Rensselaer Co., N. Y., Stephen Wilcox.

Children:

2315. Caroline Wilcox, b.——

2316. Ambrose Wilcox, b.——

Mercy Main (2301), sister of the preceding, m. her cousin James Main, son of Gilbert (497). They lived at Plattsburgh and Berlin, N. Y.

Children:

2317. Daniel T., b. about 1816; m. Nancy, dau. of Gardner Main.

2318. Hannah, b.——; m. Philander Odell.

2319. James, b.——. He removed to Illinois.

2320. William, b.——; d. young.

2321. Palmer, b.——

2322. Clark, b.——

2323. Perry, b.——

2324. Mary Ann, b.——

2325. Keziah, b.——

2326. Nancy, b.——

Isaac Sheldon Main (2311), son of James Main, 3d (2298), and Susannah Sheldon [James (285), Jeremiah (269), Jeremiah (260), Ezekiel], b., Adams, N. Y., Jan. 12, 1827; d., Philadelphia, Penn., Apr. 9, 1909; m. (1), Homesfield, N. Y., Jan. 6, 1849, Lucy A. Holloway, b., Homesfield, Apr. 3, 1828; d., Troy, N. Y., May 15, 1884; dau. of Samuel and Lucy (Baker), of Homesfield. He m. (2) Mrs. Anna M. Hunt, née Van Hagen.

Children, by first m.:

2327. George A., b., Troy, Oct. 20, 1852; m. Addie Adams.

2328. William H., b., Adams, Aug. 7, 1862; m. Hattie A. Gramm.

George S. Main (2327), b., Troy, N. Y., Oct. 20, 1852; m., Troy, Dec. 24, 1873, Addie Adams, b., Brunswick, Rensselaer Co., N. Y., Apr. 29, 1853; dau. of George W. Adams and Lydia, his wife. Mr. Main when four years old moved with the family to Adams, N. Y.; but at the age of twelve years they returned to Troy, where he received high-school education. He resided in Troy until 1890, being in the grocery business a portion of the time. In 1890 he moved with his family to Buffalo, N. Y., his present home [1909], where he is a railroad clerk. Mrs. Main received her education in public and private schools of Brunswick. Both he and his wife are members of the Emanuel Baptist Church. Res., 330 Normal Ave., Buffalo, N. Y.:

Dau.:

2329. Hila Adams, b., Troy, Oct. 18, 1886. She is a graduate of the Buffalo High School, and is a typewriter and stenographer.

William Holloway Main (2328), son of Isaac Sheldon (2310) and Lucy A. (Holloway) Main, b., Adams, N. Y., Aug. 7, 1862; m., Troy, N. Y., July 1, 1885, Hattie A. Gramm, b., Troy, May 1, 1863; dau. of Louis Gramm, of Troy. Rev. Mr. Main was educated for the ministry at Colgate University, and ordained at Waterford, N. Y., where he was pastor. He was pastor at Buffalo and Syracuse, N. Y., and at Hartford, Conn. Now he is pastor of the Memorial Baptist Church, Philadelphia, Penn. He travelled abroad twice, visiting Palestine and Egypt on the first trip. He is a lecturer. He was for two years president of Connecticut State Christian Endeavor Union. Grand Chaplin of Grand Lodge of F. and A. M. of Connecticut. He is a member of the Founders of Patriots of America; member of Baptist Board of Education of New York State for five years. He studied law before entering Colgate University. Res., 1623 No. 15th St., Philadelphia, Penn.

Dau.:

2330. Lucy Carolyn, b., Waterford, N. Y., Sept. 9, 1886. She was educated at Syracuse [N. Y.] University, and is a musician.

By the assistance of Rev. Wm. H. Main (2328) and A. A. Aspinwall, Washington, D. C. (2334), I am able to connect Jeremiah Main (269) and wife Thankful Brown, dau. of James Brown and Elizabeth Randall, of Stonington, Conn., with this Main family, the children taking for three generations the name of their progenitor James Brown, who was the son of one of the three brothers (Eleazer) who first settled in Stonington. (See B. G., p. 14.) He built his house on the west side of the road about thirty rods south of the Miner Meeting-house. This house and barn were very old in 1846, and were then torn down, and not a vestige of them remains to mark the place. It was a beautiful location. Here, on this beautiful farm, Thankful Brown (twin) was b., Oct. 22, 1720; m., Stonington,

Apr. 26, 1742, Jeremiah Main (269), b. Apr. 10, 1708; d., Stonington, 1780. The last occupant of this farm and house mentioned above was Charles Brown, who died there, and his widow Rhoda Ann Brown removed to Stephentown, N. Y., and married again, where her dau. Frances Eleanor lived and had a family. (See B. G., pp. 66 and 67.)

For the benefit of those who have not a copy of the Brown Genealogy here are inserted the records of James Brown and family, as they were the progenitors of many large Main families heretofore given with their family numbers in this book. The father of the compiler of these records hired a portion of this James Brown farm, and it was his privilege to go in and out of this old one-story house, and drink the beautiful water from this excellent well, which is now covered with a large, flat stone. He assisted in plowing, planting, mowing, and harvesting the crops from 1840 to 1845.

James Brown, son of Eleazer and Ann (Pendleton) Brown, b., Stonington, Conn., July 1, 1696; d. Feb. 2, 1750, aged fifty-five years; m., May 5, 1718, by Rev. James Noyes, of Stonington, Elizabeth Randall, b. July 4, 1696; d. Aug. 25, 1786, aged ninety-one years. Interment in Brown Cemetery. His wife Elizabeth was the dau. of John Randall and Abigail ——, whose family name and birth do not appear on record. She was the granddau. of John Randall, the progenitor of the Randall family of Westerly, R. I., and Stonington, Conn. His name first appears at Newport, R. I., from which place he came to Westerly as early as 1667, where the remainder of his life was spent. The Randall land was about four miles northeast of Stonington Borough, known as Angwilla and considered the finest land of the town. These lands join on the north the lands of Thomas Brown, and have been in the Randall name as late as 1875. These farms now [1910] are mostly owned by Elias Miner and his sons. The Randall families were highly respected and progressive, ranking high in moral character and being prominent citizens of the town.

Children, b. Stonington; since 1807, No. Stonington:

James, Jr., b. Jan. 29, 1719; d. Dec. 24, 1741.

Dau. (twin), b. and d. Oct. 22, 1720.

Thankful (twin), b. Oct. 22, 1720; m. Jeremiah Main (284a–291).

Simeon, b. Jan. 31, 1723; m. Dorothy Hern.

Ann, b. Mar. 23, 1728. Not further mentioned.

Zebulon, b. Nov. 20, 1730; m. Anna Main (301–312).

Elizabeth, b. July 31, 1732; m. Timothy Main (292–300).

Abigail, b. Apr. 23, 1737. Not further mentioned.

Joshua, b. Apr. 8, 1740; m. Joanna Rogers.

Site of Eleazer Brown's house
With the Brown Cemetery in the background

In this quiet place, above the ashes of the long-time dead, are the tablets and monuments of many of the descendants of Eleazer Brown and Ann Pendleton, his wife; and James Brown and Elizabeth Randall, his wife.

Eleazer Brown's tombstone

In Memory of
Mr James Brown
who died
Feb 2^d 1750.
in the 53th year
of his age.

In Memory of
Elizabeth Relict of
Mr James Brown.
who died
Augt 25th 1786.
in the 91st year
of her age

Tombstone of James Brown

Frances Main (523), dau. of Jonas (509) and Lydia Porter (see p. 75), b., Henderson, Jefferson Co., N. Y., Mar. 4, 1812; d., Nunda, Livingston Co., N. Y., Apr. 10, 1891; m., Watertown, N. Y., May 5, 1836, Rev. Joseph Aikin Aspinwall, b., Rupert, Bennington Co., Vt., July 25, 1812; d., Nunda, Oct. 24, 1860.

Children:

> 2331. Joseph Francis, b., Leyden, N. Y., Mar. 22, 1837; d. May 5, 1909; unm.
>
> 2332. David Irving, b., Hartford, N. Y., June 28, 1840 (2336 2338).
>
> 2333. Mortimer Clarence, b. Oct. 13, 1842; d. Mar. 8, 1846.
>
> 2334. Algernon Aikin, b., Fort Ann, N. Y., Feb. 3, 1845 (2339, 2340).
>
> 2335. Murray Channing, b., Saratoga Springs, N. Y., Feb. 25, 1848 (2341–2350).

David Irving Aspinwall (2332), b., Hartford, Washington Co., N. Y., June 28, 1840; m. Adelia A. Briggs, dau. of Philip and Delecta (Hebmer) Briggs, b. Apr. 3, 1846; d. Feb. 16, 1909. Res., Penn Yan, Yates Co., N. Y.

Children:

> 2336. Cora D., b. Feb. 13, 1865; m., Feb. 13, 1888, Edward A. Schrumn. No issue.
>
> 2337. Frank Aikin, b. Mar. 7, 1868. He was twice m. No issue.
>
> 2338. Janie B., b. Aug. 27, 1874; m., Nov. 11, 1896, Ernest H. Chapman, of Penn Yan. Dau.: Doris Jeanette, b. Nov. 11, 1897.

Algernon Aikin Aspinwall (2334), b., Fort Ann, Washington Co., N. Y., Feb. 3, 1845; m., Titusville, Penn., June 1, 1870, Martha Ann Humphrey, b., New Britain, Conn., Mar. 11, 1849; dau. of John William and Mary (Francis) Humphrey. Mr. Aspinwall was in the Civil War. He enlisted in April, 1861, in Co. F, 33d N. Y. Vol. Infantry, at Nunda, N. Y., where he was then residing. At the close of the war he removed to Titusville. In 1885 he accepted an appointment as Chief of Division in the Department of the Interior, Washington, D. C., and has resided in that city ever since. He published a genealogy of the Aspinwall family in 1901, and has been engaged for about fifteen years in collecting data for a genealogy of the descendants of Ezekiel Maine, which he hopes to publish in the near future. The author of this genealogy gives him permission to use as much as he may desire of the matter of this book that is not found in his data.

Children, b. Titusville:

2339. William Humphrey, b. Feb. 21, 1872; m., New York City,
Apr. 30, 1902, Mabel Louise Bosworth, b. Portland, Me.;
dau. of George M. and Clara V. (Smith) Bosworth. Children: (1) George Bosworth, b. Apr. 25, 1903; (2) Helen, b.
Mar. 24, 1906; d. Dec. 25, 1906. Res., Bartlesville, Okla.

2340. Clarence Aikin, b. Aug. 6, 1874; m., Waterbury, Conn., Jan.
1, 1900, Jeannette Scovill, b., Waterbury, Dec. 30, 1878;
dau. of Henry William and Elsie (Hyde) Scovill. Children:
(1) Margaret Scovill, b. Nov. 6, 1900; (2) Algernon Aikin,
b. Sept. 25, 1902; (3) Scovill Hazard, b. Feb. 23, 1906; (4)
Ellen Hyde, b. Feb. 19, 1909. Res., Washington, D. C.

Murray Channing Aspinwall (2335), son of Rev. Joseph Aikin and
Frances (Main, 523) Aspinwall, b., Saratoga Springs, N. Y., Feb. 25, 1848;
m. (1), Palmyra, N. Y., Jan. 1, 1870, Cynthia Adella Benedict, b. July 18,
1849; d., Troy, N. Y., Oct. 17, 1879; dau. of Ira and Mary (Warner)
Benedict. He m. (2), Apr. 25, 1883, Lucy Mary Holloway, b., Omar,
Jefferson Co., N. Y., Apr. 27, 1862; dau. of Daniel Webster and Lois
(Stickney) Holloway. Res., Troy, N. Y.

Children by first m.:

2341. Harry Benedict, b. Oct. 1, 1872; d. July 28, 1873.
2342. Warner Howard, b. Aug. 1, 1874. Res., New York City.
2343. Grace Maine, b. Mar. 3, 1876; d. July 26, 1876.
2344. Earl Williams, b. Jan. 31, 1878; d. Nov. 25, 1881.

Children by second m.:

2345. Murray, b. Feb. 22, 1885; d. July 6, 1888.
2346. Lucille, b. June 1, 1887.
2347. Delford, b. Dec. 4, 1889; d. Jan. 1, 1893.
2348. Lois, b. Sept. 26, 1891.
2349. Kenneth, b. Dec. 30, 1894; d. 1896.
2350. Frances, b. June 1, 1897.

Nos. 2351 to 2368 belong with the Joshua Main family.

Cyrus Gilbert (2010), son of Daniel Durfee and Harriet (Main, 1993)
Gilbert, b., Wilton, Conn., June 8, 1828; d., Wilton, Dec. 24, 1875; m.,
Wilton, Feb. 16, 1856, Sarah Scribner, b., Wilton, 1838; d., Wilton, Sept.
29, 1866; dau. of Stephen and Annace (Jennings) Scribner, of Wilton.
Mr. Gilbert served for three years in the Civil War, in Co. G, 5th Regiment

Louisa A. (Brown) Lewis (64), wife of Dr. Edwin R. Lewis
Daughter (2387), and Son (2388)

William Cyrus Gilbert
(2352)
Danbury, Conn.
Page 271

of Connecticut Volunteers, and received an honorable discharge, by reason
of expiration of term, and later a roll of honor for meritorious service,
now in possession of his son. Both he and his wife were members of the
Methodist Church.

Children, b. Wilton:

2351. Adele Gilbert, b. Mar. 6, 1859; d., Wilton, Apr. 14, 1876.

2352. William Cyrus Gilbert, b. June 19, 1865; m., Danbury, Conn.,
June 22, 1887, Virginia Godfrey, b., Newtown, Conn., Dec.
29, 1865; dau. of Austin and Esther Burr (Gray) Godfrey,
of Westport, Conn.   Mr. Gilbert received his education in
the public schools and in Stillman's Business College of Danbury. He was elected alderman for two successive terms,
and served from March, 1904, to 1907. He was elected
Mayor of the city of Danbury, Apr. 1, 1907, and re-elected
April, 1909, terms of two years each. He was appointed
member of Town Board of Finance Sept. 1, 1904, and
reappointed for the term of three years September, 1908.
He was president of the Republican Club in 1906. He is a
member of Union Lodge, Eureka Chapter and Wooster
Council F. and A. M. of Danbury; member of Samaritan
Lodge, No. 7, I. O. O. F., and financial secretary of the
same; member of Danbury Council Royal Arcanum, and
collector. He served for four years in Company G, 4th
Reg. C. N. G., under Capt. C. Queen and Capt. Frank
Nash. He was chosen Vestryman of St. James Church in
May, 1905, and elected each year thereafter. Mrs. Gilbert
was educated in the schools of Newtown, and for four years
attended the Union School at Syracuse, N. Y. Both he and
his wife are members of the Episcopal Church.

Children, b. Danbury:

2353. Pauline Adele, b. Oct. 17, 1888.

2354. Cyrus Thurston, b. June 6, 1892.

2355. Earle Godfrey, b. July 20, 1893.

2356. Leonial, b. Nov. 13, 1894; d., Danbury, Feb. 4, 1895.

2357. William Chauncey, b. Feb. 28, 1896.

2358. Helen Augusta, b. Sept. 2, 1898.

2359. Marshall Gray, b. Sept. 22, 1901.

Julian Sylvester Main (2056), son of Sylvester (2001) and Susan (Lobdell) Main, b., Ridgefield, Conn., Sept. 28, 1841; d., Ridgefield, Nov. 19,

1865; m., Dec. 11, 1862, Sarah Eliza Smith, b., Barbadoes, West Indies, June 13, 1840. She m. (2) Harry S. Winner, and they have seven children. Res., 105 No. Park St., East Orange, N. J.

Children:

2360. Nellie Virginia, b., Ridgefield, May 1, 1863; d., New York, Aug. 1, 1884; m., in 1882, Henry Charles Palmer.

2361. Julian Hubert, b., Brooklyn, N. Y., Mar. 23, 1865; m., in 1889, Emily La Croix.

Helen Ida Main (2057), dau. of Sylvester (2001) and Susan (Lobdell) Main, b., Ridgefield, Conn., Oct. 21, 1844; d., Danbury, Conn., May 22, 1889; m., June 28, 1864, John Albert Pulling, b., Brookfield, Conn., Feb. 4, 1843.

Children, last three b. Danbury:

2362. Gracie Louise, b., Ridgefield, Apr. 11, 1866; m. Arthur Edward Tweedy.

2363. Willie Arthur, b. Feb. 10, 1868; d. Aug. 24, 1868.

2364. Susie Estella, b. June 17, 1869; m., Danbury, June 10, 1891, Charles Rider. Children, b. Danbury: (1) Helen Olivia, b. May 20, 1892; (2) Marion Elizabeth, b. Nov. 3, 1893.

2365. Ward Benedict, b. Jan. 7, 1877; d. Feb. 15, 1878.

Cynthia Isabella Main (2058), dau. of Sylvester (2001) and Susan (Lobdell) Main, b., Ridgefield, Conn., Aug. 17, 1849; m. (1), So. Salem, N. Y., June 20, 1871, John S. Monroe, b., Ridgefield, Aug. 31, 1851; divorced in 1876. She m. (2), Ridgefield, Mar. 27, 1881, Frank Edwin Olmstead, b., Norwalk, Conn., Sept. 5, 1846; d., Ridgefield, Dec. 31, 1901.

Dau. by first m.:

2366. Helen Ida, b., Ridgefield, June 26, 1873; m., Syracuse, N. Y., Jan. 30, 1895, William Irving Gates, b., Mill Center, Wis., June 4, 1873. Children: (1) Florence Edyth, b., Syracuse, Nov. 5, 1895, d. July 7, 1896; (2) Hubert Perry, b., Woodward, Onondaga Co., N. Y., May 10, 1898; (3) Mildred Whyte (twin), b., Syracuse, Oct. 9, 1901, d. 1903; (4) Lillian Louise (twin), b. Oct. 9, 1901; (5) Irving, b., Syracuse, May 25, 1906.

Children by second m., b. Ridgefield:

2367. Lena Garr, b. Oct. 7, 1885.

2368. Susan Iola, b. July 22, 1892.

It is not certainly known who Timothy Main, the progenitor of this family, is, but as he lived in Stonington, as did his descendants, it is proof positive he is one of the Main family. Some of the descendants that follow are connected by marriage, and are found in different parts of this book.

Timothy Main m. Hannah ——.

Son:

2369. Jesse, m. Annie Benjamin. He lived near Dea. Allen Wheeler's, where he spent the most of his days. It was said of him that he made *cider* his only beverage.

Children, b. No. Stonington, Conn.:

2370. Charles Main, b.——; m.——.
2371. Noyes, b.——; m. Ann Mitchel. Ann
2372. Lucy, b. 1821; m. Adam Main (Simeon Main family, 138).
2373. Lydia, b.——; d. young.
2374. Luke, b.——
2375. Clarinda, b.——; m. Peleg Gallup.
2376. Clark B., b. Mar. 14, 1829 (2378–2380).
2377. Smith B., b. Sept. 8, 1832; unm. Res., No. Stonington, Conn.

Clark B. Main (2376), son of Jesse and Annie (Benjamin) Main, b. Apr. 14, 1829; m., Groton, Conn., Apr. 16, 1854, Abby E. Mitchel, sister of the wife of Noyes Main. Res., Clarks Falls, Conn.

Children, b. No. Stonington, Conn.:

2378. Frank W., b. Apr. 3, 1855; m. Henrietta Chapman. (See p. 180, 1503.)
2379. Allen T., b. Dec. 21, 1856; m. N. Mitchel.
2380. Richard Dudley, b. Dec. 21, 1859; m., No. Stonington, Oct. 11, 1885, Mary Kilkenny. Son: Wilson Dudley, b. May 1, 1887; m., No. Stonington, June 30, 1909, Belva Brown, dau. of William A. Brown and Hattie Turner, dau. of Denison S. Turner. (See Appendix II, 87.)

Florence Eliza Main (2380a), dau. of Zalmon Smith Main (2014) and Mary Hawkins, b., Hawkins, N. Y., Aug. 3, 1866; m., Binghamton, N. Y., May 22, 1898, William Albert Martin, b., Oxford, N. Y., Sept. 21, 1866; son of Wm. Albert and Eliza A. (Barker) Martin, of Binghamton. Miss Main received her education in the schools of Hawkins until 1881, then in the Newark Valley Academy until 1883, and in the Lady Jane Grey School at Binghamton, receiving diploma in 1888. She resided at Hawkins until 1893 and Binghamton until 1907. Mr. Martin was educated at Oxford

Academy, then moved to Binghamton in 1883, where he began his business career with D. Appleton & Co., where he remained four years. Then he accepted a position in the Star Chair Manufacturing Company as secretary and treasurer, where he remained four years, then accepting a similar position in another company where he remained until 1905; then he removed with his family to California, seeking a home among the orange-groves of that State, where, in 1910, he is an orange-grower at Ontario, Cal. Both he and his wife are members of the Presbyterian Church. Dau.: Ruth W. Martin, b., Binghamton, N. Y., Aug. 23, 1901.

APPENDIX

Appendix I.

Emily Elizabeth Brown (62), b. Jan. 16, 1828; m. Thomas W. Wheeler. Her records on p. 91. Dau.: See 635.

Cyrus Henry Brown (63), son of Cyrus W. and Elizabeth Stewart (Babcock) Brown, b., No. Stonington, Conn., Nov. 24, 1829; m., Ashaway, R. I., Mar. 23, 1856, Sarah Catherine Maxson, b., Hopkinton, R. I., Mar. 4, 1837; d., Westerly, R. I., Oct. 1, 1897; dau. of Horace and Lovina (Lamphear) Maxson. Her ancestry is traced to the first white child born on the island of Rhode Island. She was educated in the public schools of Ashaway and the Young Ladies' Seminary at De Ruyter, N. Y. She was greatly beloved as wife, mother, and Christian woman. Her children and grandchildren were the crowning glory and dearest solace of her life, and her last words, as she was thinking of them, were, "I must leave them, but I have led them aright" — parting words never to be forgotten. Cyrus H. Brown, compiler of these records, also of the Brown Genealogy,— with the assistance of Charles N. Brown of Madison, Wis.,— was educated in the public schools of his native town and in private schools, also taking a preparatory course for teaching at the Connecticut Literary Institution at Suffield, Conn., from May, 1849, to July, 1851. He taught for six years in the public schools of Connecticut and Rhode Island. For one year travelled in Louisiana as a book-agent, in 1853, 1854, giving an opportunity to see the country and people and their habits and customs. Soon after marriage, in 1856, moved with his wife to Brighton, Mass., and followed the provision business, in Boston and Brookline, Mass., till 1889. Then until 1897 the family in summer removed to their farm in Dover, Mass., but retained their home in Allston, Mass. Then in March the same year, on account of the illness of Mrs. Brown, came on a visit to our daughter Mrs. Geo. H. Utter, of Westerly, R. I., where Mrs. Brown passed away six months later. Here I make my home, and soon after Mrs. Brown's death I began writing the Brown Genealogy. Both were members of the Brighton Ave. Baptist Church, Boston; also their six children; was superintendent of the Sunday school for twenty-two years. United with the Calvary Baptist Church, Westerly; was chosen deacon, and teacher in the Bible school, and in 1910 still acting in that capacity.

276

Cyrus H. Brown

(63)

Author of this genealogy, Westerly, R. I.

Pages 25 and 276

Sarah C. (Maxson) Brown, wife of Cyrus H. Brown

Children, b. Brighton, which was annexed to Boston about 1870:

2381. Elizabeth Lovina, b. June 15, 1858; m. Geo. H. Utter (2407
2410).

2382. Henry Edwin, b. Apr. 5, 1861; m. Caroline C. Rollins (2411,
2412).

2383. Katherine Mabel, b. Nov. 5, 1865; m. John L. Howard (2413,
2414).

2384. Wilfred Merrill, b. Apr. 4, 1870; m. Annie C. Bradley (2415).

2385. Horace Clifford, b. June 22, 1873; m. Aldeane Kilmer (2416,
2417).

2386. Grace Emily, b. July 10, 1881; m., Westerly, Sept. 21, 1909,
Chester Denning Abbott, b., Andover, Mass., Apr. 3, 1883;
son of James J. Abbott, b. Apr. 6, 1858, and Lucy A. Blunt,
b. July 22, 1860. Mr. Abbott received his education in the
schools of Andover; after graduation entered the Massachusetts Agricultural College and, after taking a general
course, he then took a special course in the Dairy Department. He is a dairyman and farmer in Andover. Miss
Brown received her education in the Boston schools until
1897, when, on account of the sickness and death of her
mother, she came to Westerly to live with her sister Mrs.
George H. Utter, and there entered the Westerly High
School and remained two years, and one year at the Business College. She attended the Northfield Seminary for
three years; then entered the Rhode Island Normal School
and graduated in 1907. She began teaching in Andover,
and continued until her marriage.

Louisa A. Brown (64), dau. of Cyrus W. and Elizabeth Stewart (Babcock) Brown, b., No. Stonington, Conn., Mar. 21, 1832; d., Westerly, R. I.,
Apr. 11, 1888; m., No. Stonington, Dec. 17, 1850, Dr. Edwin Ransom
Lewis, b., Hopkinton, R: I., Jan. 31, 1827; d., Westerly, June 13, 1887;
son of Dea. Christopher C. and Wealthy (Kenyon) Lewis. Dr. Lewis was
not only a physician of renown, but "the beloved physician," and as a man
and neighbor he was above reproach, kind and benevolent; his home was
radiant with good cheer and sunshine. He was of commanding presence,
his fine face expressing his strength of character and keen intellect. His
wife was educated in the public schools, and in Miss Whiting's School for
Young Ladies, in Charlestown, Mass., and the Connecticut Literary Insti-

tution at Suffield, Conn. She was a true, loving companion, that "looked well to the ways of her household." In person she was erect, with a graceful form, her hair untouched by age; unselfish in character, noble, and consistent. Above all, both were earnest Christians, members of the Seventh Day Baptist Church of Westerly. They passed away ten months apart, the community sustaining an irreparable loss.

Children, b. Westerly:

 2387. Henrietta Louise, b. Dec. 8, 1854; m. Henry M. Maxson (2418).

 2388. Edwin Ransom, Jr., b. June 5, 1863; m. Mary T. Babcock
   (2419).

 2389. Hannah Browning, b. June 6, 1870; d. Nov. 4, 1876.

Gideon Perry Brown (65), brother of the preceding, b., No. Stonington, Conn., Aug. 3, 1834; d., Boston, Mass., May 26, 1898; m. (1), Brighton, Mass., Dec. 16, 1862, Mary Luella Hollis, dau. of Albert E. and Mary (Palmer) Hollis; b., Brighton, Apr. 2, 1838; d., Brighton, Feb. 14, 1870. He m. (2), June 4, 1873, Martha Corrina Hollis, sister of first wife, b. July 27, 1850. He was a wool merchant of Boston, where he spent all of his business life. Interments, Mount Auburn.

Dau. by first m., b. Boston:

 2390. Marion Luella Brown, b. Sept. 30, 1865; m. (1), Boston, Mar.
   19, 1890, Virgil M. Richard; divorced. Son: Norman M.,
   b. June 23, 1894. She m. (2), Boston, Apr. 5, 1898, Albert
   Thornton Thompson, b., Maplewood, Mass., Jan. 19, 1857.
   Res., 1910, Boston.

Children by second m.:

 2391. Adelaide Corrina Brown, b. Mar. 5, 1874; m. (1), Boston,
   Oct. 14, 1896, Herbert Watson; he d., City of Mexico, Jan.
   15, 1904. He was a wool merchant of Boston.   Dau.:
   Corrina Adelaide, b. Oct. 28, 1897.   Mrs. Watson m. (2),
   Boston, Mar. 3, 1905, Dr. Fred Drew, b., Alfred, Me.,
   Dec. 18, 1866; son of Ira S. and Lydia A. (Starr) Drew.
   Res., 1910, Boston, Mass.

 2392. George Winslow Brown, b., Boston, Nov. 29, 1876. He graduated from the English High School in Boston in 1895, and
   then went to the Massachusetts Institute of Technology,
   where he specialized in chemistry.   In October, 1899, he
   went to work for the American Woolen Co., as chemist, first
   in their Washington Mills at Lawrence, Mass., then at their

Assabet Mills plant, at Maynard, Mass., the largest woolen-mill in the world, with about one thousand looms. His duties are testing everything bought for the mills, to see that they get everything they pay for; also he has the ordering of dyes, chemicals, and soap materials; and matching the shades used in the dyehouse. Address 1910, Chemist Assabet Mills, Maynard, Mass.

Benadam Williams Brown (66), son of Cyrus Williams and Elizabeth S. (Babcock) Brown, b., No. Stonington, Conn., Apr. 4, 1836; m. (1), Hartford, Conn., Sept. 19, 1860, by D. Henry Miller, D.D., Almira M.McGlaflin, b., Windsor, Conn., Sept. 22, 1842; d., Prairie City, Ia., July 27, 1907; m. (2), Lincoln, Neb., Jan. 16, 1909, Mrs. Mary A. Baker, née Gaffron, b., Milledgeville, Ill., dau. of Anthony and Anna (Berkner) Gaffron, of Wisconsin. Mr. Brown was educated in the schools of No. Stonington, and in 1854 served as clerk for two years in Hartford. In 1856 was engaged with his brother G. P. Brown in mercantile business for a short time in Brighton, Mass., but returned to Hartford and was clerk for three years; then went into mercantile business for four years. He was in the office of Brown Brothers in Brookline, Mass., until he went West, in 1867, where he engaged successfully in farming and stock-raising. In 1879 was elected County Supervisor and Auditor of Jasper County, Ia., for eight and one-half years, being re-elected at different times. He began shipping dressed poultry to Boston, Mass., in 1867, and was a pioneer in that business; and after retiring from public office in 1888 he relinquished farming and devoted his entire time to the poultry industry. On Jan. 1, 1890, he assisted in establishing the State Bank of Prairie City, Ia., and was elected its first cashier. He retired from business in 1907. Res., Lincoln, Neb.

Children:

2393. Lee Everett, b., Hartford, July 22, 1863; m., Newton, Ia., Feb. 8, 1888, Lena McGregor, b., Newton, Nov. 24, 1869. He has been cashier of the National Bank of Newton for a number of years. Son: Charles Milton, b., Newton, Aug. 17, 1892.

2394. Minnie Laura, b., Fairmount, Jasper Co., Ia., Dec. 19, 1870; m., Prairie City, Nov. 27, 1895, Joseph L. Freeman, b., Lone Rock, Wis., June 24, 1864; son of Henry and Clara (Ballard) Freeman, who were m., Madison, Wis., Dec. 24, 1859. Dau.: Myra Josephine, b., Prairie City, July 30, 1899.

2395. Benjamin Williams, b., Fairmount, Oct. 21, 1880; m., David
City, Neb., Feb. 12, 1902, Winifred Earl Ball, b., David
City, Jan. 22, 1881; dau. of Curtis M., b., Wisconsin, Sept.
2, 1849, and Nancy (Brammer) Ball, b. Dec. 20, 1856, in
Kentucky. Dau.: Ruth McGlaflin, b., Prairie City, June 27,
1905. Res., David City, Neb.

Thomas Shailer Brown (67), son of Cyrus W. and Elizabeth S. (Babcock) Brown, b. June 28, 1838; m., Brighton, Mass., Apr. 24, 1866, Mary A. Colby, b., Brighton, July 10, 1840. He was associated with his oldest brother Cyrus H. in mercantile business in Boston and Brookline, Mass., from 1865 to 1889, when he bought the interest of his brother and conducted the same business with his son Thomas Colby until about 1904. He is now a farmer in Dover, Mass. He was superintendent of the Brookline Baptist Sunday School for a number of years. He and his wife are members of the Brookline Baptist Church.

Children, b. Brookline:

2396. Annie Belle Brown, b. Aug. 15, 1868; m., Brookline, Nov. 11,
1896, Geo. McClellan Brooks, b., East Boston, Mass., Sept.
10, 1863; son of Wm. F. and Mary (Snow) Brooks. He is a
stock-broker, Boston. She was educated in the schools of
Brookline and is a member of the Baptist Church. No issue.
Res., Arlington, Mass.

2397. Thomas Colby Brown, b. Dec. 15, 1870; m., Boston, Apr. 6,
1898, Dora Damon, b., Freehold, Penn., Apr. 4, 1875. He
was educated in the Brookline schools and was a member of
the Baptist Church. He is agent for a large creamery company, in 1910, with office at No. Delaware Ave., Philadelphia, Penn. No issue.

John Babcock Brown (68), brother of the preceding, b., No. Stonington, Conn., Feb. 3, 1841; m., Canton, Conn., Oct. 15, 1865, Lavinia Richardson, b., Windsor, Conn., June 19, 1845; dau. of John and Emily (Marble) Richardson. Mr. Brown was for a short time after marriage on his father's farm; then he removed to Westerly, R. I., and for a number of years was engaged in mercantile business. Before his marriage he enlisted in the Civil War, Aug. 11, 1862, Co. G, 21st Conn. Regt. Vol.; mustered into United States service at Norwich, Conn., Sept. 5, as 2d Sergeant. The regiment was assigned to 9th Army Corps Oct. 9, at Pleasant Valley, Md. On Oct. 28 the long march to Falmouth, Va., began (175 miles in twelve

Cyrus Williams Brown, Jr., and his wife
Elizabeth Stewart Babcock (49) and their children
From left to right, top row: (62), (63), (67), (64), (68), (65), (66), (69), (70), (71)
Picture taken Nov. 30, 1863, the last time members were all together

Residence of Cyrus H Brown (63) and family for thirty-five years
Where the four younger children were born
Allston St , Boston, Mass

days). They were without tents during the winter, exposed to terrible storms, and lying at night on the frozen ground or in the mud of Virginia, with no covering other than blankets, very scanty and thin — an experience which tested to the utmost the endurance of every man, and planted the seeds of disease and death which produced such a harvest on the plains of Falmouth, and gave to its camp the name of "Camp Death." He participated in the following battles: Fredericksburg, Dec. 13, 1862; promoted to 1st Sergeant Mar. 6, 1863; was in the siege of Suffolk, Va.; on May 16, 1864, participated in the battle of Drewry's Bluff. At this time the total number of officers and men for duty was twenty-nine. May 31 he was promoted to 2d Lieutenant, and participated in the battle of Cold Harbor and the battle of Petersburg. He was honorably discharged June 14, 1864. Both he and his wife are active members of the Calvary Baptist Church of Westerly.

Children:

2398. Cyrus Williams, b., No. Stonington, Sept. 23, 1866 (2420-2422).

2399. Lavinia Louise, b., Westerly, Sept. 12, 1870 (2423).

2400. John Howard, b., Westerly, Dec. 29, 1872; m., Glastonbury, Conn., June 24, 1908, Lucy C. Robinson, b., Glastonbury, Oct. 8, 1880; dau. of Thomas J. Robinson and Mary J. ———, his wife. Mr. Brown is a graduate of the Westerly High School and took a partial course at Brown University. He was successor to his father in the dry-goods business at Westerly for ten years; he then entered the employ of Babcock & Wilcox, water-tube boiler company, New York, as salesman, and continues in that capacity in 1910. Mrs. Brown is a graduate of the Glastonbury High School and of Business College; afterwards employed as secretary of Glastonbury Knitting Co., and held this position until marriage.

Sarah Ellen Brown (69), dau. of Cyrus W. and Elizabeth S. (Babcock) Brown, b., No. Stonington, Conn., May 23, 1843; m., No. Stonington, Nov. 29, 1863, Allen Barber, b., Westerly, R. I., June 12, 1841; son of Thomas J. Barber, b., Hopkinton, R. I., June 13, 1807, and Roxy Amy Lewis, b., Voluntown, Conn., Jan. 4, 1818; m., Voluntown, Mar., 1840; he d., Westerly, Sept., 1853; interred in River Bend Cemetery, Westerly; she m. (2) Lincoln, Neb.; d., Lincoln, Sept., 1897. Allen Barber and wife were educated in the public schools, and the Westerly High School. After their marriage they moved to Hartford, Conn., where he purchased a farm, remaining but two years, when they removed to Galesburg, Ill., in 1866, where he owned a valuable and productive farm; but again removed to Lincoln, in 1873, where he purchased 240 acres of valuable land within the city limits; here, with his son, he conducted the farm, giving special attention to stockraising. This farm was sold in 1907, they turning to more quiet life in their declining years. He is a Republican; attends the Baptist Church. Res., 1910, Havelock, Neb.

Children, b. Galesburg:

>   2401. Alice Gertrude Barber, b. Aug. 6, 1868; d. Dec. 8, 1868.
>   2402. Allen Lincoln Barber, b. Apr. 28, 1871; m., Havelock, July 18, 1908, Minnie Bird Wilhelm, b., Havelock, Oct. 28, 1887; dau. of Levi and Etta (Cunningham) Wilhelm, of Havelock. He is a farmer of the progressive kind that makes things move to a successful issue, having before him a bright prospect. Dau.: Henrietta Elizabeth, b. Aug. 14, 1909. Res., Havelock, Neb.

William Stuart Brown (70), brother of the preceding, b., No. Stonington, Conn., July 11, 1845; m., Brighton, Mass., Dec. 27, 1870, Carrie L. P. Colby, b., Brighton, Oct. 16, 1850. She was sister to the wife of Thomas S. Brown (67). She d. on the train when returning home from the South, where she had been for her health, as the train approached Washington, D. C., May 28, 1891. Mr. Brown conducted the provision business for a few years in Brookline, Mass.

Children, b. Brookline:

>   2403. Wm. Stuart, Jr., b. July 4, 1873; d. Feb. 26, 1895.
>   2404. Carrie Louise, b. Jan. 1, 1875; m., Auburn, Me., Sept. 23, 1896, Osroe L. Knight, b., Peru, Me., Aug. 19, 1857. He is a farmer at West Peru, Oxford Co., Me., in 1910. Children: (1) John Leighton, b., Waltham, Mass., Mar. 10, 1899; (2) Ralph Gerrish, b., Peru, Dec. 9, 1902; (3) Blanche Emily, b. Sept., 1904.
>   2405. Arthur Webster, b. Oct. 14, 1878; m. and divorced.

James Stone Brown (71), son of Cyrus W. and Elizabeth S. (Babcock) Brown, b., No. Stonington, Conn., Mar. 2, 1848; m., Westerly, R. I., Apr. 29, 1872, Mary Elizabeth Brayton, b., Westerly, Sept. 14, 1847; dau. of James W. Brayton, b., Coventry, R. I., Sept. 24, 1815, d., Westerly, Aug. 1, 1905, and Lucy Pendleton, b., Westerly, Apr. 20, 1813; d. Apr. 20, 1883. James Brown and his wife lived at the Brown homestead in No. Stonington until his house and barns were destroyed by fire. He gave his attention to horse raising and training up to the time of the fire, when he removed to Vienna, Austria.

Dau.:

> 2406. Ethel Irene Brown, b., No. Stonington, Dec. 3, 1874. She has been a piano and vocal teacher for the past ten years in Westerly; now [1910] at the Susquehanna University, Selinsgrove, Penn.

[Of these twenty-seven grandchildren, twenty-three are living in 1910; also twenty-five great-grandchildren.]

Elizabeth Lovina Brown (2381), dau. of Cyrus H. and Sarah C. (Maxson) Brown, b., Brighton, Mass. (now Boston), June 15, 1858; m., Boston, Mass., May 19, 1880, George Herbert Utter, b. Plainfield, N. J. He was the son of George Benjamin Utter, b., Plainfield, Otsego Co., N. Y., Feb. 4, 1819; d., Westerly, R. I., Aug. 28, 1892; he was the son of Wm. Utter, of Hopkinton, R. I., and wife Dolly Wilcox, of Whitesborough, N. Y.; m., De Ruyter, N. Y., May 24, 1847, Mary Starr Maxson, b., Homer, N. Y., Nov. 25, 1825; d., Westerly, Mar. 24, 1868; dau. of John and Mary (Starr) Maxson. Elder Geo. B. Utter, in 1844, joined with others in establishing a religious newspaper, called *The Sabbath Recorder*, which soon became the recognized organ of the Seventh Day Baptist denomination. For more than twenty-five years he edited and published that paper and had the oversight of the monthly and quarterly periodicals and books and reports of various kinds published for circulation in and by that denomination. He became interested in the *Narragansett Weekly* in 1859, a paper published in Westerly, but did not remove to Westerly with his family until Jan., 1862. He was proprietor and editor of the paper until his death, in 1892. George H. Utter was educated in the schools of Westerly and at Alfred Academy, Alfred, N. Y., until 1873, when he entered Amherst College and graduated therefrom in the class of 1877; then immediately came to the assistance of his father on the weekly paper, which had a wide circulation. In 1893 the Westerly *Daily Sun* was established, and the *Weekly* was continued as its weekly edition until 1897, when it was discontinued. *The Daily Sun* is a bright, progressive paper, having the largest circulation in Washington County. His son George Benjamin, after his graduation from Amherst College, in 1905, came upon the editorial staff, and is a valuable assistant in the conduct of the paper. Geo. H. Utter was aide-de-camp on the staff of Governor Bourne, May, 1883–May, 1885; member of the Rhode Island

House of Representatives, May, 1885–May, 1889, and the last year was chosen speaker. He became a member of the Rhode Island Senate, May, 1889–May, 1891; then served as Secretary of State, May, 1891–May, 1894; was chosen Lieutenant-Governor in Jan., 1904, serving to Jan., 1905; was elected Governor in Nov., 1904; took office Jan. 3, 1905. Nov., 1905, was re-elected Governor, and held office two years. Alfred University conferred on Mr. Utter, in June, 1906, the degree of LL.D. Both he and his wife are members of the Seventh Day Baptist Church.

Children, b. Westerly:

2,407. George Benjamin Utter, b. Apr. 11, 1881. He was educated in the schools of Westerly, and graduated from the Riverview Military Academy at Poughkeepsie, N. Y., and from Amherst College in 1905; and is associate editor and manager of the Westerly *Daily Sun.* In Dec., 1907, he received an invitation to meet, somewhere in India, his class- and room-mate in college, of Davenport, Ia., who the year of his graduation had started on a trip around the world. In less than a week after receiving the invitation to meet his college classmate he left New York, Dec. 17, with the intention of reaching that far-away land in as short a period as possible. He went to England, crossed the English Channel to Calais, France, where he took the mail train of the English-Indian mail service, across France, Northern Italy to the east coast of that country, continuing south along the Adriatic shore to Brindisi, after a ride of forty-eight hours. Here a transfer was made to steamer across the Mediterranean, through the Suez Canal to the Red Sea, the Indian Ocean to Bombay, India, where he met his college friend. The voyage from Westerly, R. I., to Bombay took *twenty-four* days. He went from Bombay by rail across to Madras, thence south, visiting the great temples of Southern India; thence to the Island of Ceylon. Then the voyage was continued west to the Red Sea and Canal to Egypt. A month was spent in Egypt, visiting Port Said, Cairo, Luxor, Assuan, Alexandria, and other places of interest, ascending the Nile River for one thousand miles. From Egypt, Italy was the next, visiting Naples, Rome, and other cities; thence to Paris, where Mr. Utter and his friend met the parents of the latter. Then a tour of Europe was made by automobile. The route included

Cyrus H. Brown (63), Wife, and Children

385   386   382   381

384

383

Picture Taken in 1889

Page 337

Group of Grandchildren of Cyrus H. Brown (63)

2110   2113   2107   2108   2109

        2114   2116   2112   2111

France, south to the coast, north over the Alps to Turin,
thence across the northern part of Italy to Venice. From
here the mountains were skirted into Austria. After a ten-
day stay at Vienna the course was into Germany, through
the cities to Berlin. After making a complete circle the
homeward voyage was begun, after seven months of travel.
This trip of a lifetime broadened his grasp of the world of
the countries he visited, and added to his store of knowledge
that which cannot be gained by books. His letters of travel
published in the Westerly *Sun* were read by thousands with
increasing interest. His intercourse with others is kind and
gracious; his frank, good-natured face bespeaks intelligence
and invites confidence. He is a member of the Seventh Day
Baptist Church and assistant superintendent of the Sabbath School. He is a member of the Republican Town
Committee of Westerly, president of the Young Men's
Republican Club, and a member of the Executive Committee of the Rhode Island Republican Clubs.

2408. Henry Edwin Utter, b. Apr. 9, 1883. He was educated in the
schools of Westerly, and was two years at the Riverview
Military Academy; graduated from Amherst College in
1906; entered Columbia University, N. Y., Sept., 1906, and
is in the College of Physicians and Surgeons, class of 1910.

2409. Mary Starr, b. Feb. 21, 1890. She graduated from the High
School of Westerly in 1909; entered Lasell Seminary,
Auburndale, Mass., Sept., 1909, for a three years' course.

2410. Wilfred Brown, b. Sept. 13, 1894. He entered the High School
of Westerly in Sept., 1909, and is to take the full course.

REVOLUTIONARY WAR RECORD OF JESSE STARR, SON OF VINE STARR, B.,
GROTON, CONN., JAN. 17, 1716.

Jesse Starr, b. Nov. 23, 1753; d. Nov. 25, 1799; m. Mary Dewey; their
dau. Mary Starr, b., Groton, Conn., Sept. 2, 1791; d. July 27, 1859; m.
Dea. John Maxson, of Newport, R. I.; their dau. Mary Starr Maxson, b.,
Homer, N. Y., Nov. 25, 1825; d., Westerly, R. I., Mar. 24, 1868; m.,
De Ruyter, N. Y., May 24, 1847, George Benjamin Utter, b., Plainfield,
N. Y., Feb. 4, 1819. The vessel on which Jesse Starr sailed was captured
June 7, 1782, by the British ship *Belisarius* and all impressed into the British
service. He was released Aug. 20, 1783, and his widow drew a corper I's

and a sergeant's pension while she lived. He was a Sergeant in the Regiment of Artificers. His taxes were abated, as his house was destroyed by the British during the War.

Henry Edwin Brown (2382), son of Cyrus H. and Sarah C. (Maxson) Brown, b., Brighton, Mass., Apr. 5, 1861; d., Newburyport, Mass., June 25, 1909; m., Boston, Mass., Dec. 3, 1890, Caroline Campbell Rollins, b., Brighton, June 23, 1868; dau. of Lot M. and Delia S. (Campbell) Rollins. Since graduating from the schools of Boston, he has been a clerk in the hardware business in Minneapolis, Minn., and in business in Boston, until his death, with his brother Fred M. Brown, under the firm name of Brown Brothers. Both he and his wife were members of the Brighton Ave. Baptist Church and Sunday School. Interment, River Bend, Westerly, R. I.

> Another link is broken
> In fond affection's chain;
> The sad farewell is spoken,
> But in heaven we meet again.

Children:

2411. Catharine Rollins, b., Minneapolis, Feb. 9, 1893. Since the death of her father, her home is with her aunt, Mrs. George H. Utter, of Westerly, R. I., where [1910] she attends the High School.

2412. Frances Campbell, b., Boston, Mar. 3, 1903.

Katherine Mabel Brown (2383), dau. of Cyrus H. and Sarah C. (Maxson) Brown, b., Brighton, Mass., Nov. 5, 1865; m., Boston, Mass., Oct. 23, 1895, John Lewis Howard, b., So. Boston, Mass., Apr. 30, 1866; son of John Henry Howard, b. Boston, and Georgianna M. (Packard) Howard, b., No. Bridgewater, Mass., Jan. 30, 1841. Mrs. Howard resides with her son, and for many years has been employed in the service of the State at the State-house in Boston. Mr. Howard is civil engineer for the city of Boston. Both he and his wife are members of the Melrose Baptist Church. Mrs. Howard was superintendent of the Kindergarten Department of the Sunday School for a number of years. Res., Melrose, Mass.

Children, b. Melrose:

2413. Elizabeth, b. Oct. 13, 1897.

2414. Helen, b. Nov. 29, 1902.

Wilfred Merrill Brown (2384), son of Cyrus H. and Sarah C. (Maxson) Brown, b., Brighton, Mass., Apr. 4, 1870; m., Stonington, Conn., Sept. 11, 1906, Annie Cutler Bradley, b., Stonington, Dec. 18, 1883; dau. of Edward

E., b. Nov. 29, 1857, and Lois Chadwick (Gates) Bradley, b. Oct. 10, 1861. Edward E. was the son of Almenus Dickerman and Amanda M. (Parks) Bradley, b. Russell, Mass. Mr. Bradley is a member and director of the Atwood Morrison Company, of Stonington, manufacturers of silk-machinery which is used in all the principal silk-mills in the world. The Atwood whir spindle is the only kind used in the spinning of silk the world over. Mrs. Brown was educated in the public schools of Stonington; two years at the Eversley House School, Southport, England; four years at the Emerson College of Oratory, Boston, Mass.; taught physical culture for one year, 1905–1906, in State Normal School at Mankato, Minn. Both are members of the Baptist Church. He graduated from the schools of Boston in 1889. His business, hardware. Res., 1910, Boston (Roxbury).

Dau.:

2415. Lois Bradley, b., Roxbury, Mass., Feb. 20, 1908.

Horace Clifford Brown (2385), son of Cyrus H. and Sarah C. (Maxson) Brown, b., Boston, Mass., June 22, 1873; m., Westerly, R. I., Dec. 30, 1902, Aldeane Kilmer, b., Meriden, Kan., Oct. 17, 1881; dau. of Richard P. and Caroline A. (Cutler) Kilmer. Mr. Kilmer was b., Syracuse, N. Y., Mar. 21, 1841; d., Garden City, Kan., Apr. 3, 1886. His wife was b., Stonington, Conn., May 19, 1845, and she makes her home with her daughter in Newburyport, Mass. Mr. Brown received his education in the public schools of Boston, and after his graduation, until Apr., 1905, was with Dame, Stoddard & Co., Boston, in the hardware business. Now [1910] with the Towle Manufacturing Co., Newburyport, manufacturers of sterling silverware, as cost accountant.

Children:

2416. Horace Clifford, Jr., b., Melrose, Mass., Jan. 8, 1906.

2417. Lois Theda, b., Newburyport, Sept. 9, 1907.

Henrietta Louise Lewis (2387), dau. of Dr. Edwin R. and Louisa (Brown) Lewis, b., Westerly (Niantic), R. I., Dec. 8, 1854; m., Westerly, Dec. 30, 1879, Henry Martin Maxson, b., Stonington, Conn., Mar. 28, 1853; son of Jonathan Maxson, b., Westerly, Jan. 26, 1816, d. Nov. 12, 1899, and Matilda Mandane Wilcox, b. Nov. 13, 1819. His grandfather also was Jonathan Maxson, b., Newport, R. I., July 4, 1782; d., Westerly, Jan. 22, 1853. His grandmother was Nancy Potter, dau. of George Potter and Mary Stillman; b., Potter Hill, R. I., Mar. 12, 1781; d. July 10, 1862. He attended the public schools of Westerly, and Alfred Academy, New York; graduated from Amherst College in 1877; taught two years in the common schools of Rhode Island; ten years in Attleboro, Mass., as teacher and super-intendent; four years as superintendent in Pawtucket, R. I.; assumed office Sept., 1892, as superintendent in Plainfield, N. J.; in 1910 holds that office. In 1904 Alfred University conferred on him the degree of Ph.D.

Dau., b. Westerly:

> 2418. Ruth Potter, b. Feb. 10, 1881. She graduated from Smith College in June, 1905.

Edwin Ransom Lewis, Jr. (2388), son of Dr. Edwin R. and Louisa (Brown) Lewis, b., Westerly, R. I., June 5, 1863; m., Westerly, Feb. 27, 1889, Mary Townsend Babcock, b., Westerly, Mar. 26, 1867; dau. of Horace and Harriet B. (Cross) Babcock. He is a practising physician in Westerly.

Son:

> 2419. Edwin R., Jr., b., Westerly, Mar. 21, 1890; d. Oct. 27, 1890.

Cyrus Williams Brown (2398), son of John B. and Lavinia (Richardson) Brown, b., No. Stonington, Conn., Sept. 23, 1866; m., Westerly, R. I., Nov. 26, 1890, Grace Louise Davis, b., Westerly, Nov. 17, 1872. Mr. Brown resembles and has the characteristics of his great-grandfather. He is in the coal and real-estate business, New London, Conn.

Children:

> 2420. Cyrus Williams, Jr., b., Stonington, Conn., Oct. 26, 1896.
> 2421. Helen Davis, b., Westerly, Apr. 11, 1900.
> 2422. Stuart Romeyn, b., New London, Mar. 19, 1902.

Lavinia Louise Brown (2399), dau. of John B. and Lavinia (Richard-son) Brown, b., Westerly, R. I., Sept. 12, 1870; m., Westerly, Oct. 19, 1892, William Dixie Hoxie, b., Gravesend, L. I., N. Y., July 1, 1866; son of John Hoxie, b., Charlestown, R. I., 1827, d., New York, 1882, and Isabella Dickinson, b., New York, Sept. 29, 1835; d., Westerly, Oct. 20, 1906; dau. of J. Jeffreys Dickinson, b., Charleston, S. C., 1796, d., New York, 1862, and Isabella Knowles, b., Liverpool, England, 1805; d., New York, 1865; interment in Greenwood, Brooklyn, N. Y. Mr. Hoxie received his educa-tion in the common schools of Brooklyn; also in the Stevens School of Technology, which he entered in 1885, graduating in 1889; then spent a year in the machine-shops of Ridon & Marsh, at the same time carrying on experimental work for Stephen Wilcox, devoting his whole time to that work. In 1891 he became associated wih the Babcock & Wilcox Company, manufacturers of water-tube steam boilers, with a capital of $3,000,000.

APPENDIX

This company built and installed the Babcock & Wilcox Marine Boiler, in 1894, and is continuing to develop the same. Mr. Hoxie came on the Board of Directors in 1896; the year following was chosen second vice-president; in 1897 and 1898 was chosen first vice-president of the company. This company enjoys a reputation that is world-wide, manufacturing at Bayonne, N. J.; Renfrew, Scotland, near Glasgow; Paris, France; Oberhausen, Germany; with offices in the principal cities on the globe. Res., 298 Washington Ave., Brooklyn, N. Y. Summer res., Westerly, R. I.

Dau.:

2423. Isabella Hoxie, b., New York City, Nov. 12, 1893. She is a student at Adelphi Academy, Brooklyn, class of 1910.

It Is Sweet To Be
Remembered

And a pleasant thing to find,
That though you may be absent
You still are kept in mind.

Thomas Harrison Brown (72), son of Thomas M. and Mercy Ann (Babcock, 50) Brown, b., No. Stonington, Conn., Oct. 16, 1839; m., Jan. 1, 1870, Amanda A. Wilbur, d., Stonington (Pawcatuck), Conn., Nov. 12, 1909. Mr. Brown was in the Civil War; enlisted in the 26th Connecticut Infantry Regt., Sept. 1, 1862; mustered into the United States service Nov. 10, 1862, in Company H — Daniel Chapman, Capt. He was in the engagements at Port Hudson, May 27, 1863, and June 14, 1863. He was discharged Aug. 17, 1863. Res., 1910, Westerly, R. I.

Children, b. Stonington:

2424. Carrie Evilena Brown, b. Jan. 22, 1873; m., Oct. 19, 1900, Frank I. Dawley. Son: Frank Irwin, b. Apr. 1, 1907.

2425. Annie Viola Brown, b. Apr. 3, 1874; m., Westerly, R. I., June 28, 1899, Wilfred H. Nye. No issue.

2426. Charles Ross Brown, b. Nov. 6, 1875; m., Aug. 1, 1898, Martha Midwood. Children: (1) Gladys Evelyn, b. July 8, 1900; (2) Charles Wilbur, b. Aug. 16, 1902.

2427. Agnes Ethel Brown, b. Nov. 15, 1876; m., Sept. 7, 1898, Louis Hohn. Son: Louis Elliott, b. May 2, 1904.

2428. Winnie Etta Brown, b. July 3, 1878; unm. She is bookkeeper and stenographer, since 1901, at Providence, R. I.

2429. Thomas Henry Brown, b. Nov. 2, 1879; m. Effie Martin, of New London, Conn.

2430. Bessie Mae Brown, b. Apr. 13, 1882; m., Westerly, Oct. 24, 1907, Herbert Pomeroy Clark, b., Westerly, Aug. 10, 1882; son of George F. and Mary Olive (Spicer) Clark. He is a compositor on the Westerly *Daily Sun,* and a member of the Seventh Day Baptist Church.

2431. Mabel Rae Brown, b. May 1, 1884; m., Westerly, Oct. 19, 1909, Henry Vincent Brown, b., Westerly, Apr. 9, 1881. He has been a clerk for E. Howard Clark since 1898, in Westerly, R. I.

2432. Alonzo Fisk Brown, b. Feb. 26, 1888; unm.

2433. Edith Idalene Brown, b. Oct. 8, 1889; m., Stonington, Aug. 24, 1909, Seth C. Johnson, b. Oct. 29, 1889.

Wm. Ellsworth Brown (73), son of Thomas M. and Mercy Ann (Babcock, 50), b., No. Stonington, Conn., July 13, 1841; m., Montville, Conn., Mar. 16, 1864, Ellen Augusta Darrow, b. Apr. 16, 1842. Res., New London, Conn.

Children:

2434. Walter Edwin Brown, b. Apr. 22, 1865; unm.

2435. Addie Mabel Brown, b. Aug. 23, 1867; m., Aug. 18, 1890, Joseph S. Collins. Son: Harold William, b. Dec. 15, 1899; d. Aug. 5, 1900.

2436. Frank L., b. Feb. 25, 1872; unm.

Hermon Clinton Brown (74), brother of the preceding, b., No. Stonington, Conn., Jan. 22, 1843; m. (1), No. Stonington, Mar. 16, 1868, Lucy A. Brown, b., No. Stonington, 1847; d. Dec. 25, 1873. Children: (1) Lucy M., d., aged six years; (2) Herbert D., d., aged four years; (3) Frank, d. in infancy. He m. (2), Stonington, Conn., June 5, 1879, Sarah J. Miner, b. Oct. 13, 1858; dau. of Dea. Erastus and Phebe J. (Breed) Miner, of Stonington. Mr. Brown is a progressive farmer of ability and thrift. Res., 1910, Stonington (Angwilla), Conn.

Children by second m., b. Stonington:

2437. J. Ethel Brown, b. Mar. 29, 1880; d. Jan. 29, 1887.

2438. Howard C. Brown, b. May 9, 1881; m., Westerly, R. I., May 26, 1909, Lovina Nugent, b., Stonington, Apr. 22, 1880; dau. of James and Eliza (Walden) Nugent, of Stonington. He is a farmer, in 1910, on the Daniel Brown Farm, Stonington.

2439. Lewis H. Brown, b. Jan. 16, 1883.

2440. Sarah Emma Brown, b. Jan. 3, 1887; m., Dec. 2, 1908, Harvey Arzamarskie, b., No. Stonington, June 15, 1886.

2441. Carl Wilson Brown, b. Jan. 10, 1895.

Stephen Edwin Brown (75), son of Thomas M. and Mercy Ann (Babcock, 50) Brown, b., No. Stonington, Conn., May 27, 1845; d. Oct. 27, 1895; m., Stonington, Conn., Mar., 1865, Mary G. Green, dau. of James M. and Susan (Gardner) Green; b. Aug. 8, 1846; d., No. Stonington, May 31, 1889.

Children, b. No. Stonington:

2442. Nellie Brown, b. Dec. 8, 1865; m., June 29, 1889, Irving H. Champlin, b., Westerly, R. I., Sept. 12, 1864; son of Henry and Mary (Horton) Champlin. No issue.

2443. Mary A. Brown, b. Mar. 25, 1867; unm.

2444. Thomas E. Brown, b. Aug. 30, 1868; m., No. Stonington, Feb. 9, 1890, Nellie M. Pitcher, b. May 23, 1871. No issue.

2445. William E. Brown, b. Feb. 2, 1870; m., No. Stonington, Sept.

22, 1897, by Rev. Richard Kemp, Catherine Mannix, b.
Feb. 20, 1874. He d. Apr. 11, 1906, by a fall from a window
while putting in window-screens. He was well and favorably
known in Groton, Conn., where he removed soon after his
marriage and had lived for nine years; he was making rapid
advances financially, being honored, trusted, and faithful. He
was a member of Fairview Lodge, I. O. O. F.; of the Loyal
Protective Legion and Home Rebekah Lodge. Interment in
Ledyard Cemetery, south of Groton Monument. Children:
(1) Maud Edna, b. July 20, 1898; (2) Wm. E., b. June, 1906.

2446. James M. Brown, b. Jan. 21, 1875; unm.

2447. Angie B. Brown, b. June 16, 1878; m., No. Stonington, Sept.
11, 1895, Latham Hull, b., No. Stonington, Feb. 6, 1870;
son of Wm. B. and Susan E. (Wattles) Hull. Dau.: Ethel L.,
b. Apr. 26, 1896. Res., 1910, No. Stonington, Conn.

2448. Susan Amanda Brown, b. Feb. 1, 1879; m., Griswold, Conn.,
Nov. 29, 1900, Andrew Franklin Tillinghast, b., Griswold,
Feb. 1, 1879. His occupation, railroad motorman. Children:
(1) Marion Louise, b. Sept. 20, 1905; (2) Helen Lenore, b.
Feb. 20, 1907; (3) George Elsworth, b. Jan. 12, 1909. Res.,
1910, Mystic, Conn.

2449. Hattie M. Brown, b. July 3, 1883; m., Westerly, May 13, 1903,
Willard Hall. Dau.: Mary Elizabeth, b. Feb. 28, 1909; d.
August, 1909.

2450. Stephen E. Brown, b. July 1, 1888; unm.

Appendix II.

This is written to show the lineage of Benjamin Peabody and Martha
Peckham (618-624), that their descendants are eligible by birth to join the
Society of the Mayflower Descendants. Benjamin Peabody resided all his
life in that part of Stonington which has been called No. Stonington since
1807. He was a lineal descendant of John Alden of the *Mayflower* pilgrims,
who landed at Plymouth Rock, Mass., in 1620. The emigrant ancestor of
the Peabody family was:

1. John Peabody, who came to this country from England in 1635,
and brought with him four children, viz.:

The birthplace of Cyrus W. Brown, Jr.
Who married Elizabeth Stewart Babcock (49)
North Stonington, Conn.
Page 24

Nathan Brown House
North Stonington, Conn.

Built by him, and on this site he was born, June 20, 1738. He was the
grandfather of Cyrus W. Brown, Jr.

Homestead of Cyrus W. Brown, Jr., and his wife, Elizabeth S. Babcock (44)

Farm purchased of the heirs of Elder Asher Miner in 1887. Here were born Thomas S. (67), John B. (68), and Sarah F. (69). The parents passed the rest of their days here.

Page 25

    2. Thomas, b——

    3. Frances, b.——

    4. William, b. in 1620; m. Elizabeth Alden.

    5. Annie, b.——

William Peabody (4), b., England, in 1620; m. Elizabeth Alden, Dec. 26, 1644; she d. Dec. 13, 1707, aged eighty-seven years; dau. of John Alden, of *Mayflower* fame.

    Children:

        6. John, b. Oct. 4, 1645; d. unm.

        7. Elizabeth, b. Apr. 24, 1647; m., 1666, John Rogers.

        8. Mary, b. Aug. 7, 1648; m., 1667, Edward Southworth.

        9. Mercy, b. Jan. 2, 1650, m., 1671, John Simmons.

      10. Martha, b. Feb. 24, 1651; m., 1677, Samuel Seabury.

      11. Priscilla, b. Jan. 15, 1653; m. Rev. Ichabod Wiswall.

      12. Sarah, b. Aug. 7, 1656; m., 1680, John Coe.

      13. Ruth, b. June 27, 1658; m., 1683, Benj. Bartlett.

      14. Rebecca, b. Oct. 16, 1660; m. William Southworth.

      15. Hannah, b. Oct. 15, 1662; m., 1683, Samuel Bartlett.

      16. William, b. Nov. 24, 1664. He removed to Little Compton, R. I., and m. (1) Judith ——, who d. July 20, 1714; he m. (2) Elizabeth ——. who d. Dec. 14, 1717; he m. (3) Mary ——. The family names of these three wives are unknown.

Children by first m.:

      17. Elizabeth, b. Apr. 10, 1698.

      18. John, b. Feb. 7, 1700.

      19. William, b. Feb. 21, 1702.

      20. Rebecca, b. Feb 29, 1704, m. Rev. Joseph Fish, pastor of the Congregational Church, No. Stonington, Conn.

      21. Priscilla, b. Mar. 4, 1706.

      22. Judith, b. Jan. 23, 1708.

      23. Joseph, b. July 26, 1710.

      24. Mary, b. Apr. 4, 1712, m. Nathaniel Fish, brother of Rev. Joseph Fish.

Son by second m.:

      25. Benjamin, b. Nov. 25, 1717.

William Peabody (19), m., Little Compton, R. I., Jerusha Starr.

Children, b. Little Compton:

      26. Rachel, b.——

27. Thomas, b. Nov. 30, 1727.

28. Hannah, b.——

29. William, b.——

30. Lydia, b.——

31. Samuel, b.——

William Peabody removed to Stonington, Conn., now No. Stonington, in 1744, and purchased a farm of 250 acres, upon which he spent the remainder of his life, dying Jan. 3, 1778. His farm was then divided between his two sons Thomas (27) and Samuel (31). After coming to Stonington twins were born to them:

32. James, b. Dec. 14, 1745.

33. Mary, b. Dec. 14, 1745.

Thomas Peabody (27), son of William Peabody (19) and Jerusha Starr, b., Little Compton, R. I., Nov. 30, 1727; m., Stonington, Conn., Aug. 16, 1761, Ruth Babcock, of Stonington.

Children, b. Stonington:

34. Ruth, b. Feb. 7, 1762.

35. Jerusha, b. Apr. 8, 1763.

36. William, b. July 22, 1764.

37. Lydia, b. Feb. 28, 1766.

38. Rebecca, b. Jan. 29, 1768.

39. Thomas, b. Apr. 12, 1769.

40. Susannah, b. Apr. 12, 1770; m. Jonas Chapman.

41. Benjamin, b. Apr. 29, 1772.

42. John, b. Aug. 28, 1775.

43. Lucy, b. June 26, 1777.

44. Lemuel, b. Dec. 20, 1778.

45. Amy, b. Feb. 22, 1779; d. young.

46. Joseph, b. Apr. 18, 1781.

Benjamin Peabody (41), son of Thomas (27) and Ruth (Babcock) Peabody, b., Stonington, Conn., Apr. 29, 1772; m. (1), Stonington, Nov. 13, 1796, Abigail Holmes, b. Mar. 20, 1779. He m. (2), Mar. 5, 1812, Martha Peckham (535).

Children by first m., b. Stonington:

47. Benjamin, b. June 15, 1797.

48. George W., b. Jan. 25, 1799.

49. Abigail, b. Feb. 17, 1801.

50. John, b. May 24, 1803.

51. William Pitt, b. July 24, 1805.
52. Giles H., b. Sept. 25, 1807; d. young.
53. Rebecca H., b. Sept. 6, 1809.

Children by second m., b. No. Stonington, Conn.:

NOTE.— The records of the following children are found on pp. 89 and 90, and all are written in that connection except Martha E. Peabody, whose records at that time had not been found, and for convenience are placed here.

54. Thomas H. (618), b. Mar. 10, 1813; unm.
55. Francis Starr (619), b. Apr. 29, 1815; m. Martha A. Phillips.
56. Martha E. (620), b. Apr. 24, 1819; m. John I. Miner, b. Nov. 18, 1808.
57. Mary (621), b. May 2, 1822; m. Cyrus W. Crary.
58. Fanny A. (622), b. June 29, 1825; m. Russell Wells.
59. Nancy (623), b. Sept. 5, 1828.
60. James Alden (624), b. May 30, 1831; m. Augusta J. Crumb.

The foregoing Peabody records are from Wheeler.

Martha Esther Peabody (620, p. 89), b., No. Stonington, Conn., Apr. 24, 1819; d., Hopkinton, R. I., Sept. 24, 1896; m., No. Stonington, May 24, 1838, John Irish Miner, b. Nov. 18, 1808; d., No. Stonington, Nov. 16, 1880; son of Elder Asher Miner and wife, Lucy Spaulding, of No. Stonington. Mr. Miner lived the most of his married life on the eastern part of the Peabody Farm. Interments, Peabody Cemetery.

Children, b. No. Stonington:

61. Frances Marion, b. Nov. 4, 1840; m. Denison S. Turner (65, 66).
62. James Oscar, b. Nov. 4, 1842; m. Etta Maria Park (67–74).
63. Charles Dexter, b. Dec. 12, 1846; m. Susan Barber (75–78).
64. Alden F., b. May 25, 1852; m. Josephine L. Maine (79–81).

Frances Marion Miner (61), dau. of John Irish Miner and Martha Esther Peabody (620), b. Nov. 4, 1840; m., Mar. 6, 1859, Denison Stewart Turner, b., No. Stonington, Conn., July 18, 1835; son of Ezekiel C. and Mary (Swan) Turner. He is a farmer. Res., No. Stonington, Conn.

Children, b. No. Stonington:

65. Frank Denison, b. Oct. 17, 1860; m. Julia E. Wells (82).
66. Harriet Miner, b. June 25, 1862; m. William A. Brown (83–92).

James Oscar Miner (62), brother of the preceding, b. Nov. 4, 1842; m., Hopkinton, R. I., Feb. 17, 1878, Etta Maria Park, dau. of Sterry and Lucy

(Slocum) Park, son of Israel Palmer Park, who m. (1), Apr. 1, 1794, Abigail Sterry. They are both members of the Baptist Church. Res., Pendleton Hill, Conn.

Children, b. No. Stonington, Conn.:

    67. Son, b. 1880; d. in infancy.

    68. Everett O., b. Aug. 13, 1881; d. in infancy.

    69. James E., b. Nov. 14, 1882.

    70. Susan Mabel, b. Dec. 29, 1884; m., Franklin, Conn., Jan. 12, 1902, George Henry Child. Dau.: Emily Fludder, b. May 26, 1905. Res., Providence, R. I.

    71. Sarah Hannah, b. Dec. 4, 1888; d., aged eleven months.

    72. Herbert Orren, b. Feb. 14, 1892.

    73. Dwight Latham, b. June 1, 1895.

    74. Willes Leonard, b. June 22, 1905.

Charles Dexter Miner (63), brother of the preceding, b. Dec. 12, 1846; d., No. Stonington, Conn., Apr. 21, 1909; m., May 20, 1868, Susan Barber, b., So. Kingstown, R. I., June 30, 1847; dau. of Joseph Denison Barber, of So. Kingstown. Res. at the Deacon Allen Wheeler homestead, No. Stonington. Place of interment, Union Cemetery.

Children, b. No. Stonington:

    75. Susan Etta, b. Nov. 5, 1870; d. June 2, 1882.

    76. Mary Ellen, b. Nov. 27, 1872; d. Mar. 1, 1881.

    77. Charles Denison, b. Aug. 2, 1879; unm.

    78. Frank Barber, b. Mar. 30, 1883; unm.

Alden Fredrick Miner (64), brother of the preceding, b. May 25, 1852; m., No. Stonington, Conn., Apr. 9, 1873, Josephine L. Maine, b., Mansfield, Conn., May 18, 1846; dau. of Carey E. and Mary (Kennedy) Maine. Res., Ashaway, R. I.

Children, b. No. Stonington:

    79. Winnifred Estelle, b. Dec. 3, 1874; m. George F. Partelo (93-97).

    80. Walter Adelbert, b. Sept. 2, 1877.

    81. Ethel Mary, b. June 8, 1886.

Frank Denison Turner (65), son of Denison S. and Frances M. (Miner) Turner, b., No. Stonington, Conn., Oct. 17, 1859; m., Apr. 3, 1890, Julia Etta Wells, b. Mar. 25, 1872. Occupation, Livery. Res., Westerly, R. I.

Son:

    82. Carroll Lavern, b. June 4, 1891; d. Nov. 12, 1899.

Harriet Miner Turner (66), sister of the preceding, b., No. Stonington, Conn., June 25, 1862; m., Hopkinton, R. I., Nov. 10, 1878, William A. Brown, b., No. Stonington, Apr. 10, 1856; son of Avery E. and Sarah E. (Champlin) Brown. He is a farmer. Res., Westerly, R. I.

Children, b. No. Stonington:

    83. Alexander Brown, b. July 11, 1879.

    84. Dora A., b. June 13, 1881.

    85. Clara M., b. Feb. 28, 1884.

    86. Myrtle, b. July 22, 1886.

    87. Belva, b. June 19, 1888; m. Wilson D. Main.

    88. Avery D., b. July 4, 1890.

    89. Frankie E., b. Oct. 29, 1896.

    90. Louis T., b. July 29, 1898.

    91. Edna H., b. Apr. 29, 1900.

    92. Bessie M., b. May 18, 1903.

Winnifred Estelle Miner (79), dau. of Alden F. and Josephine L. (Maine) Miner, b., No. Stonington, Conn., Dec. 3, 1874; m., Hopkinton, R. I., Apr. 9, 1898, George F. Partelo, b., Ashaway, R. I., Apr. 9, 1876; son of I. Frank and Mary E. (Coon) Partelo, of Ashaway. Mr. Partelo is a clerk. He and his wife are members of the Seventh Day Baptist Church.

Children, b. Ashaway:

    93. Percy C., b. Jan. 22, 1899; d. in infancy.

    94. Alfred L. (twin), b. Dec. 18, 1900.

    95. Althea L. (twin), b. Dec. 18, 1900.

    96. Mary J., b. Dec. 23, 1905.

    97. Everett C., b. May 28, 1908.

Appendix III.

The origin of the Mayne, Maine, and Main family, with different spelling of the name, came into the possession of Eli G. Main, of Waterbury, Conn.

John Mayne, son of Alexander, b., Hatesburgh, Devonshire, England: b., about 1614, Hatherleigh, Devonshire, England; d., Boston, Mass., Mar. 27, 1699; m., in Exeter, England, Elizabeth Laurie.

Children:

Rachel, b. 1640; m. Stephen (son of Abram) Preble.
*Josiah, b. 1643; m.——. They had seven children.
Priscilla, b. 1645; m. —— Carrol.
Sarah, b. 1646; m. John Bulline.
Lydia, b. 1648; m. —— Felk.
Dorothy, b. 1650; m. John A. Newhall.
Thomas, b. 1652; m. Elizabeth ——.
Hannah, b. 1653; m. —— Hayden.

Amos, a son of Josiah above, was b. 1708 and d. 1760. He was the first minister of Rochester, N. H. He was ordained in 1737 and remained in office till death, in 1760. A monument stands in the public square upon which is his figure in bronze.

In Portsmouth, N. H., Records, among the taxable persons mentioned, was one Thomas Mayne, in 1711.

[John Mayne of York, Me., "York Deeds Book," 3, Folio 115.]
John Mayne purchased of Richard Carter, Sen., his interest in home and lands at Westcustogo Royal River, Casco Bay, Me., in the year 1652.

From Plymouth Colony Records is taken the following:
Ezekiel Mayne of Scituate was summoned before Court to give "his witness" in the marriage of Robt. Whitcomb and Mary Cudworth, June 10, 1661 (Vol. 2, p. 93).

In 1666, Ezekiel Mayne was called in the case of Mary, wife of Tom Totam, town of Scituate.

In 1660–1661, Ezekiel Mayne was fined one pound ($5.00), and same year was excused from military duty because he had only one eye.

[York, Me., Book of Deeds. Book II. Folio 80.]
This indenture made in the 20th Reign of our Sovereign Lord, Charles II, by the Grace of God of England, Scotland and Ireland, defenders of the faith. That I, John Deaman, of Kittery, York Co., Maine, do for divers and sundry considerations of the sum of four score and fifty pounds in hand paid, whereof I acknowledge, do Bargain and Sell to Henry Maine and Andrew Deaman, their heirs and assigns forever, both of the Isle of Shoals, all the Stage Moorings, dwelling houses and two out houses, anchors, cables,

---

* It is generally believed that Ezekiel, of Stonington, was a child of this family.—*E. G. Main.*

etc., situate upon one of the Isle of Shoals called "Smutty Nose Island," whereof I have hereunto set my hand and seal.

A.D. 1668.   JOHN DEAMAN [SEAL].

Witnesses: WM. SEALY
                ARTHUR CHAPMAN
                PETER LEWIS

Portsmouth, the 27th day of Dec., 1669.

Personally appeared before me John Deaman, gave his oath that the above is a true copy given of his own free will and accord.

PETER WARE, *Recorder.*
ELIAS STILLMAN, *Commissioner.*

The following note came into my possession among my foreign correspondences (E. G. Main):

In the year 1679 John Main was executed in Glasgow, Scotland, for his adherence to the "Solemn League and Covenant." He was a flag-bearer at the battle of Bothwell Bridge. The flag is still in existence, torn and tattered, and still in the possession of his descendants.

The Mains have been and still are residents of Old Monkland Parish, County of Lanark, Scotland.

In the History of Westerly, R. I., page 39, appears the following: "Among the early settlers of this place it mentions the organization of a 'Sabbatarian' Church, and among its first pastors was one Arthur E. Main, 1671."

I find among my papers some *English Marriages* that may be of interest (Eli G. Main):

John Sarge and Sarah Mayne, of London, England, were married Sept. 12, 1572.

Thomas Mayne and Elizabeth Norgote, of London, England, were married April 14, 1661.

Thomas Escott and Elizabeth Mayne, of London, England, were married June 30, 1638.

Geoffrey Sire de Maienne came from Normandy, France, with "William the Conqueror," and is mentioned in Roll of Battle Abbey in the years 1041 and 1063.

Appendix IV

SOLDIERS BY THE NAME OF MAIN IN THE WAR OF THE REVOLUTION

[See Adjutant-General's Records of Connecticut, War of the Revolution]

Name	Rank	Commander	Town	Enlisted	Discharged	Miscellaneous Data
Andrew	Private	Samuel Prentiss	Stonington	May 8, 1775	Dec. 17, 1775	Continental, 3d Co.
Benjamin	Private	Huntington	Norwich	May 8, 1775	Dec. 17, 1775	Continental, 4th Battalion Troop; Sick at Stonington, May 9, 1776
David	Private	Samuel Prentiss	Stonington	May 8, 1775	Dec. 17, 1775	Continental, 3d Co.
Henry	Private	Williams	Groton		July 11, 1779	Stationed at Ft. Griswold
John	Private	Beardsley	Goshen	May 28, 1777	d. June 3, 1778	5th Reg. Services at Monmouth and Morristown, N. J.; Danbury and Redding, Conn., and Valley Forge, N. Y.
Jonas	Ensign	Hungerford	Groton	Nov. 5, 1780	Jan. 3, 1781	Militia, 1781
Lyman	Private	Prentiss	Stonington	Sept. 26, 1782	Nov. 22, 1782	Militia, 1782
Nathaniel	Private	Prentiss	Stonington	May 8, 1775	Dec., 1775	Continental, 3d Co.
Nathaniel	Corporal	Dixon	Stonington	Service June to Dec., 1776		3d Battalion, Col. Sage
Stephen	Private	Holmes	Stonington	May 8, 1776	Nov. 17, 1776	8th Reg., Col. Oliver Smith
Perez	Private	Holmes	Stonington	Sept. 30, 1782	Nov. 26, 1782	8th Reg., Col. Oliver Smith
William	Private	Hungerford	Groton	Nov. 11, 1780	July 6, 1781	Militia
Amos	Captain	Hungerford	Groton	Nov. 11, 1780	July 6, 1781	8th Reg. of Foot, in the Militia

300

MAINS IN THE WAR OF 1812

Name	Rank	Commander	Town	Enlisted	Discharged	Miscellaneous Data
John	Private	Festus Cone	Tolland	Aug. 14, 1812	Oct. 18, 1813	25th Reg., Infantry

Also in War of 1812: Abel, Amos, Chandler, Jabez, Jared, Jesse, Job, John, Randall, Rial, Russell, Simeon, Stephen

WAR WITH MEXICO

Name	Rank	Commander	Town	Enlisted	Discharged
Nelson	Private		Stonington	Mar. 16, 1847	Mar. 26, 1848

Appendix V.

[The history of these four Baptist churches was written for the Brown Genealogy, but it will be of equal interest to the families whose early homes were near one of these old churches. Although many of the children and grandchildren have removed to Western States, they will be interested in these churches where their fathers and mothers worshipped and were active members; and many still are strong and active supporters of these churches at the present day.]

FIRST BAPTIST CHURCH OF NO. STONINGTON, CONN.

In writing the records of some of the Brown families, it is found that many of their ancestors are worthy of honorable mention in connection with the First and Second Baptist Churches in what is now No. Stonington. The First Baptist Church was organized in 1743; and Elder Wait Palmer was chosen its pastor and ordained the same year.

At the time this church was organized there was but one other Baptist church in the State of Connecticut. This one was located at Groton, three miles west of Old Mystic; organized in 1705, with Valentine Wightman as its first pastor. It must be borne in mind that the date which marks the rise of this church carries us far back into the early settlement of the country — and seventy years before the Revolution.

Wait Palmer was baptized May 27, 1711; he married Mary Brown (42), daughter of Eleazer Brown (11) and Ann Pendleton. They settled about three miles west of her father's house, on that fertile ridge of land called Taugwank; afterwards they removed to Pau-hun-gue-nuck Hill, now called Pendleton Hill. At this time the settlements were few, and the church small; but their spirit and courage we admire, the elevated tone of their piety, their patient endurance of suffering, and their manly resistance of religious despotism. They were extraordinary men, made so by the grace of God.

Elder Palmer was a man of plain, common education, yet of strong, vigorous intellect, of sound, practical sense. Books he had none. The Bible alone was the man of his council, his almost exclusive study; hence he became mighty in the Scriptures. He owned a farm of ninety acres a little west of the Pendleton Hill meeting-house. He received comparatively no support from the Church, and he often preached in destitute settlements. He held meetings in Preston, where afterwards there became a flourishing Baptist church, and in Tolland also, where he baptized the celebrated Shubael Stearns and shortly after assisted with Joshua Morse in his ordination, who became the most remarkable preacher of his time. He formed a church in North Carolina, and in a short time had 606 members. He really evangelized the States of South Carolina and Georgia.

Elder Palmer baptized Simeon Brown (72), the first pastor of the Second Church in this town.

We cannot state at the close of his ministry the numerical strength of the church, but it was fast gaining strength and power. During the pastorate of Elder Palmer we have no data as to when the church was built, but find that the land for it was given by Daniel Brown (24), cousin to Elder Palmer's wife, and Thomas Holmes. The house was located two miles south of Pendleton Hill, near Zebulon York's, on the east side of the road. The compiler remembers it as a small and very old brown house, after it had been deserted from twelve to fifteen years. Mr. Palmer was the first pastor of this church, and it was at a period which tried men's souls, as he labored extensively for the diffusion of truth with our earliest ministers in the great work of gathering and planting churches. We are constrained to reverence his name and memory, and regard him as worthy to be enrolled among the noble men of his day. Elder Palmer was an active patriot in the Revolution, soon after which he died, in 1790, nearly ninety years old. Interment, half a mile south of the present Pendleton Hill meeting-house, in an unmarked grave.

The following record was found among the old records of the First Baptist Church (Pendleton Hill), asking the Second Church to give up their beloved brother, Eleazer Brown, to become their minister. Quoted as written:

"The Church of Christ under the Pastorate Charge of Elder Simeon Brown. To the Church of Christ, formerly of Elder Palmer's Charge, sends greeting, wishing, grace, Mercy and Peace, to be multiplied unto you, through our Lord Jesus Christ. To whom be glory and praise Amen.

"Beloved, whereas we on the 9th of this Instant December 1769 Received a request from you by your Messengers: that we would manifest our freedom in giving up to your Watchcare our Beloved Brother Eleazer Brown; that you may be enabled to set him apart to be your Minister and Sealer under Christ, the great Head of the Church. In answer to which we hereby send you our Letter of Reccomendation, reccomending our said Brother as one visibly Clean, and in regular standing in our Church as having a Special Gift from God to preach the everlasting Gospel.

"Wishing and praying the Blessing of Heaven to attend him, and you Amen.   "Signed in behalf of the Church —

Stonington, Decr. 9th   SANDS NILES
        1769.   *Clerk"*

302

APPENDIX

The second pastor of this church was Eleazer Brown (139), who came to this church as a licentiate from the Second Baptist Church in this town, which was organized in 1765. In this capacity he served the church for the term of four years and was ordained as pastor June 24, 1770. The ministers who assisted were Joshua Morse, Timothy Wightman, of the First Church of Groton, Simeon Brown (72), of the Second Church in this town.

Mr. Brown was a man whom God had eminently fitted for the station he was to occupy. He waited with becoming modesty for four years the acceptance of the church, yet all the time preached to the church, which watched his steady demeanor, his ripening gifts and growing worth. From the minutes of the Stonington Union Association the church numbered ninety-seven. Towards the close of his ministry there came, in 1791, a great outpouring of the Spirit of God; the seed faithfully sown began to bear much fruit, and at this revival the church received an accession of fifty-two, making the total membership one hundred and fifty-two. Elder Brown had, it is said, but little education, but was a man of strong native powers, of vivid thought and conception, and of a flowing, rapid delivery. He was rightly esteemed as one of the most eminent preachers of his day.

Peleg Randall was baptized Nov. 19, 1784, and was ordained an evangelist Oct. 25, 1792; on this occasion the aged pastor of this church with much propriety gave the charge. The old pastor, worn with long labor, was about to be taken up to his reward; but ere he departed he poured the sacred oil upon the head of his successor. This was his only pastorate, and the longest of this church, extending over a period of twenty-five years.

On the 11th of July, 1795, he fell asleep in Jesus, in the twenty-seventh year of his ministry.

Interment in Brown Cemetery, north of the Second Church.

The third pastor of this church was Peleg Randall, who succeeded Elder Brown in 1792. Dr. A. G. Palmer says of him: "His discourses were cool, deliberate, instructive, but were usually wanting in the glowing warmth and animation for which his revered predecessor was so highly distinguished. He was at times impassioned, ardent, and impressive in his delivery, often becoming, towards the close of his discourse, deeply moved himself, hence deeply moving others."

Although no general revival was enjoyed under his ministry, yet it was by no means unfruitful in the conversion of souls. At this time this church was not alone, for the Second Church was organized five miles to the south, with Elder Simeon Brown as pastor, in 1765, which must have drawn a number by letter from this church to the Second Church. Mr. Randall closed his labors with this church Oct. 8, 1813, and the church was left without a pastor.

Rev. Jonathan Miner was ordained at the First Church in Groton, Feb. 14, 1814, to which this church sent delegates; and because of the impression the candidate made upon these delegates the church resolved at once to call him to preach to them for one year. The call was accepted, and Mr. Miner took up his residence with them in the spring of 1814. During the first three months of his ministry *fifty-six* members were added to the church by baptism. The work of grace continued from year to year, as revival followed revival, up to the close of his ministry.

But there were years of comparative unfruitfulness. At the close of 1814 the church numbered one hundred and eighty-five. The next general revival under the leadership of Elder Miner commenced in the autumn of 1822 and extended till April, 1823. Many in the meridian of life were received and baptized into the fellowship of the church. Dr. A. G. Palmer said, on the occasion of the one-hundredth anniversary of this church: "These were days of childhood with many of us; but they left an impression upon our hearts which neither time nor eternity will ever efface. It was the first bright spot in our existence, the enkindling of the spiritual life within us, the lighting up in our young minds, the hope of immortality." By this revival the church received an accession of fifty-one members, making the whole number two hundred and thirty-one.

All of these years of the existence of this pioneer church, till 1830, they worshipped in the old meeting-house, and here had been gathered a large and flourishing body of spiritual members. But the time had come for the church to enlarge its house of worship. Accordingly, in 1830, they rebuilt on that beautiful plateau, Pendleton Hill, commanding a most magnificent view of the surrounding country and of the ocean, fifteen miles away. The dedicatory sermon was preached by Elder John Gano Wightman, of the First Groton Church, now [1910] Old Mystic. Elder Wightman was grandson of Valentine Wightman; his father was Timothy Wightman, the three elders serving successively one hundred and twenty-five years. Now, this First Groton Church is two hundred and five years old.

But to return: ninety-one years had now passed in the history of this church, and it had but four pastors, and under their efficient labors it had advanced from a state of extreme feebleness to comparative strength and prosperity. During this time the increasing population of the town gave to the church a larger field to draw from; hence during the closing years of Elder Miner's ministry of faithful service, we note large ingatherings to the church.

First Baptist Church

North Stonington, Conn.

(Pendleton Hill)

Organized 1743

Second Baptist Church
North Stonington, Conn.
Organized 1765

Up to this time the church had paid their ministers no salary. Elder Miner said to the church, after they had built their new and commodious house of worship, "You ought now to pay your minister a little salary."

His term of service was twenty years, terminating in March, 1834. From this time till 1837 the church was without a pastor. In 1835 another wave of revival interest came, when forty-five were received by baptism. In the autumn of 1837 another awakening began, and as the result of a faithful working church forty precious souls were gathered into the fold of Christ.

During this time the oversight of the church devolved upon the deacons, who filled their offices well; hence a most excellent report of their stewardship by constant ingatherings.

As many of the Brown ancestors participated in duties and labors of this church, from the very first and all through the century, and coöperated with it, the compiler was desirous of taking a glance at its history for the first one hundred years. The only other long pastorate of this church was Rev. D. S. Chapman's, fourteen years; he died pastor of the church. People came to the old church long distances in those early times, and it was no uncommon thing to see, hitched around and near this meeting-house, thirty, forty, or even fifty horses with saddle and pillion on their backs. That was when they were glad when they said, "Let us go into the house of the Lord."

Services have been regularly maintained all these one hundred and sixty-two years. The deacons of this church have an honorable mention, being men of God, laboring zealously for the saving of the lost, using the office of deacon well, and getting to themselves a good report.

Appendix VI.

SECOND BAPTIST CHURCH OF NO. STONINGTON, CONN.

The Second Baptist Church of No. Stonington, Conn., was organized in March, 1765, with Elder Simeon Brown (72) as pastor. Elder Brown was born in Stonington Jan. 31, 1723, a man of strong native talents; he was converted under the preaching of Whitefield, in 1745. He united with Rev. Stephen Babcock in forming the Baptist Church in Westerly, R. I., in 1750; and was baptized by Rev. Wait Palmer in 1764, being ordained the same year. His pastorate and watchful care over this church extended from the organization, in 1765, till his death, in 1815 — fifty years and eight months; a noble record to be engraved on his monument in Brown Cemetery in his native town.

His descendants may well be proud of the character and the consecrated life of so noble a man, laying down the burdens of life in his ninety-fourth year. The self-sacrificing labors and the towering grandeur of his character and the wide-spread and abounding influence which emanated from his life perpetuate his memory through many generations, leaving a shining record.

The handful of corn on the tops of the mountains grew till now the membership was three hundred and thirty-five. He served this church all these years without salary, and built the meeting-house from lumber cut from his "cedar swamp," with the assistance of his brethren.

It was without paint, both interior and exterior; with galleries on three sides, a high pulpit on the north side, with an ascent of ten stairs, enclosed with panel work. When the minister was seated he could not be seen by the audience. He stood on a small platform, and was a commanding figure. The writer was present when the last service was held in this old meeting-house, in the spring of 1845; it was like parting with one's dearest friend, and many tears were shed. It was suggested that they better let it stand, but it was taken down and the present house erected the same year.

The ceiling of the porch of the new house was the panelling taken from the pews of the old house.

The following items of interest by way of comparison are gleaned from the Stonington Baptist Association, as it was first called in the first printed minutes, which embraced churches in Rhode Island as far east as Exeter and Wickford and west to Waterford and Montville, Conn.

Stonington Baptist Association
held at
Elder Timothy Wightman's
Meeting house
in 1792
Groton.

First Church, Elder Eleazer Brown, No. 152.
Second Church, Elder Simeon Brown, " 201.
Exeter Church, R. I. (Nooseneck hill), " 254.

1811.

Second N. Stonington, No. 276.

Exeter, R. I. No. 253; First Groton 208; First N. Stonington 185.

1822.

Exeter 684; North Kingston (Wickford) 401; Second N. Stonington 320; First Groton 246.

1832.

Exeter 512; Second N. Stonington 454; Second Groton 358; First Groton 257.

From this last date to the present, 1910, all these country churches have decreased in membership; and while they still live, they have become, some of them, very weak.

The successor to Elder Brown was Elder Asher Miner, who had been for ten years associate pastor with the aged minister, and at his death became sole pastor.

The church has been, and is still, called the Miner Church, although many living at this distant day believe it should have been called the Elder Simeon Brown Church.

Rev. Asher Miner was born in No. Stonington, Conn., Jan. 30, 1772. He was the son of Thomas and Mary (Page) Miner; married Lucy Spalding, Nov. 28, 1790; and was ordained in 1805. The church is beautifully located, second only to the church on Pendleton Hill for natural scenery and picturesqueness. Elder Miner was a contemporary with Elder Jonathan Miner of the First Church and Elder John Gano Wightman of the First Groton Church.

Neither Elder Brown nor Elder Miner had the advantages of a collegiate or theological education, but both were men of natural endowments, and good understanding of the Word of God. Their highest aim and the crowning efforts of their lives were to lead men and women, old and young, to a saving knowledge of Jesus Christ, and in this crowning part of their work they were eminently successful; which is the pre-eminent work of the gospel ministry. Elder Miner had been trained in church work by his illustrious predecessor, and had spent his whole life with this church. Elder Brown had laid the sure foundation and was worthy to be followed.

There is yet one living, in 1910, who remembers this saint of God, the tone of his voice, and the people who came in large numbers to attend divine worship.

During his pastorate there were received nearly five hundred into the fellowship of this church. Although there were churches at this time in Westerly, Stonington, Mystic, much nearer, the people flocked to this old church in great numbers; so that during this pastorate the church numbered, at one time, four hundred and eighty. Elder Miner died Sept. 1, 1836, and the people still worship in the old house.

A few now, in 1910, remember Elder Asher Miner, whose whole term of service was thirty-one years. On his tombstone in Union Cemetery is inscribed:

> The gospel was his joy and song,
> Even to his latest breath;
> The truth he had proclaimed so long
> Was his support in death.

The names of some of the ministers who succeeded Elder Miner were Elder Erastus Denison, Elder John Green, who often supplied, Thomas Barber, Elder C. C. Lewis, who was a man of fervor and power, and died in the pastoral office of this church Mar. 10, 1864, in his fifty-seventh year. This new house has not witnessed such powerful revivals as did the former, many of the young people having left the country church and being found in the cities and villages all over the land.

The men of God who served as deacons should be mentioned,— at least some of them,— but nearly all have fallen asleep. Of the following, the compiler remembers all except the first: Zebulon Brown (74), brother of Elder Simeon Brown; John Stanton (b. 1753), died in 1851, at the age of ninety-eight; Josiah Brown (279), son of Elder Simeon Brown; Josiah Brown, Jr. (304); Allen Wheeler (b. 1793); Cyrus W. Brown (253); Reuben W. York. The acting deacons in 1905 are: Horace F. York, Richard Wheeler, and C. L. Gray.

Appendix VII.

THIRD BAPTIST CHURCH, NO. STONINGTON, CONN.

The Third Baptist Church was organized Dec. 25, 1828. The town of Stonington had been divided, and No. Stonington had been set off from it in 1807.

A committee of interested persons was appointed, Dec. 10, 1828, to adopt articles of faith for a contemplated church. The committee con-

Third Baptist Church
Organized 1828

Residence of George A. Pendleton
Where Cyrus H. Brown (63) was born, Nov. 24, 1829
North Stonington, Conn.

This house was built, over two hundred years ago, by Sylvanus Maxson, who owned large tracts of land. Nathan Maxson, his son, came into possession of it, and he and his wife Ruth died here; and their daughter Sarah Catherine was born and married in this house to Cyrus H. Brown (63). It has been celebrated as the rendezvous of the Sabbatarian fraternity for scores of years. Near this house is the second Seventh Day Baptist meeting-house in America.

sisted of Samuel Chapman, Rev. Levi Walker, John F. Wheeler, and reported the articles of faith. They were adopted and remain unchanged. According to custom, a council was called for recognition of the body, and it met Dec. 25, 1828, approving the organization. The sermon was preached by Rev. Wm. Bentley. Others who took part in the recognition services were: Revs. John Gano Wightman, Wm Palmer, Luther Godard, Benjamin M Hill, Jabez S Swan, Jonathan Miner, and Asher Miner. The eight persons who received letters from their churches were: Rev. Levi Walker, M.D , Samuel Chapman, David Holmes, Sally Wheeler, Phebe Walker, Lucy Chapman, Lucy Grant, and Emily Fanning.

Three days after the recognition the church received seven members by baptism, the ordinance being performed by Elder Jabez S. Swan; others united by letter and baptism, so that in June, 1829, when the church joined the Stonington Union Association, this new church reported thirty members and had several ministers as supplies, meeting at the schoolhouse In 1833 the membership was fifty.

Urged by the growth of numbers and the demands of the community, the church and society in 1833 erected the present house of worship, then, as still, a beautiful and substantial sanctuary. In a few months the amount raised was $2,000. The roll of subscribers began with. Saxton Miner, $100; Thomas P. Wattles, $100; Deacon Ezra Miner, $100; Daniel Bentley, $100, Benjamin Hewitt, $125, Rufus Williams, $100; David Coats, $100.

The lot, containing three-fourths of an acre of land, cost $125. The members of the society hold the property in trust for the use and benefit of the Baptist denomination forever.

The first acting pastor of this new church was Rev Levi Walker, M.D. He was born in Massachusetts, moved to Maine, was converted in 1804, and for a time was a Methodist circuit preacher. He afterwards became a Baptist and united with the First Baptist Church in Fall River, Mass. Mr. Walker studied medicine and entered upon his practice, meanwhile continuing to preach, and became pastor of the Baptist Church in Warwick, R. I., in 1816 He then became pastor of the Preston City Church, Conn , in 1819, and settled on a farm in No. Stonington in 1823. He preached with success in various districts, organizing the first Sunday school in the town and accomplishing much in his two professions. He died Dec. 12, 1869, aged eighty-five years and ten months. His three sons also went into the ministry

In 1834 Rev. Feronda Bestor became its pastor, and at that time the new church was dedicated. Mr. Bestor remained three years, and received thirty-eight by baptism, forty-five by letter. The church numbered at this time one hundred and twenty-eight. The church in 1837 entertained the Association for the first time, and Rev. Alfred Gates was the pastor and remained about one year. A special revival was enjoyed, and twenty-seven were admitted by baptism; and in 1837 the church numbered one hundred and fifty-two, with a Sabbath school of sixteen teachers and ninety pupils.

Rev. Alfred Gates was born in Granville, N. Y., in 1803. He studied at Hamilton, N. Y., and was ordained at Willimantic, Conn., in 1831. He was pastor at Preston, Conn., and other churches. He died at Montville, Conn., Jan. 30, 1875. The church was supplied by several ministers until 1842, when Rev. B. C. Grafton was called, under whose labors fifty-three were added by baptism. He remained about one year. Rev. Edward T. Hiscox, from Hamilton University, N. Y., supplied the church about six months, and was ordained Jan. 18, 1844, when he was called and removed to Westerly, R. I., Apr. 18, 1844.

Rev. James R. Stone was his successor. The church was enrolled with one hundred and eighty-seven members.

Levi Walker, Jr., was licensed to preach Dec. 18, 1829. Born in New Bedford, Mass., in 1811, he was converted in this town. After pastorates in New Hampshire and Massachusetts, he returned to No. Stonington, where he died in February, 1839, loved by all who knew him.

A number of young men converted in this church became successful ministers, 1842–1848, among whom were Edwin D. Bentley, Ralph H. Maine, and William H. Randall. The latter, during the Civil War, recruited a company and entered the field as captain. For heroic conduct at Chancellorsville he was promoted to major; he also served his command as captain. In 1865 he resumed the pastorate; but, failing in health, he sought restoration in Florida, but died Mar. 7, 1874, aged fifty-six years.

During the pastorate of James R. Stone, on Oct. 18, 1846, another revival began, and continued through the following winter. On Oct. 18, 1846, Cyrus H. Brown, Louisa A. Brown, Gideon P. Brown, and Maryette Burdick were baptized and received into the church. On Mar. 28, 1847, twenty-eight had been admitted into the church. The compiler retained his membership with this church ten years, removing to Boston in 1856, where he united with the Brighton Avenue Baptist Church, retaining membership there until 1898, when, removing from there to Westerly, R. I., he joined the Calvary Baptist Church.

Rev. James R. Stone, afterwards Dr. Stone, after three years of service, severed his connection with this church, much to its regret. The next to come on the field was Daniel Henry Miller, a young man who came over from the Methodist to the Baptist faith. He received ordination Dec. 15, 1847. David Coates said of him, "He will be quite a preacher when he becomes a man; he is only a boy now." His ministry here, as in all his fields of labor, was marked with energy, ability, and success. The fortieth anniversary of his ministry was celebrated Dec. 15, 1887. Rev. George H. Miner said of his early pastorate with this people: "I seem to see a young man, tall and somewhat slender in form, with a commanding presence; bold and fearless, his voice impressive and solemn, full of reverential awe. *Now* in whispered tones he utters the most tender appeals and the sweetest comforts, and as the winds rise and sway the forest trees and shake the very earth, and the belching thunders pour forth their loud rumblings, and the sharp lightnings flash and the awful tempest is upon us, so his words alternate between the gentle and the awful, the tender and the dreadful."

In April, 1849, Mr. Miller (since Dr. Miller) resigned his pastorate, much to the regret of the church, having pastorates in Yonkers, N. Y., Elizabeth, N. J., and Norwich, Conn. Dr. Miller was also chaplain in the Civil War. His successor was Rev. Orin T. Walker, of Martha's Vineyard, Mass.

It was a home-coming to Mr. Walker. His ministry commenced early in 1850, and continued until April, 1853. Many will recall his labors in the schoolhouses of Ashwillet. Mr. Walker's resignation was much regretted. He was called to New London, Conn., New Jersey, Boston, and Chicago.

Rev. Thomas W. Clarke succeeded Mr. Walker. At this time the membership was the largest at any time in its history, being two hundred and twenty-three.

In 1853 the church lamented the death of David Coats, aged eighty-seven years.

Active in the church were Rev. Levi Walker, Benj. B. Hewitt, Ansel Coats, and John C. Coats, the constant and efficient church clerk for forty-eight years, Nathan Edgcomb and Thomas Edgcomb, Daniel Bentley, the Breeds, the Grants, the Stewarts, the Wheelers, the Hillards, and Ephraim W. Maine, Joseph Frink, Capt. Babcock, Deacon Cyrus W. Brown, Samuel Thompson, Stephen Main, and good women not a few, whose records, with those of these good men, are now in the Book of Life.

The pastors from 1856 to 1910 were: Henry W. Webber, Joseph Burnett, 1857, Edgar A. Hewitt, 1860, C. W. Ray, 1862, Samuel D. Ashley, 1868, J. W. Holman, 1870, Fenner B. Dickinson, 1874, William D. Morgan, 1877, James D. Noble, 1878, W. W. Staples, 1880, J. Edred Jones, 1881,

Daniel E. Easton, 1884, Edwin D. Bentley, 1888, Francis Purvis, 1891, C. Grant Savage, 1893, Richard Kemp, 1896, Frank D. Luddington, 1899, H. A. Calhoun, 1901, and Lucian Drury, 1904-1909.

Since the organization of the church only six have been chosen as deacons: John T. Wheeler, 1834, Ezra Miner, 1834, Benjamin T. Billings, 1875, Nelson A. Brown, 1875, William H. Hillard, 1888, and Nathan S. Edgcomb, 1888.

The church has received a number of substantial bequests. From Miss Abby Miner the church was made her residuary legatee, receiving $2,343, in 1881. The church received in 1882, from the estate of Mrs. Mary A. (Crandall) Gallup, widow of John Dean Gallup, $250, on the condition that the church raise an equal amount. In 1886 it received from the estate of Oliver Sisson $150. At this time the church took from its treasury $7 to add to the fund, making a total of $3,000. From the estate of Mrs. Louisa (Palmer) Crandall, widow of Oliver S. Crandall, the church received $250. About 1870 B. F. Sisson, of Binghamton, N. Y., a native of the town, donated $100 toward a new bell for the church tower.

While there were many very worthy families of whom honorable mention could be made in connection with the church, among others will be mentioned John O. and Thomas W. Wheeler and wife, Emily Elizabeth (Brown) Wheeler and daughter, Nancy Mary Wheeler, wife of Deacon W. H. Hillard. They entertained and made a pleasant home for many ministers who came as supplies, and were also leaders of the singing in the church nearly all their lives. On the decease of Mrs. W. H. Hillard, she gave, in 1902, her piano to the church. At the decease of Mrs. Wheeler, Jan. 29, 1905, she made the church her residuary legatee, consisting mostly of her real estate, two houses and lands, pleasantly located in the village, requesting it to be sold, and the interest used as a perpetual fund for the church.

The church should hold in grateful remembrance the fathers and mothers, the sons and daughters, who have consecrated their lives to the service of God.

Baptist Church

Brookfield, N. Y.

This meeting-house is owned and occupied by the Seventh Day Baptist Society and the First Day Baptist Society. In the picture is the First Day parsonage; the parsonage of the Seventh Day Society is located in another part of the town.

In the above photograph Dr. H. C. Brown appears at the left and E. Eugene Brown at the right.

Appendix VIII.

HISTORY OF THE FIRST BAPTIST CHURCH OF BROOK-
FIELD, N. Y.

One of the principal promoters of this church was Simeon Brown, Jr., son of Elder Simeon Brown, of Stonington, Conn. He received a license to preach in 1775, being the first who had been granted a license from that church.

He emigrated from Stonington, Conn., May, 1792, with his wife and children in an ox-cart. This family and others coming from Stonington from time to time were a nucleus from which this church was formed, June 28, 1798.

Twenty people met together to consider the organization of a Baptist church. After drawing up articles of faith, the First Church of Christ in Brookfield, N. Y., was organized, Oct. 12, 1799. There in the wild woods and amid howling beasts of prey was erected an altar for the worship of God. This young church began holding meetings with their spiritual leader and recognized head in the log house of the minister, Elder Simeon Brown, Jr., and there was much interest shown among the scattered settlers. After a few years a meeting-house was built, making a more attractive and comfortable church home for the people. Elder Brown was the pastor until his death, Aug. 18, 1826. In 1837 a new meeting-house was built, to be used together with the Seventh Day Baptist people of Clarkville, which is occupied still by both churches in 1905.

This Brookfield Baptist Church has ordained nine pastors and licensed twelve to preach the gospel. It has always had a Deacon Brown since its organization, but one person of that name holding that position at the same time. During its existence it has always observed monthly communion service. In September, 1801, the church joined the Otsego Baptist Association, always being regular in its representatives and delegates. Thus by strong faith in God from the beginning, for sixscore years this church has flourished, and is still holding forth the word of life.

The following extracts are from reminiscences of Elder Brown read at the Centennial Celebration of this church, July 7, 1898:

"In personal appearance Elder Brown was more than medium height and well proportioned, being of strong build. He had light brown hair worn moderately long in thin locks, eyes blue, shaded with heavy eyebrows and a massive forehead. He was always clean shaven, and had a pleasing expression. He was fond of the chase, and in his later years would ride to a known fox trail and often do good shooting in the saddle.

"When he became too feeble to leave his home he held evening services in his own house. His last sermon was preached at his house while sitting in his chair, being too feeble to stand."

This church has had in one hundred and seven years nineteen pastors, from its organization in 1798 to 1905. The longest pastorates were Rev. Simeon Brown, Jr., from 1798 to 1826, and Rev. Holland Turner, from 1835 to 1845.

The ordinations in this church were: Rev. Simeon Brown, Jr., Oct. 14, 1800; Rev. Joshua Wells, Oct. 18, 1815; Thomas Dye; G. B. Perry, Mar. 5, 1823; Peter Latimer, May 31, 1827; Ferris Scott, July 20, 1858; O. N. Fletcher, Nov. 1, 1866; A. V. B. Crumb, Aug. 23, 1876, missionary to Burmah; R. J. Thompson, Aug. 15, 1883.

The Deacons, from organization to 1905, were: Daniel Maine, Nathan Brown, Bell Lewis, Wait Clarke, Samuel Browne, Thomas E. Craine, George Crumb, Morgan L. Brown, Don F. Maine, Avory Cole.

The church clerks, from organization to 1905, were: Andrew Coats, Asa Frink, Jr., Allen Green, Henry Brown, Randall Y. Hibbard, Don F. Maine, Ellen R. Baldwin, Catherine Crandall, Clifton Craine.

Errata.

Page 37. Truman P. Maine (168) is now [1910] in the Medical Department of Harvard College.

Page 62. Mary Annie Rider, read (435), *not* (441).

Page 66. Mary Annie Rider (435), m. James M. Cook (400-404), *not* (413-417).

Page 108. Anna Maria Main (749), *not Ann* Maria.

Page 124. Abigail (Main) Thompson, mother of Charles Dwight Thompson, is (875), *not* (872).

Page 124. Louise Billings Thompson (934), m., Nov. 29, 1909, Charles E. Hillard.

Page 133. Fidelia Melinda Maine (1039), d. Mansfield, Conn., and is buried in Groton, Conn.

Page 142. First line, Elmina Catherine (1122), m. B. F. Arnold; erase *Rev.*

Page 143. Edgar Oscar Silver, d. Nov. 18, 1909.

Page 221. Children of Frank Healy and Mary De Ette (Nichols), 1901-1904, read Healy, *not* Nichols.

"I EXPECT *to pass through this life but once. If therefore there is any kindness I can show, or any good I can do to any fellow-being, let me do it now; let me not defer or neglect it, for I shall not pass this way again."*

List of Illustrations.

MARRIAGES

BIRTHS

BIRTHS

DEATHS

MEMORANDA

MEMORANDA

INDEX

I. Nathaniel Babcock Family.

BERRY

Charles W., 28
Edwin P., 27, 28
Emma A., 29
Lucy M., 30
Sarah G., 28

BILLINGS

Lois, 15
Sarah, 18

BLIVIN

Polly, 21

BOURS

John, 17

BRADFORD

Alice N., 30
Cecil B., 31
George L., 30
John W., 31

BRADLEY

Annie C., 25

BRAYTON

Mary E., 25

BROWN

Benadam W., 25
Bessie M., 26
Carrie E., 26
Cyrus H., 25
Cyrus W., 24
Emily E., 25
George, 12
Gideon P., 25
Hermon C., 25
Horace C., 25
James S., 25
Jane, 11
John B., 25
Lois B., 25
Lois T., 25
Louisa A., 25

Marion L., 29
Sarah E., 25
Stephen E., 25
Thomas E., 29
Thomas H., 25
Thomas M., 25
Thomas S., 25
Wilfred M., 25
William D., 22
William E., 25
William S., 25

BURDICK

Mary E., 29

CANDEE

Laura, 28

CHAMPLIN

Mary, 13
William, 11

CHIPMAN

Martha E., 26

CLARK

Herbert P., 26
Joseph, 14
Susanna, 13
Thomas, 14

COATS

Hannah, 11

COLBY

Carrie L. P., 25
Mary A., 25

CRANDALL

Caroline P., 22
Ethan, 22
Jane, 11
Lydia, 13
Nancy M., 22
Wealthy M., 22

DAVIDSON

John, 15

DAVIS

Mercy, 22

DAWLEY

Frank I., 26
Irwin F., 26

EXLEY

Albert, 31
Bertha E., 31
Clarice C., 31
Edith M., 31
Florence R., 31
Lucius M., 31
Martha M., 31
Maybell E., 31
Nathan, 31
William S., 31

GALLUP

Benjamin, 23
Charles B., 23
John B., 23
Susan C., 23

GEESON

M. Elizabeth, 32

GOSS

Edwin, 24
Virginia P., 24

GOULD

Ophir, 21
Susanna, 21

GREEN

Gracie A., 30
Maria C., 28

HALL

Elizabeth, 13

NATHANIEL BABCOCK FAMILY

RICHARDSON	SPENCER	THOMPSON
Lovinia, 25	Edith L., 28	Abigail, 14
	Henry J., 28	George A., 29
RICHMOND	William C., 28	Ruth G., 30
Betsey, 22		Sarah P., 30
		Sarah W., 28
ROSS	STANTON	
Mary, 24	Abby C., 27	VOSE
	Caroline S., 23	Sarah, 14
SALTONSTALL	Hannah, 15	
Dudley, 17	Mary, 17	WALKER
	Rebecca, 13	Elma E., 21
SAUNDERS	Sarah, 14	
Elizabeth, 13		WHEELER
		Thomas W., 25
SCHWENK	STEWART	
Fred K., 30	Elizabeth, 22	WIGHTMAN
Marion K., 30		Lydia C., 22
SMITH	SWAN	WILLIAMS
Abigail, 17	Phebe, 17	Elizabeth, 18

Continuation of Babcock family names will be found in the index to Appendices.

II. Simeon Main Family.

AVERY

Albert T., 36
George A., 37
John D., 36
Thomas W., 36

BABCOCK

John D., 34
William S., 34

BENJAMIN

Nettie B., 38

BROWN

George C., 35

BURDICK

Alida M., 36
Amos G., 36

CAMPBELL

Sarah E., 35

CHAPMAN

Nellie G., 38

COON

Alice D., 36
Anis L., 36
Annie M., 35
Carroll E., 36
Chauncey E., 35
Delia A., 36
Fanny, 35
Frank, 35

Frank E., 35
Jesse W., 35
Jessie A., 36
John T., 35
Julia A., 35
Katie, 35
Marion R., 35
Mary D., 35
Nellie, 35
Raymond, 36
William E., 35
Willie E., 35

DURO

Amy D., 36
Archibald E., 36
Edward J., 36
Lucy D., 36

GREEN

Charles E., 37
Edwin M., 37
Florence I., 37
Frank R., 37
Lila B., 37
Melissa, 35

HEWITT

Abby S. C., 34

KELLY

Julia, 35

MAIN

Abby C., 36
Adam, 34
Charles E., 37
Charles H., 36

Christopher G., 33
Daniel, 33
Frances E., 34
Joanna, 33
John D., 34
Lillie A., 35
Lucy M., 34
Martha L., 37
Mary A., 36
Miner, 33
Nancy E., 37
Phoebe, 34
Prentice, 33
Prudence, 33
Richard H., 34
Simeon, 33

MAINE

Adlia E., 38
Amasa M., 38
Arthur P., 37
Betsey A., 37
Daisy G., 38
Dorothy E., 38
Dorris I., 38
Eunice A., 34
Herman, 35
Isaac, 37, 38
James W., 37
Jennie E., 38
Jennie L., 38
Lucy A., 35
Lucy M., 37
Mary A., 37
Nellie A., 35
Nettie B., 38
Park B., 35
Truman P., 37
Violette M., 38

325

SIMEON MAIN FAMILY

MILLER

Ethel C., 36
Robert C., 36
Willie W., 36

MINER

Anna, 33
Louisa, 36
Lovisa, 36
Lydia E., 33

MITCHELL

Amos, 34
Dudley, 34
William H., 34

STANTON

Donald H., 37
Gladys E., 37
John, 33

John G., 36
Paul M., 37
Ruth M., 37

WOODMANSEE

Emma L., 35

YORK

Martha, 33

III. Isaac Miner Family.

ALLEN

Emma G., 45
Eva A., 45
Ida E., 45
Jennie L., 45
Orrin B., 45

ARNOLD

Mary E., 45

BENJAMIN

Albert D., 44
Arthur D., 44
Elizabeth A., 44
Frank A., 44
Henry B., 44
Mary A., 44
Nathan, 43
Nathan W., 44
Nellie F., 43
Sarah A., 44

BREAKER

Helen, 40
Lewis C., 40
William D., 40

BROWN

Katurah, 39

BURDICK

Harva C., 41

CHAPMAN

Anna M., 48
Jesse, 39
Mary A., 47

CHESBOROUGH

Luke, 39
Luke P., 39
Martha E., 39
Mary M., 39

COATES

Alfred W., 40
Annie E., 40
Frank, 47

DEANE

Jennie M. M., 42

EGGLESTON

Ethel C., 48
Gladys M., 48
S. Curtis, 48

FENNER

Fannie, 43

GORE

Abby M., 47

GREEN

Eliza, 40

GRIGGS

Claud, 47

HULL

Jesse Y., 40

LATHAM

Abby J., 42

MAIN

Charles H., 41
George H., 47
George W., 46
Hulda, 40
Mary J., 47
Prentice, 39
Susan K., 44
Susan P., 47
William L., 44

MAINE

Arline, 46
Chester B., 46
Clarence E., 46
Dorothy, 46
James W., 46
Mildred, 46
Norman Y., 46
Ruth M., 46

MINER

Albert D., 45
Alvin P., 43
Amos P., 42
Anna, 39
Anna G., 48
Arthur, 40
Arthur C., 48
Belle, 42
Bernice C., 48
Calvin G., 40
Charles A., 47
Charles E., 47
Charles H. C., 48
Chester, 43
Clarissa, 41
Courtland P., 46

325

Denison W., 41
Dora, 48
Elias, 41
Ellen, 40
Elmina, 41
Elsie M., 43
Emeline, 41
Emma, 40
Etna, 40
Fanny, 41
Fanny M., 42
Florence M., 45
Frances E., 43
George A., 48
George F., 47
George P., 46
George W., 47
Grace E., 47
Harold C., 45
Harriet N., 40
Helen H., 43
Herbert A., 47
Hiram, 40
Irving O., 45
Irving W., 41
Isaac, 39
Isaac D., 44, 45
Isaac W., 40
Jane, 40
John D., 45
Katurah, 39

Lillian M., 47
Lovisa, 41
Lucy, 48
Lucy B., 46
Marita, 45
Martha A., 41
Mary A., 46
Mary E., 39
Maurice C., 47
Minnie, 48
Nellie M., 48
Nellie W., 47
Olive M., 43
Orrin E., 42
Palmer N., 40
Palmer W., 47
Parker, 42
Phebe A., 40
Ralph W., 45
Raymond C., 43
Roscoe R., 42
Susan A., 42
Thomas P., 41
Wilfred A., 45
William H., 43
William J., 47
Willie, 43
Zebulon B., 40

OWEN

Bertha A., 45

PALMER

Amelia M., 43
Birdsey G., 43

PARK

Clarissa M., 41

PENDLETON

James A., 41

PIERCE

Addie R., 48

RICHARDSON

Thomas F., 47

TURNER

Frank D., 44

WELLS

Clara P., 46
Horace, 46
Maryette, 46

WILKINSON

Jennie A., 43
Susan E., 42

YORK

Martha P., 40

IV. Ezekiel Main Family.

Phebe R., 193
William, 117

BALDWIN
Laura A., 171

BALL
Clara B., 181

BARBER
Benjamin, 122
Birdie C. C., 122
Charley, 161
Elnora D., 122
Ethel, 161
George, 161
Ida, 161
Mary, 79
Willis R., 122

BARGER
Ernest, 192
Grace, 192
H. A., 193
Pearl, 192
Samuel F., 192

BARKER
Hattie, 103

BARLOW
Alice R., 261
Henry M., 261
Herbert H., 261
M. Aeline, 261
Seth H., 261

BARNES
Arthur O., 125
Hattie M., 124
M. Sada, 87
Mary L., 97
Orsmus S., 125

BARNS
Annie, 95
Nancy, 246

BARR
Agnes L., 182

BARTLETT
Charles A., 134
Dorothy, 134
George, 134
Inez, 134
Lindsley H., 134
Lois M., 134
Mortimer O., 134
Rena A., 134
Wallace E., 134

BATES
W. R. S., 139

BATON
Alzada, 155

BEARDSLEY
Bessie, 237
Henry C., 237
Howard, 237
Leroy, 237

BEATON
John W., 70

BECKET
Isaac, 140

BEEBE
Maria W., 179

BEERS
Arthur P., 239
Blanche, 239
Lucretia, 237

BELKNAP
Emma A., 208

BENEDICT
Cynthia A., 270

BENJAMIN
Abby, 178
Annie, 273

Charles H., 189
Clara B., 261
Everett D., 189
Jacob D., 189
Lizzie A., 254
Mary E., 189
Nettie B., 189

BENNETT
Lyman, 265
Mark, 156
Newton, 156

BENT
Francis P., 88
Martin F., 88
William W., 88

BENTLEY
Alace L., 71
Alice M., 71
Almira, 225
Charles F., 71
Cora H., 71
Delia C., 232
Elsie W., 71
Esther M., 71
Francis J., 67
Frederick Y., 71
Florence A., 71
Gertrude M., 71
Grace V., 71
Herbert G., 71
Lydia, 71
Lydia E., 67
Mabel V., 71
Mary J., 141
Mildred M., 71
Ruth M., 71
William L., 71
William T., 71

BERRY
Emma A., 93

BILLINGS
Byron, 177
Comfort, 120

Almira B., 176
Charles H., 159
Charles L., 160
Dencie F., 160
Edwin W., 160
Emily, 153
Enoch B., 159
Estelle G., 160
Ethel G., 160
Eveline F., 160
George E., 160
George H., 160
H. Ellen, 126
Hannah F., 159
Hazel D., 160
Irving C., 69
Jessie M., 160
Latham H., 160
Lois A., 160
Sarah, 152
Wilbur, 152
William B., 160

ECKLER
Albert B., 175
Albert E., 175
Ella E., 175
Emerson T., 175
Oneita T., 175

EDGECOMB
Julia, 145

EDWARDS
Emma M., 156
Fannie E., 160
Freelove, 79, 80
George W., 160
Isaac, 167
Lydia, 128
Nathan, 167
Phebe E., 167
Ruth M., 160

EGGLESTON
Angeline, 127
Frank, 178

Ichabod, 121
Ida L., 127
Latham M., 121
Mary, 146
Patience, 147
Stiles P., 127
Thankful, 125

ELLSWORTH
Gertrude, 108

ELLWOOD
Lucinda M., 213

ERVING
Elizabeth C., 144

EVERDEEN
Elizabeth B., 131

EWART
Margaret, 220

FARRELL
Margaret F., 151

FAULKES
Charles H., 106
Frances F., 106

FERRINGTON
Carl, 221
Ithamer, 220
Lemur J., 221
Martin, 220
Mildred I., 221
Miles I., 221
William H., 220

FIELDING
Jerusha C., 75

FILLMORE
Charles D., 100
Dale, 100
Frances, 100
Frank, 100

Jennie, 100
John, 100
Millard, 100

FINAN
Elizabeth A., 181

FINNEGAN
Anna A., 256
Carrie E., 256
Grace L., 256
John, 255
John W., 256
Sarah E., 256

FITCH
Elliott G., 203
Luella, 210
L. Sherwood, 209
Lynn, 209
Sarah L., 209
Sorannus A., 203

FLEMING
Nettie A., 208

FOLEY
Catharine A., 238

FOOTE
Maryette, 235

FORBES
Delia, 129

FOSTER
Loansa, 153

FOWLER
Gertrude M., 88

FOX
Henrietta R., 225
Joseph, 225

FRENCH
Edwin W., 91

334

George F., 86
Howard V., 86
Iona G., 86
Jirah I., 85
John, 84, 85
La Fayette, 86
Latham H., 87
Leslie J., 86
Lucy, 84
Lyle C., 86
Lyman M., 86
Marion, 87
Mary W., 85
Melissa P., 85
Mildred, 87
Murray, 86
Nancy, 84
Nathan S., 86
Susan, 250
Thomas H., 86
Van Renesselaer, 85
W. Henry, 87
William C., 87
William W., 85

GREEN

Albert S., 240
Benjamin A., 142
Bessie H., 240
Ella E., 240
Emma F., 240
Hulda A., 240
Margaret A., 60
Susan B., 240
William D., 266

GREENE

Fred S., 70
Henry C., 69

GREENFIELD

Floyd, 175
Frank, 175
Iona, 175

GREGORY

Charles S., 239
Helen I., 239, 244

Lois M., 239
Mary E., 239
Matthew H., 239
Rebecca, 239
Stanley H., 240

GRIFFIN

Bertha, 217

GUNDERSEN

Theresa M., 68, 72

GURLEY

Stephen C., 128

HAECKER

Theophilus L., 196

HAIGHT

Elizabeth, 233

HAKES

Hannah, 119

HALE

Charles W., 135
Fiona P., 135

HALL

Alace M., 155
Albro, 225
Albro W., 225
Ernest E., 225
George, 225
Jennie A., 225
John M., 86
Lydia, 246
Lyman, 86

HALLIDAY

Mertie, 217

HALSEY

Alonzo, 244
Anzolet E., 244
Evelyn E., 244
James P., 244
Lela L., 245
Leland A., 245

Mabel E., 245
Nellie M., 245
William Z., 244

HAMILTON

Sarah F., 130

HANSON

George H., 116

HARRINGTON

Charles, 168
James L., 256
Jerusha, 233
William, 255

HARRIS

Adelbert, 211
Arthur, 210
Edgar, 210
Florence E., 123
George H., 67
John B., 210
Leon M., 212
Lewis H., 210
Lulu E., 212
Mary A., 218
Mildred M., 212
Susan, 160
William D., 92

HART

Charles A., 240
Gladys E., 240
Phineas, 240

HARVEY

Martha A., 180
Susan E., 131

HASKELL

Anna M., 239
Frank, 239
Hazel C., 239
Spencer H., 239

HATHAWAY

Patience, 79

EZEKIEL MAIN FAMILY

Lucy, 234
Lydia, 250
Main, 234
Mary, 244
Phebe, 243
Rollin, 234
Solon, 234

STONE
Bertha M., 177
Edith J., 238
George H., 149
George W., 149
Walter J., 238
Walter M., 238

STORMS
Ruby T., 244

STRONG
J. Frank, 131

SULLENBARGER
Bessie, 105

SWAN
Eliza, 122
Martha W., 163

SWARTZ
Anna, 244

SYMONDS
Doris E., 134
Henry L., 134

TABOR
Julia, 181

TALBOT
Belinda R., 202

TAYLOR
Ambrose B., 182
Charles, 236
Edward, 93
Ethel M., 182
Hazel L., 182
Mary A., 228

TEMPLETON
Robert L., 110

TEN EYCK
Janette, 173

TERWILLIGER
Augustus, 87

THAYER
Cora I., 56
James, 75

THOMAS
R. L., 265

THOMPSON
Abby C., 124
Bertha G., 67
Betsey, 121
Burton D., 240
Carrie E., 123
Catharine, 141
Charles D., 124
Daniel, 84
Edith A., 123
Elizabeth A., 123
Elmina B., 67
Frances A., 120
George D., 123
Harriet W., 124
Harrison M., 122
Helen M., 240
James D., 122
James W., 123
Janette L., 123
John C., 67
Lesley G., 123
Louise B., 124
Louise E., 123
Lucille B., 124
Lucy E., 121
Malcom E., 67
Mary E., 120
Maud O., 67
Sally B., 120
Thomas, 120

Willard A., 240
Winthrop E., 123

THORNTON
Charles, 216
Frederick, 216

THORP
Annie E., 223

THURSTON
Abigail, 119, 129
Edward, 51

TIBBALS
Edith D., 112

TILTON
A. Mary, 159

TOMPKINS
B. Fitch, 210
Brownell, 209
Mary E., 218
Rose L., 221
William, 219

TUCKER
Arthur R., 226
Hattie M., 167

TULLAR
Austin M., 132

TURNER
Alfred, 132
Amy E., 132
Charles G., 151
Charlotte L., 132
Cynthia, 132
Eliza A., 132
Henry E., 132
John, 184
Mary J., 132
Maud, 184
Melinda, 132
Minnie, 184
William O., 132

354

V. Appendices.

Appendix No. 1.

APPENDIX NO. 2

Appendix No. 2.

ALDEN

Elizabeth, 293

BABCOCK

Ruth, 294

BARBER

Susan, 296

BARTLETT

Benjamin, 293
Samuel, 293

BROWN

Alexander, 297
Avery D., 297
Belva, 297
Bessie M., 297
Clara M., 297
Dora, 297
Edna H., 297
Frankie E., 297
Louis T., 297
Myrtle, 297
William A., 297

CHAPMAN

Jonas, 294

CHILD

Emily F., 296
George H., 296

COE

John, 293

CRARY

Cyrus W., 295

CRUMB

Augusta J., 295

FISH

Joseph, 293
Nathaniel, 293

HOLMES

Abigail, 294

MAIN

Wilson D., 297

MAINE

Josephine L., 296

MINER

Alden F., 296
Charles D., 296
Dwight L., 296
Ethel M., 296
Frances M., 295
Frank B., 296
Herbert O., 296
James E., 296
James O., 295
John I., 295
Susan M., 296
Walter A., 296
Willes L., 296
Winnifred E., 297

PARK

Etta M., 295

PARTELO

Alfred L., 297
Althea L., 297
Everett C., 297
George F., 297
Mary J., 297

PEABODY

Abigail, 294
Amy, 294

Annie, 293
Benjamin, 292, 293, 294
Elizabeth, 293
Fanny A., 295
Frances, 293
Francis S., 295
George W., 294
Giles H., 295
Hannah, 293, 294
James, 294
James A., 295
Jerusha, 294
John, 292, 293, 294
Joseph, 293, 294
Judith, 293
Lemuel, 294
Lucy, 294
Lydia, 294
Martha E., 295
Mary, 293, 294, 295
Mercy, 293
Nancy, 295
Priscilla, 293
Rachel, 293
Rebecca, 293, 294
Rebecca H., 295
Ruth, 293, 294
Samuel, 294
Sarah, 293
Susannah, 294
Thomas, 293, 294
Thomas H., 295
William, 293, 294
William P., 295

PECKHAM

Martha, 292, 294

PHILLIPS

Martha, 295

ROGERS

John, 292

Appendix No. 5

History of the First Baptist Church of North Stonington, Conn., 301-305

Appendix No. 6

History of the Second Baptist Church of North Stonington, Conn., 305-308

Appendix No. 7

History of the Third Baptist Church of North Stonington, Conn., 308-312

Appendix No. 8

History of the First Baptist Church of Brookfield, N. Y., 313, 314

THE NATHANIEL BABCOCK

AND

EZEKIEL MAIN GENEALOGY

IS NOW PUBLISHED and ready for DISTRIBUTION.

It also includes two families, the ISAAC MINER and SIMEON MAIN families, brought down to the present time.

TESTIMONIALS.

A few who have already received the genealogy show their appreciation of the book. Herewith are extracts from letters signed by their number and page in the book.

" Your years of work show up in a satisfactory manner and you can feel proud of it. Like the Brown book, it is a lasting monument to you for generations to come. It is a great pleasure to see it dedicated to my brother and sister. Words fail to express my appreciation." (81) p. 27.

" I have given the genealogy a cursory examination and extend to you my hearty appreciation of your work." President of the Randall Association.

"I wish to compliment you upon the exceedingly fine book you have compiled and published. Everyone says that such a compilation takes a large amount of time and work; yet no one can comprehend the work unless they have traced remote degrees of kindred and compiled the detailed work. You may send me another book, bound in half morocco." (87) p. 32.

"This is a very fine work, and I assure you that I appreciate it. Would like to have you send me another copy." (614) p. 88.

"The Book is wonderful! What strikes me the most forcibly is your father's and mother's pictures. They have such a life-like look, it seemed they would speak. I prize the book highly." (377) p. 60.

"I really do not know how you could ever write so much. It is a grand work. I cannot conceive how one mind, one hand, could ever do so much; surely you have the———" L. C. M.

"The book is a beauty and so far as I can see it is all right, and I am much pleased with it." (2055) p. 242.

"I am much pleased with the Genealogy you sent me, but regret that we did not have a picture of Father in the Book." (2204) p. 261.

"You have certainly produced a book of great interest and value to the descendants and will also be to future generations." (1077) p. 136.

The letter of Eli G. Main of Waterbury Conn. was particularly interesting and appreciative. I sent it away and it has not been returned. Compiler.

"The genealogy arrived safely and in good shape. It is a fine volume and I feel immensely proud of it. I am very grateful to you for having taken up the work and having it published; for now it is in shape to be preserved from generation to generation. I take pleasure in tracing my kindred, and it has put me in touch with some of whom I had lost all trace and not heard from in many years. The illustrations are all fine and especially the one of my Father.......... I want to thank you for the immense amount of gratuitous time and labor you have expended in behalf of the Main family and which I trust is appreciated by all.

The book will be as a monument in memory of your "labor of love" for long years after we all have passed over." (2380) p. 273.

A copy of the genealogy has been presented to the Westerly R. I. Public Library by, (2399) p. 288., and the librarian gives a long testimonial appreciative of the book, in which he says in part: "Unlike most compilations, the work is exceedingly interesting even to those whose names do not appear in the book. The historical matter is one of the most pleasing features of the work. The book is not simply a record of names: it contains many biographical sketches. In family lines there have been famous men and women, and their names have not been allowed to pass without some appropriate sketch of their achievements........ It has been a labor of *love*: yet the result will certainly furnish much happiness to a large number of descendants of these and kindred families."

A newspaper article says in part:

" It is surprising how a man so advanced in life could possibly go through the time, trouble and expense of preparing a book containing such an amount of valuable information. It is a work of painstaking, a determined and successful effort to enter into the minutest details of family records, and it shows the

author and writer t be a master of the arduous task. The
book will be a recuited by every man, woman and child connected with ·   in this book.." (955) p. 127.

.u .u.   r article says in part:

"I ish .o .ecord my high appreciation of the work of Mr.
Cyrus H. Brown of Westerly R. I., in the collection of this vast
amount of data. Mr. Brown has given generously of his time
and energy, for which he expects no remuneration whatever,
simply desiring reimbursement for the money actually expended in publishing the genealogy. I sincerely hope he will be
promptly accorded the loyal support of those whose ancestors
he has given a permanent place in history by the production of
this splendid volume." (1067) p. 135.

From the Everett Press Co., Publishers, Boston :

" You certainly have had a difficult task, and one that would
have discouraged the average man from the start. Without
wishing to flatter you I must state that your energy and tena-
city of purpose are remarkable. Most of us find it difficult to
do the things that we really have to do without going out of
our way to find other troubles ; still if it were not for just such
men as you a great many things would remain undone. I only
hope the people who are interested in these books thoroughly
appreciate your efforts. I also hope there will be some financial evidence of this appreciation. Tell your acquaintances
that they not only want the book, but they have got to have it.
They owe it to themselves and their family to have it in their
library." The book is waiting for you.

After reading these testimonials, send for a book to

CYRUS H. BROWN,

WESTERLY, R. I.

CPSIA information can be obtained
at www.ICGtesting.com
Printed in the USA
BVOW06s1055181117
500758BV00021B/358/P

9 781117 501178